D0878206

ALSO BY SUSAN EISENHOWER

Breaking Free

The Making of a Soviet Scientist
(memoirs of Roald Sagdeev, co-author)

MRS. IKE

Mrs. Ike by Susan Eisenhower is the second book in the Capital Classics series—a trade paperback imprint from Capital Books in association with Washington literary agent and author, Ronald Goldfarb, who represents some of the Capitol City's most distinguished authors. The series features works by prominent authors in a variety of fields, whose books have never before been available in trade paperback, reissued with "questions to ponder" sections to make them more accessible to college students and reading groups. Other titles in the series include:

Finding My Voice by Diane Rehm

Mrs. Ike

Portrait of a Marriage

Susan Eisenhower

ISBN: 0-9846-8420-4
ISBN-13:   9780984684205

For my daughters,
Caroline, Laura, and Amy

ACKNOWLEDGMENTS

Writing a history brings with it special challenges, and I am deeply grateful to many people for their assistance: Ron Goldfarb, my agent, for his unfailing support; Elisabeth Sifton, my editor at Farrar, Straus and Giroux, who did a magnificent job of editing this book; Linda Tuck, her assistant; Jeff Seroy and Leslie Herzik, in publicity; and Karla Reganold, who tirelessly worked with me, even over vacations, to complete copy-editing changes on time.

I would also like to thank all those at the Eisenhower Library and Museum in Abilene, Kansas, for their enormous contribution to this work. I now understand why the Eisenhower Library has the reputation of being one of the very best in the presidential system. My thanks go to Dan Holt, director, Martin "Mack" Teasley, his deputy, and Jim Leyerzapf, who never failed to help me find a reference, even under the tightest of deadlines. Appreciation also goes to Kathy Struss, for her ready response in finding photographs both well-known and obscure, and Denis Medina, curator of the museum.

I very much appreciate the support and assistance of everyone at the Eisenhower Farm, a national historic site in Gettysburg, Pennsylvania—especially Carol Hegeman, who offered her time and help at every turn. I am also grateful to Larry Adams, curator of the Mamie Eisenhower birthplace, and the many others—too many to list—who offered help along the way, including George Feltner, who dug deep into his personal papers to find an article he had written about the early Carlsons; John Mott, former curator of Culzean Castle in Scotland, who helped me secure permission from the Queen of England to publish her letter to my grandfather; and countless others, like Sue Jehl and Mary Jane McCafree Monroe, who allowed me to interview them and who offered photographs from their own personal collections. I am indebted to them all.

My thanks also go to my husband, Roald, who of all people gave me the greatest encouragement, my daughter Caroline, who read the manuscript and helped with the source notes, and my daughters Laura and Amy, who put up with the idiosyncrasies of an author in the throes of an all-consuming work.

Finally, and most important, it should be said that quite literally this book could not have been written if it had not been for my parents. My mother, Barbara, conducted crucial interviews with Mamie and others before their deaths, offering them to me along with the fruit of her work—as well as unfettered access to family letters and photographs, so many of which have never before been published. The sizable collection of Mamie's letters to her parents, which were in my mother's possession, will now, for the first time, be available to scholars at the Eisenhower Library.

I am also deeply indebted to my father, John, for his generosity of time and spirit. He unstintingly made himself available on the shortest of notices for both interviews and factual or interpretative checks. I discovered that his memory (when checked against Mamie's letters) is flawless and his perspective absolutely invaluable. I must also say that picking his brain as I did and discussing the issues outlined in this book gave me insights not only into my grandparents' life but also into his. I am blessed for the discovery, and I will remember those countless occasions on which we spoke as personal treasures—they were, without a doubt, the most enjoyable part of writing *Mrs. Ike.*

CONTENTS

FOREWORD

This year marks the fiftieth anniversary of Dwight Eisenhower's election, in 1952, as President of the United States. It was a contentious nomination process, pitting Eisenhower, the wartime hero, against Robert Taft, "Mr. Republican." It culminated in perhaps one of the last cliffhanger conventions of the modern age. At issue within the Republican Party was America's role in the postwar world. After a hard fought victory at the convention, Eisenhower went on to beat Governor Adlai Stevenson and win the Presidency in a landslide.

This paperback version of *Mrs. Ike* is being published now in this fiftieth anniversary year. Its hardcover version emphasized the life of Mamie Eisenhower. In contrast, this new paperback version underscores the Eisenhowers as a couple. This is appropriate. Until *Mrs. Ike*, few if any historians gave Mamie Eisenhower her due as Dwight Eisenhower's helpmate. Ironically, during the Eisenhower presidency Mamie Eisenhower was seen as a colorful First Lady, with a quick wit and a tireless commitment to making the White House "everyone's house." She was known as a brilliant manager and a practiced perfectionist.

In the intervening years, however, Mamie retreated to the shadows of history, relegated to the list of wives who were but caricatures of themselves. Little mention was made of Mamie's real contribution as a soother, an influencer, and a problem-solver.

As *Mrs. Ike* reveals, from the outset Mamie played a crucial role in Ike's development from a Kansas farm boy to a sophisticated leader of leaders. Her own well-traveled upbringing played a role. But just as important was her well-honed sense of humor and joie de vivre. Mamie helped Ike relax and unwind, so utterly essential in high stress, high impact jobs. She was also accomplished at entertaining, and through her skills she helped create and solidify a network of friends and contacts that proved to be an enormous asset in Eisenhower's rise to power.

Furthermore, though the subject of First Ladies has become a popular research topic in its own right, many historians still compare Mamie with many of her contemporary counterparts, like Eleanor Roosevelt, Bess Truman, and Jacqueline Kennedy. As *Mrs. Ike* demonstrates in so many instances, Mamie considered herself not the wife of a politician but an Army wife who found herself resident of the White House. In that respect Mamie is far better compared with other Army wives who became First Ladies—like Martha Washington and Julia Grant—than she is the wives of the politicians who preceded or succeeded Ike in office.

Finally, with the events of September 11, 2001, *Mrs. Ike* reads and feels, at times, like a story that is set in another historical time. Yet sometimes the contemporary parallels are evident. Threats to our security, for example, have changed in character, but not so how people deal with the anxiety of danger or the loneliness of staying behind while loved ones fight abroad.

Other differences between the eras are more sharply obvious. A once open and accessible government, for instance, now functions behind metal detectors and guards with automatic weapons. Technology has also speeded things up. Letters that used to be written with care and ceremony have given way to email and impersonal faxes. Unscheduled hours, a critical resource for synthesis and contemplation, are now crowded out by ever increasing demands for our attention. As time races by, the very lack of it seems to undermine our ability to connect with ourselves and with others.

In many ways, then, *Mrs. Ike* is a story of another era: the days when it took a month to go to the Far East and secretaries worked only with typewriters and carbon paper. But it is also about something more enduring than the way things used to be. *Mrs. Ike* is a personal and intimate account of a couple, their sorrows, their passions, and their unwavering belief in this country. They served America during the most pivotal events of the twentieth century, from the First World War and the Great Depression to World War II and the beginning of the space age. With modesty, humility, and the judicious use of power, Dwight Eisenhower led, in every sense of the word, those that Tom Brokaw calls "the greatest generation."

During more than fifty years of public service, Ike and Mamie helped shape the United States we know today; and they gave all of themselves in the process. As much as this story is uniquely theirs, it is also a tale of America with all of its raw possibility. That makes it a timeless story that can be told in any era.

—Susan Eisenhower
Washington, D.C., May 2002

INTRODUCTION

My grandmother was buried in the gold-and-white organdy gown she'd worn the night she and my grandfather celebrated their fiftieth wedding anniversary. When the funeral was over and the guests had departed, her coffin, which sat on top of a flower-draped bier, was lowered into place—next to the remains of her husband and near the grave of their three-year-old son. I thought of how profoundly symbolic it was that she was laid to rest in this way. A sentimentalist to the end, she had already chosen her burial garb, and it said everything about what she'd valued most in her eighty-two years: her family and her marriage and commitment to Ike.

Mamie's death in 1979 was all but dismissed by the press at the time, though poll after poll had placed her at the top of the list of America's Most-Admired Women. Most of the national newsweeklies carried only two-paragraph obituaries, and nearly half the story was dedicated to the rumors about my grandfather's supposed affair with his wartime driver, as if Mamie's "role" as an allegedly wronged wife had defined at least that much of her life. But it is not surprising that this was the prevailing attitude at the time. The women's liberation movement had shaken the country, and Mamie's apparently self-effacing devotion to one man seemed outdated and irrelevant to many. The implication was that Ike had behaved as other generals had done during the war, since his driver was an attractive, independent divorcée and Mamie was, it seemed, an overly anxious, bedridden burden of a woman.

Even at the time, I recognized that Mamie was being grossly underestimated. Her critics knew little of army life and even less of her relationship with Ike. Most of the people who wrote about her knew nothing beyond her apparent frivolity and obvious reliance on her husband. But much of Mamie's banter had been a way to hold the public at arm's length. My mother recalled that during the 1940s, when Mamie and other Eisenhower family members were first thrust into the public eye, she had cleverly held off the press with "clichés to guard their privacy."

If the public thought of Mamie in terms of empty generalizations, I had had a peek into Mamie's inner life in the decade following Ike's death in 1969. My, how she regaled me with stories! I often visited her at the Gettysburg farm, mostly to keep her company during those lonely and difficult days. As she rested in bed, books piled on Ike's side so she'd miss him a little less, I would perch next to her on a delicate French chair and listen to her captivating stories of how they'd met and what they'd been through together. She was always disarmingly open about her feelings on the topic of love and marriage—even her own intimate relationship with Ike. She liked to talk about it, and I figured it was her way of keeping him alive in her mind.

Mamie was always the first to admit that her life as an army wife had been "no bed of roses" and that marriage to Ike had not been without its problems. Nevertheless, Mamie had been resourceful, and the deep respect she had for her husband stopped her short, more than once, from denouncing their hardships forever. From all she told me, I also surmised that there had been an enormous physical attraction between them.

Not until years after her death did I appreciate what she'd really been through. One day I came across a pile of family papers, letters which Ike had written to her and her parents and which had never been published. Several years later I discovered an even larger collection of Mamie's own letters, also unpublished; some had only just been removed from the darkest corners of the basement at our family home.

In striking contrast to the view of Mamie Eisenhower held by those who dismissed her, what I knew and now read revealed a young girl and then woman who had been free of the constraints of a conflicted self-image. She had been centered, confident, and unapologetic about who she was. Despite her deep belief in the family and in traditional American values, she also had no difficulty dispensing with common dictates if she found them stuffy or nonsensical. She was her own woman, who knew her mind and lived life *her* way.

Through great hardship and disappointment she developed a personal philosophy that made her remarkably independent and resilient in many ways—important attributes she brought to her partnership with Ike. She had to have had a spine of steel to survive the difficult early years of their marriage, their prolonged and painful separations, and a way of life that dropped her in posts in Latin America and the Far East, as well as in war-ravaged Europe after both the First and Second World Wars. This broad international experience made her unique, by the way, among First Ladies.

It can be said that Mamie experienced a full range of human emotion: from great love, devoted friendship, and public adulation to loneliness, humiliation, and devastating tragedy and loss. She accomplished much and contributed significantly to her family and her nation. But most of all, she met her challenges and triumphs in her own distinctive style.

On the day she was buried, I stood crushed amid the crowd of mourners and grieved as others did. I would miss her throaty but musical hello on the other end of the phone, and the intimate times we had shared on my grandparents' beloved sunporch or around the long dining-room table she had spent years saving the money to buy. But most of all it would be her vital personality and her no-nonsense approach to living that I would miss and remember long after her passing.

Rs. Ike

CHAPTER ONE

BELONGING ON AMERICAN SOIL

*I*n the mornings the sun streams through the sheer curtains that veil the silk-draped windows of my grandparents' bedroom. Looking eastward to an open field, one sees the flagpole that flew the American flag and Ike's five stars, standing proudly against a landscape dotted with grazing deer and white-tailed rabbits. The faint smell of Yuram, Mamie's favorite perfume, lingers upstairs, and despite a few changes, inevitable with time, her presence can still be felt in those rooms.

Mamie Eisenhower was a woman of sparkle and life, with a ready wit and a coquettish flair for making people feel special. To a grandchild, she was something to behold: a powerful personality wrapped in satin and silks whose hair was tied at the top with a pink ribbon. I can still see her propped up in that bed, with a pastel print bed jacket and her honey-colored curls drawn back with a lace bow. She was clearly a woman who relished her femininity and lived it to the hilt.

Mamie favored pink, perhaps because it accentuated her flawless milky complexion and her clear, glittering china-blue eyes. Mamie knew about those things—how to set herself off to her best advantage. She once confided, "You have to use the gifts you have. I know I have beautiful eyes and I use them."

My grandmother had a huge collection of dressing gowns, dresses, hats, handbags, gloves—all lovingly arranged in delicately scented closets. Her garments were made in all the colors of the rainbow, though she once confessed to my mother that she hated blue—which, she said, she had been forced to wear as a child. Her dresses filled nearly every closet on the second floor of their Gettysburg home. Some were from the most exclusive fashion houses of Europe and New York; some she'd purchased off the rack at Penney's, or Penné's, she'd say as a joke on herself. There was a democracy to her closet. All dresses, no matter what the cost, were hung in luxurious splendor, treated to padded hangers and fragrant sachets.

Once, when someone criticized her during the White House years for wearing a youthful flowered halter-topped dress, she declared, "I hate old-lady clothes and I shall never wear them."

Despite Mamie's penchant for bargain hunting and visiting five-and-dime stores, she loved quality—fine antiques, rich silks and brocades, and the best china and sterling silver money could buy. Bedsheets had to be linen or satin, never percale; nightgowns had to be silk, never nylon; and carpets had to be wool (my, how she abhorred the sight of footprints on their pile!).

Even though my grandparents' home in Gettysburg was a farm-house, it reflected Mamie's love of beautiful things as well as her appreciation for formality, which was belied by her breezy unpretentiousness. There was only one room that was austere and merely functional: my grandfather's nap and dressing room, just down a short hallway from the bedroom they shared. It was the one spot in the house that had been bypassed by Mamie's touch—a concession to their differences in both outlook and upbringing.

Since Mamie treasured elegance, I always wondered how this pampered daughter of a wealthy Midwestern businessman had survived the rigors of the old army; how she had managed thirty-five moves in as many years. She always made light of the ordeal, with a toss of her head and an instant quip. "I've kept house in everything but an igloo," she'd say with a wink.

Mamie all but cluttered the house in Gettysburg—the first and only one she and Ike had ever owned—with a vast collection of knickknacks, memorabilia, and photographs of friends and family. She lovingly kept every small present that her "boys," Ike and their son, John, had given her over the years. She could remember with intimate detail the whole story involving even the most modest of gifts. One of what she called her prized possessions was a simple rose-quartz night-light, special because the boys had given it to her after a day of shopping en route to the United States from the Philippines in 1938.

Remnants of my father's childhood could also turn up in unexpected places. My sister-in-law Julie once opened a drawer and found an old piece of paper folded into quarters containing a tooth with the string still attached. On the paper, written in pencil, was a message in a young boy's script: "Dear Tooth Fairy, please leave my tooth."

Mamie's sentimentality was also directed toward Ike. In a girlish way, she kept his handsome West Point picture on her dressing table, amid lipsticks, perfume bottles of every description, and the silver dressing-table set he'd purchased for her in the Philippines. On the bottom of the meticulously polished silver frame, from which a cadet standing with ramrod erectness looked out, he had written: "For The dearest and sweetest girl in the world."

Surprisingly absent were pictures of the countless famous people she and Ike had known; there was also little evidence of the White House years. In truth, the framed photos on her dressers and tabletops expressed her real interest, which was in celebrating those she loved, including a diverse group of children, grandchildren, and great-grandchildren—not all of whom were her own. Along with photos of us, she also kept photographs of the Secret Service men's offspring as well as those of her devoted houseman and cook, John and Delores Moaney.

I always took those pictures of other people's children for granted, knowing the intense interest Mamie lavished on their families. But I was especially curious about the faces of people to whom I was related, particularly the black-and-white images of little girls of the Victorian period with large bows and lace dresses; of a young woman in a high-necked blouse, with her hair swept back; of a row of family members at a reunion just after World War II; and of a pensive youngster we all knew to be my father's deceased brother, "Ikky," who'd died at the age of three and a half. These photographs more than any others were a sharp reminder that Mamie had been born in another era, though she had presided over the 1950s and lived through the tumultuous 1970s. Mamie was, in fact, a Victorian, if often a headstrong one.

On November 14, 1896, Mamie Geneva Doud made her entry into this world. It was some three decades after the Civil War, at a time when America's potential was bursting from every verdant corner. She was particularly proud of her father's side of the family—mainly because of their "ancient" American roots and because they had accomplished so much. She felt a sense of belonging on American soil so strongly that she shrugged it off as unremarkable that by the time she became First Lady she had already "wowed the sovereigns and shopgirls of three continents," as *Look* magazine once noted. "I've *never* had any social ambitions," she once told a friend. "I didn't have to. I had my place in this world and I knew it. I came from a long family of Americans. I didn't have to prove anything."

Her father, John S. Doud, whom we all called Pupah, traced his ancestry in America back to 1639, when his forebear Henry Doude came from Guilford, England, and helped to establish a community of the same name in Connecticut. Pupah's family moved several times, eager to take advantage of new opportunities as America's transportation system developed. His parents, Royal H. Doud and Mary Sheldon Doud, migrated to New York State and settled on a farm in Turin. Later, with the completion of the Erie Canal, they moved again to Rome, New York, where they established a wholesale grocery business named Foote Doud and Company. This enterprise laid the groundwork for the family's affluence in the years to come. And in Rome, in 1870, John Sheldon Doud was born, the third son and fourth child of their nine-year marriage.

When Pupah was six years old, his father was one of the first men to go into the meatpacking business, which eventually necessitated another move, when railroads superseded the Erie Canal as the primary mode of shipment. The Doud family, now with six children, joined the nation's westward thrust, packing their belongings into railway cars and heading for Chicago. There, Royal Doud successfully established a meatpacking enterprise and eventually opened a subsidiary in another booming town farther west, Boone, Iowa.*

Pupah was a rawboned man of the world who had run away from home three times by the age of eighteen. On one occasion he worked as a cook on a Mississippi riverboat before returning to his parents and their business responsibilities. At the age of twenty-four, after an early classical education at Northwestern and Chicago universities, Pupah took a job as traffic manager in the Boone sub-

---

*Originally known as Montana, the town was renamed Boone in honor of Daniel Boone's son Nathan.

sidiary of his father's company, Montgomery Live Hog Buyers. When Royal retired some years later, he left the ownership of his considerable holdings in the hands of his three sons, Eli, James, and John.

It could not have been long after Pupah's arrival in Boone in 1893 that the Carlson family, and their beautiful daughter Elvira Mathilde, came to his attention. Her father, Carl Carlson, was a successful businessman who'd also gained prominence in the community as a visible and influential force in Republican politics. John was attracted to Elvira's quick wit and her delicate Nordic beauty, she to his managerial flair and swashbuckling sense of adventure. Despite Elvira's tender age—she was sixteen at the time—they married in the Carlson home on Monona Street on August 10, 1894.

If Pupah was the offspring of early English settlers, Mamie's mother, Elvira Carlson Doud (we all called her Nana), was the product of newer immigrant waves. She was a first-generation American whose ties with Sweden were still very much intact. Her father, Severin Carl Jeremiahson, born in 1848, had immigrated to the United States in 1868 from Sweden, where he had served as a confidential messenger for a wealthy family. He landed in Boston, changed his surname to Carlson (adding "son" to his first name, Carl, which was a common practice in Sweden), and then went to Canada, where he dabbled in various part-time jobs. But not long after his arrival in the New World, a Swedish friend suggested Boone, Iowa, as a place to settle. The Chicago and Northwestern railroads had just extended their lines westward, and opportunity in the growing Iowa town seemed to be boundless. So just before Christmas in 1868, Carl Carlson arrived in Boone. He stayed in a boardinghouse for a while, doing odd jobs in town. In April 1869, he sent for his wife, Johanna Maria—Mari—and their firstborn son, Carl Rudolph (later known as Charlie), who were still in Sweden. When they reached Boone, the family rented a small farm and Carl worked as a regular hand at a flour mill. He was eventually paid a bonus with a house and a lot, enough to sustain the total of his seven children. Of the Carlson children, only three survived to middle age: Eda Wilhemina, an upright religious woman who never married; Elvira Mathilde; and a son, Joel, the youngest.

Boone was good to the Carlson family. In time Carl acquired

the mill, which he ran with his son Charlie, a young man who had already gained work experience as a postal clerk and then as a master mechanic on the Chicago and Northwestern railroads. They named the mill Carl Carlson and Son.

Notwithstanding the Carlsons' growing prosperity, they maintained their deeply religious ways. Swedish Evangelicals, they belonged to a denomination noted for its severity and strictness. The family held both morning and evening Bible readings and prayers, as well as attending Sunday services.

Eda earned her living as a milliner and served as church organist and vocalist for more than fifty years. My father, John, still recalls the times Aunt Eda (known as Auntie) would take him to church. The preachers regularly gave their parishioners "hell" even for the slightest transgressions, like going to the movies. "Oh my God, it was worth a whole sermon."

Elvira, or Nana, a woman her grandson John described as "an odd mixture of Victorian propriety and outgoing friendliness," was also religious, but unlike her gaunt and pious sister Eda, she was too fun-loving to become deeply absorbed in the church. As a tomboy, she was proud, even in her later years, of how she pitched a ball and played the harmonica.

As well as preserving their religious convictions, the Carlsons maintained their ties to the old country. They kept a picture of the Swedish royal family on a dresser in the one-story house they built and later enlarged. They also spoke Swedish at home, a practice that was largely carried on by Auntie and Nana throughout their lives.

Like many other immigrant families, the Carlsons sponsored a nephew on Mari's side of the family, also called Carl. Mari, the matriarch of the family, found time while meeting the demands of a sizable family to write about him to his mother, her younger sister, Mathilde, who'd remained in Sweden. In one undated letter, the sobriety of purpose that characterized their lives was evident in even the most mundane exchanges: "Carl is capable and kind and that I know you will be glad to hear and we are glad over this too," she wrote in Swedish. "He comes home each evening in the week so I know he has no objectionable companions, and he works every day . . ."

Mari Carlson's nephew was a joy to his adoptive family, but the Carlsons' own beloved son Charlie was to meet a tragic end. In

1895 he hitched a ride on a speeding Chicago-Northwestern train and, standing on top of a cattle car as it went under a low bridge, he was decapitated. The entire family was devastated by his death. A photograph of Charlie was enshrined in the parlor in sacred memory of the family's firstborn son. No longer interested in continuing to run the company he had built with Charlie, Carl Carlson sold his shares in Carl Carlson and Son to the Doud family, which also had interests in the milling business. This, in addition to the John Doud–Elvira Carlson marriage the previous year, further cemented the alliance of the two families.

After their wedding Nana and Pupah stayed in Boone, making their first home on Carroll Street, only blocks away from the Carlsons. A year later (the year Charlie died), their first child, Eleanor, was born. The following year, a second daughter, christened Mamie Geneva Doud, was born in the same house.* Because she weighed only four pounds, her uncle Joel grumbled that she looked like "a little picked chicken."

The success of Pupah's meatpacking ventures eventually prompted the Douds to move to Cedar Rapids, nine months after Mamie was born. It was of Cedar Rapids that she retained her first childhood memories: of the frontier town's wooden walkways, of the goat her family kept (presumably as a pet), and of Jackson school, which she attended across the street from their house.

In Cedar Rapids, Nana gave birth to two more daughters, Ida Mae in 1900 and Mabel Frances in 1902. Pupah was so disappointed that he had not yet had a son that he nicknamed his two younger daughters "Buster" and "Mike," respectively. By now, Nana, twenty-four, had been married only eight years and already had four children to cope with. Although Pupah could provide her with some domestic help, she sorely missed the company of her tight-knit family. Cedar Rapids was only a short train ride away from Boone, so on the weekends the Douds would take the grandchildren to visit the Carlsons. The winters were very cold, Mamie recalled, and when they came from Cedar Rapids, Grandpa Carl-

---

*Contrary to many accounts claiming that Mamie's real name was Mary, she was indeed christened Mamie Geneva Doud. The intention may have been to name her after her grandmother Mari, but then her parents may have decided that one Mari was enough. The name Geneva was chosen because of her mother's captivation with the popular song "Lovely Lake Geneva."

son would meet them at the railroad station with the horses and sleigh. To stay warm, they put buffalo robes lined in red felt over their knees, and used covered hot bricks as foot warmers.

Mamie also spent part of her summer vacations with her grandparents. "In the summer the sleighs were hoisted to the top of the barn for storage," she recalled, and there was "a large cherry tree outside the kitchen door, and when the fruit was ripe there was always a ladder against the tree so we could climb up and gather cherries and eat them."

Despite many happy occasions with her Carlson grandparents, Mamie chafed at their somber rigidity, which perhaps contributed to her headstrong rebelliousness. "On Sundays, we'd visit Boone. After we'd been in the Swedish Church with Grandma and Grandpa, which of course we couldn't understand, we'd come home and all we could do was sit on the steps and watch people go by. We couldn't play cards. We couldn't do anything. It was the Victorian age and you weren't allowed to do anything. It was awful."

The pressures of child rearing and perhaps marital difficulties sent Nana into a "decline"—a worrisome state that prompted Pupah to take semiretirement from his business and move the family to Colorado Springs. He was thirty-six years old, but he already had a fortune rumored to be in excess of a million dollars—money enough to ensure that his young family would live comfortably even if he never worked again. Colorado Springs, however, did not turn out to be a boon for the family at all. The city's high altitude was blamed for a serious heart ailment that Eleanor developed, and consequently the family moved once more, this time to Denver. Mamie herself had developed a rheumatic heart before she was ten, but she was far more robust than her older sister. She recalled that from the time Eleanor's heart trouble started, her sister was an invalid. Frail but sweet-natured and patient, "Eleanor could ride in a carriage, but she couldn't ride a bicycle, skate, or ride a horse—the things that the rest of us could do. Eleanor had round-the-clock nurses from the time she was eight years old." To alleviate water retention, a side effect of her condition, the doctors placed tubes in Eleanor's legs and abdomen to drain off excess fluid. Her illness was gruesome, and Mamie remembered "seeing the festering all around those little tubes, and her abdomen was so distended."

The Douds quickly settled into Denver society, eventually buying a brick house of "Denver Square" design located at 750 Lafayette Street, only blocks away from the city's wealthiest section. Fashionably located, 750 was staffed with several servants who took care of the four-bedroom, one-bathroom house.

At the turn of the century, Denver was a booming Western capital, already established as *the* place to be in the summertime. Wealthy families in the mining and cattle businesses centered many of their social activities there, making the mile-high city the Palm Springs of its era. In 1906, it was a city of second-generation wealth, "self-consciously staid and proper on the surface, but still surging with youthful vitality; the place to which miners and cattlemen came to spend the wealth they dug out of the ore-packed mountains or raised on their 10,000-acre ranches on the plains."

Denver society regarded people who'd made their fortunes in mining as much more aristocratic than those who'd found wealth in the meatpacking business, but the Douds had little pretensions in that respect. They were quiet people whose social life revolved around a few close couples and their families. Still, like so many others in America at the time, they lived by Victorian mores, which placed great importance on what other people thought of them. My mother once told me she had never met a family who seemed to care about appearances as much as the Douds did. And my father would often laughingly recount that his grandmother was always concerned that all her daughters (and later their children) wore only clean and mended underwear, "for fear" of shocking the doctors if they should be "in an accident."

As in other households, the maiden aunt in the Doud family was also a peculiar institution. Although Nana and Pupah had a handful of servants, Eda was expected to pick up the slack when she visited Denver for any length of time. "Auntie got the short end of the stick," my father recalls. "As the maiden aunt she was the one who did the dishes while the others sat in the living room. She was treated like the housemaid—that's the way it was done in those days."

Despite their nineteenth-century sense of propriety, the Douds set great store by being modern. They were not big entertainers, but on Sunday evenings they would have an open-house buffet for any friends who wanted to stop in. Aside from the sumptuous spread, these evenings revolved around the poker table in the

Douds' brand-new "recreation room" in the basement. Mamie was always proud that her parents were among the first people in Denver to have such a game room. Boasting a piano, a pool table, and a Victrola, it was the center of family life and a fetching place to entertain her many beaus.

It is not surprising that Pupah was among the first to conceive the idea of a "rec" room. He was an avid innovator and enthusiast of all the latest gadgets and devices. Automobiles, or horseless carriages as they were still called, were perhaps his greatest passion. In 1904, while the family still lived in Colorado Springs, he bought a green Rambler, the first car in town. Later came an Oldsmobile, a Winton Six, a Packard and a Pierce-Arrow, and then a Steamer, a seven-person touring car that he kept in mint condition.

In 1910, the Douds started spending their winters in San Antonio, Texas, where they rented a sizable house on McCullough Street, in one of the most fashionable neighborhoods in the city. To ensure that its spacious hallways, wide verandas, and well-clipped lawns were properly prepared in advance, a few days before their own departure the Douds would put two maids on the train for San Antonio to steward the family's household and wardrobe items and see that Nana's electric car survived the trip. Then the family and two more servants would wedge themselves into the touring car and set off for Texas, over muddy and potholed byways hardly developed enough to be called roads. According to accounts, they kept a shovel strapped to the running board so they could dig the car out of any hole or trench. One flat tire could jeopardize the whole trip, necessitating a team of horses to tow them into town. Despite the inconveniences, Pupah, ever the adventurer, insisted on making the trip by automobile.

With time on his hands, Pupah had ample opportunity not only for getting out and about but also for showering attention and resources on his family of growing girls. Mamie occupied a special place in his affections, and he nicknamed her "Puddy." She recalled, "Our whole life was centered around [our] family . . . [We] went on camping trips with friends, and in the mountains we rode burros and climbed and fished. We had picnics together; we'd go out in the evening to the parks and listen to band concerts. [There was] a lake, and if you were very good, Papa would take you on [a] launch. It was your big excitement to buy popcorn ... It was all very simple."

Pupah liked to indulge the girls with special treats and outings of all kinds. This was evident in a letter he wrote to Mamie's ailing older sister, Eleanor:

Doud and Montgomery
Live Hog Buyers
February 20, 1911

My Dear Little Eleanor,
... Your letter came this morning and you certainly must feel good to be able to write so long a letter as this was. I'm sorry that the $5.00 would not buy both the Kamona and the slippers but I'll send you another $5.00 when I send the $15.00 for the March kiddie fund to Mother ...

I think when we go east we will stop in Gettysburg to see where that big battle was fought. It was the turning point of the war and really the greatest battle of the civil war & I have always wanted to go here. They have guides and carriages to take visitors everywhere ...

... I have had letters now from everyone but Puddy dear—she has not found time yet but will pretty soon I know. Mikey makes up for her tho every once in a while one turns up from her and I am glad to get them ...

The Douds set great store on having fun. Mamie would later recall little tricks Pupah used to play on his four daughters. In Cedar Rapids they were among the first to have a telephone, and Papa would arrange for a neighbor to call up and act as Santa Claus. And in those early years, Mamie asked for and received jewelry. One year Santa brought her a diamond chip set in filigreed gold.

Each holiday was marked with lavish intensity, and all pretexts were used as an excuse to celebrate. The Douds decorated the dining table for every holiday: pumpkins and ghosts for Halloween, hearts for Valentine's Day, even flags for George Washington's birthday. "It was a girl family," Mamie told us later, and Mr. Doud feted his little girls in every way possible.

But perhaps the biggest dates in the year were the birthdays. In Denver the Douds would begin a procession at the top of the long carpeted staircase with the birthday girl at the head. Singing "Here Comes the Bride," the parade would snake down the paneled stairs and into the dining room, where everyone would gather around the long mahogany table and sing "Happy Birthday." If you were the birthday girl, Mamie remembered, "you were to take your place at the table and Papa would bow and seat you."

Even if their father was away, a birthday remained the most-anticipated day of each daughter's year. On November 15, 1911—the day following her fifteenth birthday—Mamie wrote to her father in Boone, where he was surveying his business interests in the stockyards.

Dear Papa,
I had the most lovely birthday and was remembered by all. I was going to write you yesterday but mother said to wait. I'm glad I did for I can write to you on my new stationery. Oh daddy, thank you so much for the five dollars. I decided to put it in the bank which will make me seventy dollars, isn't that just fine?

Mother gave me some pink silk for a dress—it certainly is a dream, a pair of white kid gloves that come to my shoulder, a dollar from aunty, a pink silk scarf and two beautiful hair ribbons and a petticoat to go with another new dress. Don't you think I was well remembered? . . .

Your loving daughter
Mamie

P.S. I was looking through my letters yesterday and found the letter you wrote on my 14th birthday.

But despite a rather indulgent approach to his little ones, Doud was very strict. "Papa was the head of the family," Mamie recalled. "[Mama] leaned on him [to provide the] discipline. [You'd be] sent to bed while it was still light outside and you'd be put in your little bed and all you could do was to look out of the window and watch the children out there playing." Even after his daughters had married, John Doud, true to form, locked the Lafayette Street door at 11:00 p.m.

"The women of the house beat him down," my father later observed, "but Pupah was still very authoritarian. Later, my mother [Mamie] would say with a quiver (when recalling some misdeed), 'Mr. Doud would have never allowed that.'"

But for all the attention and discipline, Mamie was often manipulative. Regarded as the most beautiful of the Douds' four daughters, she had her father wrapped around her slender and well-manicured little finger. Once, he punished her for some wrongdoing by having her ringlets cut off. She had always wanted curls, so she threw a tantrum. "I made such a fuss, they cut off my sister's hair, too," Mamie recounted, even though Eleanor didn't want her hair cut. "They did it to pacify me; in other words, I got my way."

Although Pupah understood that Mamie's strong-minded ways had to be reined in—and he took many opportunities to tell her so—secretly he must have admired her spunk and resourcefulness, qualities the two of them shared.

At some point in the first decade of the century, Pupah began traveling more and more on business. He'd be away from the family for six months at a time. During his long absences he would make his headquarters the stockyards in Boone or Chicago. My father, John, who spent many summers with the Douds in Denver, said that when Pupah was on the road, "his living, sleeping, and dining room contained hardly more than a cot, a table and an old-fashioned telephone, and a single light bulb hanging by a wire from the ceiling." While he was gone, Nana was left with a houseboy and a cook.

It is not known if there were problems with the family business in Chicago and Boone, or whether Pupah's long absences from his family were a reflection of some marital discord. But semiretirement did not sit well with him, and he did not have nearly enough to do to absorb his energies. Perhaps he needed and wanted to reinvolve himself in business. But it is also possible that business provided a Victorian front for a kind of temporary separation from his wife. Family lore suggests that occasionally Pupah may have had other romantic interests. If so, this would have caused Nana great pain. Whatever the reasons for his absences, however, the Douds maintained the appearance, if not the reality, of marital fidelity.

It's difficult to make sweeping speculations about what kind of pressures Nana and Pupah lived with during those decades. In the space of seven years—by Mamie's twelfth birthday—all four of her grandparents had died. These were mournful events that must have had a huge impact on family life. In November 1901 Pupah's father, Royal, died in Chicago, after a discouraging trip to the Klondike, where a business venture to sell supplies to Alaskan gold prospectors had failed. Seven years later, his wife, Mary, also passed away. But the deaths of the Carlson parents must have been even more traumatic. Nana, who was given to periods of depression, had always been especially attached to her family. Mari died in July 1906, and Carl in 1908.

The Carlsons' religious faith seems to have brought them some comfort in dealing with these losses. In a letter from cousin Carl (who now called himself Charles) to relatives in the old country, he broke the news of Mari's passing and revealed a fatalistic philosophy that Mamie would eventually adopt, especially at times when her life seemed to be hopelessly beyond her control.

In Swedish Charles wrote:

Boone, Iowa
July 19, 1906

Beloved Parents, Brothers and Sister, also other relatives!
You will no doubt be surprised to see a letter from me written in Boone. But I must inform you of the great and unforeseen sorrow that I must come here to participate in my dear and beloved Aunt's funeral. I received a telegram on Monday evening that she had died at noon . . .
    She had a record of righteousness, which is her legacy. First because she was a righteous wife and mother, whose mother love extended even to me during my long stay with her . . .
    When I read through this letter I find I neglected to state what sickness she died from. She had gallstones, felt sick at first about three months ago. She became better, but had pains quite often and during the latter period daily, so on the

7th of July they found an operation was necessary. She went through it quite well and this was the only hope for her recovery, but things took a turn and she died on the 16th in the hospital. They were all at her death bed. She was willing and ready to leave though she would have been glad to stay. But she said, "Not my will but God's." So it was God's will and desire to take her from us.

Charles

To Mamie, those seven years must have seemed as though they were spent in perpetual mourning. Family tradition dictated that when a death occurred, family members were to stay up with the body for one full night. The casket always remained open. Perhaps this old custom was meant to make sure that the deceased had really died, to avert the accidental burial of a loved one who might be imperceptibly alive. It may also have derived from frontier practices of guarding against the possibility of wolves carrying off the body. Whatever the reasons, the ritual made a dramatic impression on the young girl.

However, none of the deaths that seemed to surround the young Doud family prepared Mamie, or any of them, for the untimely passing of her sister Eleanor on January 18, 1912. Feeble and frail during her years of medical problems, Eleanor died of heart failure at the age of seventeen. In keeping with the family tradition, her body lay in an open casket at home; then a service was held for her at the Corona Street Presbyterian Church, where the Douds worshiped and the children went to Sunday school. All the town, it seemed, turned out to pay their respects to Eleanor and her family. One of the Douds' neighbors observed, "I never saw people sorrow so for one not their own." Among the swelling crowd, they reported, there was "an intimate sense of loss."

Eleanor's death had occurred in the most severe part of the winter months, and it was too cold to bury her until spring. The body was kept in a crypt in the Ivy Chapel at the Fairmount Cemetery until the ground thawed and she could be permanently interred. Nana was so distraught about her daughter's death that she visited the cemetery every day, taking the younger children with her. "We would catch a streetcar which was just a half block away, with one change," Mamie recalled. "[We] could get right out at the cemetery and just take about twenty steps to this church where my sister was."

After Eleanor's burial, the entire family went to the grave site once a week after Sunday school to put fresh flowers at her headstone. Fairmount was a relatively new cemetery at the time, but the Doud plot was already surrounded by a few marble mausoleums with Doric columns and elaborate tombstones with statuesque angels. The family would stand at the site of Eleanor's grave in silent contemplation for some time, no matter what the weather. Mamie later remembered the sounds of the wind whispering through the yew and cypress trees, and the cooing doves which abounded at Fairmount. She bridled at the solemn regularity of these visits and the sorrowful haunting sound of the birds. Whenever she'd hear such sounds later in her life, she told us, her mind would go back to those bleak days.

Years later, she said that she thought it was very wrong for parents to make young children focus on death so much. "It's bad psychology," she'd say simply.

Of the two sides of the Doud household—the morose on the one hand and the fun-loving on the other—there can be no doubt that Mamie determined that she would always strive for the latter. Years later her friend Kate Hughes, the wife of General Everett Hughes, said she thought Mamie always tried to "push death away," even at the risk of upsetting her mother. No matter what the occasion, even in the most trying circumstances, Mamie would make a special effort to minimize sadness, trying to create amusement and laughter wherever she went.

To help take the children's minds off the tragedy of Eleanor's death, Pupah organized a trip to Chicago several months after her burial. In Chicago, the metropolitan magnet for all the Midwest, his three remaining daughters could indulge themselves in a shopping spree and visit their Uncle Eli and Aunt Minnie Doud, who lived on the outskirts of the city.

Pupah had some words for Mamie as she set off on that trip. Affectionately but firmly, he warned her to watch her manners and be a gracious guest. He realized that Mamie was growing into womanhood, but he took advantage of his special relationship with her to scold her for her directness, a sensitive point that one might have expected Nana to raise.

Doud and Montgomery
"Buyers of Live Hogs"
Boone, Iowa
June 3, 1912

My Dear Little Puddy,
No word has reached me this morning of your safe arrival tho possibly a card may have come on the 10:30 train. I shall go up to the P.O. soon and see if there is anything from you. I am not worried for I know that you are OK ... I know that you will have a good time in Chicago dear & you will try to so act as to make us proud of our little daughter. Don't talk too much and be awfully careful of saying things that offend or hurt. I mean like calling attention to Auntie's yellow spots & that she is getting old. She knew all of these things but it hurt her to know that others noticed them. That is your great fault—that you speak without thinking & in so doing hurt those who love you best. You have done it to Auntie, to Uncle, to your Daddy while you were here & often to Mother. I know that you do not mean any harm but you should watch your little "clapper." We miss our little Puddy and very much wish that you were here but if you have a good time in Chicago & get stronger thru your trip I shall be glad. When you are short of money you have only to write your Daddy for more. Don't spend what you have foolishly but do more than your share of the theater, the luncheon, and the soda expenses, always remembering Louise & Aunt Minnie while God has been good in this & other ways to us. Try in every way to do as our little mother would have you do & do nothing that God would think wrong in you. Dad loves you dearly Puddy dear. I'm always tired and always homesick but I love you nonetheless & I am glad that I am able to let you have your little trip. My kisses to you Puddy & I am always

Your loving
Father

Mamie was reaching the age when young society women went to finishing school. That June, Mamie was graduated from the elementary and intermediate Corona Street School, now called the Dora M. Moore School, named for its first principal. For a short time thereafter she went to East Denver High School, when the family was in the city, and Mulholland School in San Antonio, when the family wintered in Texas. Though very bright, Mamie was at best a mediocre student. Her formal education had been constantly interrupted by travel, illnesses, and death. When she developed rheumatic fever at the age of eight, she had been taken out of school for the better part of a year. Later, when her parents decided that wintering in San Antonio might bring positive benefits to ailing Eleanor, Mamie had again been taken out of school for nearly the entire period of their absence. On another occasion Nana contracted pneumonia and was sent off to Pueblo, Colorado, where she was hospitalized for two months; within weeks Pupah had packed up the family and relocated everyone to be with her.

In fact, the Corona Street School, only blocks away from Lafayette Street, was the only school that Mamie attended for more than a year. But despite her lack of "studious education," she was highly regarded by her teachers for being dependable and thorough. Mamie's eighth-grade teacher, Miss Hamilton, reported, "If you wanted a job well done, you gave it to Mamie."

Pupah didn't care about the girls' grades in school, only that they passed. His attitude reflected the notion that a society lady's education would be gained at home or through tutoring, certainly not in public high school. Most of what Mamie needed to learn about running a house with servants, managing domestic financial accounts, and taking her rightful place in society would be gleaned at home. The Douds had always been most serious about giving Mamie and her sisters the proper training, and they were taught how to embroider and sew and to prepare special items for their hope chests, which would be opened when they married. Mamie also took piano lessons, demonstrating an excellent ear—a talent she inherited from her father. And on Saturdays she took ballroom-dancing lessons.

For the school year 1914–15, the Douds enrolled Mamie in Miss Wolcott's, a finishing school (whose motto was "Noblesse Oblige") for daughters of prominent families in Denver. Miss Anna Wolcott, the sister of Colorado's senator, Edward Wolcott, founded and ran this school "for ladies of refinement," and it survived as a Denver fixture until 1924.

By now Mamie, regarded as one of Denver's most captivating belles, was consumed by her social life, enjoying the attentions of the eligible sons of the city's best families—men who belonged to clubs that arranged movie outings, dinner dances, and picnics for its members. Mamie's childhood friend Eileen Archibold recalled that she was utterly feminine, with a distinctive sense of style—a young woman who dressed in "adult finery at every opportunity." "When the rest of us were still getting kicked in the shins by boys, one of [the boys] gave Mamie a snakeskin. It was a real honor . . . Boys swarmed around the Doud house . . . [and] as she grew older they took her dancing and dancing and dancing."

Indifferent to her lessons and impulsive and determined by nature, Mamie insisted on leaving Miss Wolcott's after only a year to join her family for their annual pilgrimage to San Antonio. As in the past, the family squeezed into their six-passenger touring car, with Pupah and Nana in the front, Mamie, Buster, and Mike in the back, and Landers, the houseman, and Dawson, the cook, in the jump seats. She would return, she told her best beaus, in early June. But it was in San Antonio that Miss Mamie Geneva Doud would meet the man she would eventually marry.

CHAPTER TWO

THE WELLSPRING OF HIS IDEALISM

ℳy grandparents' marriage was the union of two people from backgrounds of glaring contrasts, which must have made for much of the attraction but also some of the friction between them. If Mamie had been raised in a wealthy "girl family," as she would call it, Ike had grown up in a struggling "boy family" that at times had all but teetered on the brink of poverty. The third of seven sons born to Ida and David Eisenhower, Ike knew nothing about such things as money allowances and trips to big cities for shopping sprees. Unlike the Douds, who enjoyed a pampered and coddled lifestyle at 750 Lafayette Street, Dwight's parents lived in a small white clapboard house on Fourth Street, decidedly situated on the wrong side of the railway tracks that divided Abilene, Kansas, in two.

The scholarship on Dwight's German ancestors is still far from definitive, but the one thing historians appear to agree on is that the Eisenhowers were descended from ancient German stock that originated in the Odenwald, in Germany. Some Eisenhower historians say that Ike's ancestors were German warriors who pledged themselves to pacifism in the sixteenth century and fled persecution by migrating to Switzerland. But recent scholarship suggests that the Eisenhauers, his direct ancestors, may have been Lutherans who migrated to the Saarland from the Odenwald, where they worked as potash burners for a glass factory in Karlsbrunn. It is believed that the family lived there for a generation or more before emigrating to the United States. In 1741, Hans Nicols Eisenhauer and his three sons, who are registered in church records in Karlsbrunn, embarked on an arduous trip to America that lasted some six months. Sailing on the *Europa*, which left from the Netherlands, they arrived in Lewes, Delaware. After a thorough medical examination and a visit to the courthouse, where they had to pledge their allegiance to the British Crown, they are thought to have encountered a Mennonite community known as the River Brethren (because their baptisms took place in rivers), which they joined to take part in William Penn's "Holy Experiment."

The name Eisenhauer was anglicized to Eisenhower sometime shortly after their arrival in North America. Putting down roots as farmers in eastern Pennsylvania, they eventually sold their landholdings and settled again in Elizabethville, in Dauphin County, near Harrisburg.

Jacob, Dwight's grandfather, was by all accounts the most dynamic of the sizable brood of second-generation American Eisenhowers. He became a River Brethren preacher whose passionate pacifist oratory was delivered in German, the only language of the sect. His skill and compelling message were so renowned that he was capable of attracting large crowds.

Although the pacifist teachings of the Mennonite community precluded a fighting role for most Eisenhower men when the Civil War broke out, the family opposed slavery. In fact, some members of the Eisenhower family actually disobeyed the tenets of their religious order and fought for the Union in that conflict. Although Jacob preached the message of peace, he made his feelings known by naming one of his fourteen children (six of whom lived to maturity) Abraham Lincoln Eisenhower. Three months after the Battle of Gettysburg, waged within sixty miles of the Eisenhower farm, Jacob's wife, Rebecca, gave birth to another son, David, who was to become Dwight's father.

In the 1870s, a sizable contingent of the River Brethren decided to pack up and move west. The Eisenhowers sold their Elizabethville home for $8,500, and the family, including Jacob's elderly father, Frederick, traveled by train to Kansas with enough household possessions to fill fifteen carloads.

The location chosen by the River Brethren community was Abilene, Kansas, the terminus of the Chisholm Trail and the Kansas Pacific (later Union Pacific) railroad. Although the town was surrounded by fertile land for growing crops and grazing cattle, Abilene had a godless reputation. As the railway junction for the cattle business, the flat, dusty town attracted many of the elements that made the Wild West famous. Cowboys just in from herding their cattle had to wait around for the animals to fatten up before loading them onto railway cars for shipment. Saloons and brothels awaited the bored and restless cowhands, and Abilene's infamous Texas Street was "a glowing thoroughfare which led from the dreariness of the open prairies into the delight of hell itself." With time on their hands, the drunken cowhands often turned to brawls and shootouts.

Wild Bill Hickok eventually brought order to Abilene in the 1870s, but the continuation of the railroad west did as much as the rule of law to calm the raucous town. Hickok's presence was a recent memory for the citizens of Abilene when the Eisenhowers arrived, and one of their neighbors claimed to have been a deputy of Wild Bill's.

The Eisenhowers and other members of their sect settled on the edge of town. Jacob acquired a large tract of land for one-seventh the cost of the old property they'd sold, and the family resumed farming. The River Brethren remained a close-knit community, easily identified by their men's long beards and their women's distinctive bonnets.

The men in David's family were farmers and veterinarians, and he was among the first of his sect to move away from the community, attending Lane College, a Mennonite establishment in Lecompton, Kansas. He had aspirations to become an engineer and took the necessary courses, combining them with classical subjects. Despite the incongruities of these two disciplines, David retained his appreciation for the classics and was able to read the Bible in ancient Greek. It was at Lane College where he met Ida Stover, a beautiful young Virginia woman with merry eyes and a serene smile.

Like David, Ida was of German stock and also a member of the River Brethren. Her family had come to America in one of the German waves of immigration in the early 1700s. The Stovers had settled in Lancaster County, Pennsylvania, before moving to Mount Sidney in the Shenandoah Valley, near Staunton, Virginia. Ida, one of eleven children, was born there on May 1, 1862.

Ida, too, subscribed to pacifism, a conviction born of the horrors of the Civil War. Before her third birthday, the Union Army, under General Sheridan, had waged a campaign in the Shenandoah Valley so devastating that "a crow flying over it would have to carry its own rations." The campaign had rivaled Sherman's march through the Deep South for its cruelty and destruction. Even two years later, "charred ruins of home and barns...blackened soil where straw and hay stacks had burned...decaying trees of uprooted orchards...[and] wrecked bridges and railways" littered the landscape.

Before Ida reached her fifth birthday, her mother died. Simon, her father, was unable to cope with eleven children under the age of seventeen, so he parceled them out to nearby relatives. Ida was sent to live with her maternal grandfather, William Link, who became her legal guardian when her father died in 1873.* With money she inherited from her father, she sustained herself through her high-school years, then took a job teaching in Limestone, Virginia, near Mount Sidney, putting away as much money as she could for a college education. Higher education for women was not something Virginia ladies were supposed to aspire to, so when other members of the River Brethren moved westward, Ida was ready to join them to pursue her education. In 1883, she left Virginia for Lecompton, Kansas.

Ida was a popular young woman at Lane College, but David Eisenhower's persistence and seriousness impressed her deeply. One of their sons, Milton, later recalled that his father was "a man of few words, undemonstrative, with a sort of quiet dignity. He appreciated personal friendships above everything except his religious beliefs"—a part of his nature he shared with Ida Stover. Before either of them had finished college, they decided to marry. The ceremony, on September 23, 1885, was performed in the college chapel. As a wedding present David's parents presented them with $2,000 and 160 acres.

Despite the generous gift, David had decided early on that he would not become a farmer. He also broke with another family tradition after 150 years of life in America: David was the first Eisenhower to refuse to speak German to his wife and children. After seeing beyond the world of his parents' Kansas farm, he didn't want his children to be different, set apart, or limited in their opportunities. Mortgaging their land to his brother-in-law

---

*The Links had immigrated to the New World from Switzerland, where the family had lived for a century after leaving Germany. So perhaps both versions regarding Ike's European ancestry are correct.

Chris Musser, David and Ida moved to Hope, Kansas, twenty-eight miles away, where they planned to open a general store. David's early experience with the store was successful, and soon he and Ida became the proud parents of a son, Arthur.

This might have been a joyful time in the lives of this independent young couple, but business problems created by a farm depression doomed the store. Small shops like the Eisenhowers' often carried the cost of the farmers' purchases until the crops were harvested and paid for. With David's customers unable to pay their bills, the store went bankrupt in 1888. The disaster meant that the Eisenhowers lost everything except their clothes, a few household items, and Ida's ebony piano, at which she loved to play hymns. Ida, pregnant again, stayed in Hope to oversee the settlement and closure of the business and await the birth of their second son, Edgar, while David left for Texas to find a job on the railroad, first in Tyler and later in Denison. A few months later, Ida joined David with the two young sons.

Less than two years later, on October 14, 1890, David Dwight Eisenhower was born.* The infant took his first breaths and cried his first cries amid the deafening sounds of a violent thunderstorm that lashed the sides of their tiny clapboard house. Perhaps his arrival, under such conditions, was an appropriate metaphor for a young boy who later, with the help of his mother, learned to tame his fearsome temper.

Now with three children, the Eisenhowers felt the pinch of poverty, and their letters home must have revealed something of their plight. After two years in Denison, David was offered a job for fifty dollars a week by the Belle Springs Creamery, which was run by the River Brethren, in Abilene. It entailed twelve hours of manual toil a day, but this was enough to provide a stable living for himself and his growing family.

The young Eisenhowers now made their home in a tiny house not far from the creamery. Because they had no money for a crib, Dwight was ensconced in an open bureau drawer. In these confining quarters, another son, Roy, was born to the Eisenhowers in 1892. Years later, Roy's wife would recall a family story that said, "when Roy was born, Father Eisenhower—quite in fun, of course—[said he] was going to pack his suitcase and leave because

---

*The sequence of his names was changed when he went to West Point.

Roy was a boy." Yet three more boys were eventually born to the Eisenhowers. In 1894 Paul arrived, though he died of diphtheria when he was only ten months old; Earl was born in 1898, and the youngest, Milton, came in 1899.

The Eisenhowers' growing family necessitated their moving to a more sizable frame house, at 201 Southeast Fourth Street. Fifty years later Ike observed that even this larger house had less floor space than his office at the Pentagon.

*A*lthough David and Ida Eisenhower were also children of the Victorian age, their lives were lived without the hypocrisy that so characterized that era. Keeping up appearances had no importance for them, but rather Christian openness and a deep commitment to religious principles prevailed.

David and Ida instilled these values in their sons by example. David, as his son Arthur later recalled, "had no use for alcohol. He didn't smoke. He was very much opposed to the races [as well as] cards. Work was his recreation." They read the Bible daily, and on Sundays they held prayer readings and hymn sings at the Eisenhower house. Edgar once said, "Religion to my father and mother was a way of life; they lived it. They believed in the brotherhood of man and, as a result, they were neighbors in the truest sense of the word. Mother was a slave to her friends and neighbors. We all learned a true sense of service from her."

The Eisenhowers were a strong moral force in their children's lives, but life was hard. Ida, who had six growing boys to contend with, was an able home manager, and the boys rotated chores: tending to the animals, cultivating their own vegetable plots, cooking, washing, and, for the older ones, even taking care of their younger brothers. As my grandfather later told me, "We always felt needed," a feeling he thought had a positive effect on their upbringing. He would tell my siblings and me that his family was poor, "but we never knew it"—such was the dignified and self-confident atmosphere that predominated in the Eisenhower household.

The Eisenhower sons were expected to work—both on their studies at school and on their chores at home. If they wanted any spending money, they had to earn it by selling the family produce, often door-to-door on Abilene's northside, where newly rich railwaymen, bankers, and ranchers built their homes and opulent mansions.

"To me this was distressing," Edgar would later remember. "[Prospective buyers] would go over the vegetables we had to offer and select the nice ones and pay us a meager price for them. Some would cast aspersions upon our produce. In a boylike way I resented that. I developed then a feeling that the railroad tracks separated the classes in Abilene—those who lived north of the tracks thought that they were just better than those who lived south of the tracks. Being older than Dwight, I was probably more sensitive about this. I talked to him about it years later. He said he never had any such feeling."

"We were a cheerful and vital family," Ike recalled. "Our pleasures were simple—they included survival—but we had plenty of fresh air, exercise, and companionship . . . The daily prayers of my parents did not fail to include a plea for the hungry and weary and the unfortunate of the world."

Ida, the central figure in the boys' lives, was idolized by all of them. So great was her influence, she was, I believe, the wellspring of Ike's idealism. She taught her sons, by example, the serenity and fulfillment that could come from devoting oneself to a higher and larger idea, but she never forced her children to espouse any specific cause. Ike later recalled that "her sincerity, her open smile, her gentleness with all, and her tolerance of their ways, despite an inflexible loyalty to her religious convictions and her own strict pattern of personal conduct, made even a brief visit with Ida Eisenhower memorable for a stranger. And for her sons, privileged to spend a boyhood in her company, the memories were indelible."

Ida's calming influence was especially significant in focusing the considerable energies of her passionate third son, Dwight. Of all the boys, Dwight, she noted, "had the most to learn." But his emotional intensity was coupled with intelligence, and her quiet, steady authority helped him to direct his gifts.

This was no small task in the rough-and-tumble environment of Abilene. Despite their parents' religious conservatism about pastimes such as cards, the boys were exposed to many of the wild pioneer elements. Dwight, for example, was befriended by a hunter-fisherman named Bob Davis who'd taught him poker percentages so thoroughly that, in Ike's words, "It was not remarkable that I should be a regular winner." He and his brothers were also athletes and ready to defend their honor with their fists—as part of the "frontier code." According to Arthur, Edgar and Dwight "were so tough at bare-knuckle combat in their early teens that they became champions of the southside of Abilene against the north. One long fight to a draw that Dwight had had with a north-side champion was remembered for years in their little town . . . [It was] an example of sheer courage and endurance." But by 1905, the boys had grown older, and north-south rivalry with fists had less appeal than contests for female attention. And the southside "boasted" more pretty girls than the north, among them, Gladys Harding, Ruby Norman, the four Curry sisters, and Winnie Williams.

Despite the distractions of small-town life, Dwight showed academic promise in school. "History was always Dwight's passion," Joe Howe, a local newspaper editor, remembered. He allowed Dwight to borrow his books, which he had in abundance. "Among his favorites were the *Life of Hannibal* and stories of the Punic Wars."

Ike loved Greek and Roman history and found it so engrossing that he was often guilty of neglecting his other studies and his chores. His mother, who normally revered scholarship and learning, became annoyed enough to lock up his books in a closet. "This had the desired effect for a while," Ike recalled. "But one day I found the key to the closet. Whenever Mother went into town to shop or was out working in her flower garden, I would sneak out the books."

Given the family's financial situation, prospects for intellectual development and a college education seemed limited. Arthur, the eldest, abandoned plans for a university education and took a job first as a janitor and then as a clerk at the Commerce Trust Company in Kansas City, rising eventually to the position of vice president. Ed and Dwight had made plans to help finance each other's college tuitions. Ed enrolled at the University of Michigan, where Dwight would later join him, and Dwight took jobs in Abilene so that he could send Ed money. But then, encouraged by one of his closest friends, Everett "Swede" Hazlett, Ike began to think about joining him in trying to secure an appointment to the United States Naval Academy at Annapolis.

"It was not difficult to persuade me that this was a good move,"

Ike recalled, "first because of my long interest in military history and second because I realized that my own college education would not be achieved without considerable delay while I tried to accumulate money." But Ike was disqualified from the Naval Academy because of his age: the cutoff for admissions was twenty, and he would be twenty-one at the start of term. Still, he was eligible for the Military Academy at West Point, and he eventually secured an appointment when Senator Joseph Bristow's first choice failed the physical examination. Many people in Abilene had written letters of recommendation to the senator in his behalf, and each had something to say about the integrity and "unimpeachable honesty" of the applicant's father, David.

Securing the West Point appointment "was a great day in my life," Ike later said. His mother, however, was genuinely disappointed and saddened. "It was difficult for her to consider approving the decision of one of her boys to embark upon military life . . . [but] because she and my father always insisted that each boy should be the master of his own fate, she kept her own counsel."

In June of 1911, Ike boarded a train and headed for West Point on the Hudson River. He had saved the money to meet the required deposit and his transportation costs, and he left to begin his new life with only the last of his savings, a five-dollar bill which he carried in his pocket.

Ike had many friends in Abilene with whom he'd formed close bonds. Hazlett was one, but there were others, including schoolmate and confidant Ruby Norman, with whom he stayed in touch. The hardest parting, however, came when he said goodbye to his parents. Ike's choice of the Military Academy only underscored the fact that his parents did not have the money to send him to a private civilian university, for at least part of the attraction of West Point was the prospect of getting a college education at government expense. But Ike had had to put aside one of the basic tenets of his religion, pacifism, to do so—a decision that must have been more painful than either of his parents could admit. Milton, who was with them on the day Ike went away for good, later said that after the train left the station, Ida returned to their house and excused herself to the bedroom she shared with her husband. From the hallway, he could hear her crying, something he had never heard her do before.

· · ·

$\mathcal{D}$wight had difficulties adjusting to West Point and proclaimed that if he or any of the other new entrants had had time to sit down and reflect on the harassment and the demands placed on them, "[we] would have probably taken the next train out." But his investiture at the academy gave him a new sense, almost a religious perspective, on the way he viewed himself in relation to his country. "From here on in," he recalled near the end of his life, "[I knew that] it would be the nation I was serving, not myself." It was then that Ike, along with his classmates, made the West Point motto of "Duty, Honor, Country" their own.

One of the driving passions of Ike's tenure at the Point centered around athletics, most notably football. Although he was lean and muscular at five-foot-eleven and 152 pounds, his enthusiasm made up for what he "lacked in tonnage." He was already recognized for his skill at the sport when, just before the Army-Navy game of 1912, he suffered a serious knee injury during a game against Tufts. The entry about him in his graduation yearbook, written by his roommate P. A. Hodgson, alludes to this incident, his greatest disappointment:

> At one time [Ike] threatened to get interested in life and won his "A" by being the most promising back in Eastern football—but the Tufts game broke his knee and the promise. Now Ike must content himself with tea, tiddledywinks and talk—all of which he excels . . .

Dwight was in the hospital for several days while the doctors worked to untwist his knee. Not long after, he jarred it again, ensuring that his football days were over forever. "I was almost despondent," he later recalled, "and several times had to be prevented from resigning from the army. Life seemed to have little meaning. A need to excel was gone."

Writing to Ruby Norman, he complained, "I sure hate to be so helpless and worthless. I'm getting to be such a confirmed grouch, you'd hardly know me." He added that he had "never had such a protracted case of the blue devils in my life."

Eisenhower's disciplinary record suffered badly: he took up smoking, which was prohibited at West Point, had several reprimands from the authorities, and started to play poker in earnest. Ike's winnings took care of many of his expenses, and the game at least offered some outlet for his feelings of profound frustration. Nevertheless, his record suffered. In class standing for discipline, out of 162 cadets Eisenhower stood 125th.

Just before graduation in 1915, authorities warned him that his injured knee might prevent him from getting a commission in the army. Eisenhower is said to have replied sarcastically, as the passionate often do when psychologically preparing themselves for rejection, "It's all right with me." But the prospect was enough to prompt him to send away for information on how to become an Argentine gaucho, the Midwest equivalent of joining the French Foreign Legion.

Ike spent his leave during that summer of 1915 in Abilene. As the days wore on, he apparently developed a crush on, or perhaps even fell in love with, an old schoolmate, Gladys Harding, the daughter of the wealthy owner of a freight company. Apparently, Ike raised the prospect of marriage to Gladys, but the proposal was neither rejected nor accepted. It is still not known if the indecision reflected her parents' reservations or her own doubts about being an army wife and sacrificing her dreams of a career as a pianist. Ike's declaration might also have been no more serious than the sort made by a young man on the verge of entering new and unsettled circumstances. Whatever the case, that season of his discontent was also the last summer he would spend in his hometown.

When it became clear that Ike's commission was going to come through, he applied for assignment to the Philippines, a request that was rejected. Instead, he was ordered to report to the 19th Infantry, stationed in Galveston, Texas. Long-smoldering trouble with Mexico was threatening to break into open confrontation. As a consequence, a greater number of regular army troops had been stationed along the border, all the way from California to Brownsville, Texas. As Ike set off for Galveston, floods forced the regiment to disperse, with one group going to Utah and the other to Fort Sam Houston, a few miles outside San Antonio. Ike was assigned to "Fort Sam," and it was there that Mamie Geneva Doud would make an unforgettable entry into his life.

CHAPTER THREE

AN ATTRACTION OF OPPOSITES

*J*ohn Doud "always had an itchy foot." Two winters after Eleanor's burial, the family resumed their annual pilgrimage to San Antonio. They also planned and took excursions to Cuba and to Panama, where the canal had just opened. On another occasion they visited Pupah's sister, "Aunt Susie," in New York and followed this with a tour of the Great Lakes region.

In 1915, Mamie made her debut in San Antonio. It was arranged by a local judge and his wife, a woman who, Mamie recalled, had an "aristocratic Virginia background." Ever since the Douds had started traveling to San Antonio for the winter, Judge Robert P. Ingrum and his family had taken them under their wing, enjoying meals and Sunday excursions together.

One afternoon the two families went out for a Sunday drive, this time deciding to visit the judge's sister-in-law, Lulu Harris, whose husband had been moved with the 19th Infantry to Utah. She had been permitted to stay on at the barracks in Fort Sam Houston, managing their small quarters and looking after their two young sons.

The Douds had had virtually no exposure to the army. They had only been to Fort Collins, outside Denver, for an occasional band concert in the summer. Without any real knowledge or understanding of army life, Mamie surveyed Lulu Harris's situation and felt sorry for the woman, stuck there on an army post with her two children, waiting for her husband to return. But she didn't give the young mother's situation any more thought than that.

As the families sat on the front porch of the Harrises' barracks that afternoon with two young officers, Leonard T. "Gee" Gerow and Wade H. "Ham" Haislip, the two men called to another officer coming out of the building across the street. Dwight Eisenhower, his hat squared forward and wearing side arms, was Officer of the Day and therefore had pressing duties. With little time for small talk, he was briefly introduced to the visitors but could not stay. He took notice of Mamie, though, and asked her if she would like to accompany him on his rounds.

Gerow and Haislip had warned Mamie that Ike was known as the "woman-hater" of the post, an attribution due perhaps to his disappointment with the unsatisfactory situation between himself and Gladys. But Mamie apparently received the caution as an inducement rather than a deterrent. "Though I loathed walking," she told my mother, "the challenge was too much for me. So, I said, 'Certainly, I'd like to,' and I never walked so far in my life." She was wearing tightly laced beige boots she had just purchased on the visit to New York. "They were the last word, but they were *not* walking shoes."

"If she had been intrigued by my reputation as a woman-hater," Ike said later, "I was intrigued by her appearance." Mamie must have well concealed the agony her feet were in because Ike described her as "vivacious," "attractive," and "saucy about the face." As he told a journalist during the war, he had also admired her "clear blue eyes that were full of impertinence." Mamie recalled that as they walked, Ike said matter-of-factly, " 'Now Miss Doud, this is an army post, and the men in the barracks are not expecting ladies. I suggest you keep your eyes to the front.' Of course I immediately looked both left and right." Either in spite or because of her impishness, Ike was clearly interested in the young Denver debutante.

Mamie, too, was intrigued. She admitted that the lean, broad-shouldered soldier with a magnetic smile was "the handsomest man" she had ever met, a far cry from the society boys at home, whom she described as "lounge lizards with patent-leather hair."

Captivated by Mamie's flirtatious charm, Ike called her the next day, but the Douds had gone fishing with one of her many beaus. He persisted, though, in the face of one of the busiest social calendars of any young woman in San Antonio. "What did he expect?" Mamie exclaimed. "I was booked solid. It was my debutante year!" Undaunted, "Louie [the lieutenant] from Fort Sam" called two or three times a day for the next three weeks.

On the evenings Mamie wasn't available, Ike would come and sit on the wide veranda of the McCullough Street house and talk to her parents until she returned.

Finally, Pupah stepped in and told Mamie to "stop her flighty nonsense or the 'Army boy' [will] give up in disgust." Several weeks after their initial encounter, Mamie finally agreed to have dinner with Lieutenant Eisenhower at the St. Anthony Hotel, after which they took in a vaudeville show at the Majestic Theater. Eventually she stopped accepting other men's invitations and saw Ike whenever he had free time, often dining at inexpensive Tex-Mex restaurants and occasionally dancing on the St. Anthony roof.

By the end of that year it was obvious to Pupah that Dwight Eisenhower was an ardent and most probably a serious suitor. He wrote to his daughter while he was away on one of his business trips.

December 6, 1915

My Dear Little Girl,
You are *Dad's* little girl even though you are grown up & 19 & you are still little Puddy to Father. Dear me while I was walking thru the park tonight, thinking of you all, it came to me that some time, maybe soon, you would be leaving us to be some one's little woman, just as our little Mother & other Little Mothers before *her* have done & the lump came up into Dad's throat. I don't want you to leave us soon. The pigs and what I can make by being here, all seemed so insignificant beside my having to be away from home & you all. So I thot that I'd write you a little letter this evening thinking perhaps you'd be hurt because I wrote to Buss & Micky before you, tho that was because their letters came 1st & had you beaten them I'd have answered yours before theirs. I'm oh so glad that everything is so pleasant for you there my Puddy, & Dad hopes that you can keep well and still have good times. I'm glad too that Mother got you the shoes & the hat & I hope you can have another dress this month if Mother thinks best, even if it does exceed her limit. Next month if you still wish to "horse back" and the Lieut [Eisenhower] wants you to ride, perhaps we can manage a "habit" too . . . I have been very busy and tomorrow we are to have 12 or 14 cars which

means get up early to have my work begin early & write Mother a little letter before my hogs come . . .

This is not much of a letter dearest but "Unc" is to take it down & is ready to go. I feared that to morrow would go by without my having a chance to write you dear so I am sending you lots & lots of love & many kisses. Be good to Mother dolly—She is so worthy of all our love & care & we know we never never can repay her for her many sacrifices for us *all*.

Ever your loving
Father

Tell Minnie [Nana] I wish I were home.

Further evidence of Eisenhower's seriousness came at Christmas. When Mamie opened a neatly wrapped package, she was astonished to find a heart-shaped sterling-silver jewelry box, and she understood immediately that she would need her father's permission to keep Ike's gift. For a woman without a formal engagement, receiving such a present in those days would have been unacceptable. After much cajoling, Pupah agreed to let Mamie keep the silver box, if only because her initials had been engraved on it and Ike could never return it to the jewelers.

Despite his extravagant gesture, Lieutenant Eisenhower was rather noncommittal in describing Mamie when writing to old friends like Ruby Norman. Also, Gladys Harding was still in touch with him and had, in fact, recently sent him an expensive Christmas present, though he also seemed to take her overtures with some passivity. An undated letter sent to Ruby makes all this clear:

Dearest Ruby,
'Tis a long time since I've written you, n'est-ce pas? I've really started several times—but always something happens—and I get side-tracked. It's ten o'clock now—I'm on guard and sitting here in the guard house . . .

The girl I run around with is named Miss Doud, from Denver. Winters here. Pretty nice—but awful strong for society—which often bores me. But we get along well together and I am at her house whenever I am off duty—whether it's morning—noon—night. Her mother and sisters are fine—and we have lots of fun together . . .

I suppose you and Miss Miller are quite some gay butter-flies, yes? Go to it—I'm for you. I'd have a good time myself but my money won't hold out. Toward the end of the last of each month—I have to hibernate and wait for pay day—awful! . . .

My roommate is going into aviation. I tried but I can't make it until next September. I'll get a lot more then—if I can get in—and maybe I can make ends meet then. Ha ha. You know me, I'll never have a sou . . .

Heard from Gladys about 2 weeks ago. She sent me a fine smoking jacket for Christmas. Mighty nice of her I thought.

I coached a football team for a little school here this fall. They gave a dance not long ago at a big hotel, and I attended. When I entered the ball room everybody stopped and started clapping and cheering. I blushed like a baby—Gee! Surely was embarrassed. I made a run for a corner, believe me.

Well girl—write to me—I'll try to do better on writing hereafter—and sometime, if you're interested I'll tell you all about the girl I run around with *since* I learned that G.H. cared so terribly for her work.

Good night—
as ever
Dwight

As the early winter rolled on, the relationship between Ike and Mamie intensified. Ike was captivated by the utter femininity of "Miss Doud," a creature who embodied all the mystery of another world. She was unlike any woman he had ever known. And Mamie was overwhelmed by Ike's sex appeal and masculinity, a trait she had not encountered among the society boys who courted her. Mamie and Ike's very polarity would be the basis of their volatile but electric lifelong attraction.

There was never really a formal proposal. Over time, Mamie told us, "We took it for granted that we'd marry."

Eisenhower must have been aware of the prize he had stolen from Denver's social elite, but he did not seem worried about keeping Mamie in the style to which she had grown accustomed. Perhaps she had reassured him on that point, or possibly he imagined he would supplement his income with poker winnings. Whatever the root of his confidence, by now he must have realized that

Mamie would be a wife with few conflicting priorities—a far better prerequisite for an army wife than a woman with even fledgling career aspirations.

When they decided to become engaged on Valentine's Day, Ike presented Mamie with his West Point class ring, from Bailey Banks and Biddle. Tradition dictated that the fiancée of a West Point graduate should wear a miniature of her husband's class ring as her engagement ring. But when Mamie heard of this, she balked. She wanted a miniature of nothing. She wanted a full-size copy of "the real thing," she explained.*

Despite the solemnity of Ike's presentation, Pupah was not home at the time. He was in Iowa on business again, so Nana refused to let Mamie wear the ring until Mr. Doud had given his consent. It was not until March 17 that Ike could properly ask for Mamie's hand.†

Pupah most certainly had doubts about Ike's proposal. No matter how much Mamie said she didn't care about her soldier fiancé's income, he was well aware of the problems she faced. She took for granted the comfortable life she led, but in the army she would have severe financial constraints and would never have a permanent home. "But Papa could see we were wild about each other," Mamie later said, "[and] all I wanted was that man."

Her father finally conceded that "there was no reason why scrimping and saving would not lay a foundation for an enduring marriage." But he warned that he would *not* give Mamie an allowance, and she would have to live within her husband's means.

When Ike came to ask for Mamie's hand, Pupah replied that he had not anticipated that Mamie would be married so young, but said he would approve the marriage if they would wait until November, when Mamie would turn twenty. All seemed to be settled, and the happy couple began to discuss wedding plans when Pupah's approval was nearly withdrawn. One evening when Ike was

*Mamie wore the full-size copy of Ike's huge class ring throughout her life, but during the 1952 campaign she had to take it off when she shook hands, since otherwise it left her fingers black and blue.

†In evidence of Mamie's love of celebrating special days, she often marked both Saint Valentine's Day and Saint Patrick's Day as the anniversary of their engagement, leading the columnist Betty Beale to comment in April 1948 that friends of Mamie Eisenhower "claim that she has more anniversaries than anyone they know."

at the house, he mentioned that he had applied for and been accepted into the army's aviation section, which would mean a fifty-percent increase in monthly pay. To a soon-to-be-married man who earned only $141.67 a month and was still in debt to his father, this was badly needed money.

Pupah had other ideas. He thought that becoming an aviator and taking a wife were incompatible. Flying was a dangerous experimental endeavor. If Ike became an aviator, he said, he would rescind his consent.

Ike left the Doud house that evening to consider the situation. "After looking at the matter, seriously, but not grimly," he later recalled, "I phoned the Douds and made a date to see the family once more. When I arrived I announced that I was ready to give up aviation. It turned out that my decision was an immense relief to the family because Mamie had been raising quite a fuss. She understood the way I felt about getting into flying."

Mamie's support for Ike's aviation ambitions gave him an insight into the tenacious loyalty she would invest in him throughout her life. Unlike Gladys Harding, Mamie knew her own mind and had no hesitation in trusting her own instincts, even over her father's objections. Mamie's support must have also signaled to Ike something of her stubborn determination, a trait that would be necessary for overcoming the difficulties of army life.

Before the Douds' departure for Denver, Ike gave Mamie a carat-and-a-half diamond set in platinum as her "real" engagement ring, going into significant debt to do so. She was thrilled with the ring and wore it on her slender left hand, while the copy of his massive class ring was worn with pride on her delicate right hand. "The diamond must have cost a great deal," Mamie said later, "but to Ike, the sky was the limit and money never meant much to him except to obtain some specific end."*

With plans set for a November wedding, the Douds again headed north, and Mamie was with them. The couple would have to content themselves with long-distance correspondence during the months until their marriage. Ike took his new responsibilities soberly and eagerly. "As a symbol of my new seriousness and sacrifice," he recalled, "I stopped smoking ready-made cigarettes,

---

*Ike managed to pay back his debt to his father and his installments on the ring quite quickly, through his poker earnings.

which were about $1.00 a carton, and went back to rolling my own."

*M*eanwhile the political situation between the United States and strife-ridden Mexico was deteriorating rapidly. Mexico was embroiled in civil war, and in October 1915 President Woodrow Wilson recognized General Venustiano Carranza as the de facto president of the "Constitutionalist" government. Mexican rebel Pancho Villa, in defiant opposition to Carranza, began raiding U.S. border towns in retaliation, and the situation became so serious that General John J. Pershing was sent south to mount punitive expeditions into Mexico and the National Guard was called up from as far away as Chicago. The looming conflict was intensely felt in a place like San Antonio, so close to the border.

Although Ike's and Mamie's letters of this period have not survived, the tension of the mobilization must surely have been reflected in their correspondence, an exchange that prompted them to advance the date of their wedding. Mamie later told my mother that the border situation was so serious that "I was worried I would lose him . . . I was making my own plans and not thinking about Papa and Mama, who were with Auntie in Boone."

However, there was one major obstacle in their way. Leaves for officers had been canceled except for emergencies. Ike, determined to marry at the earliest possible opportunity, used a favorable impression he had once left on the commanding general to wheedle a ten-day leave.

When Mamie told her parents about the change in plans, they were "speechless." The Douds were perfectly aware that such a short engagement would raise eyebrows and encourage gossip that the wedding had been *necessary*. But Mamie's stubborn defiance finally won the day. "Well," she had retorted firmly, "Ike is on his way and we have only ten days."

Many things weren't possible to do for a wedding on such short notice. A church ceremony had been planned but had to be canceled in favor of a service at home. Mamie's dress had to be purchased "off the rack," since a custom-made dress would have taken too long to make.* Furthermore, Mamie had expected to

---

*Later, Mamie had the dress modified and wore it to cocktail and dinner parties.

complete her hope chest by November. The chest, with its silver, linens, and embroidered towels, would have been of great value in her new army setting, but it could not be finished in time for a July wedding. Nevertheless, Mamie cared little for show and ignored the details that might have mattered to other society women of her age.

In the last week of June, Ike departed Fort Sam Houston for Denver and the start of his leave, but floods in Texas delayed him by a day. Arriving in the Colorado capital with a hastily purchased ring in hand, he also announced that he had just been promoted to first lieutenant. That meant twenty more dollars a month; it was a lucky promotion on his wedding day.

On July 1, 1916, at noon, the bride was escorted on the arm of her father down the paneled staircase that had been part of the procession route for their childhood birthday romps. Ike, who had come to the house two hours early, had had to remain standing while he waited, so he wouldn't crease his dress-white trousers. Next to the fireplace in the music room, with an English pastor officiating, Ike and Mamie exchanged their wedding vows, which were followed by a formal luncheon in the Douds' adjacent dining room.

That evening, the newlyweds took a train to a small resort near Denver in Eldorado Springs, where they spent a few nights. Then, back at 750, they helped address wedding announcements and prepared to leave for Abilene, where they would visit Ike's parents. A few days after the Fourth of July, Mamie and Ike boarded the 5:00 p.m. train, scheduled to arrive in Abilene at 3:00 the next morning. It must have been an emotional parting for Mamie and her parents: the Douds, who had always placed such an emphasis on family, were losing "little Puddy" at a very young age to a nomadic and uncertain life that would take her far from their Denver–San Antonio axis. But no matter how many doubts or reservations Pupah and Nana may have harbored about their daughter's long-term prospects, they were already attached to their new son-in-law and couldn't help being touched by the happiness Mamie radiated.

The train ride to Abilene was long and uncomfortable; though it was evening, temperatures were at their seasonal peak. As the lights of Denver disappeared into the hot midsummer night, Mamie opened her face-powder box to dust the shine off her nose and, to her surprise, discovered that her younger sisters had filled the box with rice. As the monotony of the train finally quelled the day's excitement, she and Ike closed their eyes for the few short hours that remained before they reached Ike's hometown.

When the train finally pulled into the Abilene station, Mamie and Ike looked for his father and at first could not see him in the darkness of night. Then they caught a glimpse of David Eisenhower standing alone on the platform. Mamie later recalled that she thought it was strange to see her new father-in-law in his shirtsleeves. She had been raised in a social circle where men always wore jackets outside the home.

After the short ride to the Eisenhowers' homestead, Mamie was surprised again, this time by the size of their small clapboard house, and incredulous that Mrs. Eisenhower, with help from the boys who were still at home, did all the cooking and cleaning herself. Mamie was amazed that the Eisenhowers did not believe in alcohol or cards and "went to bed early and got up very early." In other words, she concluded, "they were completely different from my family."

As the young couple had only a few short hours in Abilene—they were due to leave for San Antonio that morning at 11:00—Ida had prepared a large brunch in their honor, complete with fried chicken ("I'd never heard of such a thing!" Mamie later exclaimed). Before sitting down, Mamie excused herself to go upstairs to freshen up. On her way back down, she caught sight of Ike's youngest brother, Milton. "You must be my new brother," she exclaimed brightly. "I've always wanted to have a brother!" She rushed to the bottom of the stairs and planted a kiss on his cheek. Telling me this story years later, Milton added with a laugh, "And I've been her willing slave ever since!"

Mamie got along well with the elder Eisenhowers, whom she called Grandpa and Grandma, though she readily admitted she had little in common with them. Years later she admitted that on subsequent visits to see her parents-in-law she would hang out of the upstairs window to smoke her cigarettes, hoping she wouldn't be caught. Perhaps because of this gulf between their lifestyles and outlooks, in the coming years she and Ike spent considerably more time with the Douds. Their gaiety and sense of fun were vastly different from the tone of the more austere Eisenhowers, whose family motto was "Sink or swim, survive or perish."

"The Eisenhowers were so rigidly Pennsylvania Dutch, I don't think Dad [Ike] communicated on a confidential basis with his father, *ever*," John recalled. "I think Pupah regarded Ike as a son, or at least his ally among the distaff. And Nana just doted on him."

Mamie, too, had her theories: "Ike loved the warmth of our family. He had never been used to that soft side of life, being raised in a household of six boys. The Douds were sentimental and demonstrative and a very close family."

As the years passed, both the determination, hard work, and idealism of the Eisenhowers and the sensitivity and fun-loving nature of the Douds found expression in Ike's character; he was a man who possessed, in the opinion of many, "extraordinary balance." Mamie, the nineteen-year-old bride, was also transformed by their union. Over the years, she would be shaken from her protected and pampered lifestyle, and raised to maturity in a demanding army system where efficiency and competence were expected and sacrifices taken for granted. The process of growth was long and enlarging, but ultimately the merging of opposites would be the making of them both.

CHAPTER FOUR

"MY DUTY WILL ALWAYS COME FIRST"

<img_1>amie had been raised like a Southern belle, to do nothing but run a great house, manage the servants, and please a man. She was strong-willed and determined to do this, not merely to prove to her parents that she could but also to succeed at the task itself.

Still, Mimi, as we always called her, found that she faced challenges for which she had not been prepared, especially as she had been, by her own reckoning, "rotten spoiled." She was accustomed to being able to cajole her father for a new dress, a vacation, or a special outing pretty much any time she wanted one. Expense had rarely been spared. Pupah was right that making ends meet on Ike's salary would be difficult.

The Douds made Mamie's initial transition into army life a little easier with a generous monetary present and the remaining fund they'd put aside to pay for the wedding. Mamie used some of the latter to buy furniture. With the former the young couple bought a secondhand car.

Of Mamie's new responsibilities as a young wife, she most enjoyed trying to make their two-room quarters livable. They were given some wedding presents by their closest friends on the post, and Mamie also had a few items from Denver to help adorn the place. In the living room she laid down a red Khiva rug that had been in her hope chest, and in their bedroom she placed a green Oriental rug from the music room at Lafayette Street. She knew how to sew and embroider, so she set about making curtains from some brocade she had brought from Denver. She also rented a piano for five dollars a month—an essential expense, she proclaimed.

As much fun as it might be to fix up a home, Mamie was ill-prepared for even the most basic tasks of housekeeping. Growing up, she never even had to make her own bed, let alone scrub floors. She also knew virtually nothing about cooking or preparing food. (She must have taken to heart her mother's simple formula: "If you don't learn to cook, no one will ask you to do it.") So for the first few months, at least, the Eisenhowers spent forty dollars a month to take their meals at the officers' mess across the street.

But money was tight, and, as Mamie would say, she had to "squeeze a dollar until the eagle screamed." Many times the couple were down to their last twenty-five cents when payday dawned. So she allowed Ike to teach her some basic cooking skills, and they started to eat simply at home. Eventually she learned how to put a meal on the table, but Ike, who took great pleasure in cooking, was always regarded as the family expert, concocting specialties like beef stew, vegetable soup, and charcoal-broiled steak.

Mamie remained romantically captivated by her handsome husband, but she still had a good deal of maturing to do. "Shortly after we were married," she recalled years later, "we had our first fight. I was angry; I struck out at his hand. My ring came down on his and shattered his [amethyst] stone. He said, 'Well, young lady, for that display of temper you will replace this stone with your own money.' "*

The words "that display of temper" made a deep impression on Mamie, and she soon learned to bite her tongue, but she readily admitted she did not always succeed. But in the early years she was not above using, however unsuccessfully, such old emotional tactics to get her way—even if she had little support for this from her family. "After we were married, I learned quickly not to run to [Nana] seeking comfort when my husband and I had a spat. She always sided with Ike."

"In our family we had always said what came to mind regard-

*Mamie claims that Ike knew that she could use some of the savings she had put away from the Douds' wedding money.

less," she later said. "If feelings were hurt, tearful reunions quickly followed and all was forgiven." My father confirmed this: "The atmosphere in the Doud household was always emotional. The ladies, particularly Nana, Mike, and Great-aunt Eda, possessed a remarkable capacity for weeping and screaming at each other and then falling on each other's necks, making up an hour later." As Mamie eventually matured, she came to play, in Ike's absence, "the role of peacemaker."

Ike was nonplussed by Mamie's outbursts, which he gradually got her to control by sheer dint of his own imposing personality.* Throwing tantrums, no matter how small, was utterly counter to his upbringing. In fact, from his earliest years he had been painstakingly encouraged to restrain his passionate temper and find other ways to express himself, though his impatience, especially with stupidity, later became legendary.

*I*f Mamie was unused to the give-and-take so central to matrimony, being an army wife was even more foreign to her. She got her first real taste of it not long after their wedding when Ike was made provost marshal of the post. His responsibilities included keeping order at the military installation among "untrained soldiers with time on their hands." Conflict was particularly acute between the regular army and the National Guard, which had recently arrived in Fort Sam, and keeping the peace required Ike to spend many evenings on duty, late into the night. The rough-and-rugged atmosphere at the post must have terrified the former Denver debutante, for until her marriage Mamie had never even spent a night alone in a house. Now, long, empty nights became commonplace, as she would wait by herself till the early hours of the morning when Ike would come in. One night, Ike told her he had been ambushed and nearly shot.

Since there were only a few women on the post, and it was teeming with unrest, Ike recalled, "there were times I was frightened for Mamie." He gave her a .45 pistol and carefully showed

---

*Even during and after the White House years, recalls Mamie's secretary Mary Jane McCafree Monroe, "When she stepped out of line, he might say something like: 'Now, Mamie, this is the way you want to do it.' "

her how to use it in case of intrusion. She listened and "took it all seriously." Later, he decided to check and see how prepared she was to handle the weapon. He told her to pretend someone was breaking in and threatening her. Ike remembered that "she went to look for [the gun] . . . She had hidden it behind the piano, inside a bedding roll, under other possessions . . . so far buried that she couldn't have gotten it out in a week, much less a hurry." Ike could see that Mamie would never be able to defend herself under such circumstances, so he abandoned such tactics and "decided to keep on trying to make the camp safer."

To a young woman with romantic notions about love and marriage—and utterly accustomed to being the focus of attention—Mamie and Ike's first separation a month after their wedding must have also come as a shock. When Mamie cried and complained that Ike was leaving her, he put his arm around her and said gently but firmly, "My duty will always come first." Mamie understood by the seriousness of the exchange that he meant it.

Pride was then, and continued to be all her life, one of Mamie's strongest emotions. Sometimes it could stand in the way of a happy outcome, but it fostered tenacity and, ultimately, strength. So if Mamie felt fear or loneliness, she did not discuss it with her parents, nor would she admit that her family's warnings about the financial hardships had been well founded. The intensity of her love for Ike aside, she knew she'd "made her own bed," as she put it later, so she figured she'd better make the best of it, though Ike's priorities were painfully hard to accept.

ℬecause Mamie knew people in San Antonio society, and Mrs. Ingrum introduced her to other young married women, she had some relief from the day-to-day life on the post, where a rigid protocol all its own prevailed.

The "old army" between the wars was hidebound in tradition. It was a small force, with slightly more than 120,000 enlisted men and 14,000 officers, the most elite of whom had been trained at West Point. It was not until the First World War that the army had gone from a small constabulary guarding against Indians to a force with the potential for rapid expansion and utilization of industrial resources. But perhaps because of its size and because its posts and camps were far-flung, the army was a closed, familylike community that was virtually self-sufficient, a world apart from civilian life. And those who were steeped in army values regarded service as far superior to the motivating formula of moneymaking "on the outside."

Many of the customs and rituals observed in the armed forces were borrowed from Europe. At that time, for example, an officer's commission from West Point, by act of Congress, declared that the recipient was "an officer and a gentleman." Ballroom dancing was part of the curriculum at West Point, and cadets were also expected to master the fine art of carving meat. Upon graduation, cadets ordered calling cards along with uniforms.

On post, the tradition of calling on one's superior officers was strictly observed. If an officer had a wife, she was expected to accompany her husband on such calls. A properly attired wife wore a hat and gloves for each twenty-minute stop—a visit no longer than the time it took to smoke one cigarette. If a drink was offered, it could be consumed, but the visitors would be expected to leave promptly thereafter. All such calls had to be made within twenty-four hours of arriving at a new post.

Superior officers who were called upon were expected to return these visits within two weeks. If one made a call and found no one at home, an officer would leave two of his cards, one for the absent officer and one for his absent wife. But a wife would leave only one card for her counterpart, since etiquette dictated that no impression be left that a lady had been calling on a man. Once the attempt had been made to make the visit, the callers would not be expected to return.

On Ike's arrival at Fort Sam, before he met Mamie, he and his friends Gee Gerow and Ham Haislip had tried to circumvent this formality by finding the times when officers and their wives would be out, and then one of the three would go and leave everyone's cards. Once, in this way, Ike called on a senior officer and his wife and, confirming they were out, left his card and those of his two mates; the next day he was horrified to discover that Gerow and Haislip had actually been at a picnic with that very officer and his wife. No doubt Mamie's presence in Ike's life made lighter work of such protocol obligations. And she was an incalculable asset not only in formal army circles but also in smoothing out the rough edges of the Kansas farm boy.

.   .   .

*I*f Mamie's first year of marriage was a big adjustment,* one of the bright spots she could count on was her parents' arrival in San Antonio in time for Ike's birthday on October 14. The Douds also stayed in the city through Christmas that year. In a letter to Santa, otherwise known as Pupah, Mamie revealed something of her wish list.

December 15, 1916

Dearest Santa Claus:
There are just a few things which I would like for *you* to bring me this year—a pretty work basket which sits on legs—a pair of mahogany candle sticks— a white silk petticoat, and a corsage bouquet of violets and valley lilies-(artificial) and Santa dear if you can squeeze in an electric grill...I hope you won't have to work too hard on X-mas Santa Claus—I must close for this year,

> Your loving little friend,
> Mamie Doud (Eisenhower)

Not long after Christmas, before the Douds returned to Denver, Mamie found out that she was expecting a baby. Her parents, and especially her sisters, anticipated the event with great excitement. But the joyous news was contrasted with new and disturbing political developments. That April President Wilson sent a message to Congress urging that it declare war against Germany. Though he had won reelection in 1916 on a platform of neutrality and minimal preparedness—advocating that the United States government should try to mediate a peace between the belligerent parties—Wilson changed his position after Germany began unrestricted submarine warfare and sank many American ships. This declaration of war cast into question the fate of the young Eisenhowers, with Ike facing the possibility of going to the front as Mamie prepared to give birth to their first child.

---

*After their first year of marriage, Ike presented Mamie with a cameo, set against a black background, for their first anniversary. For each of the following ten years, he gave her a diamond that was placed in her wedding band.

Bad news followed soon: Ike and Mamie were crushed to discover that the 19th Infantry would be split and Ike would be ordered to take up with the 57th. In those days, a soldier expected to be with his regiment for virtually all his career, and to be separated from the 19th was to be wrenched from many close friends, like Gee Gerow and Ham Haislip. Ike's new position as supply officer gave him the responsibility for three thousand recruits who had been recently mobilized and sent to Leon Springs, a little more than twenty miles from San Antonio. Mamie was not permitted to accompany Ike to this camp, where rigorous training was under way.

The Douds had returned to Denver, and in Ike's absence Mamie stayed alone at Fort Sam. During those many lonely evenings, she worked on making a christening dress for the child she was expecting; there was little else to do. Occasionally she was included in some social evening, but most nights she stayed home, working in the silence of their small quarters, without a radio or any other form of outside entertainment. How had she become part of a life so uncertain she could not even know where her husband would be when her baby was born?

One weekend, exasperated because she had not seen Ike for some time, she decided to take their car and drive to Leon Springs. "Our car sat idly in the garage because only Ike could drive it," she remembered. "I got tired of having him so near and yet so far away. One weekend when he could not come home, I decided to go see him." The fact that Mamie did not know how to drive did not seem to daunt her in the least. Before she left at 5:00 a.m., she called Ike and then set out before anyone else was on the road. Later she couldn't quite recall how she got the automobile started—maybe she found a soldier to crank up the engine. But she was miraculously able to drive almost the entire twenty miles without applying the brakes, which she knew only vaguely were somewhere on the floor. She was lucky that she survived unscathed, as she had to cross several sets of train tracks on the way to Leon Springs.

When Mamie arrived at the gates of the camp, Ike was waiting for her. "Ike, jump on," she shouted. "I don't know how to stop the thing." Ike recalled many years later, "It was difficult to judge who was in more danger—the men on their way to war or the women on their way to the men."

While others from the 57th went to Europe, Ike, to his disappointment, was assigned to Camp Oglethorpe, Georgia, where he was to train officer candidates in trench warfare at a simulated battlefield site. His departure for Georgia late that summer was a particularly difficult parting. Mamie was in the last trimester of her pregnancy, and she dreaded and worried about his absence, though there was nothing she could do. Ike was firm about his aspirations: from Oglethorpe, he wanted to go to the front in Europe. That was what he had been trained for at West Point, he told her; he had and would continue to apply, repeatedly if necessary, for the opportunity to go into combat.

Mamie, alone, prepared for the birth of the baby. Nana, who was recovering from surgery, agreed to come back to San Antonio to be of help when the baby arrived. Fort Sam Houston had no maternity facilities. "It was no place for a mother or babies," Mamie later recalled. They had to fashion a hopelessly primitive, makeshift delivery room out of nothing much more than a table and a chair.

On September 24, Mamie went into labor. She and Nana caught a ride on a mule-drawn wooden wagon that made the rounds of the post, providing rides from one point to another. When they got to the infirmary, Mamie was placed in a small windowless "labor" room, while Nana, on the okay from the doctor, stepped out for a snack. While Nana was gone, Mamie's labor suddenly progressed, and before she got back, a healthy baby boy had been born. The delivery went so well that Mamie was given only a little gas and remained utterly alert. "It is lucky that babies came easily to me," Mamie told me, dreading to imagine what might have happened if there had been any complications.

As she held this small life in her arms, she mused on how much the infant looked like her husband. When Nana returned—shocked and upset that she had missed the delivery—Mamie told her that the baby would be called Doud Dwight, and then she immediately nicknamed him Little Ike. Within days, this nickname was shortened to Ikey and then Ikky.*

Nana immediately went to the post exchange to send a telegram

*Decades later, people spelled the name as Icky, but in all the letters written during his lifetime, the name is spelled Ikky—and that is the form I have chosen to use.

to the baby's father, on maneuvers in Georgia. It was three days before Ike found out that he had a son. Meanwhile, Pupah drove down to San Antonio with Auntie, Buster, and Mike. With all the Douds now in San Antonio, life for Mamie promised color, fun, and laughter again.

Mamie refused to move back to the Douds' McCullough Street home. Determined to be completely independent, she declined any help from her parents, but soon, given the confining nature of having an infant in their two-room quarters, she began to go to her parents' house during the day, always insisting on coming back home to Fort Sam at night.

During this time, Ike was transferred to Fort Leavenworth, Kansas, to train second lieutenants. Just after the Christmas holiday season, he was given special emergency leave to visit Mamie, who had contracted a severe case of pneumonia from a bad cold caught during one of the many holiday parties she'd gone to. With no antibiotics to treat the affliction, as Mamie remembered only too well, "you either came through or you didn't." Ike had only three days to visit his stricken wife and meet his new son for the first time. After his departure, Mamie, weakened by her illness, went for a time back to Denver with the family. There she stayed while Ike waited to hear whether or not he would be sent to the front in France.

In Leavenworth, Ike was increasingly frustrated that his many requests to go overseas had been rejected: "I seemed embedded in the monotony and unsought safety of the Zone of the Interior. I could see myself, years later, silent at class reunions while others reminisced of battle . . . [This would have been] intolerable punishment. It looked to me as if anyone who was denied the opportunity to fight might as well get out of the Army at the end of the war."

Ike's pleas to go to the front had come to naught; indeed, the War Department issued a reprimand to him for "second guessing his superiors." When he learned the news, Eisenhower snapped that his only sin had been to volunteer for combat. Despite his unhappiness, Eisenhower had an internal rule that he would put the best of himself into any job he was assigned, and his determination was noticed by at least some of his fellow officers. One soldier at Leavenworth wrote after his arrival, "Our new Captain

Eisenhower, by name, is, I believe, one of the most efficient and best Army officers in the country."

To Ike's "elation," he was ordered to Camp Meade to join the 65th Engineers, the parent company organizing a tank corps for overseas. But before reporting for duty, he rushed back to San Antonio for another brief meeting with Ikky and Mamie. Then, in mid-March 1918, convinced he was going overseas, he was ordered to Camp Colt in Gettysburg, a deserted campsite where the 65th Engineers would form what was to be called simply the Tank Corps. Since Ike had last been with his family, he had been given two promotions and increasing responsibility. Yet despite his success, Mamie must have wondered if and when she would ever start a proper married life: she had barely seen Ike during Ikky's first seven months.

Word then came that in April they could join Ike in Gettysburg, where, as commander of the Tank Corps, he now had some prospect of finding housing for the three of them. Mamie's excitement at seeing Ike grew as she and Ikky neared Pennsylvania, but she noticed with some concern that bad weather was setting in. What had been showers earlier in the day was turning to frozen rain. By the time they arrived at Gettysburg's small gingerbread train station, heavy snow was falling. Matters were made worse by the fact that Ikky was running a fever, and his condition would soon be diagnosed as chicken pox.

Ike had sent an aide to greet his weary family at the station, for the unexpectedly heavy snowstorm had created a crisis at the camp and he couldn't come himself. Colt had been set up as a summer camp and there were no provisions for the winterlike conditions; as commander, Ike had to find heaters for the tent city erected around Lee's statue on Confederate Avenue.

If this was a less than graceful family reunion, the accommodations into which Mamie and Ikky moved with Ike also left a great deal to be desired. Secured on a temporary basis, this first home was a tiny "two-up two-down" that reeked of stagnant damp, and the only heat source was a potbellied stove downstairs. In Denver, the Doud house had gas and electricity; Mamie had never seen a potbellied stove, let alone known how to make one work.

Mamie had a difficult time settling in and making the house

functional while she cared for the baby. Ike was working hard and was rarely at home. She wondered why she'd come to Gettysburg at all, she told my mother later. But then in June things began to improve. The Eisenhowers were able to move into the Alpha Tau Omega fraternity house, part of Gettysburg College. While the students were on vacation, they had a couple of months to spread out in this considerably larger space. The rambling Victorian house had a huge ballroom but, incongruously, no kitchen, so Mamie had to improvise by washing dishes and laundry in the bathtub. Given the primitive facilities for preparing even the simplest food, more often than not they took their meals at the camp.

"It *was* a very difficult time for me," Mamie later recalled. "I couldn't get [help] of any kind. I think I probably weighed about a hundred and two pounds and I had this baby to carry up and down these steps" (the stairs were all the more formidable because of the very high ceilings). Hiring help from the surrounding community was impossible because of the strain the camp had placed on community resources. The town of Gettysburg had been turned upside down by the enormous influx of soldiers. When Mamie first arrived at Camp Colt, there had been only five hundred men in the encampment, but by that summer of 1918 the camp served as both a mobilization and a disembarkation point, and the numbers swelled to ten thousand men and six hundred officers. The locals made considerable effort to accommodate this massive buildup. Canteens were started in church basements, and families willingly made room in their homes for the soldiers' wives and children.

By the end of the summer, with college beginning again, the Eisenhowers had to find new housing, and the lodgings in the town were already overstretched. A lawyer familiar with estate property in the area received permission for the twenty-eight-year-old camp commander and his wife and son to move into a small brick house on Spring Street. It was Ike and Mamie's first real home together.

That July, Pupah and Buster arrived in Gettysburg for a visit. Buster was a maturing seventeen-year-old who shared many of her older sister's qualities. Like Mamie, she was petite, gregarious, and popular with the young Denver men. Mamie was delighted by the company Pupah and Buster provided, filling the lonely hours while Ike was consumed by his work. She'd come to rely on Buster while she was in Denver waiting to rejoin Ike, and she had missed her younger sister since coming to Gettysburg. Buster's moral support and unflagging high spirits had made the girls uncommonly close.

Mamie was especially sorry when the two-month stay with Pupah and Buster was over. Fortunately, however, the two departed for Denver before an influenza epidemic hit Camp Colt. By the time the strange outbreak was diagnosed, several people had died, and herculean efforts were made to contain the contagious killer. Hospitals were overwhelmed, and every church was utilized to accommodate the overflow of dislocated family members, while the patients were isolated and quarantined at Camp Colt. Ike remembered those tragic days just after the disease had overwhelmed the community:

> The week was a nightmare and the toll was heavy. The little town had no facilities to take care of the dead ... there were no coffins. We had no place to put the bodies except in a storage tent until they could gradually be taken care of more suitably ... As the number of sick mounted rapidly ... the whole camp was on edge. No one knew who was going to be stricken and death came suddenly.

Doctors were frantically giving the men every kind of inoculation imaginable to try to arrest the spread of the disease. With Ikky and Mamie with him in Gettysburg, Ike admitted he was "desperately worried" that either of them might become ill. With few options, Ike agreed to allow a doctor to use experimental sprays and syrups on his family. "We were fortunate," Ike remembered. "Not a single person in my headquarters command or my family contracted the flu." By the time the epidemic was over a week or so later, one hundred seventy-five people had died.

Ike had had a great deal to contend with during his tenure as commander of the camp. In recognition of his service, he was promoted to lieutenant colonel.

As the weather grew colder, preparations were made to disassemble the camp and move it to a warmer climate. Ike expected that when everything had been packed up, he would be leaving for France with the last group of trainees. His orders were for Camp Dix and embarkation on November 18.

At just that point, amid rumors of an armistice, a devastating telegram for Mamie arrived from Pupah in Denver, informing Mamie that her sister Buster had died. Shortly after she and Pupah had returned to Denver, she had developed a kidney infection, which had turned into nephritis. As her illness progressed, she had gone blind and then passed away finally on November 9.

As soon as the news arrived, Ike penned a letter to Nana, expressing his profound condolences and revealing some of his own shock.

November 9, 1918
Gettysburg, Pa.

My Own Dearest Mother:
Dad's telegram arrived about 7:30 tonight, and we are heart broken. And how our hearts bleed for you tonight. Our own little darling that we all loved and adored—and of whom *you* were *the* mother. We can feel *your* grief and mother mine— please believe that, in this hour, the children left to you are sending out their love and affection to you—to do their best in consoling you and strengthening you in this trial.

Mamie has repeated over and over "poor mother," "poor mother"—and tomorrow she starts to you. I cannot come— duty prevents—but even now I know that the love you bear your children tells you that my heart and my love are with you.

To me it seems that the truest monument our darling has left to her memory is the lesson of patience and sweetness she has taught us. I hope I may have learned that lesson well enough that from this day on I may also show those traits in dealing with my fellow men.

Your devoted
Son

With Ike's departure for Europe and the funeral in Denver both pending, Mamie stayed up all night packing her clothes and some things for Ikky. It was agreed that she would remain with her parents in Denver while he was gone: Mamie's presence there would be welcome during this period of mourning, and Ike would be sure of her safety during his absence. The next day, Ike rode with Mamie and Ikky on the morning train to Harrisburg, where he put his wife and son on the overnight express to Chicago. After a layover of a few hours, the two would continue on to Denver. Amid the large, bustling crowd in Harrisburg, they said goodbye, not knowing when they would meet again.

As Mamie and Ikky tearfully settled into their seats, their train passed through little towns all along the great Ohio Valley. Church bells began to ring, and Mamie wondered if it was a signal that the armistice had been achieved. In Chicago, she had the news confirmed: jubilant people were openly celebrating, and Mamie and Ikky were caught in their joy, unable to move through the teeming crowd, unable to find their platform for the Denver train.

Ike's safety was now all but assured, but Mamie's grief over Buster's death and her physical discomfort were exacerbated by having to deal with cartloads of luggage and, more important, a small hungry child who was worn and fractious from the long trip. To her dismay she discovered that Chicago stores were closed to mark the end of the war, and she couldn't get milk for Ikky. Pupah's brother Eli eventually came to the rescue, picking up Mamie and Ikky at the station and taking them to Oak Park for the night.

The next day they resumed their trip to Denver for Buster's burial, where she would be interred next to their sister Eleanor at Fairmount Cemetery.

CHAPTER FIVE

A GRIEF THAT WOULD BREAK
THE HARDEST HEART

With news of the armistice, Ike, left behind in Gettysburg by the "war to end all wars," now had to report to Camp Dix and later to Fort Benning, while the War Department tried to figure out what to do with the Tank Corps. The task was now demobilization, and eventually Ike was sent back to Camp Meade.

Since Mamie was gone, the responsibility for packing up the house, before reporting to his new assignment, fell to Ike. Mamie later recalled that she did not see her things for years—and when she did, Ikky's high chair was missing and the coffee percolator that she'd been so proud to own still had coffee grounds in it. Even though the war was over, there was no housing for families at Camp Meade. Only the highest-ranking officers had quarters, so Mamie remained in Denver, waiting for the situation to change. "It meant a brief spell of loneliness," Ike said, "brief, that is, meaning interminable."

That summer the army planned to put together a truck convoy to cross the entire country, and word came that the Tank Corps would be permitted to send two observers; Ike volunteered to go.

As recently as 1916, the army had been mostly horse-drawn, and trucks had just come into use. They had been utilized during the American incursion into Mexico in 1916 but had been unreliable on the bad Mexican roads. Now, less than a handful of years later, the convoy would test the maneuverability of military equipment on a larger scale and determine how military personnel could maintain that equipment on the move.

The convoy was given an elaborate send-off by many Washington bigwigs when it hit the road finally at 11:15 a.m. on July 6, 1919. The caravan was to traverse the old Lincoln Highway and cover 3,200 miles to the West Coast. Ike later recalled that "all drivers had claimed lengthy experience in driving trucks; some of them, it turned out, had never handled anything more than a Model T." Along the way, at least half the roads were dirt, and "the roads varied from average to non-existent." During sixty days of grueling travel, they averaged 6.07 miles per hour, or 58.1 miles per day.

No doubt during this cavalcade there were plenty of letters between Mamie and Ike, but the only surviving piece of correspondence in family hands is a postcard Ike sent her from the road. The scenic side showed a photograph of the convoy crew, and on the other side he wrote:

June 18, 1919

Dearest,
I am not in this picture—but I thought you'd like to see it.
Love you heaps and heaps.

Your lover

As the convoy made its way west, the tired crew was recognized and sometimes celebrated in each small town. This was good for considerable local excitement. When the convoy went through Boone, Iowa, for example, on July 25, 1919, the town paper was full of the news, reporting that the convoy took a thirty-minute stop while the Red Cross served refreshments to 280 army personnel. Miss Eda and Joel Carlson, said the account, were on hand to greet their nephew Dwight Eisenhower. After refreshments, he was interviewed, saying diplomatically, if non-committally, "I can't say too much of the condition of the Lincoln Highway."

With the convoy wending and weaving its way across the Midwest, in a pique of impetuousness Mamie decided she wanted to meet Ike en route. Appealing to her father's sense of adventure, she persuaded Pupah to rev up the family touring car and meet the convoy in South Platte, Nebraska, where Mamie and the

Douds drove with it for three or four days—as far as Laramie, Wyoming.

At the end of the summer, the convoy reached San Francisco. There Ike secured four weeks of leave and came back to Denver to help the Douds prepare to motor south to San Antonio. Midway, torrential rainfall washed out the roads, and Ike, Mamie, Ikky, Nana, and Pupah were stranded for a week in Lawton, Oklahoma. With time on their hands, they played cards and listened to bulletins about the World Series. When they finally reached San Antonio, Ike returned to Camp Meade, charged with finding some housing for his family so they could be reunited again. In three years of marriage Ike and Mamie had spent less than half of it together, and they both understood the importance of trying to start again the family life that had been theirs for that short, chaotic period in Gettysburg.

A month later, Ike phoned Mamie to say he had found a room in Laurel, Maryland, where they could stay, but there was not space enough for Ikky. The Douds, however, were more than happy to look after their grandson while Ike and Mamie had some time together and a chance to look for more permanent housing.

Late that fall, Mamie arrived in Laurel, near Camp Meade, but she stayed only a month. Ike worked extremely long hours, and their rented room was some distance from the camp. Because of power shortages, there was no electricity in this tiny one-room walkup from 6:00 a.m. to 6:00 p.m., and as the winter days grew shorter, Mamie would often find herself sitting in the dark waiting for Ike to come home so that they could dine at Halverson's boardinghouse, the only place in the vicinity where one could get a decent meal. In the gloom of this environment Mamie missed Ikky terribly, and it was probably during one of those twilight hours that she decided she would go back to stay with her parents in San Antonio until the army assigned them some kind of quarters on post. Later, in reflecting on this dismal chapter, she said she told Ike she "couldn't take it any longer." Leaving Laurel, she regretfully recalled, was the first time she'd ever "given up and thrown in the sponge."

The separation was no better, though. Ike wrote to Mamie's parents after her return to San Antonio, and the strain it created is evident.

November 16 [1919]

Dearest Mother:

I hear from Mamie so infrequently that I have no idea how you all are getting along. Sincerely trust though that you & Daddy are fine . . .

We are very busy—but seem to get nothing accomplished. So few men are available—and so many different things to be done—that mainly we seem to be chasing ourselves in a circle.

About 2 days ago I received a letter that Mike wrote me in September. Had certainly chased me about a bit. I want to write her this p.m.

Would you mind, when you have time, writing me about Ikky—Yesterday I did get a letter from Mamie—first one in over 2 weeks—but she said practically nothing about any of you. So please tell me about Ikky & daddy & yourself.

Yesterday was the day set for reductions. Heard nothing—so I'm still calling myself "Koinel."* Great joy! But no telling how short-lived it will be. No use of fretting ourselves though!

How has your trip turned out? Has it made you a little happier to get to the sunny climate? How I hope it has! I think you are wonderful—I like to be around you & daddy.

I try to be patient & cheerful—but I do like to be with people I love.

The best of everything to you & daddy—& I hope the trip has made you both much happier and that the change is giving your mind a rest.

Devotedly your
Son

Within a few months of Mamie's departure, the army decided to allocate to married officers a few unrenovated wartime barracks. Ike and Mamie would be eligible for one, but they would have to pay for the improvements with their own money, just as they would have to furnish it themselves. In early summer Mamie came to help Ike remodel the dilapidated quarters. Ike and a few of his

*This refers to postwar rank reductions. After "Koinel," he drew a cartoon of himself.

friends installed a kitchen and a bath, refinished the floors, and partitioned the rooms. For an outlay of eight hundred dollars, an awkward little space had been turned into an acceptable home.

The remaining problem was how to furnish the place. "When we left Fort Sam," Mamie recalled, "on the advice of another army wife, I [had] sold all our furniture except the Oriental rug. She advised me to travel light, sell everything when we moved, and then pick up what we needed in the new place. But it was many years before I could gather the money together to replace all that I had sold."

Now they had to make do in the starkest of ways. "I took orange crates and made a dressing table out of them. I got some cretonne and little thumbtacks and covered up the orange crates," Mamie later recalled. And she found other sources for furnishings. The Red Cross building, in the main part of Camp Meade, had been closed at the end of the war, and the furniture donated for its lounge had been thrown away. Piles of it were sitting in a dump. By combing through the refuse, Mamie acquired a rattan chaise and an octagonal table. Ike said, " 'Oh my God, Mamie, you're not going to keep that?' I said, 'Yes, I like it—I got it off the dump heap.' "

"We slept on army cots and I would get cretonne and make covers for them, so it would cover the head and foot. At that time we were getting Japanese print material . . . I would get it by the yard and I made draperies. You just did anything to make it look decent."

With their quarters now transformed into a real home, Ikky joined his parents, and the family was reunited for the first time in more than a year and a half.

Army life, with its family features, meant that everyone was essentially in the same boat. Perhaps that was one of the things Mamie liked best about it. "You moved in, and if it was a hot day, someone brought you over some lemonade, or some sheets . . . or cooking pans, if your [things] had not arrived . . . We all did it, everybody helped out." Mamie was not the only army wife trying to bring order to this makeshift way of life. There was camaraderie on post, born of the hardships and forged in the experience of living in the same "old broken-down quarters."

Although Ike and Mamie were always struggling, their next-door neighbors at Camp Meade, the George Pattons, unlike the Eisenhowers, had between them a considerable fortune, which enabled them to renovate their quarters in style and staff it with servants. Money was regarded as such a help in an army career that no attempt was made to hide it. Once, when Patton had to fulfill the army's equitation requirement at Fort Leavenworth, he was excused because he had brought his thirteen polo ponies with him for training. That didn't hurt Patton one bit, as the prestige of having his horses with him outweighed the special exception.

Despite the difference in financial means between the Eisenhowers and the Pattons, there was no gap between the households. Ike and George were close, regularly meeting in their off-hours to discuss Tank Corps business and playing poker twice a week. They also worked closely on the range together. Once, both Patton and Eisenhower were nearly killed during maneuvers when a cable snapped, whipping within inches of their faces at machine-gun-bullet speed, with enough force to slice tree branches and saplings like a razor. Such experiences tended to have a bonding effect.

The wives, however, were not on intimate terms. Mamie did not exactly regard Bea Patton as a contemporary—she was perhaps ten years older than Mamie—and they shared very few interests. To Mamie's mind Bea, the mother of three, was a matron—a type she would never agree to become, no matter what her age, no matter how many children she had.

Despite the makeshift conditions on the post, the officers' wives were expected to entertain. Formality on the post dictated that even in social things the wives had to live up to a high standard. Officers entertained officers, regardless of rank, and junior officers would often entertain their superiors, which was not only encouraged but expected. In the old army an officer's simple talents were not the only factors for promotion; a popular and socially sophisticated wife was an enormous asset. This created the necessity for a unique partnership between husband and wife. Mamie referred to the work she shared with Ike as "our career," and she was always conscious that, in her words, "a wife plays a very big part [in it]. If she doesn't measure up, or if she's a troublemaker, a gossiper, or she doesn't know the proper things to do, these things all play a great part." She "bought into the partnership idea strongly," my father concurred. "When one of their acquaintances was made a general in 1940, she said, 'I don't know how that man ever made brigadier general, his wife is simply awful.'"

Given the challenges, Mamie began to fit into the army

system. As one might have expected from her life before she married, she was good at entertaining, a breezy, engaging, and polished hostess who always made people feel welcome. Camp Meade, like many army posts, relied on its own resources for recreational diversions for the officers and their men, and Mamie and Ike entertained constantly, adopting the Doud tradition of a Sunday buffet open house, often followed by card games or songfests. The lively atmosphere that prevailed at their quarters earned it the name "Club Eisenhower," and it became a virtual hangout for Ike's contemporaries.

In addition to entertaining officers on post, Mamie frequently served as hostess at receptions thrown in honor of high-ranking officials who came up from Washington, sometimes for as many as one hundred guests. Though social faux pas were rare, the most glaring one Mamie made in those years came when a number of Washington dignitaries, including Secretary of War Newton Baker, visited Meade. At one gathering Baker was overwhelmed by officers' wives singing the praises of their husbands. When they'd finished, the secretary turned to Mamie and asked her what she thought *her* husband was good at. Looking at him directly, she replied pertly, "My, he plays an awfully good game of poker."

When Ike found out what she'd said, he was furious.

"But everybody knows you're a good soldier!" she said, hotly defending herself.

In fact, it was true that Ike was highly regarded, but it was also true that Mamie knew very little about his work. During that era in the army, women were not allowed to go into headquarters or to their husbands' place of operations. They weren't even permitted in the Officers' Club until evening. Wives were expected to stay at arm's length and tend only to domestic matters.

Yet it is also true that Mamie did not feel compelled to know the details of Ike's work. "I never felt like I had to help Ike in any way, except in making as nice a family life as possible," Mamie once said. "I thought he was perfectly capable of paddling his own canoe. It just never occurred to me to give him any advice on his business. That was his."

For the first time in their army life, Mamie was a deeply contented wife. She had an irresistible little boy whose father was a handsome, well-liked officer. Most of all, after all their previous separations they were a united family, settled into a home they had fashioned for themselves.

Ike, too, recalled those happy times: "Barracks or not, Mamie, Icky and I had settled down to a fuller family life than we'd ever known. Icky, naturally, was in his element and he thoroughly enjoyed his role as center of attention. For a little boy just getting interested in the outside world, few places could have been more exciting than Meade. Deafening noises of the tanks enthralled him. A football scrimmage was pure delight. And a parade with martial music set him aglow. I was inclined to display Icky and his talents at the slightest excuse, or without one for that matter. In his company, I'm sure I strutted a bit and Mamie was thoroughly happy that, once again, her two men were with her."

In the fall of 1920, Nana, Pupah, and Mike came for a visit. They also brought Aunt Eda, who missed "her baby" Ikky, whom she had looked after while Mamie had been in Laurel and then at Meade. The Douds were surely gratified to see the Eisenhowers leading such a harmonious life, and they were delighted by the popularity Ikky enjoyed among the young officers, who made him a Tank Corps uniform and declared him "Mascot of the Corps." After a brief visit the elder Douds returned to Denver, leaving Eda and Mike to stay on. Mamie sent them all the news.

Dearest Folksies:
. . . Poor Aunty has one of her spells to-day and is in bed and besides its raining pitch Forks . . . Ikkie seems the only cheerful one around here . . .

I just think Ikkie's pictures are *marvelous*. Am so pleased with them. Mother it was darling of you to have them made. Will you order ½ dozen more of smiling one for me—be sure and send me the bill for them . . .

If you can . . . I wish you'd gather all my old dresses together and send them to me. Aunty says there were so many I could use. I think in the bottom drawer of Ike's trunk is my marriage certificate which I must have. Also I have to write to S.A. [San Antonio] for Ikkie's birth certificate cause if anything should to happen to Ike I couldn't get his pension from government unless I had both of those papers. Also I think

you might as well send my tea wagon and Ikkie's cedar chest
... Ikkie had a fine birthday. Mrs. Hitt made a lovely birthday
cake and I had ordered two sunshine cakes from Baltimore so
he had plenty—we sang here comes the bride for two nites
and burned candles out—ha ha. You know him and his happy
birthday cake. He re'cd everything on earth—animals, drum,
horn, suitcases, dolls, Tank and goodness knows what not.
Everyone got him some thing and the house is littered with
trash ... Ikkie is fine and certainly enjoys himself. He's as
brown as a berry and is quite a moving picture fiend—and we
go every other nite. He pesters the life out of us until we take
him ... I must quit now. Besides my sweetheart [Ike] just
came home and so I must get lunch. Bye bye—see you later—
as Ikkie says.

Your Puddy

That fall, with only Eda and Mike remaining, the Eisenhowers'
social schedule seemed especially full. Eda wrote to Joel that
"everybody seems so friendly, all officers and their families stick
together and always up and going—just like one big family." She
had been a guest at a small dance, Auntie confessed, but added,
"Please do not mention this to any of the Booneites. I'll get in
bad for sure, horrors. I enjoyed myself and have had a very good
time so far."

The next month Eda reported to her younger brother, Joel, that
a surprise party had been given for Ike's thirtieth birthday, and he
was presented with a beautiful silver cigarette case with a small
tank engraved on the inside and the words, "Col. Ike a friend
indeed."

It was a golden moment, with the promise of many more to
come. Just before Christmas, for which Mamie had festively decorated their quarters, the Douds returned for the family holiday.
But on the eve of the Nativity, the tranquillity of the Eisenhowers'
lives was shattered.

There have been many accounts of how three-year-old Ikky
died, but perhaps the most poignant, in its simplicity, is the account Mamie gave to my mother nine days before her death:

Nana was taking care of Ikky. I had gone into Baltimore with some of the other officers' wives on the post. We were shopping for Christmas presents for the enlisted men's children. We had a Christmas tree for them and we were planning a party. I returned that evening and was told that the baby had not been feeling well that afternoon. He seemed to be sick at his stomach. I called the doctor and he came right over. He said that he would be alright, that he must have eaten something that did not agree with him. The baby seemed feverish to me, so I took him to bed with me to soothe him. He seemed to get worse and finally his little body was burning up. We didn't call the doctor back, because we thought, too, he had a stomach ailment, but the first thing in the morning we called him. "We think you better put him in the hospital where the nurses can keep an eye on him," they said. We had gotten a little red tricycle for him for Christmas and the Christmas tree was all trimmed downstairs. As we walked past the tree to take him to the hospital, he smiled and pointed to the tricycle.

If he had broken out it wouldn't have been so bad, but he didn't. The nurses weren't paying any attention to him. On one visit we could see him running up and down the halls in the hospital. The nurses weren't keeping him in bed. There wasn't anyone else in there. Nobody was entertaining him or anything. He was a child, you see, accustomed to having Ike, myself, or Mama, someone around all the time.

Finally, we called the doctors from Johns Hopkins. The doctor said, "He has scarlet fever." The army doctors admitted they didn't know anything about scarlet fever. There was not much the Hopkins doctors could do either. [They put him in quarantine] and we were told we would just have to wait it out. We would go over and see him and wave and throw kisses to him through the glass partition. Ike would sit on a porch just outside his room and talk to him. They wouldn't let me go in his room, but they finally let Ike.

[Then] the meningitis set in. Within a week he was gone. The night he died, I was home with such a heavy cold they thought I might be getting pneumonia. Ike had gone to the hospital and later, near morning, Ikky died in his arms. We never talked about it. I did not ask him, because it was something that hurt him so badly.*

News of Ikky's death on January 2, 1921, spread like wildfire through the post. When arrangements were made to take the body to Denver for burial, an honor guard from the camp escorted Mamie and Ike and the little casket to the station, and the same men who had declared Ikky "Mascot of the Corps" carried the boy's remains onto the train.

In Denver, the casket was placed in front of the fireplace, banked with flowers, in the same music room where Mamie and Ike had married only four and a half years before. Ikky was interred at Fairmount Cemetery next to Eleanor and Buster, who had died only two years before. After the services, Mamie and Ike returned to Camp Meade by train, stopping for the night in Chicago. Both tried to think of other things, but the boy's death utterly consumed them. Not long after their return, Mamie wrote her parents.

Tuesday 11:30 a.m.

Dearest Folksies:
Daddy's sweet letter came this morning and oh how good it did make me feel. I just had a feeling I would hear from some one of you to-day. It seems good to be home but the emptiness sure does hurt. I've just wandered around all morning. Ike & I didn't sleep an hour all Friday nite. We felt so terribly

---

*My own understanding of the previous sequence of events is the following: Ike's wartime rank was finally reduced to captain; by December he had been promoted again to major, which brought with it another seventy dollars per month. With this new financial stability, Mamie and Ike thought at last they had enough money to get some help with the house and the youngster, and they hired a maid. They later surmised that Ikky had contracted scarlet fever from the maid, who had been exposed to the disease before coming to work for them—though she had failed to disclose it, possibly not knowing herself that she carried it. In the correspondence of the period, a woman named Carrie is mentioned a great deal. Carrie, who helped Mamie with housework, herself became ill around the same time that Ikky died. It is possible that she may have been the same maid; in any case, only later did they hypothesize that this is how Ikky had become fatally ill.

low at leaving you all . . . Sunday was a very tiresome day and we went to bed at 8 o'clock but didn't sleep well. Sheets and Robertson [young officer friends] met us in Baltimore and we had breakfast in the station, coming right home . . .

Barnholtz had the house spotless and very much dressed up—even to a rosebud put on my pillow, which amused me considerably . . . The men made a beautiful chest for Ikkie's toys—all painted and varnished with a lock and handles on either end. Sheets said so many soldiers came to him and wanted to do something for Ike. Wasn't it sweet of them? . . .

Ike is up to his ears in work—which is good for him. Carrie is still in the hospital but will be out shortly. Tameraz has had Diphtheria and is just recovering. Poor old Tam—guess he was so worn out he couldn't fight it . . . Ike's brother Arthur and a friend are coming to-morrow—suppose they will only be here for luncheon. So B & I are going to commissary now to stock up. B. Harris is in the hospital taking the rest cure. She almost had a nervous breakdown. Mrs. Haynes' dog Sandy that Ikkie was so crazy about was run over & killed by a truck yesterday. She felt so badly. Dears I sure miss you all so much and I do hope nothing will prevent your coming back to Meade . . .

Want to get this off in afternoon's mail. So bye bye. Oh so much love for you all.

Your Mamie

In a letter a week or so later, Ike described for Mamie's parents their reentry into life at Meade in a more upbeat fashion, devoid of the emotional references Mamie had offered so forthrightly:

Our first week at home has been a busy one, especially for me. They have instituted a lot of innovations in administration—and I have been vainly trying to catch up. Among other extra work—I have to pass an exam in the new Law Book next Wed. and must submit a resumé of a Tank book of 450 pages—*some job*!! . . . The football squad took the smiling picture of Ikky we had given Barnholtz—and had it enlarged—tinted & framed & presented to us.

Ike's reference to Ikky's picture is matter-of-fact, but he displayed uncharacteristic sarcasm when referring to the specialists who had attended Ikky before his death.

> I haven't received the statements from the specialists yet. Other bills & expenses were 650 dollars—which of course included last month's expenses. Tell Mother that the nurse *must* have been good. She charged fifty dollars for 4 days . . . Your devoted son

Two days later Mamie wrote some of the same news, though she was more open about the crisis.

January 31, 1921

Dearest Folksies,

. . . I do think the verse is the sweetest I've ever read. When I feel so badly it helps me so much. I've read it a dozen times already. Ike and I had a very bad nite last nite. I just thot something would surely burst inside of me. I find the hardest time is when I go to bed and I can't go tuck him in—and the many times I think I hear him in the nite. I *know* I shouldn't write all this—but I get so full up I have to tell someone and I know you all share my feelings—and understand.

Teddy—Porks White—and Tommy have been to call and many others—they try not to let me get lonesome. Carrie is out of the hospital and stopped here on her way home but I was in Washington. Said she was writing me a note. The football squad had the laughing picture of Ikkie enlarged tinted in oils and framed and presented to us on Wednesday. Wasn't it sweet of them. Most have been to see it. I have it hung in the living room over the wicker couch where every time I come into the room I can see it. It certainly does hurt, but I can't learn any sooner to face it all. Re'cd some lovely cards . . .

I am so nervous and restless it is hard for me to write so I know you will understand why my letter is so disconnected. Ike is attending two schools a day beside his Brigade work and is quite upset and never home except in eve . . . No, Mike Sheets does not live in our house but mighty near it. I don't know what we would do without him.* He certainly is a comfort to us both . . . Remember me to everyone. We do miss you all so much and need you. We feel like a couple of lost kids. Love you love you and here's so many hugs and kisses I can't count them for everyone of you.

Your Mamie

While the community was still reeling from Ikky's death, tragedy struck again. The wife of Sergeant Haynes, who lived near the Eisenhowers' quarters, was hit by a truck and lived only a few hours. In a letter to Mamie's parents, Ike noted that "we are in

---

*Everyone, it seems, was deeply affected by the tragedy. Mamie wrote her parents that Mrs. Hitt's maid "lost 10 lbs in the three days following Ikkie's death and . . . carried his picture with her constantly." Mrs. Hitt worried about her employee and sent her home for a "change of climate." Mike Sheets, who was a tower of strength to Mamie, was himself in a state of profound grief. In a letter to Mamie's mother he described the impact of Ikky's death—some five months after his passing.

June 8, 1921

Dear Mrs. Doud,
I received your very kind letter. I thank you very much for placing the roses on Ikky's grave. I love him so much and think of him very often. You and your family should be proud in the knowledge that he is your own. I am proud, and I was just only his friend. We will all see him again some day and be happy with him. When we will also understand that God is indeed kind. But that we just did not understand Him or His workings while on this earth. This would be a much better world if we understood more about Him. The reward he offers is much greater than the effort required to live a proper life. I am suffering a great loss, more than I am able to appreciate, in my ignorance of God and his teachings.

There is nothing important to tell you. You no doubt receive all the news from Mrs. Ike. She is quite happy, and they are going out quite often. They miss you very much indeed. It is quite possible you would not understand how much I miss you. I have never before felt quite so "shot up" as I did the night of your departure from Baltimore. You know, strange as it may seem, I sometimes get lonesome. At such times, to some extent, I realize what I have missed and am missing. But I guess that is best.

I received the picture. It is very sweet.

Please remember me to Mr. Doud and give my very kind regards to Mike.

Yours,
A. M. Sheets

the midst of more sorrow." But despite their own grief, Mamie was mobilized into action.

Everyone is sad—[Mrs. Haynes] was well liked. It seems we are having more than our share of distress—

Mamie is wonderful. She is helping—very much—and is as brave as she can be. We have taken in all the relatives and are feeding them. Her mother is expected tonight—and she is to stay at our house. So all in all—we are much upset—and busy.

We both send our love to you all. Mamie said she'd write as soon as she could get her bearings once more. It is particularly hard on her—as Carrie has not returned to work.

Much love from your
Devoted Son

The Eisenhowers remained at Camp Meade until the beginning of the new year, 1922, and went on living in the same quarters where the tragedy had occurred. They both mourned in their own way, but each blamed him- or herself for having taken Ikky's presence in their lives for granted. Ike may have regretted the time he had been separated from his son, and Mamie may have been tormented that she had not been with him in his last hours. Ike mostly kept his own counsel, but Mamie expressed herself more freely in the moments when she could no longer put on a cheerful face. Ike later recalled that "no matter what activities and preoccupations there were, we could never forget the death of the boy." It was the one disaster from which, he said, he never fully recovered. And "for Mamie, the loss was heartbreaking, and her grief, in turn, would have broken the hardest heart."

TROPICAL CHALLENGES

*I*n 1960, just before Mamie left the White House, my grand-mother gave an interview to *Better Homes and Gardens* in which she was quoted as saying, "Giving up a baby is the hardest trial a young couple may have to face." In noting the special nature of this couple, the magazine observed that "not success, but trag-edy first made Ike and Mamie something more than average."

The death of Ikky had a profoundly maturing effect on both of them. As my sister-in-law Julie once asserted, Ikky's death "closed a chapter in the marriage. It could never again be unblemished first love. Ike was no longer the untried idealist, Mamie no longer the blithely romantic spirit. They now regarded each other with open eyes."

Ike threw himself into his work. Mamie, despite her lifelong desire to "push death away," was forced to confront it head-on. She had just turned twenty-four, and already she had lost all four of her grandparents, two of her sisters, and now her firstborn child. Making sense of the tragedy was utterly bewildering for her, and she may have soothed herself with the notion that it had been God's will. Certainly by the end of her life, she had come to ex-plain the many imponderables she'd encountered in that way.

Ikky's death was not a topic that was ever easy for Mamie and Ike to discuss. When they did speak of him, they would do so only in a positive, if wistful, way, referring only to the young boy's life. Every year on the anniversary of his birthday, Ike sent Mamie yellow roses—yellow was Ikky's favorite color—and they had a plant fashioned in the shape of a heart put on his grave. But they never marked the day of his death; in fact, Mamie insisted she couldn't remember what it was.

Mamie worked hard at being the cheerful soul. As Lieutenant Sheets had written to Nana some five months after the tragedy, Mrs. Ike is "quite happy, and they are going out quite often." The gay frivolity she radiated was Mamie's own heartfelt attempt to keep them both from what Ike saw as the "ragged edges of a breakdown."

Though separated in some ways by an unbridgeable sorrow, in their wordless grief they clung tightly to one another. It was an act of love but also of bravery that ten months after Ikky's death Mamie became pregnant again.

Sometime during that fall of 1921, the Pattons had invited Ike and Mamie to dinner to meet Brigadier General Fox Conner, one of Chief of Staff John J. Pershing's protégés, who was making a brief visit to Camp Meade. The conversation centered around Patton and Eisenhower's ideas for enhancing the Tank Corps. Impressed by Eisenhower's abilities, Conner wrote Ike not long after that evening and asked him to be his executive officer for the infantry brigade in Panama. Ike decided to accept Conner's offer and put in for Panama. The War Department initially rejected his application, but eventually Conner cut through the red tape with a direct appeal to Pershing, and the orders came through. By the end of the year, Ike's appointment was official. Even though Mamie already knew she was pregnant, when she heard confirmation of their new assignment she refused to let Ike ask to change his orders to a post somewhere in the States.

Before leaving Camp Meade for New York, where they would board an army transport ship for the Canal Zone, General Samuel Rockenbach, the camp's commanding officer, gave a going-away party in honor of the Eisenhowers. That evening he presented Mamie with a "handsome silver vase inscribed: To the Mascot of the Tank Corps Football Team." It was a bittersweet goodbye. Camp Meade had been their first real home together as a family, but it was also the place where Ikky had died, bringing not only a devastating void to Mamie and Ike's life but a wrenching sadness to everyone at the camp.

.   .   .

*G*oing to Panama would have tested all of Mamie's strength at the best of times, but now, with her pregnancy, even more so. Since attempts to construct a canal across the Isthmus of Panama had begun at the end of the last century, thousands of people had died there from yellow fever and malaria. In fact, when John F. Wallace, the first American engineer to take over the project from the French, packed for his sojourn, he was said to have included among his possessions two metal coffins, in case he and his wife should die from any of the dreaded tropical diseases. His successor in 1905, engineer John F. Stevens, proclaimed that there were three troublemakers at work on the canal: "Yellow fever, malaria and cold feet—the greatest of these [being] cold feet." Almost two decades had passed since Stevens's assessment, but Panama was still considered to be on the fringes of civilization.

Often a worrier, Mamie may well have been frightened at the thought of going to this insect-infested zone, pregnant as she was with a child she deeply desired and anticipated. But she did not go out of naïveté or mere curiosity—she had traveled to Panama before marrying Ike and she knew what she was getting into. She did it as proof of her faith in and commitment to her husband.

By January 1922, Ike and Mamie were in New York to board the army transport *San Miguel*. There was a brief delay because their ship was offshore responding to an emergency, leaving the two of them stranded with nothing to do but wait and "[survive] on cheap meals and free museums." But when the transport returned to port, the Eisenhowers loaded their Ford onto the ship and went on board to secure their accommodations. Since Ike was commander of the troops on the ship, they were slated to get a "decent" suite; but, as Mamie recalled later, unexpectedly "some general on a joy ride" decided to travel to the Canal Zone, bumping them from a more spacious cabin to a tiny cubicle with a one-seater couch and a cramped double-decker bunk.

Somewhere around Cape Hatteras, the ship hit a violent tropical storm. Mamie, suffering from morning sickness and claustrophobia, was not about to sleep on the bunk. Instead, with one of the worst cases of seasickness she ever had, she clung to the small couch just below the porthole, scarcely able to lift her head.

January is the tropical-storm season in the Caribbean—which became abundantly clear as the ship entered those waters, with stops in Puerto Rico and Port-au-Prince. Before they reached Balboa, a storm had just passed through, and when the ship finally docked, hot, steamy blasts of air hit them as they emerged from their cabin. Weakened from the turbulent passage, Mamie soon remembered the reasons she had been warned that for "proper grooming, two complete changes of clothing would have to be washed and ironed every day." She had arrived in Panama!

When the contents of the ship were unloaded, the Eisenhowers, already grim from their ordeal, discovered that their Ford had been seriously bashed about in the storm and whatever parts of the car hadn't been all but irreparably damaged had been stolen.

Arrangements were made to send their luggage to Camp Gaillard, the army post where they would live, and then, with the help of an aide, they caught the train that connected the Atlantic and Pacific coasts of the isthmus, a nineteenth-century system that was dirty and crowded. When they reached the point along the canal nearest Camp Gaillard, they alighted at a stop connected to the camp by a catwalk that crossed the top of the lock. While it was wide enough for a car, special arrangements had to be made to use a vehicle, so Mamie and Ike used the normal means of walking: holding on to a rope. "For Mamie," Ike recalled later, "it was the worst possible avenue of entry into a foreign station."

Camp Gaillard was perched on the edge of the Culebra Cut, which was constantly plagued by mudslides. Tons of land often fell into the canal, which would then have to be dredged, while mudslides interrupted traffic and undermined the stability of the locality. No one could say, when the sun went down at night, what the condition of the cut would be the next morning, but Ike tended to downplay the problem. Years later he was horrified to discover, when flying over the Canal Zone after World War II, that the entire post where he and Mamie had lived had slid into the canal and had had to be laboriously dredged out.

Ike and Mamie were assigned to quarters next to General and Mrs. Conner in a two-story house. Built on stilts, it had been erected by the French at the turn of the century. The house had been unoccupied for nearly a decade, and the jungle had all but reclaimed it. Thick vines wound around the wire screens and lattices that substituted for windowpanes. The porch, collapsing from damp and mildew, opened into the house itself, which was infested with lizards, spiders, cockroaches, and snakes. The jungle screamed just feet from the door. Their first night in Panama, Mamie remembered, a rat gnawed on the leg of a nearby chair all night long.

Bats, one of the most distasteful of the jungle pests, had been imported into the Canal Zone by the French, who had hoped that they would consume the mosquitoes carrying yellow fever. At night the bats would pour out of the jungle and "bombard the house." It was illegal to kill bats, but Mamie became so upset about one that had gotten into the bedroom one night that she made Ike kill it with his ceremonial dress saber. The sight of her husband jumping around the bedroom flailing a sword in pursuit of the small winged animal made her laugh. Douglas Fairbanks had nothing on her dashing Ike, she concluded.

As Mamie discovered almost immediately, bedbugs were also a concern. "Once a week, you'd take your bed and put the legs in cans of kerosene, and you'd take paper and light [the metal bedframe]." This would kill the bedbugs lining the bedsprings. Mattresses also had to be aired and fumigated weekly, and electric light bulbs were used to reduce the effects of mildew on clothing and important pieces of furniture, like the piano Mamie rented.

"Mrs. Conner thought I was namby-pamby because things didn't bother her," Mamie later remembered. "But to have bats crawl in under the door at night and fly around was not my idea of a good time. Then when those huge cockroaches would jump at you from the top of the door, I mean, those things I wasn't used to. Anyway . . . I wasn't feeling my best."

By late May, Mamie had achieved an "uneasy peace with her surroundings." The house had been renovated and the jungle pushed back, and she had cut her hair—to the style that would stay with her the rest of her life. One interviewer who spoke to Mamie just after she became First Lady noted, "Mrs. Eisenhower [was] positive that she cut her hair for comfort and not to conform to the prevailing fashion."

Mamie also fell into a routine with the other army wives. Daily shopping was done mostly at the post shops and commissary. But often the women went into Panama City to take advantage of the wide array of goods that were sold straight off the ships from America, Asia, and Europe. To do this, they would have to walk along the narrow lock to a waiting jitney that would take them to the city, where they could shop for knickknacks and visit the duty-free store. In this way Mamie soon acquired rugs, brass tables, and fine accessories for the house, and she was able to add to her collection of Minton china.

At the same time, she also played a key role in a major charitable effort to establish a maternity hospital for the wives of enlisted men of the Puerto Rican regiment. General Conner had allocated a small building for this project, and the ladies of the post set to work to make it sanitary and habitable. No funds were forthcoming, so every cent for the project had to be privately raised. Mamie became absorbed in the job, organizing the committee to hold card parties, picnics, and dances to raise money for the effort. In the end, they raised about one thousand dollars, enough in those days to "make the clinic a reality."

As Mamie's pregnancy advanced, the question of where she would have her own baby became an issue of paramount importance. Sometime that spring, Mamie's parents visited, and a decision was made.

Mamie wanted to have the baby in the new maternity clinic she had helped establish: "I was all ready to put up with this rugged business. It was alright with me . . . but my father and mother came and gave one look and said, 'You're going to Denver.'" With a month or two to spare, Mamie left the Canal Zone for Colorado. During her absence, she and Ike stayed in touch by writing one another frequently. In a letter I found more than seventy years after it had been written, my grandfather conveyed all his news, always concerned that Mamie should be well cared for.

June 3

My Sweetgirl:
I have been on the range all morning—and am hot and tired. It was very muddy and we slipped and slid all over the place. Seems as if there is very little news—all I know out of the ordinary is that Florence Conner had been right sick for several days. Some sort of fever—the doctors are not certain what it is. Heard Mrs. Cudlip was operated on for appendicitis. Looks like it was imperative to get it these days to be in fashion.

Played 3 games of chess last night—so I didn't get to bed until 12. Some dissipation! The rest of the Post went to the dance. I mailed your money on the 31st. I am mentioning it only because if the letter went astray—this one will let you know to notify me.

Getting sort of used to the wet season. Rains considerably ... my leggings, boots & etc. mildew unless I watch them closely. Oh yes!! Had the ceiling torn out of the bathroom and replaced to get rid of bat dirt. Has been terrific lately—and I was fed up with it. Will have it painted afterwards, but I don't suppose it will ever dry.

Dearest—will you please look in your valuable papers & see whether you have following things:

```
Policy—[$]10,000—govt
   "       [$] 2,000—Nat. Ins. Co.
   "       [$] 3,000—army mutual
   "       [$] 7,500—(accident) Royal
```

and receipts for same to show they are all paid to *date*. I'd keep the receipts for a policy in an envelope with the one to which it pertains. I know I ask you about these things right often—but I always want you protected.

In addition to above—in case of my death there is due you from the government—6 months pay, and the part of the months pay I have already earned. I have accounts in 2 banks. Riggs and American Foreign Banking Corp—Panama. I don't know whether I even told you, but you know *you* have fifty dollars left in your bank down here.

Now don't go wondering *why* I'm telling you all this. It is simply that I like to keep your memory refreshed on these things, so you can get your dues in case of any accident.

Because you see dear, I love you.

Much love to Mother & Mike—

Your devoted
Lover

P.S. I found the receipts I mentioned and am enclosing, D.

Ike came to the United States for the birth of the baby, arriving just before Mamie went into confinement. On the night the baby was born, Mamie and Ike had been playing cards with friends. After retiring for the evening and as Mamie changed into her sleeping attire, Ike read aloud as he often did, this time from a book of short stories by Ring Lardner. One of the stories was so funny that Mamie was convulsed with laughter. Ike looked at her seriously and said, "You'd better stop laughing so hard or I'll be taking you to the hospital."

His passing prediction was right. Mamie's water broke and she went into labor immediately. Nana, concerned lest the start of an engine wake the neighbors and alert them to the event, prevailed on Ike to roll the car out of the driveway before starting it. Anxious to get on the road, Ike pushed the vehicle out, jumped into the driver's seat, and stepped on the gas. Nothing happened.

"Ike," Mamie prompted, "you have to start the ignition."

Chagrined, Ike turned the key and they were off. Mamie found the whole incident so funny that, as she later put it, the baby was literally laughed into the world.

The Eisenhowers' new son, born on August 3, 1922, was named John Sheldon Doud Eisenhower in Pupah's honor. His birth was a joyous event; never was a baby so deeply desired or loved. As Ike later recalled, his birth "did much to fill the gap that we felt so poignantly and so deeply every day of our lives since the death of our first son . . . The most absorbing interest in our lives was the growth [of the baby into a] walking, talking, running-the-whole-household young fellow."

Ike stayed for the christening and left three weeks after John's birth. Mamie remained in the States for another two months. Before she left Denver, her parents urged her to take a nurse to help her look after the infant in Panama. So Katherine Herrick, a large woman about Mamie's age who had been working at Denver General Hospital, was employed, staying with the family for four years. And sometime that fall, Katherine, John, and Mamie left for Panama via a fruit boat from New Orleans. Pupah paid their way.

From the vessel, Mamie wrote to her parents. Her anxiety about leaving the safety of American shores for the wilds of Panama was obvious:

Tues, 10 p.m.

Dear Folksies:
Just a note to let you know we expect to land about six a.m. and gee but we will be glad. This has been a terrible trip—rough all the way and Katherine and I haven't felt so good altho we didn't lose any of our meals. Johnnie is fine and has been an adorable baby. The crowd aboard is as punk as usual and the ship is dirty. I shall never try a Wed. boat again . . . just think, a week tomorrow since we sailed. Hope Ike got the dope on the landing of the ship—for I am anxious to turn all responsibility over to him . . . Won't I be glad to see him waiting for me on that dock . . . [I] will cable you tomorrow about our safe arrival. I sure love you all very very much and I wish you could see how Johnnie has grown in the weeks since we left. He's getting so smart and grown-up. Am crazy to know what Ike will have to say when he sees him . . . Your little farewell card was so sweet Mother dear and we didn't feel so awful [sic] alone after reading it—darling little mother I love you so much and seems like I miss you more than ever this year—guess cause I was home so long. Goodnite we must turn in now as 5 o'clock will come soon—oodles of hugs and kisses to all.

Your Mamie

Mamie's return to Panama was not all she'd hoped for. Although she again settled into a routine, Ike spent a great deal of time away from the camp, and many of the evenings he was engrossed in discussion with General Conner. Since coming to Panama, the two men had formed a close personal and intellectual relationship, and Conner, as a mentor, invested time and energy in his young protégé's future. "One of the profound beliefs of General Conner," Ike later recalled, "was that the world could not long avoid another major war . . . He urged me to be ready for it."

Conner had an extraordinary library and he encouraged Ike to use it. Ike did so with passion, reading everything from Shakespeare, Plato, and Nietzsche to technical essays on military campaigns. Books like Carl von Clausewitz's *On War* and Matthew F. Steele's *American Campaigns* were absorbed and discussed. Many of their philosophical brainstormings were conducted during maneuvers—they were often on horseback as many as eight hours a day. But these deep analytical assessments also went on during the warm, languid evenings after dinner. The tropical sun set as late as ten, and often Ike and Fox Conner would talk well into the darkness of night.

It's not surprising that Mamie felt left out. Ike was so consumed by his readings and his exchanges with Conner that Mamie surely did not get the attention she needed—especially as a new mother. She may well have been suffering from a kind of postpartum depression, and certainly life in Panama did not provide any of the distractions that might have helped take her mind off things.

Mamie understood the importance for Ike of Conner's attention, but her possessiveness, which she always claimed was natural for women, also inspired jealousy. Ike's professional responsibilities, which often took him away from home for weeks at a time, increasingly distressed her, but she put on a brave face when writing to Pupah.

Dearest Daddy,
Just a note to go out in this a.m.'s mail to let you know we are fine. Ike got away yesterday a.m. and I got up at 5:30 and went down to where they bid him farewell—it may be five weeks but probably only two. We are not afraid and have loads of parties to go to as the ladies are having "hen parties." Am having a "Tea" Sunday afternoon from 4:30 to 5:30 for 60 ladies—quite a mob but will pass an awfully lonesome time of day. Johnnie is fine and can sit alone now—also squeals like a little pig. He weighs 18 lbs and starts cream of wheat gruel and vegetable soup to-day. I took some Kodak pictures and gave them to a soldier to develop out here but he is very slow and I haven't re'cd them back. I do hope they are good cause you can't imagine how that rascal has grown— he surely has your head and profile—it is so funny. You'll just love him to pieces. To-day is Valentine's Day—"will you be my Valentine?" I have no conception of time down here and never realized that date was near until yesterday . . .
Your Puddy

Ike's absences and his growing absorption with General Conner's future war scenarios began to tell on Mamie. Virginia Conner, the general's wife, later observed that Mamie and Ike seemed to be "drifting apart." Mamie became physically run-down and suffered intermittently from digestive problems. She also harbored fears that in this wild, untamed part of the world John might fall ill, and she knew she could not bear another painful loss.

Sometime the following year, Mamie all but fled to Denver. Decades later she reflected on her reasons: "I was down to skin and bones and hollow-eyed; so ill I'd have to walk all night long. The porch was screened on three sides and I would walk all night listening to mosquitoes buzz. I could hear the monkeys scream in the jungle and I felt like screaming too. I don't know what it was, but there was something about the tropics that got me. I just could not sleep—I would walk and walk. It was terrible. My health and vitality seemed to ebb away. I don't know how I existed."

When she left with John and Katherine, Ike begged her not to go, but Mamie was adamant. His imploring words, she later admitted, stayed with her for the rest of her life. This trip to Denver had come at one of those defining moments that occur in every person's life, and from the vantage of 750 Lafayette Street she was able to take stock of her marriage and the life she had led for nearly eight years.

Under the watchful eye of her parents, Mamie's health improved and she started to see old friends and classmates again. She could not help but notice how her girlfriends were living: theirs were lives she could understand. These women had husbands who quit working at dinnertime and spent the evenings with their families. They were bankers, lawyers, and doctors who led predictable lives in clean, safe places.

But as Mamie began to feel better, she was able to take a harder look at the men themselves. As secure and stable as their lives seemed to be, Mamie realized she would not want to be married to any of them—she missed Ike. And she had also finally outgrown home.

Mamie understood that to stay married to Ike she would have to be even more uncomplaining and more accommodating to his career needs. If that meant endless hours alone, she would have to adjust; there could be no other way. She would also have to make a greater effort to enter into whatever part of his life was open to her. She would have to learn to share at least some of his recreational interests, even if that meant a special effort to become sportier or more companionable.

At this turning point in her life, Mamie was infused with a new sense of dedication. Once she had recommitted herself to her life with Ike, she was anxious to leave Denver at the earliest possible moment. With her return to Panama she threw all her efforts into keeping up with her husband and providing unstinting support.

[Undated—simply Thurs.]

Dearest Folksies,

I sure was tickled to receive three letters from you all yesterday. Gee how home sick for you it did make me . . . Its been nearly a week since I wrote you all. Sure am busy these days. Ike & I ride every morning from 7 to 9. Am doing pretty well but wish I could learn faster. Thank you Daddy dear for the check. Now that Ike has given me my rose Minton china for X-mas, I can use my allowance for my linen . . . expect to have a couple of dinner parties a week now that I have the fixings. The linen table cloth is fine Mother. Have a splendid new butler and my cook is a wonder. I'm sitting pretty sure enough. Johnnie is fine and is the idol of the "Post" and as good as gold. Climate agrees with him fine and Katherine seems satisfied. Am gradually getting Ike housebroken again but its a hard job. Going to the Generals to dinner to-morrow nite before the hop—wear my red organdie. This Post is sure gay these days. Went to bridge club this PM but didn't win prize of course and to a party yesterday. There is to be a large horse show in Panama City around X-mas and Ike is busy getting his horse in shape, riding about six horses a day . . . Am very contented and happy and my house is lovely and my new dresses greatly admired. In fact everything is rosey—I know you'll be glad to hear that. Mrs. Conner had a cousin arrive from N.Y. to-day for Betty's wedding so I guess there will be loads of parties for the two.

I think of u so much and wonder if all is well. Everyone is asleep but I was restless and had to write you. I am so busy keeping up with Ike I don't get a minute—he's become very gay since I left and must be amused every minute. If I don't there are others who are waiting to do so—paper's run out— so goodnite. I love you all heaps—

Your Mamie

Despite the gaiety of the parties and the camaraderie on the post, Panama, it seemed, was still a hardship station in every way. But Mamie had gained new resolve. She now knew the good and the bad of her life, and she would try to live in harmony with both. Army life made extraordinary demands on her husband, indeed on them both, and she did not have the dependable proximity of family and friends. As my mother described it, army life was like a kaleidoscope, where people were "meeting on army posts all over the world, separating and reshuffling at still another post in ever-widening concentric circles, to spend a phase of life together and then separate again." It was heartbreaking and often lonely, but now it too had become the fabric of her life.

At the end of his Panamanian tour, Ike was presented with the Distinguished Service Medal for his outstanding services at Camp Colt during the war. And Mamie was inspired by what that meant. "I knew almost from the day I married Ike that he would be a great soldier," she reflected later. "He was always dedicated, serious and purposeful about his job. Nothing came before his duty. I was forced to match his spirit of personal sacrifice as best I could."

CHAPTER SEVEN

THE LAST RAYS OF A BRILLIANT SUN

*W*hat Mamie seemed to have gained most from her Panama experience was the chance to rededicate herself to her husband, to reconnect, to belong again. The next fifteen or so years, before their posting in the Philippines, were among the happiest of their marriage. Mamie was in her physical prime; she had her men, Ike and John, with her; she was occupied and felt needed; and life was full of adventure and friendship.

Mamie was terribly relieved in 1924 when they received word that they would be leaving Panama—but so was Ike. By the time their orders came through, the Conners had already returned to the United States, and there was little left for them at Camp Gaillard. To Ike's dismay, however, he was instructed to go to Camp Meade again. Meade, in their minds, was associated with tragedy, and a portion of his duties, nearly identical to those of times past, would involve coaching the football team.

The old army placed great importance on fielding a winning football team, so the best army coaches were assigned to Meade, where they were charged with "beating the marines." At this stage in Eisenhower's career, however, football, a game that had once been his own personal obsession, had now been put aside for serious professional aspirations. He was crushed at the assignment, having hoped instead for a posting to Fort Leavenworth and its Command and General Staff School (C&GS), a highly competitive war college restricted to the army's crème de la crème. Command and General Staff School at Fort Leavenworth pitted 275 of the finest officers in the United States Army in direct competition— each selected by his branch of the service as its best. The success of the C&GS graduates during the First World War had demonstrated that this was a "necessary stop" on an advanced career path.

After returning from Panama, Eisenhower made efforts to secure selection for C&GS from the chief of infantry, but his applications were all to no avail. A prerequisite for attendance was Infantry School, and the chief's office was convinced that without it he'd fail. While Eisenhower was still at Meade, Fox Conner sent word: "No matter what orders you receive from the War Department make no protest accept them without question."

Soon Ike received instructions to proceed to Fort Logan, Colorado, to take up an assignment as an army recruitment officer. This would have been regarded as a demotion, but Ike took Conner's advice and reported to the post without complaint. Mamie was convinced that Conner was working behind the scenes on Ike's behalf.

Fort Logan had its compensations. Though the work was not challenging and Ike often had time on his hands, the post was located near Denver, and Mamie could see more of her family.

They had been at Logan for less than a year when Ike was finally ordered to Command and General Staff School. General Conner knew it would be hopeless to convince the chief of infantry that Ike should have this appointment, so to secure it Conner circumvented infantry and had Eisenhower selected from the adjutant general's quota—a clever maneuver that came right in time: in one more year, Ike would have been ineligible because of his age; no one older than thirty-six was permitted to attend.*

When Ike got the news he was elated. "I was ready to fly—and needed no airplane," he recalled.

Nevertheless, facing his well-prepared competition, Ike wrote Conner expressing some doubts about his ability to measure up. Conner assured his protégé: "You may not know it," he wrote, "but because of your three years' work in Panama, you are far better trained and ready for Leavenworth than anybody I know

---

*Everett Hughes, one of the instructors at C&GS, observed near the end of his life that World War II was fought by the men who had been at Leavenworth. "They had all [been given] the same problems and tackled them from the same angle. They spoke the same language. When a man wrote an order, he wrote it in Leavenworthese and everybody else understood it."

...So well acquainted with the technics and routine of preparing plans they will be second nature to you. You will feel no sense of inferiority."

Mamie understood clearly what this opportunity meant for Ike. If he were to graduate in the top third of his class at Leavenworth, he could be marked for a star in due course. So as soon as they arrived in Kansas, Mamie threw herself into the task of setting up their home as quickly as possible. Her formula was simple. The first priority was to hang paintings, unroll rugs, and put out cigarette boxes and framed photographs everywhere. The rest, with considerable work, would eventually fall into place, but at least a sense of home could be instantly created.

The Eisenhowers' quarters were in Otis Hall, a space that was really two apartments side by side. There was a kitchen at the back, but the two were not joined in any other way, so if you wanted to get from one side to the other, you had to go out into the hall through another door. This inconvenience, however, did not dim Mamie's enthusiasm for her new digs. Four bedrooms was more than ample for their small family, and it gave Ike two rooms on the top floor where he could establish a "model command post"—for his studies. This upstairs retreat was "off bounds" to everyone but Ike's closest friend and fellow student Leonard T. ("Gee") Gerow, with whom he would be studying during their late-night sessions.

One of my father's earliest memories was of "the night I invaded Dad's attic study, normally off limits. He and his friend . . . Gerow . . . were poring intensely over a large table, eyeshades protecting them from the glare of a brilliant, low-hung lamp. I was too small to see what was on the table but stared in wonderment at the huge maps tacked on the wall. The two young officers were going over the next day's tactical problem. Dad and Gee welcomed me with a laugh and shoved me out the door in the course of half a minute."

Mamie's work at Leavenworth was simpler but no less demanding. She had to provide Ike with the tranquil atmosphere needed for the rigors of study, ensure that Ike and Gee were allowed concentration unbroken by the sounds and disturbances of a rambunctious three-year-old, and, in her own relations with Ike, be patient and undemanding in everything.

There were many other army wives who were also left to shoulder domestic burdens alone. During the nine-month course, the women looked after their homes and children and occupied themselves by giving modest supper and card parties. The commanding officer of the post had decreed that no alcohol could be consumed at Leavenworth, but Mamie later recalled that his strictness inconvenienced no one: the atmosphere of studious seriousness was part of the way of life there.

During this assignment Mamie became very close to Katie Gerow, Gee Gerow's wife. Katie had been a registered nurse during World War I and had met Gee overseas. She knew her way around the army, and while their husbands worked, Katie did much to teach Mamie the ropes, to show her how one could contentedly survive the nomadic life of the army. She suggested to Mamie, for instance, that she should always have something yellow in a room, to give it "sunshine." This may have accounted for Mamie's lifelong love of yellow roses and gladioli. And, of course, Katie's friendship also helped fill the emotional void left by Ike's utterly single-minded approach to his studies.

At the end of the arduous course, the Douds came from Denver for Ike's graduation in June 1926. Some hours before the ceremonies began, word began to filter in that Ike was number one in the class. It was later confirmed that he had indeed received the highest average, followed closely by his dear friend and study mate Gee Gerow. Ike's excitement about his class standing was matched only by Mamie's, and he thanked her from the bottom of his heart for making the sacrifices necessary for his complete concentration, as well as for her moral support and optimism throughout the year. What Mamie had done had required a kind of maturity she could not have summoned before Panama. She had now passed muster as a real army wife.*

.   .   .

*This did not change from generation to generation. My mother told me that by the time my father, also an army officer, had reached advanced army school, the wives got diplomas called PHT's, "Pushing Hubby Through."

Before Ike took up his next assignment, he and Mamie joined his brothers and their families for an Eisenhower reunion in Abilene. Then they went on to his new assignment at Fort Benning, Georgia, where he was to coach yet another football team. "They took a guy who'd graduated number one in his class," my father later observed, "and then sent him to coach football. What a jar that must have been . . . But the army loved football, in fact they lived for it, and I don't think they considered it an insult at all."

In some of the photographs of that era, Eisenhower looks like a man marking time—a posture not at all comfortable or compatible with his personality. His own intellect and temperament strained to be challenged. To add to his concerns and frustrations, in the winter of 1926–27 Mamie fell ill with a digestive ailment and was taken to Walter Reed Hospital in Washington, where she would remain for several months. During this lengthy confinement, John stayed in San Antonio with Mamie's sister Mike, a woman my father later described as being "full of zip and rebellion." She had developed a reputation as the family hell-raiser early on. She had played pranks on Ike and Mamie when they were courting, and a few years later created a family crisis when she drained Pupah's precious supply of bootleg gin and replaced it with water. True to form, she eventually eloped with Richard Gill, a wealthy Texas entrepreneur, while John, aged three, was the only witness.*

When Mamie was discharged and John had returned home, the Eisenhowers again found themselves in the throes of a move, this time to Washington, D.C. At the end of the season, Fox Conner had recommended to General John J. "Black Jack" Pershing that he use Ike's writing skills to produce the guide that was to be written on the American battlefields in Europe for the Battle Monuments Commission, which Pershing chaired. The job required the writer to absorb massive volumes of official reports, statistics, and maps, then analyze them and put them in coherent and read-

---

*Years later, Mamie wondered if her sister had become an unreliable caretaker. When my father was seven, Mike and Richard had taken him off to the country outside Denver, and had gotten as far as Central City or Leadville when she suddenly thought to call 750 Lafayette Street to alert them to their whereabouts. John recalled, "The family—Mother was there at the time—thought I'd been kidnapped, and Mother had taken to her bed."

able form. It was a comprehensive education in the terrain of Europe, but Ike was given only six months to complete the task.

While Ike diligently poured himself into Pershing's pet project, Mamie set about establishing their new home in an apartment building called the Wyoming, where they lived "comfortably but far from lavishly," first in a two-bedroom and later in a three-bedroom apartment. The Wyoming, famous for its marble hallways with elegant Corinthian columns, was solidly built, with high, gracious ceilings and detailed cornice work. It was also located in one of the most attractive areas of Washington, just off Connecticut Avenue, next to a sloping field that led down to Dupont Circle. Even decades after they had left that apartment, Mamie would highly recommend it to her friends.

The Wyoming had never permitted tenants with children, but friends supported their cause and assured the building's management that "John would be no difficulty and that he was a quiet little boy, whose father was a strict disciplinarian."

Despite the pressures of turning out the guidebook, Ike's work was a great success, eliciting a glowing letter of commendation from General Pershing, which said: "[Eisenhower] has shown superior ability not only in visualizing his work as a whole but in executing its many details in an efficient and timely manner. What he has done was accomplished only by the exercise of unusual intelligence and constant devotion to duty." His reward was acceptance into the Army War College at Fort McNair, which, like C&GS, was established for an exclusive group of students selected by the army chief of staff. Preference was given to graduates of Leavenworth to "apply the knowledge they'd already acquired."

*Y*ears later Mamie told us that she intervened only twice during Ike's career. One of those occasions related to the Eisenhowers' next move, in 1928. Ike was given a choice of working on the General Staff at the War Department or revising the Battle Monuments guide to World War I by annotating his earlier work, *American Battlefields of France*, so travelers to Europe could follow it in situ. Ike wanted to take the General Staff job.

"A major never had been [offered such an opportunity]," Mamie recalled. "[The War Department job] was terrific, and oh, Ike just wanted that worse than almost anything. [But] I said, 'Honey, let's go to Europe. Let's take this assignment. This gives us the opportunity to see the Old World and travel.'... Very much against his will he went." Because of Mamie's devoted support he may have thought he should concede at least this one assignment, though he later complained of personality clashes among those he worked with on the commission.

The Eisenhowers left for Paris on the luxury liner *America* in August 1928. Pupah and Nana came along to see Europe for the first time and to help look after John while Mamie went apartment hunting and Ike settled into his new job. Because of weather delays in Southampton, England, where the *America* stopped, the weary travelers did not board the boat train for Le Havre until midnight; customs delays confronted them in France. At about 3:30 in the morning, they arrived in Paris, but no one from the commission or their travel agency was there to meet them. They decided finally to put their fate in the hands of a taxi driver, who sped through the streets of Paris in search of a small pension that would accept the tired travelers in the middle of the night. At last they settled in a reasonable spot, but Ike vowed the next morning that he would establish a rule at the commission: no one, no matter what his rank, would ever arrive in France without being met.

The Eisenhowers and the Douds stayed in a hotel while Mamie spent her days tracking down leads on apartments. She had a great deal of help from the American Embassy and the wives of the commission's officers, but finding an affordable apartment in Paris was not easy. Since the war, there had been a severe housing shortage and most apartments were either unacceptably primitive or too elaborate and expensive. Her search finally bore fruit and they settled at 68, quai d'Auteuil, on the right bank of the Seine. Before long, Club Eisenhower was again established, and George Horkan, one of Ike and Mamie's closest friends, dubbed the nearby Mirabeau Bridge "Pont Mamie."*

The location couldn't have been more convenient. It was a short distance from the McJanet School for American children that John attended and just around the corner from the Battle Monuments

---

*My father recalls that during their year in Paris, Ike once jumped into the Seine near "Pont Mamie" to save the life of a drowning Frenchman. It never received attention at the time, Eisenhower being then an unknown American army officer.

Commission's offices. Ike walked to work in the mornings and came home for lunch most days.

Nana and Pupah stayed for a few months in France, managing some outings with Ike to the battlefields, and after things were settled a bit, they went to visit Nana's extended family in Sweden. By Christmas Day 1928, the Douds were back in the United States and Mamie wrote them about how her schedule in Paris was shaping up.

Dearest Folksies,

. . . I am sorry if my letters haven't arrived in time for I have tried to watch the boats: It is very difficult for me to write three times a week. I take John to the hospital* at 3 PM . . . You can imagine how I have to jump to get J. and Ike off at 8:45 every a.m. Then my French lesson at 12—which lasts till luncheon [at] 1:30. Then take Ike back to office, call for J. at school—call for Mary & Bo† at hotel and back at hospital at 3. By the time we finish it is already dark and I hit for home—for you know how I hate to drive in this town after dark. By the time dinner is over and I am in bed, believe me I'm ready for the hay also: this last week has been unusually hard for I've had to shop in between times—you know these stores Mother in ordinary times . . .

Saturday p.m. Ike and I went out . . . and bot a beautiful tree—quite large. Ike spent the eve putting a stand on it, with John's tools & old nails from our packing boxes, he made a keen job of it . . . So before dinner last eve J & I tied little candies (wrapped in bright colored paper to-gether) to hang on the tree . . . J got a big kick out of it all . . . it is the prettiest tree we ever had. When John went to bed he was all thrilled and could even hear the bells in Santa's sleigh.

. . . At ten o'clock the Horkans phoned to come down. We told them to come out here so with the Stylers and four bot-

---

*John was seriously ill for a while and required outpatient care. In a letter sent several weeks later, Mamie told her mother not to worry: "I'm watching him like a hawk."

†Mary Horkan and her son, George, nicknamed Bo, who was my father's closest childhood friend.

tles of champagne they arrived . . . They left at one—luckily
I had all the presents under the tree and all packages wrapped
so it was fun—[though] it is rather pitiful to see us all trying
to forget we're away from all our familys . . . when I looked at
the little bunch of stuff under J's tree I could have wept . . .
I'm glad that everyone likes to come here and they say it is
so homey and bright—guess were mighty lucky.

John was doing well in school—his grades were better than
ever—and Ike was absorbed in his work, though he often complained that it was going too slowly. Mamie took French lessons
three times a week and struggled to keep the household on an
even keel. This was not always easy with the troublesome language problem, and Mamie was also well aware of anti-American
feelings in Paris. "If you didn't speak their language," she later
recounted, "you had a hard time getting around to buy food or
clothes or anything else. Only special stores would have signs in
the windows that said 'Interpreter.' "

Mamie also found it hard to deal with the two-person staff she'd
hired—a *femme de chambre* and a cook. "They were quarrelsome
people," she thought, who would fight among themselves all the
time. Mamie eventually fired them both. These domestic ups and
downs were not lost on Ike, who remarked on them as he outlined
the progress of his work to his parents-in-law.

Feb. 11 [1929]

Dear Dad, Mother, and All:
In the last week we have had a new cook who is doing all the
work and who has been most satisfactory. We are crossing our
fingers. She is a *Dane*—and the reason we think she is doing
well is because she does not talk French. She speaks English
fairly well. She has been very economical so far—and Mamie
has breathed many sighs of relief so far. Today she has had a
notice of a telegram—and she seems to be sure that she is
receiving bad news from home. Mamie fears it is a stall to
pave her exit to take another job. Would not be surprised as
she has a friend at the other end of town . . .

General Pershing arrives at Cherbourg tomorrow and [Xen-
ophon] Price left today to meet him at the port. Won't make

so much difference to me, as my work is rather set apart from that of the others. The rumor is that he will remain in France a long time . . .

Dad, do you remember when we were trying so hard to locate the exact spot on the road out of Loissons at which we were supposed to stop, and you made the suggestion that we locate there a small stone marker? Well I told Price your idea—and finally we took it up with the French govt, to get permission for the erection of such stones. It is practically settled now and we will put up about 20 of them altogether. They will be small "orientation" tables made from a single stone . . . No inscription except "Erected by the American Battle Monuments Commission"—although I told Zen he should also put J.S.D. "consulting architect." . . .

We are tickled that France looks better to you in retrospect & that you are figuring on a trip here this summer. We feel certain you'll like it here better this time, and least there is a poker game every now & then . . .

Devotedly your
Son

That winter in France was a particularly harsh one. For the first time in thirty years there was so much ice on the Seine that it was unnavigable. On March 13, Mamie observed that the conditions were beginning to wear on everyone. "Ike says he's dying by inches not getting any exercise and hopes he will live till spring when he can go someplace and play golf," a sport he had taken up at Leavenworth as relaxation between his intensive study sessions. Mamie exclaimed, however, that Ike "really looks fine, except his hair—which is nearly gone. It has come out faster in the last six months than in the last two years—too bad."

As the weather improved, Ike began to make more and more day trips to battlefield sites, usually leaving at 6:00 a.m. and coming back after dinner. Mamie sympathized: "Two hundred miles on cobble roads is hard riding."

Springtime in Paris captivated the Eisenhowers, and Mamie and John began to join Ike on his trips. They planned excursions around Paris itself—taking John and his friend Bo Horkan to such places as Malmaison, to see Napoleonic artifacts, and to Les Invalides, to see the tomb of Napoléon himself. They also went farther afield. Mamie's enthusiasm for these outings and the knowledge she acquired en route speak volumes about what this experience must have meant to her.

April 17, 1929

Dearest Folksies:
...We left last Thurs. for a trip with Ike, staying the first nite at Lille, France. It was a rotten day snowed for three hrs and rained the rest but we were very comfortable in the Packard with the heavy robe—didn't get to see much of Lille cause the weather was so bad but saw from the car the old city walls and fortifications which were very interesting and looked as old as the world. Tuesday nite we were in Gent [sic] Belgium and it is a pretty old town—had a lovely day there for sights. The marvelous old St. Bavons cathedral with the world renowned pictures by the Van Eyck brothers "The Adoration of the Lamb" and Rubens "Conversion of St. Bavon"... From Gent we went to Ypres and you can't imagine the number of British cemeteries...It was terrible....Ypres has 65,000 names of British unknowns just around [it]. You can't imagine such loss: and the largest cemetery "British" is right outside Ypres called Tyne Cot. 50,000. It is a beautiful spot and they keep up their plots so well but not like ours—of course we only lost about 75,000 over here in all.
   Sunday nite we spent in Amiens. The cathedral there is the loveliest I've seen and is the finest of the gothic cathedrals— also the largest in France. All Sunday we traveled over the Canadian front and John found 3 helmets for the boys and himself. There are many spots that have never been reclaimed, barbed wire, helmets and all things from the trenches still in the fields. Doesn't seem possible after 10 years but I guess some of the districts were so ravaged and poor that it will still be many years before things are back to normal... John is keen and these trips are fine for us both—we eat like mad and get fresh air all day.

The family also traveled through the Meuse-Argonne region, where they treated themselves to picnic lunches and long walks on the battlefields. Mamie reported in May that "they are burying

3 soldiers that have *just* been found—just think after all these years." But the ghoulish discovery did not stop her from speaking with enthusiasm about their trip to Verdun, not to mention a forthcoming trip to the château region of the Loire Valley with some students and parents of the McJanet School later in the spring. "Aren't we seeing the country, tho?" she was prompted to exclaim.

My father vividly remembers that trip to Verdun. A significant portion of the city still lay in ruins, and he was especially impressed by the "strong point" called Fort Douaumont. "As we approached the door to this grim, squat monster, a human skull—with one tooth—grinned at us from a recess," he recalled. "Without hesitation Bo and I decided that this was the time to leave and go to the bathroom. Dad, his mind on his business, was annoyed. Somehow our natural needs were taken care of and we stumbled our way through some of the eerie, dank passageways, with occasional dim lights to guide our way."

The touring party also visited the Trench of Bayonets. There, during the war, French soldiers had been going over the top of the hill when they were struck down by a German shell and buried with their bayonets still sticking out of the ground. The site had been preserved by the French government as a memorial.

As intriguing as these trips were, they were not without hazard. Remains of the war could easily be found everywhere, and French farmers were sometimes killed by undetonated shells and grenades. One day John was getting ready to kick a pineapple-shaped object he'd encountered, when their driver stopped him in horror. There in Verdun, at least one possible tragedy had been averted.

Exploring France as a family surely gave the three Eisenhowers a special sense of companionability. Rarely, outside this European experience, would they have the opportunity to travel together in such a stimulating yet uncomplicated way. Ike was pleased that Mamie was enjoying the outings and gratified that John appeared to be getting a great deal out of his time in France. Both parents noticed how quickly he was growing up and developing his own interests, and they were especially pleased that he had taken to the French language with such ease. Mamie wrote her parents: "I wish you could hear Bo and John parle avec il c'est tres bien et tres droll."

John was now seven years old, twice the age Ikky had been

when he died. Although Mamie "talked about Ikky a lot," John belonged to Ike and Mamie in a way Ikky had not. Ikky was gone before he'd developed into a young boy with ideas and skills of his own. But John, shaped by the love and attention of his parents, had become a person in his own right, with an inquiring mind and his own special brand of humor.

These shared experiences—the sheer joy and satisfaction that came from making discoveries together—left unforgettable memories for them all. "The weather is marvelous now," Mamie wrote her father that June, "and one forgets the long bad weather. If we couldn't forget some of the bad things in this life, we wouldn't have the courage to continue, would we?"

*B*etween these field trips, the Eisenhowers enjoyed going to nightclubs and "kicking up their heels." Their outings on the town were sometimes noted. During the winter the *New York Herald* reported, "The soirée dansante at the Union Interalliée last night brought many Americans to the club for dinner and dancing. One of the largest parties . . . was given by Major and Mrs. Dwight D. Eisenhower." And the *Chicago Tribune* noted that same evening: "Major and Mrs. Dwight D. Eisenhower entertained a few friends [sixteen couples] yesterday evening, commencing with a cocktail party at their home in the quai d'Auteuil and taking their party on later to the dinner dance at the Union Interalliée." "Our dinner went off beautifully," Mamie exclaimed to her mother triumphantly.

The Eisenhowers also went to the theater more often that spring, this time "on their own steam" and not as someone else's guest. "We are able to see the show that has 'Old Man River' in it—whatever that is," Ike reported.

*A*fter John's school was finished for the academic year, my grandparents still had no idea how long they would remain in France, but Ike told Mamie it would be some months before the guidebook would be finished. The threesome planned to spend the summer traveling around Europe before returning to the United States. Before setting off on their excursion, Ike checked himself into the American Hospital in Paris, where he was placed under observation for intestinal trouble he'd had for several years. Ike had been given "all kinds of tests" in Washington, and his condition did not appear to be serious, but he said it had worsened. Mamie tried to reassure her parents that Ike was in "wonderful shape except [he has] just a little high blood pressure." They hoped, she said, that what he had was just that "tropic germ that can be cured easily." Given the problems Mamie herself had with digestive ailments, perhaps they were linked with or indicative of something they had both picked up in Panama.

On Ike's discharge, the family set off on a summer of travel, from the Riviera to the Alps, staying in everything from an elegant villa in the most glamorous of resorts to modest pensions in small, remote villages.

The first leg of the journey was in Italy. Mamie, Ike, and John left Paris on July 5 and drove the 635 miles to the resort of San Remo. They had to replace a fan belt en route but otherwise made very good time. Mamie was enraptured with the Riviera. She drove fifty miles of the trip and later recalled that the Mediterranean Sea was the "bluest water" she'd ever seen. She was also taken with the beauty of Côte d'Azur cities like Nice, Cannes, and Monte Carlo, which, she said, reminded her of Havana. They had been invited to stay with friends of her sister Mike and husband Richard Gill, the Warren Kings, who owned a glorious estate in San Remo. Mamie reported that their home was a delight, with "wonderful large rooms and high ceilings" as well as "old furniture [that] makes my mouth water." And from a pavilion overlooking the sea on the Kings' estate, you could "[pick] marvelous plums right off the trees in the garden."

John developed whooping cough on the way, but recovered quickly enough to be able to enjoy weeks of what vacation remained, and his illness did little to dampen the effects of this complete rest for Ike and Mamie. In a letter to her parents on July 15, Mamie, who'd earlier confessed that she had become "pessimistic" about finding good help, marveled at the servants and service that was extravagantly extended: breakfast in their rooms, ice water by their beds every night, clothing that had been worn the day before whisked away each morning and returned freshly pressed or laundered in the evening. "We will be rotten spoiled when we leave here."

Mamie described the routine they developed for themselves:

Ike is just in his glory after breakfast; he & John go down to
the beach and after they've had a sun bath then they sit in
the Pavilion till just time for luncheon . . . after luncheon I put
John to bed till about 5:30. The men play billiards or all four
play a game on the table called Pacheti. Then I take a nap
& so do the Kings but most time Ike goes back to beach. We
have dinner at 7:30. Then we play hearts or a game called
Jeunne Main [sic]—just the easy going life we need . . . The
cook is a wonder and we eat like mad. Kings are dieting but
not so the Eisenhowers. I weight 107 lbs . . . I'm brown too
but poor Ike stays red which makes him furious.

From the estate they took short jaunts with the Kings in their
fashionably long limousine. In Monte Carlo they had dinner at the
famous Café de Paris and gambled a modest sum at the casino
(and won). They also went to Genoa, where Mamie bought John
a miniature Tower of Pisa, which he was "keen about."

The three-week holiday was a leisurely romantic adventure that
left certain images permanently fixed in Mamie's mind. Just before
their departure, she wrote:

Last night we sat in the garden after dinner and watched the
moon shining on the water with the lights of the city along
the coast. It was a beautiful sight. Ike in a white suit, me in
a white dress . . . stretched out in steamer chairs . . . like the
setting for a musical comedy, with all the lovely Palms in the
moon light too. I can't tell you how happy we are.

The Eisenhowers, anxious not to "wear out their welcome," left
the next day. Before departing for Paris, Ike and John went down
to the sea for one last swim. The water had been rough the previous days but was calm enough for a last lingering dip.

On their return to Paris, there were still the final touches to be
done on the guidebook, and Mamie had to prepare for their move
back to the United States. They would spend a month in Paris
before taking one more trip that August, with Helen and Bill
Gruber, who was also part of the commission. With Ike having
received orders for Washington, it would have to be a shorter trip
because their projected departure for the United States had been
moved up from October 1 to September 15.

The Eisenhowers sent John to a summer camp run by the McJanet School and then set off on their last journey together on the Continent. Fortunately, a diary of the trip was made by Ike and Bill, who kept it alternately. The record retains the images of a carefree trip, full of adventure and fun.

In the introduction "the boys" noted that the purpose of the trip was to "see something of France, Belgium, Germany, Switzerland, and possibly Italy and Austria." But time was short and they could not stay in any one place very long. The first half of the journal was written by Ike and included mileage progress, cost of gasoline, and meal expenses. It also contained many vivid descriptions of scenery as well as a running commentary on the antics of Mamie and Helen.

Wednesday—Aug. 28
Starting Point. Paris—10:30 a.m.
Mileage at Gate—19389 . . .

We are "travelling light"—with very few clothes and intend to stay in reasonably priced hotels, and live very simply.

We put a baggage rack (price $4.00) on our running board where we put part of the luggage to relieve the congestion in the back seat of the car, which is a standard Buick sedan.

Out of Paris we began to have trouble with the fan belt which bothered us continuously until Bill had the happy idea of turning over the belt. No further trouble with *that*!

Route led us via Chantilly, Senlis, Compiegne—St. Quentin—Cambrai—Mons to Brussels, where we stopped at the Wiltcher Hotel. Rooms $2.70 each plus 10% taxes.

The most amusing incident of the day was the discovery, by a Belgian customs official of a bottle of scotch we were carrying with us. We finally were permitted to carry it along upon paying 54 cents tax. Bill had a remarkably hard time opening the bag in which the whisky was (we hoped) well concealed.

After Brussels, the foursome made their way through Belgium, heading for Germany, a country none of the passengers had visited before. "At the junction of the Sambre and the Meuse at Namur [Belgium]," Ike noted in the diary, "we saw the old forts high up on the prominent hill which rises between the two rivers. At the time of its construction its builders must have thought that it would be forever impregnable. The Germans reduced it easily in 1914."

Near the German border, the group took a little breather, which was recorded in a diary entry of extraordinary irony. Ten years later, the war would break out and Ike would, eventually, be given the command to crush the German enemy.

We seemed to experience very definite exhilaration upon leaving Belgium and entering the Fatherland. Maybe that's because both Bill and I have our family roots in this country as our names testify.

On September 2, after a trip through the Rhine Valley, culminating with "tea" at the famous Castle in Heidelberg, the Buick headed for the Black Forest. It met with universal enthusiasm.

We struck directly to Pforzheim—where the girls did a little shopping. After an hour there we started southward through the heart of the famous Black Forest. The trip was beautiful. All of us agree it was the best day yet. The vistas through the gaps in the dense forests which cover the heights, down beautiful narrow valleys beggar description. Little villages nestle along the rushing streams, and everywhere the country seems cool, fresh and clean.

We ate lunch by the roadside and voted it the best one we've had all because the surroundings were perfect. Only a few of the roads are at all dusty and the smell of pine, cedars and the freshly cut hay in the valleys adds to the feeling of peace and contentment a visitor is almost compelled to experience in this region.

We have been enthusiastic about Germany, the people as well as the beautiful landscapes. It is hard to describe the little differences one detects between the people of one country and those of another. However, one of the big points we have noted is the friendly way we have been treated everywhere. Bill, in German which impresses the rest of us tremendously, has made inquiries of dozens and dozens of people as we have come through the country. Without excep-

tion we have received courteous and correct replies ... We
like Germany!

On September 3, the adventurers began their Alpine "experience."

Left Neustadt ... lake 2500 ft above sea level ... Brilliant
morning sun. Tiny craft skimming the sparkling surface. Boat-
men's bodies tanned to a nut-brown. Glistening green slopes.
Exhilarating air ... At some points the highway is built into
the sides of very steep slopes so that the view below is rather
terrifying. After gazing into one of these chasms, Mamie suddenly announced that in case she fainted she would like us
to know there was smelling salts in her hand bag! So far we
haven't had to use them.

The next day, they moved south of Lucerne, along the lake
whose scenery was "the finest" they'd seen. The "intensely green
slopes of the bordering hills, and the great barren snow-crested
peaks in the background all combined to create a picture of appealing beauty," Ike wrote. The group tried to take some photographs, but he explained the futility of it:

All of us know that the results can give scarcely a hint of the
beauty, the romance, and the splendor which Mother Nature
has poured so lavishly into this spot. Helen, in particular, simply bubbled over with delight ...
After leaving the lake the road led up the valley of the
Reuss River through a canyon-like valley toward the back-
bone of the Alps. Mamie suffered her customary reactions
when travelling a dangerous looking road and when ascending
in altitude and as a result tonight has an attack of indigestion.
We put up here at a splendid and expensive hotel, determined to have one evening when all modern comforts and
conveniences are ours.

On Thursday, September 5, they arrived at the Hôtel du Nord
in Interlaken at 3:00. They had gone only sixty-five miles, but the
route had been "chock-full of thrills." Then they headed south-

east over the Furka Pass. This harrowing experience was laid out by Ike in hilarious detail:

It is 2431 meters high and the road leading through it is constructed as is usual in such regions. Many hair pin turns, switch backs, steep banks on one side and sheer drops on the other compel careful driving and strict attention to the road. Fortunately the car functioned perfectly.

We soon learned that neither of the ladies has any decided preference for driving in the mountains, and the farther we went the more caustic became the back seat remarks about husbands with such poor taste and lack of sense as to suppose for one second that their wives came to Switzerland to ride through the Alps. Cannot we see mountains from the bottom as well as from the top? Do you know I'll be so nervous I won't be able to eat for a week? Think of the nightmares I'll have of this experience! My Gosh, go into first speed! I'm going to shut my eyes! How much longer does this last?

These remarks repeated in various keys and with many variations were eventually succeeded by a profound silence, flavored with a distinct odor of smelling salts coming from the back seat of the car.

And so we reached the summit!

By this time neither Bill nor I had the temerity to explain to the girls that we had to descend the Furka Pass (the second highest in the Alps) and climb immediately over the Grimsel Pass. We conversed (in tones we were sure they would overhear) concerning the slight climb we had next, and talked volubly of the fact that it was a full 1500 feet lower than the one we just topped. (It actually is about 900 feet lower).

We started the descent and Bill and I agreed that we'd be ultra-conservative, keeping the engine in first speed and proceeding so slowly that the girls could not possibly be frightened. All to no avail! Helen's difficulty comes from the fact that she hates any height, and in some places the drop on the exposed side of the road must be a full thousand feet. Naturally that seemed quite high. Mamie had no particular thing to complain of except that she hated it all, she was frightened, she was faint, and above all she was sure we were headed for a nice plunge over the cliffs. The yawning chasms seemed to have a fascination for them both, and much as they dreaded the prospect they could not help gazing down into the terrifying depths. We noted however that both leaned well toward the inside, no matter how much they gazed out the other.

We met many cars and the huge busses filled with passengers required so much room to make the turns that it was possible to pass them only on the straight stretches, and then only in the wider parts, as the road as a whole is quite narrow.

We had a few moments of real thrills when, in attempting to pass one of their busses, its front wheel became engaged with the baggage rack on our running board. As we were on the outside, and the drop at that particular point was several hundreds of feet, it is not difficult to imagine that even skillful drivers like Bill and I were a little bit concerned.

Immediately they touched, both cars were brought to a dead stop and I hopped out to examine this situation. It was not serious and with slow careful backing while I beat the rack away from the bus wheel, we were soon able to get back into the little pocket where we remained while the bus went on past.

During the occurrence Bill and I were so busy that we had no time to consider all the various possibilities of the situation. The girls however, pinned in the back seat, and perfectly helpless to do anything, could not be blamed for letting their imaginations run riot . . .

Since Bill was behind the steering wheel, with the left side of the car against the bus, and his right front wheel very close to the edge of the precipice, he could do nothing but hold tight and wait for instructions from someone who could tell him how things stood.

I was the only one who could get out at once, and as quickly as I saw that the car was not in a particularly dangerous position, was concerned only in straightening out the mess. It was however useless to attempt an explanation to the girls, since from their restricted view they were in imminent danger of taking a nice drop down the mountain side.

Mamie's first thought was that she and Helen could not get out, and this idea naturally intensified the qualms and fears of the moment.

Since Helen realized that Bill had to stick with the car, her idea was to get Mamie out and then, come weal or woe, she and Bill would meet it together. One point not yet clear to any of us including Helen, is how she expected to get Mamie out as long as she (Helen) stayed in, for Mamie's only possible means of exit lay directly through the point [where] Helen was sitting.

Later, Helen surprised the rest of us giving a minute description of the people in the bus, the actions of its driver, and the amusing antics of one passenger who stood up to address his fellow tourists and give them, in an excited voice, advice as to what to do at the moment.

It seemed odd to us that these inconsequential things should have made such a clear cut and definite impression on her at a time when she felt there was an even chance that the next second would find her tumbling down the mountain side.

When finally we reached Gletsch, in a deep canyon on the headwaters of the Rhone, and the ladies realized that we had another tremendous climb in front of us, all criticisms previously made concerning the choice of the day's route faded into insignificance compared to the remarks then addressed to us. Strangely enough when [they] paused for want of breath, a lack of a sufficiently expressive vocabulary to give vent to their inner most feelings, the silence was more expressive and more disturbing for us than were their most sarcastic remarks.

Although at the beginning of the day's trip, Bill and I had been more amused than otherwise by the girls remarks which we felt were mostly for our benefit, by this time we were not only convinced of their sincerity, but deeply concerned about the possible later reactions.

Fortunately, for us all Grimsel Pass was baby's play after the Furka Pass experience, and everything went off smoothly and pleasantly.

As far as Bill and I were concerned we experienced a very real and welcome reaction, when, the worst of the last descent being over, the girls began to yelp for lunch . . .

.   .   .

With the crisis over, they could only stand in awe of the beauty they had just encountered.

> From the standpoint of scenery the trip was magnificent. Long deep pine-covered valleys extending away for miles, mountain streams trembling down the mountain sides in precipitous falls of hundreds of feet, huge barren peaks frowning at us from the opposite sides of narrow gorges, their crests covered with snow and at their feet beautiful little mountain lakes all combined to make the trip one, which from the standpoint of scenic beauty, will never be forgotten by any of us . . .

The Eisenhower-Gruber expedition ended on its seventeenth day. During that time, they covered eighteen hundred miles through four countries. The remaining time before their departure was short, as the Eisenhowers were due to leave Europe permanently, sailing on the *Leviathan* on September 17. Before going, Ike and Mamie were given a royal send-off by their friends the Ellises, who threw a party in their honor at Laurents on the Champs Elysées—"pour tout [sic] la commission." After the dinner, the group went dancing until the wee hours of the morning, ending up at the Eisenhowers' for eggs and coffee at 6:30 a.m.

When the time for the Eisenhowers' departure arrived, the regulars of Club Eisenhower waved them goodbye at the train station. Later, when the threesome arrived at the ship, they discovered that their friends had sent gifts of candy and toys for John, and telegrams, baskets of flowers, and two dozen yellow roses for Ike and Mamie. "We know they all hated to see us go and we liked them all so much," Mamie later recalled.

The time in Paris had been in many ways a bright interlude for the Eisenhowers. The next year the Nazi party became the second largest in Germany; three years later, Hitler became the chancellor of Germany; ten years after the Eisenhower-Gruber expedition, a war began that would consume the terrain they had traveled with such carefree abandon. And Ike himself, who had so curiously and enthusiastically encountered the land of his ancestors, would be tapped to command the Allied forces against Nazi German power.

But in 1929, if the coming conflict made sounds like faraway thunder, they took no notice; nor did they gaze on the distant brewing clouds. For a moment at least, the holidaymakers had enjoyed the last rays of a brilliant sun.

CHAPTER EIGHT

WAR DEPARTMENT, WASHINGTON

One month after my grandparents and father arrived in Washington, the stock market crashed, ushering in one of the greatest crises to face the United States since the Civil War. After some uncertainty about the length of their posting, they decided they would take up residence again at the Wyoming, this time in number 302, a three-bedroom flat. Because of the Depression, many apartments were available at affordable prices for people like Ike who had a regular, stable income. Within easy reach of the War Department, the building attracted a number of army notables, including Ike's boss, General George Van Horn Moseley, and General George Symonds. Gee and Katie Gerow, from Leavenworth days, and Elise and Dick Ellis, from Paris, were also in the Wyoming.

Ike was deeply engrossed in a project for the War Department, reporting directly to General Moseley, who had been on Pershing's staff during World War I. He was charged with studying ways of mobilizing American industry in the event of a war. There were widely differing opinions about how the industrial sector should be financed and managed for any future war effort, and Eisenhower and his boss leaned toward many of the ideas promoted by Bernard Baruch, who had chaired the War Industries Board during World War I. "It was a long, irksome job," Ike later recalled. "Many people in the Department were flatly opposed to Mr. Baruch's ideas." But when Douglas MacArthur replaced General Charles Summerall as chief of staff of the army in 1930, his "arrival gave new impetus to our work and it was certainly a morale boost."

Despite the workplace frustrations, when the Eisenhowers arrived in Washington, Club Eisenhower reassembled. In addition to the many visitors passing through Washington, such as General and Mrs. Conner and even Mrs. Connelly, Mamie's French teacher from Paris, the regulars—Ham Haislip, the Gerows, the Ellises, the Sam Beaches—were joined by Ike's brother Milton, who worked at the Department of Agriculture, and his wife, Helen, as well as their good friends Ruth and Harry "Butch" Butcher, who ran station WJSV, a subsidiary of CBS. Ike and Mamie also saw a good deal of the George Pattons, who were posted at Fort Myer at the time, where Patton was commanding a squadron of cavalry. They were also close to other friends from the War Department, like Everett and Kate Hughes.

To save money, in the evenings Ike and Everett often walked back together from the War Department on Pennsylvania Avenue. When they got to the Wyoming, Everett would phone for Kate to come join them for an impromptu get-together.

Although Kate Hughes had been with Mamie at Leavenworth, she only first got to know her during those Wyoming Apartment days. Twelve years Mamie's senior, Kate thought that "Mamie always seemed like a sort of helpless little creature—at least that's the way I looked at her when I first met her. She wasn't athletic, she didn't like to go outside, she took care of herself and was sort of frail in a lot of ways." But Kate recognized that Mamie was special in so many respects, despite her seeming fragility. She told my mother that Mamie was not exactly regarded as a great beauty, but "men were very attracted to her. She was direct, honest, sincere, but also flirtatious and lively." The quality that Kate admired most was Mamie's devotion as a mother. "In any running around we did, we had to be back at that apartment when John came home from school, come hell or high water. She was there for Johnny and I thought that was wonderful."

Johnny, by now a tall, lanky eight-year-old with an engaging nature, was subject to growing pains—"violent leg aches, due probably to so much running around on concrete sidewalks and alleys," he later recalled. "Many was the time I would call out in the middle of the night and Mother, bleary-eyed, would come into my room and rub my shins. With all her maternal manifestations of affection, this rubbing of leg aches in the wee hours of the morning I remember with the greatest feeling of warmth."

Perhaps because of the untimely death of Ikky, Mamie was protective of John and tended to worry about his health and safety. She would bundle him up every morning to go to John Quincy Adams School, literally just around the corner, in a muffler, a hat and gloves, and "other accoutrements." "Like any other youngster," John remembered, "I had the geography of the Wyoming Apartments well figured out and knew exactly the point where I would disappear from the sight of her window. Then off would come the gloves, the muffler, and the hat, and I would join my friends for a game of 'work up' baseball."

"He's marble-crazy right now," Mamie reported to her parents in a letter dated November 10, 1930. "[John] takes them to school but I advised him not to play for 'keeps' yet until he learn[s] to shoot better—he's practicing right now on the rug." "Keeps" brought with it the notion of loss, and Mamie was taking no chances. Since returning from Paris, she did her best to be as frugal as possible. For example, she and Katie Gerow often shopped at the commissary at Fort McNair, and they'd take a taxi home; but they would get out at Florida Avenue, at the bottom of Connecticut Avenue, and walk up the steep hill to the Wyoming, packages and sacks in hand, to save a few cents on the taxi fare. Mamie also watched for sales, carefully choosing the best buys. Often she would regale her parents with purchasing victories like the one she declared just after the new year of 1931: "Yesterday Katee [sic] & I went shopping. She bought 2 hats & I one. Mine is black satin and had been $13.50. I got it for $3.00." On another occasion she boasted: "I got a beautiful brown lace eve dress the other day at Garfinkels—had been $60 and got it for $14.50. It's a peach." She showed little of this enthusiasm when shopping for Ike's clothes, though it was an important task, given that army officers did not wear uniforms while on active duty at the War Department, yet their appearance and grooming were always a part of their evaluations.

With the Eisenhowers on a limited budget, Pupah paid for a maid for Mamie. Though money was tight, that would never be reason to become less formal with the help; on the contrary. Deannie, who was with the family the longest, wore a white organdy apron over stylish uniforms, blue-and-white stripes for the morning, black for the afternoon and evening.

Housekeeping, even with help, was arduous, dictated very much by the mandates of the seasons. Mamie had to make sure that

during the summer the wool rugs and silk lamp shades were replaced by straw mats and paper shades—necessary steps for keeping the un-air-conditioned apartment as cool as possible during the
hot and humid Washington summers. And with Mamie's devoted
adherence to any number of seasonal celebrations, housekeeping
was in the truest sense of the word a full-time occupation.

Even with the assistance of her parents, Mamie, who had begun
to manage the family money, later said she still didn't know how
they survived financially. They had to pay rent, utilities, and telephone, and Ike got five dollars a week to pay for carfare, lunches,
and incidentals like razors and cigarettes. As she would discover
not long after coming to the Wyoming, Ike saved pennies and
quarters from this very allowance for his birthday and anniversary
presents for her, dates still lovingly celebrated in early Doud tradition. Just days before Mamie's thirty-fifth birthday, Ike wrote
her parents about all the arrangements:

> Johnnie & I are giving Mamie 3 knives & 3 forks of her new
> silverware. I got hold of a little money of which she knew
> nothing. Therefore she'll be all the more surprised & de-
> lighted with the present, I think. Johnny is all excited & very
> mysterious about it. We'll do a lot of marching & singing any-
> way. I think Mary, George and Bo [Horkan] are to be in to
> dinner—so Johnny's party will be complete.

Each year for their anniversary Ike also gave Mamie a piece of
the sterling-silver tea set she was assembling. Completed in 1935,
it was one of the most cherished of all her possessions. With a
twinkle in her eye, she told a reporter in the 1950s, "The day Ike
gave me the kettle, I knew he really loved me, [because] he had
to just about stop smoking to afford that."

To each gift Ike would affix a special card with some handwritten sentiment on it, as he did on their anniversary, July 1, 1931:

> Darling,
>   July 1 is a reminder to me that my good fortune in getting
> you has borne interest for another twelve months. That you
> have stood me for fifteen years is only another proof that you

are the outstanding woman in the world—and since you love
me—you are the *world* to me.

Your lover

Tight budget or not, Mamie and Ike mingled with some of the
most powerful people in Washington. Some they met through his
brother Milton, who came eventually to hold important posts during both the Republican and the Democratic administrations, but
many others were associated with Ike's own work at the War Department. And Mamie had already begun to make her mark socially, pioneering a seating style that she later brought to the White
House: "This week will be a busy one—doing the last odds and
ends on my party. Am still hoping for the E table—Will be like
this [illustration]. Then no one has their backs to the room."

Mamie managed all this with the help of an occasional check
from Pupah, which she kept in a slush fund for little luxuries, like
entertaining on special occasions. Once, she and Ike invited Secretary of War Patrick J. Hurley and his wife to be their guests for
dinner at the Willard Hotel. Mamie had charmed the secretary on
a number of occasions and the Hurleys accepted. It was perhaps
a bit audacious for a major and his wife to entertain a cabinet
member, but Mamie was unconcerned. "They had been wonder-
fully kind to us, so we couldn't see why we shouldn't return their
hospitality," she remarked.

Mamie and Ike chose the Willard not only because of its reputation as one of Washington's finer hotels but because they got
special rates there as members of the Saturday Night Dinner
Dance Club. In preparing the evening, Mamie spared no expense.
Decades later she told a reporter, "The party flowers cost almost
as much as it took to feed us for a week. Added to the dinner
check, they really upset our budget."*

For their regular entertaining, Mamie devised several set menus
for which she'd calculated the costs. Depending on their cash flow,
she'd get out the menu appropriate for their financial situation at
the moment. Although she was willing to splurge if she thought it

*Mamie and Ike had also been entertained by the assistant secretary of war,
Frederick H. Payne, and his wife. Mamie set about throwing a party for them,
but the details of it have been lost.

would help her husband, she made little pretense about their financial status and refused to put on what she called "airs."

In November 1931, Ike and Mamie were invited to join his boss, General Moseley, and his wife for dinner. Afterward they went to the Armistice Ball, which was attended by 15,000 people "milling around" a room made to look like the Café de la Paix during World War I. The next day Mamie, writing to her parents, declared, "I looked grand last night . . . my black velvet was a knockout. All the ladies were crazy about it and finally I had to tell them it was 4 years old and made-over."

*D*uring those Wyoming years, my father spent the summers with Nana and Pupah in Denver and with "Grandma and Grandpa" Eisenhower in Abilene. Mamie and Ike may have sent him out West so that they could have a break themselves, but it is also clear from the letters that his grandparents were also clamoring for time with him.

Young John traveled alone to Denver by train. Mamie and Ike would arrange for a redcap to meet his train in Englewood, near Chicago, and help him make his connection for Denver. They always gave him some spending money, which he would save, much to his delight. "It was a safe society in those days," my father has explained. "Nobody ever worried about sending a boy on such a trip alone."

During those Denver summers John would play pool in the Lafayette Street house's basement and throw baseballs. He also occupied himself with a tree house and by riding his bike in the neighborhood. Eventually he went to YMCA camp and took tennis lessons. Among the most memorable times, however, were the occasions when Pupah would teach him how to play the piano. When his grandfather got behind the piano, he displayed a kind of joie de vivre that was otherwise rarely exhibited. Sitting with Johnny beside him, he'd pound out the chords, his head thrown back in merriment. "I remember admiring his gold teeth, and certain gaps in his teeth I could see when he laughed so hard," John remembers.

Having John with Pupah and Nana in Denver afforded Mamie the opportunity to have some time utterly free of concern about her son and his health and safety. In July 1932, just after John had begun YMCA camp, Mamie exclaimed: "I am thrilled over what you're doing for John at YMCA . . . No, Mother dear, I don't worry about him a second, I know so well how you bend over backwards taking care of him."

Mamie wrote again:

Well, I did wonder why I hadn't had a line from any one in over two weeks but decided you just didn't feel like writing. I never dreamed of John being sick. Of course I am disappointed he's had such a time as I had expected big things in a health way from him this summer in that health resort. However I know there wasn't a stone left unturned in his care taking and only feel sorry you have so much responsibility thrown on u-all. I was so thrilled over the YMCA swimming— but I'll trust your judgement about his return for after all you see him & know his state of health better than I do now. Whatever you decide to do is OK . . .

It is surprising that Mamie and Nana were so calm and restrained on the subject of John's illness. Many accounts have suggested that Mamie was obsessed by John's health and safety, especially in view of Ikky's tragic death. Perhaps her reaction in this case showed a growing maturity on her part; it certainly wasn't because her memories of Ikky had dimmed. In fact, she frequently mentioned Ikky's birthdays in her letters to her parents, and she never failed to remark on her sisters' deaths, especially when the anniversaries of them came up or when she knew her parents would be on their way to the cemetery. "I pictured you two going to Fairmount," she wrote that summer, "to look after our darlings."

During those summers of 1929–35, my father distinctly recalls, the Sunday outings to Fairmount Cemetery were religiously observed. With fresh flowers in hand, they would replace the "wilted stinking ones" on the family graves left from the week before. "It was hard-going for a ten- or eleven-year-old boy," he told me. "[Once, my grandparents] overheard me complaining to a friend, and I was silenced for a day."

John would also visit his other grandparents in Abilene. Everything about the two households was in stark contrast. "I remember gushing over [going to Abilene] because it was so informal. They'd allow me to sit on the front lawn eating chicken legs—the chicken [which] had been alive about two hours before—the one whose head I had helped whack off. And they'd let me sit there in my undershirt. As I would enthuse over [the informality in] Abilene, it was a hint to the Douds. But they would say, 'Of course, it is just a hick town.' "

*I*n John's absence, Mamie and Ike enjoyed summer activities not possible during the more hectic pace of the school year. Deannie would take the summers off, and Ike and Mamie would be masters of their own household and schedule. "We are getting along fine and think it is good for us to be alone and get acquainted again," Mamie wrote to her parents. "Ike has been a perfect dear to me and helps so with the housework." On another occasion she recounted, "I walked six holes [of golf] with Ike and practice[d] a bit and we came home at 7:30. Ike was so pleased and we intend to do it any eve the spirit moves us. We really had lots of fun together—listened to [the radio] then the Prize fight and then to bed."

The family harmony notwithstanding, both Mamie and Ike were deeply concerned about the effects of the deepening Depression. Mamie began to take an interest in the outcome of the 1932 election. It is surprising that she seemed so riveted by a process that was off-limits to professional soldiers and their families. It was army practice that officers and their wives did not vote (a tradition that ended after World War II), and the expression of a political opinion was confined to intimate family members or friends. While this was certainly the case in the Eisenhower household, they were sensitized to the political scene, with Ike's position at the War Department and Milton's as part of the administration.

"The principal topic of conversation these days is politics," Ike told his parents-in-law.

You enjoyed going to the Senate and the House so much it is a shame you had to miss this particular session of Congress. The personal and political differences seem to be more bitter than usual, with the result that various members take great delight in calling names and hurling vituperations at one another. I suppose most of it is done for effect, but nevertheless it makes for splendid headlines for Washingtonians to read the following day. Katherine [Gerow] and Mamie are fully determined to go down to the Senate soon and spend a whole day.

Political decisions made in Washington had as big an effect on the Eisenhower family as they did on every other American family. The Depression's bite was being felt by Mamie and Ike even though he had a stable job. Pupah was also having financial difficulties in the stockyards, and Auntie had been suffering from reversals in her millinery business. "Am terribly sorry about Auntie and her work," Mamie had written to her parents as early as October 1, 1931, "but can see there is very little biz."

In Washington, Mamie also had her worries. The Wyoming was in receivership, and there were twenty-eight vacancies in the building, a number that was growing monthly. Mamie was concerned that they might have to move out because the building had been allowed to deteriorate so badly. But they decided to wait until a new owner could be found, to see if they would get a reduction in their rent and if the new management would redecorate the premises.

Washington was not spared the sight of homeless women and children roaming the streets in search of food and shelter. As the Depression progressed, unemployment would reach 25 percent of the nation's workforce. With evidence of the deepening economic crisis everywhere, the sights and smells of poverty were beginning to penetrate the core of Mamie's contented, rather sheltered existence. She wrote her parents:

> Yesterday I spent the morning and $1.50 in phone calls calling people for the Parent-Teacher's card party on Fri. Such a job, and this AM I was out at nine, calling in person on the families who didn't have phones. Believe me this is the last time I'll let myself in for anything like that again . . . Such queer dirty apts as I saw this AM—felt like I should have been disinfected when I got home.

Not all the Eisenhowers' confidants were under the Depression's screws. Gee Gerow and his wife, Katie, left the United States at the end of 1931, he for China, she to the Philippines to wait for him. A postcard from Katie in Manila, where the cost of living was low and Westerners could live luxuriously on very little, described a lifestyle at stark odds with that in Depression-ridden America. "You don't have to do a thing but draw your breath," she reported to Mamie.

Mamie probably thought little about Katie's characterization of life in the Philippines. With no inkling of what lay in store for her, she did not give significance to Katie's words. Instead, she was utterly absorbed by the constraints the Depression put on their lives in Washington and what should be done about them. Accustomed to wangling almost everything she really wanted, she was concerned that in all probability Ike would be subject to a 10 percent pay cut.*

Mamie was disappointed that circumstances precluded the acquisition of a piano. She told her parents that Ike had rejected out of hand the idea of a lease-purchase arrangement, saying that paying for it that way would make "you finally hate the sight of [it]." Mamie lamented that without practicing she might lose her knack for playing, an unpleasant eventuality, especially, she said, as "it is my only parlour trick..."

The Depression hit across all social and economic lines in America. In 1932, mobs looted department stores and food markets in Detroit, Chicago, and New York. In the countryside, vigilante groups lynched mortgage foreclosers as they fanned out across America's farmland. But no crisis was as poignant or as indicative of the times as the Bonus Men's March on Washington at the end of July. A band of 18,000 to 20,000 World War I veterans descended on Washington to collect their "adjusted compensation certificates," or "bonuses," which Congress had created in 1925 to be paid to them like a pension in 1945. With the severity of the Depression and a high percentage of unemployment among the group, they had assumed that the "deferred bonus was identical to a deposit in the bank." And they had come to collect.

Decades later, Americans would be used to the sight of teeming protesters and their tent cities sprawled across Washington's open spaces. But in 1932 there were deep suspicions in the Hoover

---

*This would be all the harder, given that the new Wyoming management was now asking $130 a month while refusing to do any redecorating of the building.

administration, shared by General MacArthur, that the demonstration had been organized by provocateurs and was "animated by the essence of revolution." The Bonus Men occupied abandoned buildings near the Capitol and built a shanty tent city on the other side of the Anacostia River. When construction in the Capitol Hill area necessitated their evacuation, the District police were sent in and a riot ensued. Overwhelmed, L. H. Reichelderfer, president of the Board of Commissioners of the District of Columbia, wrote to President Herbert Hoover requesting the assistance of the army. "The presence of Federal troops in some number," he wrote, "will obviate the seriousness of the situation and result in far less violence and bloodshed."

MacArthur decided to take control of the army units being sent to the scene, where five hundred to six hundred troops would bring the situation under control. Among the officers ordered to the site were his aides, Dwight Eisenhower and T. J. Davis. George Patton and his units were also called up from Fort Myer.

Ike felt "close enough" to MacArthur to challenge his approach to the crisis directly:

> I told him that the matter could easily become a riot and I thought it highly inappropriate for the Chief of Staff of the Army to be involved in anything like a local or street corner embroilment (of course this was no street corner matter—but it still did not require the presence of the Chief of Staff in the streets). General MacArthur disagreed, saying that it is a question of Federal authority in the District of Columbia, and because of his belief that there was "incipient revolution in the air" as he called it, he paid no attention to my dissent. He ordered me to get into my uniform.

An hour later Ike, properly clad, reported back to the War Department.

Johnny was at home that afternoon. He remembers his father, in a desperate hurry, flinging things from his closet, mumbling unmentionables under his breath. "Dad kept his clothes in the large closet in my bedroom," John later recalled. "He was a good sport, I thought, as he allowed me to leave my electric train standing on the floor, thus making travel around the room hazardous. My most vivid recollection of our shared accommodation is that of watching...him come home in a big rush to don his uniform. General Douglas MacArthur was heading out to the Anacostia Flats to meet the Bonus Marchers in person, and he wanted his aides in uniform. Dad's language as he struggled was not of the best, but his anger was not directed toward the Bonus Marchers; it was directed toward his 'damn' boots, which he had a hard time pulling on. Officers' uniforms included boots and breeches in those days."

MacArthur commanded the columns of men (and a few tanks) to cross the bridge, but before the troops reached the veterans, the wooden huts and shanties began to burn. Ike was always adamant that the troops had not started the fires, because they were "too far away." But he concluded: "The veterans, whether or not they were mistaken in marching on Washington, were ragged, ill-fed, and felt themselves badly abused. To suddenly see the whole encampment going up in flames just added to the pity one had to feel for them."

Ike warned MacArthur that after the fire the press would want to interview him and advised him not to return to the War Department lest he let himself in for questioning on what was a political and not a military matter. But in this, too, MacArthur was unwilling to listen to counsel. At 11:00 p.m. on that eventful evening, in an impromptu news conference MacArthur suggested that the country had been facing a dire threat that could directly or indirectly lead to a "takeover."

"I have never seen greater relief on the part of the distressed populace than I saw today," MacArthur told the press. "I have released in my day more than one community which had been held in the grip of a foreign enemy. I have gone into villages that for three and one half years had been under the domination of soldiers of a foreign nation. I know what gratitude means along that line. I have never seen, even in those days, such expressions of gratitude as I heard from those crowds today."

The whole incident did nothing, in Ike's view, to alleviate the distress of the veterans or enhance the reputation of the army.

A few days after the crisis had passed, Mamie wrote her own account of those events to her parents.

Saturday 2:30

Dearest Folks.

... *Well* if we didn't have excitement here Thursday with Bonus men. I had taken Helen G & Bess Mc* to Commissary and in return stopped over at Bess's to check groceries. When I reached Apt at 3:10 there were clothes from front door back—walked into Ike's room and boxes bags and boot trees all over. I thot [sic] he had been called out for military something, but what? No note. No phone call or anything. I phoned downstairs and asked had Ike gone out in uniform. Yes, he had left almost 10 minutes before—in uniform. I called Helen G. to see had Bill gone—no—she knew nothing but would call office. [It] was ¾ hr. before we could get information that Ike had gone as Gen McArthur's aide to quell the riot. Troops having been ordered out from Ft. Myer & Washington & Meade. At 5:30 Gen McA's sec, called & said Major E didn't know when he would be home. Then did I get excited—streets filled with extras. We had been going to Grubers' for dinner. I went & after dinner we rode downtown to see sights—everything that could turn a wheel was out. At 9:30 streets were cleared by tear gas and marchers pressed across Dis. line. About 11:30 the big camp we saw from "old Iron sides" was in flames, Ike got home at 1 o'clock and was out again at 7. Fri. ...

... [It was] such a terrific day for heat. When he came in he didn't have a dry rag on & his good uniform soaked. Washington police could do nothing with the mob altho they (Bonus) were unarmed. But what they did with stones & bricks was something ... To-nite Bess Mc is giving a supper party for 21—with poker and bridge afterward. I've just washed my hair & Ike has gone out to play golf and after I finish this am going to take a nap. Everyone gathered over here last nite to greet the returned "hero" ha ha and get all the dope first hand ... Ike is fine except the tear gas started his eye off again.

Everything is quiet now altho city still under "martial law." Maybe Ike will be able to write a clearer description of what he did. Of course you all have read everything in the papers.

*Helen Gruber and Bess McCammon.

But talk about a compliment to one Dwight D. only officer taken with Gen. Mc except Davis. I'll bet there was gnashing of the teeth in some quarters . . .*

It is ironic that along with the story of the Bonus Marchers Mamie enclosed a private letter for her father in which she thanked him for helping them out with their own difficult financial situation:

Dearest Daddy,
Your letter and present came this a.m. and many thanks. Yes it is quite a [lot]—50 some odd dollars reduction out of an already insufficient pay check and your help will be doubly appreciated . . . poor Helen Gruber had a savings account in one of those Chicago banks that failed. She lost $900.00. Col. Robbins was here the other day and Ike said he was pretty low about finances [the economy] in Iowa. We are hoping rents will go down but no chance I guess until this gov't Board gets to work on it . . .

Your Puddy

Despite Pupah's help, money remained tight and anxiety high. The rear axle of the family Buick they called Bessie broke while Ike was driving a friend home one evening. He had to return in a taxi. Mamie realized that repair of the car would have to come out of her budget, and she had already paid more than one hundred dollars in repair costs since May. That summer she also discovered to her horror that moths had somehow infested the closet where they stored winter clothes. She was saved by a visit from Ike's parents not long after this discovery: Ida gave herself the task of mending the moth-eaten items so they could be back in service by the fall.

On another occasion, John's overcoat was lost, stolen from the

---

*Mamie's account is interesting for many reasons, mostly because it is clear that she was not attuned to the finer points of Ike's disagreement with MacArthur. She was principally happy that her husband had received the recognition of his boss in carrying out the assignment. This, I believe, is a further indication that Ike did not share the details of his work life with Mamie, and that the separation between work and home was very much in place even during such dramatic times.

back of their unlocked car. Chiding her son for his apparent care-lessness, she wailed: "Don't you know it takes me a whole month to save ten dollars!"*

As for many other people during the Depression, the constant financial pressure would always stay with Mamie, and it prompted some, in her old age, to criticize her for being downright miserly.

*I*ke had been in Washington for three years and now he was eager to move on. He had originally thought that he would be at the War Department for only six months, while waiting to assume a command somewhere, but now the length of his tenure was ri-valing that of any of his previous assignments, though he had con-sidered a number of other possibilities, including at least one overseas posting.

During the summer of 1932, Katie Gerow wrote from the Phil-ippines:

August 9

Dearest Mamie,

Don't pass out at the appearance of a letter from me but I still love you even if I seem to have ceased to function with a pen.

We are back in Manila and settled into our own house. It is really lovely—large, cool, comfortable and we have been able to make it very attractive with my Shanghai purchases ...

We wish for you everyday and how Gee did long for Ike in China ...

Lots of talk out here about foreign service being extended to three years. If we stay well and in our present mental at-titude it would not make us mad at all. You'd better come out ... Love to the "gang" and a heart full from we two to you three.

---

*This incident took place in the winter of 1933, and, according to Mamie's letters, the coat was never found, despite the reward they offered for it. "I hope someone is warm with it," she wrote to her parents on January 23, 1934.

Gerow was not the only officer who had by now approached Ike about taking up a position outside Washington. Aside from talk about going to China, Ike had also requested a transfer to San Antonio, and other offers had been proposed. However, with Mac-Arthur unwilling to relinquish him and with added financial pressures, Mamie and Ike even began to talk about leaving the Wyoming and moving into free army housing at Fort Myer. In a letter dated October 27, 1932, Mamie outlined the considerations for her parents:

We had thot [sic] of asking to be sent to Ft. Myer but afraid of schooling problems again. Post would be beautiful and John could have riding lessons but [it] would necessitate keeping old Bessie and getting a new car for Ike [who] would have to have transportation to the War dept. We don't know whether its settled or no. If Roosevelt gets in there may be a new chief of staff and that would change the complexion of things . . . I so hate to take [Papa's] check every month when he is hard pressed. Ike says we're sure to get another pay cut—that there's already rumors about it as soon as Congress meets again.

The army was indeed bracing itself for the possibility of another pay cut. "Everyone expects to do very little socially this year," Mamie reported in the midst of what had been traditionally known as "the season." "There is an order out telling the army to throw no big parties this year & [to put nothing] in the paper as we are afraid of another cut in salary—say nothing about this to anyone," she begged her parents.

Despite their concerns over their financial situation, with characteristic loyalty and support Mamie was ready to dip into their hard-to-come-by savings. Ida had written to say that she was worried because Ike's father, David, had fallen ill and had been laid up for more than two weeks. Mamie knew that Ike was "very upset" about this news and would want to "get a plane ride west" as soon as possible. She told her parents she would "insist on his taking some of our savings and go if there is no other way." To Mamie, family things always came first.

.   .   .

That fall, Franklin D. Roosevelt was elected president of the United States. A month later, MacArthur learned that he would be retained as chief of staff for another two years. Ike was appointed as his personal assistant in February 1933, a job that brought with it some flexibility in choosing his own hours but a workload so heavy that he often would not get home until 7:30 or 7:45 in the evening.

Despite the obvious confidence placed in Ike, the new assignment brought no salary increases—nor did it offer a command of troops, which Ike had been dreaming of. The new appointment simply meant two more years in Depression-ridden Washington and two more years to become more closely associated with General Douglas MacArthur as an indispensable member of his inner circle.

CHAPTER NINE

A CIRCLE OF FRIENDS

*T*he Eisenhowers had never lived in any one place longer than they had at the Wyoming, and life had taken on a predictable, welcome pattern—the closest thing that Mamie would ever experience to normal civilian life.

As things began to pick up again, with the advent of the New Deal, the Wyoming management started improving the building. During the summer of 1933, when John was in Denver with his grandparents, Ike and Mamie moved out of number 302 into a smaller flat downstairs, while the kitchen of their apartment was modernized, another bathroom added, and a wall knocked out to enlarge the living space. "We have been moving for over a week, and yesterday finally got the last trunks, etc. in the big closet. I might just as well have moved out of Washington as moved from one floor to another," Mamie wrote her parents. However, she was excited about the changes she was making to the apartment and was already planning to hang new curtains and acquire new furnishings.

Despite this encouraging upswing in their domestic setup, a pall descended over the Eisenhowers that summer with the news that Mamie's dear friend Katie Gerow had been seized with some mysterious ailment in the Philippines, an illness serious enough to warrant debate among her physicians as to whether her treatment should be administered in the United States or Japan. "But she won't leave Gee," Mamie said, worried. "Too bad they still have over a year [to their tour]." With nothing more than secondhand information of her ailment, Mamie and Ike were utterly "undone" by the news.

That summer Ike, too, fell ill, with a progressively worsening back problem that had become chronic. He began desperately seeking advice about finding a cure, for such a medical problem could jeopardize his job security and future career. By November his physical condition had worsened and Mamie voiced her concern to her parents: "Ike's back has been bothering him so much he has been going to a Dr. down town—a medico osteopath—$5.00 per—so far not much improvement. He's afraid to go to Walter Reed [Army Hospital] for fear they will retire him. Drs. are retiring men right & left these days . . . Something has to be done for the poor dear, as he can hardly stand erect." Ten days later she reported that Ike's civilian doctor was so intrigued with his case that he proposed treating him for free, a generous offer the Eisenhowers didn't feel they could accept.

Still, despite Ike's medical situation and worries about its effect on his job stability, the Eisenhowers approached Thanksgiving that year full of gratitude to have their home and family intact. They decided to give to the Community Chest as well as to a larger group of charities, concerned that the Depression had affected the viability of these organizations, since many of the contributors were government workers who were strapped for cash. "We have a good, warm home and plenty to wear—and good friends . . . a lot to be thankful for," Mamie wrote.

*A*side from these cares, it was a contented time in Mamie and Ike's marriage. Though both were strong-willed people and occasionally quarreled, John would later say that they never argued in his presence and the only complaints he ever heard his mother voice were about Ike bringing home work from the office.

John and his father were also close. Ike was a tough disciplinarian, but he and John shared many warm moments, and his affection for his son was conveyed without doubt. "Dad and I rose about the same time, just before eight," John remembered. "We shared a bathroom . . . and the time was spent constructively. In those morning sessions I was grilled without mercy on multiplication tables, so that I was always weeks ahead of my class. And no errors were tolerated. But the morning bathroom sessions were not all devoted to schoolwork. We had time to talk about things in general and we had our laughs. For some reason, possibly to save time, Dad and I often shared a tub of bathwater. Usually I would bathe first while Dad was shaving, and Dad would then climb in after me. One morning Dad decided to dispense with this usual ritual, but I was insistent. My determination that he bathe that day must have puzzled him, but finally he gave way. The result was rewarding. Dad stuck his foot in the water and let out a howl that must have been heard throughout the Wyoming Apartments. Blue, shivering, but delighted, I leaped out of the freezing water and charged laughing into the bedroom to tell Mother of the success of my prank."

In addition to family life, Mamie and Ike had a close circle of friends they called "the gang," who lent one another warmth and support. There were many card parties and evening gatherings, everyone's birthday was remembered, and they always shared Christmas. In reading Mamie's letters of the period, I am astonished by the extent of the gift giving among the adults. And everyone in the gang remembered John, too, at Christmas, on his birthday, and at his graduation. As just about the only child born to any member of the group, John became their de facto mascot. And he returned their affections. Once, he read a novel about medieval comrades who became blood brothers, and, intrigued by the notion of it, he devised a ritual similar to the one he'd read about in the book. It required that members of the secret society prick their fingers and mix their blood together in a glass of water. Each male member of Club Eisenhower was subjected to "the ordeal": Gee Gerow, Everett Hughes, P. A. Hodgson, Sam Beach, Ham Haislip, and no doubt others. "This initiation procedure could hardly have been pleasant for the adults, administered by a child," John conceded, "but it created in me—and I know in them also—an unusual affinity. For years thereafter they referred to me as Blood Brother John. When they finally passed away, one by one, I always felt grief similar to that of losing a second father."*

As most of the men worked six days a week, Sunday was a

---

*"I came to know all these men well," he recalled in later life, "but, of course, had no yardstick with which to measure their potential greatness." Two of them, Gerow and Haislip, became four-star generals during World War II; Everett Hughes later became inspector general of the European theater and, after that, chief of ordnance.

special day, and both Ike and Mamie liked to sleep late. John, no doubt under Auntie's persistent influence, made an effort to persuade his parents to go to church with him. While Mamie may have had some flashes of conscience about it, she insisted that Sunday was the only day of the week when Ike could stay in bed and relax, and, she reasoned, she needed that time, too. Given the seriousness of Ike's chronic back problem, the argument seemed to satisfy John completely. So he would get up early, dress in coat and tie, and walk to a church he had chosen for himself, one which was attended by some of his schoolmates.

In the years before the Gerows went to the Philippines, John recalled, "My parents had the most wonderful ways of spending Sunday, I thought. They wouldn't move a muscle until 5:00 in the afternoon. Deannie (our cook) wasn't there, so Dad would do all the cooking. Then they'd call the Gerows, and they'd come down and get out these big ten-gallon tins of denatured alcohol that Dad and Gee had bought from the bootlegger [this was before Prohibition was repealed in 1933]. They kept the tins in the very ample coat room just off the living room. Ten-gallon tins are awkward, so they needed to syphon the booze into smaller bottles for later mixture with grapefruit juice or whatever. I was allowed to help. This is where I learned the principle of the syphon; thus the performance was cast in the light of educating the young."

Other Sundays, when duty called, Ike, Mamie, and John would dress up in their finery—Ike in striped pants and derby, Mamie in a silk frock with gloves and a fashionable hat—and in their 1927 Buick, "Bessie," they'd drive around town to various apartment buildings. While John waited in the car, they would make their formal calls, prescribed by rigid Washington protocol. Mamie would get into the spirit of the outing, but, my father remembers, "This was a chore that Dad detested and he made little secret of it. On rare Sundays Dad would play golf . . . Though he played little, he went after the game with the same intensity as in later years. The golf tees consisted of small, wet piles of sand, molded to a desired height. Dad had a powerful swing but a horrendous slice to go with it. He seemed to wind up in the alfalfa an inordinate amount of the time, the air punctuated with certain expletives that I had thought were unknown to adults—only kids."

.   .   .

*A*s John moved into adolescence, Mamie maintained a calm and rather sympathetic attitude toward this new stage. After his return from Denver in 1934, Mamie noted that "Ike just follows the kid around, he's so pleased to have him home and my eyes are big as saucers over how big & grown up he is. His hands fascinate me, they are so large & mannish. No dimples anymore."

But Mamie would often have to reassure Nana on the subject of John's adolescence. She chided her mother for unfounded worries. "I am sorry you worry so about John dear but as you said they have to go thru all stages. We knew before he left for Denver about the strip poker, but it was all talk. They played here right under my nose & all they lost were keys—neck ties etc . . . I do watch him mighty close & Ike talks to him a great deal. I'm sure you needn't worry yet. The age that scares me is 15 to 20."

John, a successful and popular student, was, in actual fact, the least of his parents' worries. With MacArthur's tenure as chief of staff of the army nearing an end, the subject of what next was never far from their minds.

Various officers around the country had made numerous attempts to secure Ike's services on their staffs without successfully wresting him from MacArthur's grasp. Nevertheless, Ike was not without options. During this time, he was also offered a very attractive civilian position. A newspaper chain, familiar with the high quality of his work on *American Battlefields of France*, offered him five times his salary ($3,000 a year) to be their military correspondent. There were many advantages to taking the job—the Eisenhowers could stay in Washington indefinitely, they would have few financial concerns, and he would be free of the frustrations of his current job, so far from the troops he longed to command. Ike discussed the matter with his brother Milton, but it was perhaps Mamie's advice that he considered most. It was the second and last time she intervened about a career move.

"Well, Ike," she said, "I don't think you'd be happy. This is your life, and you know it. Now true, there's not any money in it, but we have other personal things that make up for lack of currency."

Mamie's willingness to continue to live the uncertain existence that was army life was a huge factor in Ike's remaining in the service, especially as she would have been the biggest beneficiary had he left. But Pupah's checks also made remaining in the army possible, a gesture that until now has gone unrecognized.

Mamie's unqualified support may have contributed to the fuss Ike made over her inconsequential thirty-eighth birthday in 1934. By her own account, she was "overwhelmed" by what she admitted was the first surprise birthday party she had ever had in her life. In a letter to her parents, she said,

> Well what a birthday I had. Of course, the doorbell rang at 7:30 and there was your telegram. I didn't open it tho till [we were] at the table. We marched with Ike & I singing and John playing the harmonica. Then the fun started . . .

Mamie opened all the presents from Ike and John—they gave her six dessert knives, and John, who had gone shopping by himself, bought her a "large glass button" with rhinestones in the middle. "Bless his heart," she commented. "He said 'Mother it will look pretty on a black dress' and it really is quite pretty. I love it." Then Ike took Mamie to the film *The Merry Widow*, and Ann Hodgson asked them in for cocktails.

> I knew Ike had asked them for dinner so we all piled back here and imagine my surprise when we walked in to hear a loud chorus of "Happy Birthday to You" from Milton & Helen—McCamons—Horkans—Dick Ellis & Capt Evans—John and Bo. I was completely overcome. Ike, John & Deannie had gotten up this surprise party and it was a dandy . . . Everyone thought it was so cute of the boys & just entered in 100%.

Those joyful moments were among the last carefree ones for some time to come. MacArthur's term as chief of staff of the army was drawing to a close, and in his retirement he was planning to go to the Philippines as chief military adviser to the Philippine government. He asked Ike to join him. When Ike hesitated, MacArthur "lowered the boom," making his request an order, pointing out that Ike had been his chief assistant for so long that bringing in a new person would make his job much more difficult. "I was in no position to argue with the Chief of Staff," Ike later recalled.

Just as family debate raged around the question whether Mamie and John should join him overseas, Katie and Gee Gerow arrived back in Washington from the Philippines. Gee had been assigned to the War Department and Katie was immediately sent to Walter Reed Army Hospital. In a letter of June 5, 1935, Ike reported to Colonel Daniel Van Voorhis, one of their mutual friends, on the crisis.

As you probably know, Katheryn underwent a very radical operation immediately upon arriving in Washington . . . The doctors decided that the only treatment possible under the circumstances was to use the X-ray and that a further operation was out of the question . . . Katheryn herself is brave and hopeful and when not suffering excruciating pain is very lively and vivacious. Mamie, Gee, and I all try to do what we can in keeping her spirits up and in occupying her time pleasantly.

The Gerows rented an apartment on California Street, only two blocks away from the Eisenhowers. Katie was virtually bedridden, but Mamie would visit her every day, sometimes for the whole day. The Douds sent Katie a present from Denver, and frequently Mamie would try to break the monotony by taking her for rides in the car, to places such as Mount Vernon. "It's heartbreaking to see her," Mamie told her parents. "Of course a miracle could happen but I don't see how . . ."

The night before Katie died, Mamie, Ike, and John took an evening meal to the Gerows, and they told John about the seriousness of her illness. "Is Katie going to die?" John remembers asking them in surprise. The next morning at 6:25 she passed away. Gee called Ike immediately. Dressing quickly, he left the Wyoming and was at the Gerows' apartment by 6:45 to make the funeral arrangements. Mamie recalled that Katie had been conscious and aware of them on that last evening before she died. "Poor little girl suffered so terribly," Mamie said.

June 25, 1935

I've had a terrible time trying to write this week. I just couldn't get my mind on it. Last Wed was Katie's funeral after which I brot [sic] the family here for luncheon. It was so much better than letting them go back to apt. Have been over to see them this AM. They are all still in a haze and poor Gee is sunk. *All* his friends rally around but there are so many hours when one has time to think . . .

It now looks like Ike would get his secret orders about Sept. 17th for Philippines—sailing about October 4. We have talked and talked things over and have practically decided that John & I will stay on here in Washington till we see how the thing is going to turn out. John can finish his last grade school year, which he is most anxious *to do*. I don't want to go over there & this *way* at least one of us can have John. I do hope you can come and stay with me at least part of the time—It wouldn't pay me to move into a smaller apt as rents have gone up so and it would mean storing a lot of things. Do you think you could come and be with me? This job may peter out or Ike might not be able to stand the climate and then we would be in a mess. I hate to let him go alone but he would live at Hotel (which the Commission is taking over) or at the Army-Navy Club. I don't want to go away so far from u-all and after Katie's experience I'm *scared*. Of course we still have a couple of months and something may happen to the whole thing. Such a mess this whole thing is. I don't know whether this is all very clear or not—so hard to write about these things . . .

That summer Mamie and Ike stayed in Washington. They'd thought about taking a vacation with the Hodgsons to New England and Canada, but Gee was moving to a smaller apartment and Mamie said, "[He] seems terribly low and needs us."

Ike was also busy getting ready for his departure. Much to his annoyance, MacArthur had not put a limit on the length of his tour. While he was packing up and preparing to leave for an indefinite time, Mamie was living for the possibility that something might happen that would change these plans; she thought perhaps the climate in Manila would make his back "play up" and he would request a transfer. She couldn't bear to break up their apartment, which had come to mean so much, and she was frightened of living again in the tropics.

It is also quite possible that Mamie attributed Katie's mysterious ailment, which was probably cancer, to the Philippines. Consumed on occasion by immobilizing fear, she may well have worried that she too—a woman with a weak heart and intermittent digestive problems—could contract such an illness while there.

Whatever the reasons, Mamie was doggedly stubborn about staying behind, at least for a year, and there was little that Ike could do now about her decision. For him, the only bright spot was the prospect that he would earn considerably more money in the Philippines and could bring his own staff officer with him. He chose James B. Ord, a West Point classmate and dear personal friend. But these advantages were of little compensation for his failure to persuade Mamie and his unwillingness to force her to come.

Ike and Mamie had known and enjoyed many intimate and happy years together. This separation would be wrenching, and Ike feared being away from John. He must have remembered the other separations he had had from his young family and the tragedy of Ikky's death, which had deprived him of unexperienced moments forever. Certainly enough death had surrounded the family that he did not have the luxury of taking anyone for granted. That summer, Ike gave Nana a sorrowful account of their family crisis:

> . . . I deeply appreciate your generosity in arranging the [camping] experience for [John].
>
> I miss him more this year than ever before. Possibly its because I've got this Philippine thing staring me in the face and I realize that we'll be separated for many months at the very least. I hate the whole thought—and know that I am going to be miserable. On the other hand Mamie is so badly frightened (both for John and herself) at the prospect of going out there—that I simply cannot urge her to go. My thought is that either I will be able to send her favorable reports as to the conditions of health education etc. that she will be willing to come next June, or that I will come home within a reasonably short time. I can only hope for the best—as the idea of being separated from my family has nothing for me but grief . . .
>
> As you know Mamie considered several plans for her winter's sojourn including Denver, San Antonio & here. She

chose the last because of John & his convenient schooling here with old friends—as well as for the fact that it may avoid an extra move.

But I do hope that you & Dad or you alone or Auntie can spend almost the full time with her. I think she will be writing you today or tomorrow.

With lots of love to all of you—

As ever your devoted
Son

Before his departure for the Philippines, Mamie gave Ike two photos—one of John and one of herself—which she had taken and framed. Then as planned, in September, just after John's return from Denver, Ike left—first to see his parents in Abilene and the Douds in Denver, then to catch the train for San Francisco. From there he sailed for Manila. Upset by being separated from Mamie, for her birthday one month later Ike sent her a radiogram, a message similar to a telegram: "Many happy returns of the day. So long as I live I hope to be by your side on all your future birthdays. Much love, Ike." He had also sent Gee Gerow money for four dozen talisman roses for Mamie, and Gee told Mamie that Ike had sent him full instructions on what color the roses should be and what was to be put on the card. "They were exquisite," Mamie told her mother, "and the card read, 'Each rose is a message of my devotion.'"

Mamie was touched by the gesture and admitted it had made her feel good, but she was troubled and felt sad—perhaps even guilty—about a letter Ike had sent her from Shanghai some days earlier. "He was terribly lonesome," she wrote her parents. "Said it was a trip for lovers—scenery is beautiful . . . He'll feel better with time."

Most probably she knew deep in her heart that she had, in some measure, let Ike down. She had failed to meet the arduous challenge she had set for herself after Panama, hiding, perhaps, behind John's last year at school as a way to avoid going to another tropical hardship post.

In a letter to John, some weeks later, Ike wrote:

Once in a while I have a radio from Mamie, but very few letters, so far. However, since I know that she can radio to me if necessary, I always assume that she and you are well, as otherwise, she'd let me know.

So far I've not been able to decide in my own mind whether you'd like to be here or not. Everyone who has been to Baguio says that that is a wonderful place, and I think this city would be all right if a fellow had a nice place in which to live. But such places are hard to find.

Please give Mamie a great big kiss for me . . .

As ever your devoted
Dad

Except for Ike's absence, life took on the predictable pattern it had in other years at the Wyoming. While Club Eisenhower could not be said to have continued, those of the gang still in Washington entertained Mamie regularly and she them. Gee Gerow, in particular, made it his special mission to look after her, just as he took John on outings and fulfilled requests sent to him by Ike. On one occasion, Ike sent Gee twenty dollars and asked him to buy John a new tennis racquet. This Gee did with a great splash, taking John out to luncheon first and then swinging by his office to show John around before finally purchasing the new equipment. One can only imagine that looking after Ike's wife and son gave him something other than his own grief to think about, and they, too, were immeasurably grateful.

For Christmas 1935, Gee and a Lieutenant Kumpe, whom Mamie mentions in her letters but who remains a mystery otherwise, went out into the cold, windblown streets of Washington to select a Christmas tree for Mamie and John. On Christmas Eve, the remaining members of the gang assembled to help Mamie and John trim it.

Mamie was concerned that Ike was in the Philippines for Christmas, all alone without any family. They exchanged letters and radiograms; Mamie's packages arrived safely and on time. Gee no doubt helped Ike get his Christmas presents under the tree at number 302—along with Gee's own presents for John and a silver cigarette case he had bought for Mamie.

Nearly every night that holiday season, Mamie went out—culminating in New Year's Eve, which she spent with Captain Horace Smith and his mother. After some party-hopping, they dropped in to see Milton and Helen Eisenhower. Mamie reported to her parents that she got home at 3:45 and was too tired to go to any more parties that holiday season.

Throughout the winter and spring, Mamie had no shortage of activities to occupy her, and no lack of friends to see or escorts to lend their arms. "I'm having a pretty hard time getting along on $400.00 bucks but can do & John & I are very comfortable and happy," she wrote to her parents on February 13. She even confided that she had been the "belle" of the ball at one spring gathering she'd gone to in a new dress and pumps. That comment may have raised an eyebrow or two among the appearance-conscious Douds.

Whatever her deepest feelings, Mamie made a life for herself during Ike's absence, and word of her apparent independence and resourcefulness no doubt made its way to Manila. The thought of Mamie out and about probably grated on Ike, who felt the forced separation from his family had been all but an intolerable sacrifice, one that had been agreed to only in deference to his wife's fears.

Mamie was hoping that Ike would get fed up with the Philippines and that her move out there would be unnecessary. But her hopes were dashed in February when she got word that Ike's medical problems had disappeared miraculously. Mamie wrote her parents with the news.

I still don't know what Ike's plans are, he keeps talking of John's and my coming out there. [But] since they pulled the ulcerated tooth his back is well. No lumps or twinges. Says he feels better than in years. So in that case it will probably be hard to get him back to the states. As long as he stays out there under McArthur's thumb no one will ask for him here. Its too bad, however I'm not worrying [as] so many things can happen before I have to make decisions—at any rate I wouldn't leave USA till October.

Mamie noted, however, that Ike's letters were "far from cheerful," and as time progressed she wondered aloud if he cared as much as he had when he left. "I haven't had a letter from Ike in over two weeks. You know he always acts queer in tropics & if he's not coming home I feel I should go out there—altho I don't think he's very keen about it," Mamie wrote her parents. "I can't understand why he's never answered Dad's letter . . . [Also] He's never told me how much extra pay he's drawing or what rank he's holding."

It must finally have dawned on Mamie that Ike was not going to come home at the end of the year, and the realization may have shocked her into making a final decision. She began to plan for the move and assemble what she would call her Philippine trousseau. "Gee says, 'Doll yourself up and knock their eyes out'— doesn't that sound like Katie?" she wrote her parents on April 29, 1936.

Despite the advent of spring and the pleasure Mamie got from taking walks around Washington "for exercise," the anticipation of impending change hung over everything. It was as if she were trying to breathe in and experience the last moments of something that would soon be gone forever. Their years at the Wyoming had been precious times centered around her family, her home, and a community of couples she had come to love. Having close friends, indeed being a good friend, had become and would continue to be one of the central passions of her life. Soon the packers would be in her apartment, shipping out the contents of a place she had renovated to her own specifications; a home she had decorated, for the first time, in a proper fashion—without youthful and amateurish attempts to improvise. "[It's] hard to realize we won't be in this apt, very much longer," she wrote. "Been here so long seems like home." By her own reckoning she was also moving into middle age, which may have contributed to her dread at ending this contented chapter of her life. But she understood that she would have to go to the Philippines if she wanted to stay married to Ike.

In May, Dick Ellis, part of the gang at the Wyoming, died, and again Mamie gave a luncheon for the relatives after the funeral—"like I did for Katherine the year before." The woman who had been living with Dick's wife, Elise, while he had been in the hospital also lost her husband during those days: "So Tues. will be another funeral," she wrote.

After proudly attending my father's graduation (at which Nana had predicted she'd cry, and she did when John gave his speech as class president), Mamie had one more piece of unfinished business to attend to before she and John departed. Mamie and Gee went to Arlington National Cemetery to lay flowers on Katie's grave—a spot she had visited before. "Poor fellow," Mamie wrote of Gee that day, "[he] will miss us terribly."

The Hugheses, too, she knew, would also hate to see her go. "Kate and Everett are fine friends," she commented sadly. "Everett all but wept when he bid farewell to #302. Many a good time we all had here." Kate became the custodian of the piano that Mamie, with pluck and discipline, had finally saved enough money to purchase, and Gee was given the family power of attorney to take care of any business that might have to be conducted in their absence. Except for the piano, everything else was put into storage. This was army life, after all, a hard and often thankless commitment to duty and service. Mamie would do this for her husband, the man she loved, despite the personal sacrifice. Still, something about this move was more difficult than the others.

Mamie had no way of knowing it at the time—though instinct may have told her—that the life she left behind at the Wyoming would represent essentially the last years of *all* ordinary life for herself and her husband. The war that Fox Conner had predicted would soon break out. The Japanese had conquered Manchuria and were preparing to invade northern China; in Europe Hitler and Mussolini had moved against internal opponents and were preparing for the most destructive war the world had ever seen.

After the cataclysm, nothing, including the old army and the people who had been part of it, would ever be the same again.

CHAPTER TEN

"I'VE LEFT NOTHING BUT GOOD FRIENDS"

*T*he Philippines would be a challenge as great as Panama had been for Mamie. In unfamiliar surroundings once again, she and Ike had to cross the difficult terrain of army life and negotiate a new relationship with it and with each other—all this against the backdrop of one of the most culturally diverse countries on earth.

With the Tydings-McDuffie Act passed by the United States Congress in 1934, the Commonwealth of the Philippines was established the following year as a kind of semiautonomous state in transition to full independence, which would be realized twelve years thence, in 1946. The Philippines had been in American hands since 1898, when the United States had acquired the territory for $20 million, as "part of the spoils of its 'splendid little war' against Spain."

U.S. military rule in the first years had brought about an insurrection that eventually led Congress to authorize the president to establish civilian rule; in 1901, William Howard Taft was appointed the Philippines' first American civil governor.

As Spanish control of the islands had done after 1565, American authority brought a unifying identity to this ethnically diverse region. Among more than seven thousand islands—eleven of principal importance—one found Negrito, Indonesian, and Malay cultures and as many as eighty languages, as well as a wide range of dialects and religious traditions.

During the year Mamie had remained in Washington, Ike and Jimmy Ord worked under General MacArthur's command to begin the process of creating and shaping modern armed forces for the Philippines—one of the prerequisites for any independent country. Even though they were building an army from scratch, money was woefully scarce, and the recommendation for a $25 million army was slashed in the blueprint stage by more than 50 percent. The Philippines got a budget of no more than $8 million.

Ike's first year in Manila brought with it not only the challenge of this pioneering work but also the difficulties of working for MacArthur under these unorthodox circumstances. Two incidents in 1936 seriously strained their relationship. On arriving in the Philippines, MacArthur had received word from the War Department that as a *former* army chief of staff he would be reduced in rank from a four-star to a two-star general. This demotion may have had something to do with his desire to acquire the rank of field marshal in the Philippine army—a prerequisite for respect, he felt, in this Asian environment. When MacArthur informed Ike that he too should accept the rank of a general officer under the same scheme, Ike objected. He told MacArthur it was "pompous and rather ridiculous to be the field marshal of a virtually nonexisting army," and also counterproductive for either of them to accept any rank at this point. Ike refused for himself, but MacArthur went ahead with his investiture, becoming the Philippines' highest-ranking officer.

The other incident involved MacArthur's idea of holding a military parade in Manila to give the people some sense that their country was meeting its goal of establishing its own military force. MacArthur ordered Ike and Jimmy Ord to assess the costs and begin preparations. When Philippine President Manuel Quezon heard about the possibility of troop movements for this purpose, he was furious and confronted MacArthur, who expressed "unhappiness with his staff" for exceeding their orders. Both subordinate officers, Eisenhower and Ord, believed that MacArthur had double-crossed them, and the resentment lasted for some time.

One great compensation for strained officer relations was the interesting task of establishing a Philippine Air Corps—not only for enhancing overall military capability but as a means for officers to review the camps established in and around the archipelago. In 1936 Ike and Jimmy set up an airfield and selected a few students to begin on the rudiments for this capability. Ike also took up flying himself, rising early in the morning for flight instruction at Camp Murphy before going to his office in the walled city of Manila at 8:30.

Aviation in those days, little more than thirty years after Kitty Hawk, was a primitive affair. Flying occurred quite literally on a wing and a prayer. Ike later recalled the adventure:

> One had to react alertly to changes in sound or wind or temperature. The engines were good but the pilot who asked too much of one, in a steep climb, for example, learned that the roaring monster could retreat into silent surrender. The seat of the pants was a surer guide to navigation than the few instruments and beacons we had. The pilot depended on his eyes scanning terrain for landmarks and on his ears to tell him that all was well under the cowling . . . To attract the attention for a landing or a message, we buzzed a building until its occupants ran out. They never knew whether we were just visiting or in trouble. To communicate was a simple matter: you wrapped a message around a stone and dropped it as close as possible to them. We did have maps. One slight problem was [that] the tropical landscapes, viewed from several thousand feet up, bore slight resemblance to the best map.

During his four years in the islands, Ike escaped at least two potentially fatal flying accidents, the first when he and a pilot narrowly missed smashing into the side of a mountain and the other during one of his first solo flights. A sandbag strapped to the plane to serve as a stabilizing ballast broke loose and fell against the control stick. Ike narrowly avoided crashing; he was finally able to gain control of the stick, but it was a close call. Despite these brushes with death, Ike was an enthusiastic and devoted student who'd finally, after more than twenty years, managed to return to his dreams of being an aviator.

In October 1936, Mamie and John left for the Philippines from fog-shrouded San Francisco aboard the army transport *Grant*. Ike was waiting to greet them at the dock in Manila after their twenty-seven-day journey. When Mamie caught sight of Ike, she was shocked. During her absence, he had shaved off all his hair ("What hair?" she'd later quip).

Family folklore says that after they embraced and left the dock for the Manila Hotel, Ike said to her in a terse but jocular way: "I gather I have grounds for a divorce, if I want one."* My father, John, doesn't remember Mamie's reaction to these words, but their arrival in the Philippines was the beginning of another long, painful adjustment for them both.

ℳamie and John arrived in Manila just before the presidential elections between Alf M. Landon and Franklin Roosevelt in November. John, who was years away from voting, had been supporting Landon and followed the election very closely. After the results were tabulated, Ike and Mamie enrolled him in the Bishop Brent School, an Episcopalian mission turned boarding school high in the mountains outside Manila, near Baguio. With John cheerfully settled, it took Mamie no time to realize that reconnecting with her husband was not the only adjustment she had to make. General MacArthur, Mamie recalled later, had requested that she and Ike live in the Manila Hotel, where Ike had spent the previous year and where the general's doctor also resided. MacArthur's doctor was in charge of overseeing kitchen procedures in the hotel, and his supervision inspired confidence that all the food was properly handled. "You had to be very careful out there," Mamie remembered. "You couldn't eat any fresh vegetables and if you did, they had to be boiled before you could serve them. Many times you were never sure whether your Filipino servants had done that."

Ike and Mamie had a two-room suite in the un-air-conditioned wing of the hotel. Given the tropical heat and the need for ventilation, there were complications that involved issues far beyond simple physical comfort. At night the hotel staff would come to pump clouds of spray from a flit-gun and then unfurl the tentlike mosquito nets from the top of the canopy over their bed. Mamie,

---

*Family interpretation of this has always been that Ike was referring to the fact that she had not sat at home during the period they had been apart. There has never been a suggestion that he was accusing her of violating her wedding vows.

claustrophobic since childhood, never got used to sleeping under such an oppressive arrangement.

Coping with the heat was one of their biggest problems. To obtain some relief in the evening, they'd go to the movies because the chairs were comfortable and the theaters were air-conditioned. During the day she and Ike liked to have lunch in their rooms, she wrote, so "we can eat in our underwear and be cool."

Mamie was again living in a climate hospitable to mosquitoes, lizards, and other crawling things. And during the rainy season, from May to November, the Philippines were frequently bashed by typhoons and shaken by earthquakes. In the late summer of 1937, the island of Luzon, where Manila is located, was hit by an earthquake of even greater magnitude than the one that destroyed much of San Francisco in 1906. The epicenter was only six kilometers from the city. Mamie and Ike had been out to dinner the evening the quake took place. When they got back about 10:30, they found the hotel "in a panic." At their suite they discovered, to their alarm, that their huge *aparador*—a giant movable closet that stood against a wall—had fallen across the side of the bed where Ike would have been sleeping. "It surely would have crushed him," Mamie wrote her parents. "I sat up all nite with my clothes on . . . The darn things scare me pink." No matter how long Mamie stayed in the Philippines, she never got used to the quakes. "[They made me] feel so helpless," she explained, leaving her with a "stiff neck and wobbly legs."

Mamie also bridled at the Philippines' paternalistic culture. She called it a "man's country, [where] the 'master' is the whole cheese." She admitted this got her "burned up" sometimes.

She also faced several issues that had arisen between herself and Ike during their year apart. While Mamie had been in Washington, Ike had looked for and found companionship among a wide range of people in Manila. He had put together a bridge group that met in the afternoons, and he belonged to a circle of people with whom he played golf. In addition, he had often been an extra man at dinner parties, deciding on and organizing his time any way he pleased. Perhaps the most unsettling discovery for Mamie was that one of Ike's favorite golf partners was a woman named Marian Huff, the wife of Sidney Huff, a naval officer who also worked on MacArthur's staff. Sid Huff did not seem in the least bit concerned that his wife was often on the course with Ike, but

Mamie minded very much indeed. It didn't seem to occur to her that she had been escorted around Washington by a number of male friends during her year alone. But jealousy knows no logic nor does it respect reciprocity, and proud Mamie fought with the conflicting emotions of embarrassment and possibly even humiliation.

My father, John, has been skeptical that Marian Huff was anything more than a golfing companion, but "Mother had the idea that she was at least a rival." Perhaps Mamie felt a twinge of guilt for not coming out right away. She may have also had something more painful to reconcile: a feeling of inadequacy. Given her less than robust health, her husband's energetic golfing partner must have reminded her of her own physical shortcomings.

This fact of life was only underscored some months later when, angry with Ike for their failure to see eye to eye on this or some other issue, Mamie decided to leave Manila and pay John a visit at his school in Baguio. It was a five- to eight-hour drive on the winding mountainous roads, in and out of countless villages where "pigs, children, chickens, and carabaos [were] all in the road." The 185-mile trip, leading up five thousand feet, was more like six hundred miles, because of both the traffic and the route. Sergeant Harold Lauderdale, Ike's driver, was at the wheel that day, careering around the bends and shooting through the villages at a faster than normal speed. On the way through one barrio, Lauderdale hit a young girl who had been playing in the road. The car immediately stopped, and within minutes it was clear that the child was not killed or even badly injured. But in no time at all, what seemed like everyone in the village had surrounded the car and some local officials arrived. After a lengthy ordeal Mamie and her driver were allowed to proceed, but, according to my father, "Mother was scared to death."

By the time Mamie reached Baguio, she had apparently broken a blood vessel in her stomach and had started vomiting blood. She was rushed to the hospital, where she lapsed into a coma, and for some weeks her condition was regarded as life-threatening. When Ike received the news, he made the two-hour flight to Baguio and stayed by her side until the crisis passed.

Since the rainy season had started, with its intemperate heat and its uncontrollable squalls, Mamie stayed in Baguio for more than a month. But her illness may have had an unexpected salutary effect:

the disagreements with Ike that had surfaced after her arrival began to disappear, and any unpleasantness that may have revolved around Mrs. Huff all but vanished with the torrential rains.

Meanwhile, my father settled successfully into boarding-school life. Even though this meant that he no longer lived at home, his absence from his parents' day-to-day life did nothing to diminish their pride in him and his accomplishments. Through both travel and school, he was taking full advantage of being in the Philippines, and the culture seemed to intrigue and stimulate him. It was precisely this attraction that constituted at least one small family crisis, eventually resolved by Mamie's intervention.

During the summer of 1937, Ike and Mamie allowed John to travel to the southern islands with one of his classmates, Jack Cook. The two boys traveled on the motor ship *Legazpi*, and when they got to Mindanao, a Philippine army officer gave John a white cockatoo with a badly healed broken wing. John was delighted with the gift. He had been hoping to find such a bird and was also on the lookout for a monkey, which he planned to take home with him as pets. John named his new bird Oswald, a creature whose entire vocabulary consisted of one word, "*agop*."

"On docking in Manila," John later recalled, "I took Dad aboard and introduced Oswald to him. Real outbursts of temper were rare with Dad—and he almost always recovered immediately—but when he became angry, he was spectacular. This time he outdid himself. 'There's nothing I hate worse than parrots and monkeys!' he roared. I thought this was a little illogical but was at least relieved that I hadn't found my monkey.

"The incident created a temporary family crisis. Dad refused to sit in the same room with Oswald, but the door between our bedrooms was open. And every time Oswald said '*agop*,' I could see Dad wince, even from the rear. In short order, Oswald was relegated to a small room where the hotel elevator boys congregated; Mother saved the situation by calling a friend, Clare Richards, at Fort McKinley, who had both the facilities and the zest for giving Oswald a good home. The whole matter turned out happily."

Among the most important social events of 1937 was General MacArthur's marriage to Jean Faircloth, a petite brunette in her thirties, from Murfreesboro, Tennessee. They had met aboard a ship while the general and his mother were traveling to Manila and Jean was making her way on a round-the-world cruise. The wedding was a surprise to most people who knew MacArthur; nearly everyone had thought of the general as a confirmed divorcé. But Mamie declared, "He'd done right well for himself," though she confessed that "we didn't think she'd ever get him."

Mamie's letters home told of an intensive schedule of afternoon card parties and evening soirees. Next to Shanghai, prewar Manila was reputed to be, in the words of one journalist, "the gayest, most hospitable city in the Far East." Mamie concurred that it was the "partying-est place" she had ever encountered. A small elite of five hundred people (out of the five thousand Westerners living in the city) entertained often and all but exclusively among themselves. Mamie and Ike had many invitations to Mansion House, the U.S. high commissioner's residence, as well as to Malacañang Palace, where the Philippine president held his receptions and dinners. As Ike's relationship with President Quezon grew, so too did the number of invitations to the palace. Ike also played bridge with Quezon and went on occasional short outings to fish.

The gaiety of official life in the newly established commonwealth notwithstanding, the winds of war blew ominously through the capital. In July 1937, Japanese forces captured Peking and "subdued" Shanghai. By December Nanking fell, as the "Japanese army ran amok through the ruins of the captured Chinese city . . . raping, cruelly torturing, and killing more than one hundred thousand defenseless women and children."

As the Japanese pushed their invading forces farther into China, the U.S. authorities advised that all military dependents there be evacuated to the Philippines. American and European residents of Shanghai, Tientsin, and Tsingtao flooded into Manila, and their children swelled the ranks of the Brent School, where John was studying. On December 12, the American community was shocked when the Japanese attacked a United States gunboat, the USS *Panay*, moving down the Yangtze River. Even though Japan apologized and agreed to pay reparations, tension was growing between the two nations.

As cooler, more tolerable temperatures arrived at the end of the year, the Eisenhowers decided to take the Christmas break in the southern islands with Major Anderson and his wife, old friends from Camp Meade. While docked up at the Chinese Pier in Zamboanga, they watched as young boys dove for pennies thrown overboard by passengers on foreign ships. Mamie was absorbed and a little unsettled by all that she saw. On January 17, she wrote about "the famous Chinese Pier, which extends a mile out to sea with thousands of Chinese living and dying on it." They started back for Manila on Christmas night and hit the tail end of a typhoon. The boat rolled and pitched for sixteen hours. "None of us were sick but Mrs. Anderson & I were scared to death."

Mamie's willingness to risk such adventures may have been part of a conscious effort to become sportier and more companionable for Ike. If so, there was even more to the plan. Not long after their return, she took up golf with Marge Clay, wife of Lucius Clay. "I am rotten," Mamie confessed, "but I have to work off some of the fat on my rumpus—besides, the fresh air will be good for me. Ike is so pleased about it."

Moods were surely lifting, perhaps because General MacArthur's own spirits were soaring. With the birth of the general's first child, Mamie thought, the MacArthurs were "as happy as can be." "This a.m. I went over to see Jean MacArthur," she wrote her parents. "Her baby came last Monday—a boy weighing 7½ lbs. He is a darling—as small babies are. She had a very easy delivery—went to the hospital at 3 a.m. and Arthur was here at 9:20 a.m. Some luck for a woman of 39 years old and a first child. I took her a lovely embroidered piña cloth baby pillow—she or the baby can use it. She looks great. Am glad that's over for I worried about her."

With MacArthur mellowing, Mamie suspected that Ike liked things in Manila well enough to request assignment there for another year at the very least. Mamie was determined to try and get into the spirit of the place and enjoy the glamorous and leisurely pace, a way of life described as having "an elegance and a sense of time passing slowly on wide verandas." The exotic charm of it all was well captured at a lawn supper they attended in late January 1938. It was the first time Mamie had ever seen a whole pig roasting on a spit. The hosts had arranged for a piano to be brought out onto the lawn, and with the delicately lighted gardens and a full moon overhead, everyone sat around the piano and began to sing. "We didn't get home until 1:30—which is late for us these days," Mamie wrote her parents, but "[you have to] picture Ike leaning back & warbling his head off."

Within weeks, however, a series of upsetting events culminated in another tragedy. One afternoon Ike came home from the office with a pain in his "belly," and Mamie called the doctor. After examining him carefully, the doctors thought he had food poisoning and gave him medicine for it—to no avail. For twelve hours the doctors contemplated surgery to remove what they were beginning to suspect was a bowel stoppage, but after further treatment "they straightened him out."* Ike remained in the hospital for more than a week.

On his last Sunday there, Jimmy Ord came to say "So long" before making a short trip to Baguio. As Ike recalled, "He mentioned he was taking one of the Filipino students as a pilot. 'No you don't,' I said. 'Get one of the American flight instructors. They'll be glad to do it.' [Jimmy] laughed and said, 'Our Filipino boys are doing really well. I'll use one of them. I won't be gone more than a few hours. See you late this afternoon.' " As Jimmy and his Filipino pilot neared the airstrip in Baguio, Jimmy thought he'd drop a message for the Fairchilds, mutual friends who lived in the area, but while the pilot tried to circle, the plane stalled and crashed. The pilot was unhurt, even the plane was relatively undamaged, but Jimmy had been leaning out of the cockpit when the crash occurred and his seat belt snapped. His chest was crushed by the impact.

Mamie had to break the news to Ike, recounting the ordeal to her parents:

> It was a terrific shock to us all, and of course I worried about the effect it would have on Ike. Poor Jimmy died two hours after he was hurt. Of course, Ike from his sick bed made all the funeral arrangements and supervised the different boards that had to meet . . . Thursday the funeral was held. I didn't think I could make it—but I did . . . I am so thankful Ike is O.K. [but] poor Emily and the children. My heart aches for them. Ike will miss Jim terribly for they had worked & planned together for such a long time.

*This was a precursor to the ileitis attack that Eisenhower suffered during his first term as president of the United States.

Mamie regarded Ord's death as another one of those turning points that necessitated a reevaluation of the important things in life. Not long after, when Nana and Pupah complained about a burglary at 750 Lafayette Street while they were out, Mamie advised them to forget about the stolen things. "The accident has made me realize we worry too much over trifles."

Ord's death took all the zest out of Ike's work. Jimmy, he said, had been "not only a congenial fellow . . . but a top flight officer. He helped me make light work of the heavy chore of building defenses out of little or nothing." Mamie wondered if Jimmy's death might change the way Ike felt about their life in the Philippines, but she herself had come to understand that there were a number of advantages to living there, the most significant of which was the financial break it afforded them. "We've been financially on easy street for the first time in our married life," she mused. John was going to the best school, and "we're having pretty near anything we wish." In contrast to the many years it took Ike to save enough money to give Mamie the silver tea set, that Christmas Ike gave her a monogrammed silver dresser set.

But Ord's death, so much more important than the extra money, exposed to her the foreignness of their surroundings, and Mamie longed to return to the United States. The looming presence of the war also made her apprehensive, and it was a subject never far from the minds of those in the small Western community. At the Manila Hotel and at the Army-Navy Club, Ike was astonished to find that Hitler had many sympathizers. Endorsement from the Spanish community could be interpreted as approval for Hitler's support of General Francisco Franco during the Spanish Civil War, but the reasons for it among the Anglo-Saxon community were all but impossible to explain. Though army officers traditionally abstained from talking politics, Ike's anti-Hitler feelings were well known, especially among the Jewish community in Manila, where he had friends. In 1938, Ike was made an appealing offer by a Jewish committee from the area who asked him to accept a job to relocate Jewish refugees in the Philippines, Southeast Asia, or anywhere else they could be settled. They offered him $60,000 a year, with a commitment to put five years of his salary in escrow, which he could draw on at any time if he were to become "separated" from his work. Ike declined the offer, saying that the army was his life and that he wanted to serve in it in the coming war.

In February 1938, Major Richard Sutherland arrived to replace Jimmy Ord. The Sutherlands were well known to the Eisenhowers from the Wyoming, where they too had lived in the early 1930s, and from the Battle Monuments project in Paris. Mamie could tell that Ike was pleased. Perhaps Sutherland's arrival infused Ike with renewed enthusiasm for his job, or perhaps he felt he had not yet completed the tasks he had come to the Philippines to accomplish. Whatever the case, it was clear to Mamie that Ike wanted to stay on, and the only remaining question was whether or not the War Department would allow him to do so.

Mamie had become philosophical about the prospect and was determined to stay by Ike's side to the best of her physical ability. Before coming to Manila, she had not calculated the damage done by her refusal to accompany Ike in 1935, a decision that had stunned and hurt him. She now seemed to understand clearly that marital fence-mending had to come from her side and if she stayed close to him they could restore the harmony that had been theirs at the Wyoming. "You know I am pretty level-headed about what I know is right," she wrote her parents. "I made a terrible mistake in not coming out here with Ike. It's up to me to rectify lots of things."

Mamie was wary about ever giving Ike advice again about his career or about where they should live. They had both had a fine social time in Europe, but Ike had not enjoyed working with his immediate superiors on the American Battle Monuments Commission, and Mamie suspected she had pushed too hard for the opportunity to go to Europe. History had not yet demonstrated to Ike the value that his intimate knowledge of the European terrain would have in the coming war.

Mamie had had to learn the bitter lesson once more: she had to accommodate to Ike's own decisions, no matter how disruptive they might be for her. "I told him he would have to do what he wanted, as I didn't want any comebacks like the France detail. You know how he always blamed me for that." If they stayed in Manila another year, Mamie told her parents, "I know it is going to be a blow to you—but what can I do? You know Ike, I told him the other day that it has taken me 22 years to find out that the only way I can get along with him is to give him his own way *constantly*. Luckily John is very happy in his school."

Approval for a fourth year came through from the War Department, and Mamie wrote with fatalistic sadness: "It must be for the best, or the dear Lord would not have it so."

As March wore on, Mamie got used to the idea of remaining in the Philippines and assured herself that the time would go quickly. She bought a pair of golf shoes and started spending more and more time on the course, admitting that she could not play well but declaring that she liked the sport. "Tomorrow I hope to go out for a game of golf. That always makes me feel better," she remarked.

Ike, she noticed, was pleased by her enthusiasm for the game and invited her to play with him and his friends, but she declined, afraid to hold up the group. "Yesterday Ike and I went out and played 9 holes of golf and we plan to go out this p.m. and do the same. Ike gave me lots of good pointers yesterday and my game improves. I like it swell."

Mamie was counting the time before a three-month leave they would take to the United States that summer. The doctors had recommended that she undergo gynecological surgery, which the Douds' family doctor would perform. She was eager to see her family and friends, many of whom where still in Washington. Unfortunately, the travel time, round-trip by ship, took up almost two-thirds of their three-month leave, which Mamie deeply regretted. "I wish I wasn't such a sissy about airplanes," she confessed to her parents, "because we could come home one way via clipper and have so much more time in the States. But I am scared." She knew only too well how unreliable the clipper service was to the Philippines. Flights were constantly delayed by bad weather. Furthermore, passage on a ship to the States for her and John was going to cost $2,000 in gold, four months of Ike's salary—in other words, "a whole lot of money."

Before the leave they had a busy social calendar, which included card parties and luncheons and glittering soirees at the Malacañang Palace. Mamie also lunched occasionally with Jean MacArthur. Although there was friction between their husbands, Mamie liked her and felt close to her. She also enjoyed stopping in to see the progress of the MacArthurs' baby, by now nearly a toddler. Mamie reported to her parents that she saw "little Arthur MacArthur ... he's sure getting to be a 'Buster.' Looks more like Jean now than the General. Jean says, 'Don't say that in front of the General cause he wants him to look like him.' Hardly any conceit. Oh! No!"

In Mamie's own difficult moments in the army she had come to value and respect other women, regardless of how her husband got along with their husbands. This loyalty for those she liked would extend not only to Jean MacArthur but also to Bess Truman. In the Philippines, Mamie had a group of very close friends. In addition to Jean MacArthur, there were Ann Nevins, Kitty Smith, Marge Clay, Louise Caffey, and others. And as the war progressed and the national security of the Philippines would eventually be in serious jeopardy, she worried about them as she would have her own family.*

These relationships were the keystone of Mamie's life, and in a very real way that connectedness to loved ones compensated for her frustrating inability to put down roots. With ever-increasing devotion, she invested all but the same intense loyalty in her dearest friends that she did in her family, overlooking many of their foibles or indiscretions.

Mamie also remained loyal to friends who had died. Katie Gerow was an example. When Mamie got news in the Philippines, via a friend, that Gee Gerow had remarried without telling her himself, she scowled, "That rascal." Though she remained devoted to Gerow, she found it hard to accept his new wife; and even when Gee was promoted to general a couple of years later, it was Katie she thought of. "Wasn't it slick Gee was made a general? How proud Katie would be," she'd written her parents.

To clear her social obligations before their departure, Mamie planned to give a huge dinner party in the Palm Court of the Manila Hotel for seventy-five people that May. "It should be lovely," she declared. "The garden will be decorated in colored lights with easy chairs to loll in." After the affair was over, Mamie thought the party "a great success." Rain had started after the

---

*Mamie was later relieved that she and Ike left Manila when they did. Nevertheless, some sense of nostalgia must have overwhelmed her when she heard of the sinking of the *Empress of Britain*. They had had cocktails aboard the ship when it came to Manila on a world cruise.

main course had been served, but the spacious ballroom opened up for the dancing, which she and Ike "enjoyed heaps."

The Manila social season was coming to a close, and "most evenings [they'd] put on their kimonos, eat dinner and then read till bed time," but Mamie managed to do a great deal during those days, considering the humid heat and absence of air-conditioning. Unlike the picture of the bedridden wife painted by virtually every Eisenhower biographer, Mamie stayed remarkably active, especially given that she was facing major surgery in a month's time. She entertained and fulfilled the social obligations beneficial for her husband and his career; it was a question not only of physical strength but also of mental fortitude. Mamie looked after herself by taking siestas and resting when she could, but at the back of her mind was always her concern about "keeping up" with her husband.

As time passed, however, Mamie would learn that the trade-off—for attempting to play golf, for instance—was that the effort might turn into a source of conflict. She would eventually find that her relationship with Ike was more comfortable when she concentrated on doing what she did best—leaving him to his own activities, which included cooking and, later, gardening. There is evidence she might have become adept at both these pastimes, but she hesitated, perhaps because she was unwilling to encroach on things that gave him pleasure—and, in doing so, unwittingly create competition between them. Determined and strong-willed as Mamie was, eventually she would ensure that their activities were separated by domain and taste. As long as she had her own territory to command, she would leave Ike's career and some recreational choices to him, no matter how big or how far-reaching the effect on the family might be.

*R*ight after John's school ended for the summer, on June 26, 1938, the Eisenhowers left for the United States. Ike was going to Washington to lobby for more aid to the Philippines, and Mamie would undergo her surgery in Colorado, recuperate, and then join him in Washington. Sixty people came down to the dock to bid the Eisenhowers bon voyage when they sailed from the Philippine capital on the *President Coolidge*. "It was a grand send-off, such gorgeous flowers—presents and liqueurs . . . The nice friends and things done for us is what makes me sorry to leave, but I didn't shed a tear at leaving Manila, and never even stayed on deck to see us out of the breakwater."

Outside the insular world of Manila, evidence of the war was everywhere. The *Coolidge* made several stops en route: one was in Hong Kong, where they rode a rickshaw from the boat to the ferry and stayed at the elegantly appointed Repulse Bay Hotel for a night; the other was in Yokohama, where they decided to do a little sightseeing. As they went through Japanese customs, the authorities, aware of Ike's military background, stopped him and questioned him at length. Finally, Ike lost his temper and said, "I want nothing here—only to spend a few damned yen in your country." His sharp words seemed to work, and the family was permitted to enter the city. The three of them thought it was curious, though, that sightseeing guides with excellent English volunteered to take them around the city at no cost. Ike was convinced they were intelligence agents.

That summer John stayed in Denver while Mamie underwent her surgery in Pueblo, Colorado, which she got through without complications. During her convalescence, Ike and Pupah spent ten days traveling through Hell's Half Acre, Yellowstone, and many other Western landmarks, and in early September Ike met Mamie in Kansas City—so they could make the rest of the way across the country together by train.

The Washington visit was a moderate success for Ike. Although money and matériel were in short supply, even for the American military, he made modest headway in securing arms and aircraft for the Philippines, even if outdated ones. And for Mamie it was exhilarating to be back in Washington, though her recuperation put limits on her activities. She treasured the opportunity to see some dear friends, especially a few who had made up the old gang. In October, the Eisenhowers made their way back across the United States, stopping in Denver once more, en route to the Philippines on board the *Empress of Japan*, a Canadian Pacific liner.

On the ship Mamie was anxious to have rest and quiet after a long and socially taxing trip; Ike, suffering from a bout of chronic bursitis, found a satisfactory bridge foursome that served as a distraction. Mamie wrote:

Two nights out of Victoria [we] were awakened by all the noise from gongs and then high pitched singing. The Chinese were giving a play on the steerage deck and the room boys & coolies were all donating their money for the war in China. It sure was weird at 1:30 am. All the Chinese help aboard came from Canton—of course they were sunk when Canton was captured. Our table boy for instance had his whole family there and [can't] find any trace of them—pitiful.

The ship docked in Kobe, Japan, and also in Shanghai, where evidence of the war and of recent bombing was everywhere. They all breathed a sigh of relief when they left the war zone, Mamie wrote.

Far and away the best thing that greeted them on their return to Manila was the assignment to a new suite of rooms in the air-conditioned wing of the Manila Hotel. It also had the advantage of a staggeringly beautiful view of Manila Bay from their windows. "I am sure I will be a different person knowing I can rest coolly," she said, "and I have no unpleasant memories of the apartment and we [can] start out fresh." Mamie was also encouraged that her closest friends thought she not only looked younger but seemed more relaxed and confident. In no time at all, the luncheons, card parties, and evening gatherings started up again, with formal outings to Mansion House and Malacañang Palace, which always glittered like "fairyland." Mamie reestablished her close relations with Jean MacArthur, and with Marge Clay, Anne Nevins, and Mildred Hodges.

As pleasant as all this seemed, the war in the Far East was ever present. Even the popular and swank Manila Hotel was feeling the effect. As hostilities expanded, Mamie noted, virtually all pleasure travel ceased to "come out this way."

Mamie was quietly counting the months when they would return to the United States permanently. Many decades later she recalled, "[I] used to lie in my bed and look at that Manila Bay and see those boats go out. They'd get smaller and smaller, and [I'd say] 'Oh, there they go home.' " But at least her relationship with Ike was well and truly back on an even keel. "Ike is grand and sweet like his old self, and we are very happy," she wrote. On Valentine's Day of 1939, he sent a huge bouquet of flowers to their suite, with a note attached:

My Valentine,
This bouquet is to celebrate the 23rd anniversary of your class ring.

Your lover

At the end of that spring, Ike took John on a long trip to the rice terraces north of Baguio. Mamie had no complaints. She was always happy when her boys had something planned together, and in Manila she had the company of her friends. "I was well cared for," she recalled, and "Ike sent me telegrams all along the way."

In May the army personnel in Manila were full of talk about changes in Washington. Word had just been received that George C. Marshall had been appointed chief of staff. "We are a-gog over the news," Mamie wrote her parents. "He is a great friend of Fox Conner and at one time asked Ike to come to Benning to be on his staff. I do hope he'll remember us kindly." Soon Ike unexpectedly received orders to go to Fort Lewis, outside Seattle, which surprised him. His tour in the Philippines had not yet been completed and the Philippine government didn't want him to go. Moreover, he had put in for San Antonio as a first choice.

Relieved and excited as Mamie must have been about the news that they would be returning, she was all too conscious that John would be miserable about leaving his school before the end of his senior year: he "still can't see why we won't leave him out here to finish his last year. Of course we wouldn't think of doing such a thing. He didn't seem to think much of our going to Fort Lewis." She added, "We always seem to have problems."

John was not the only one lobbying to have the Eisenhowers extend their tour. President Quezon, who had come to rely heavily on Eisenhower for his counsel, literally offered Ike a blank check to remain in Manila. Ike could not accept his generosity; he was determined to return to the United States and prepare to fight a war he had been training for all his adult life. Quezon later tried to give him a $100,000 annuity policy as a token of his appreciation for all Eisenhower had done for the Philippine nation; again Ike turned down his offer.

In September Germany invaded Poland. Mamie, Ike, and John sat in the Manila apartment of Howard and Kitty Smith, tensely listening to the crackling voice of British Prime Minister Neville Chamberlain announcing Great Britain's declaration of war against

Germany. France immediately followed suit. Days later the Germans torpedoed the British liner *Athenia*—a move reminiscent of the sinking of the *Lusitania* during World War I.

The last months of their stay in the Philippines required a kind of grim humor and stamina. The Eisenhowers weren't the only people leaving the islands, and many farewell parties were being thrown. Mamie also had a considerable packing job in front of her. To clear customs, every item had to be listed and valued, from shoes and athletic equipment to underwear. While working at this mammoth job, Mamie was also getting increasingly worrisome letters from her parents, who seemed to be overly concerned about everything, and especially about what seemed to be the faltering marital relations of her younger sister, Mike, and her husband, Dick Gill. Mamie advised them to rise above the upsetting situation. "Mike after all is 37 years old and if she doesn't have any sense now she never will have any," she wrote her parents sharply. Then, more soothingly, she concluded, "Try to take these things as calmly as possible. It's hard to do when people concerned are close to you. Just remember everything in our lives is already written and all our worrying will not change a thing." The anniversary of Ikky's birth was one more reminder of the unfathomable reasons things happen. "Yes, Ike and I talked about Ikky on September 24th," she wrote, "and what a big fellow he would have been—doesn't seem possible. Thanks for going out, and tell Mother Bake [a neighbor] she was sweet to give him flowers."

Mamie had no way of knowing what would happen to her husband next, but she eventually concluded that Ike had a special destiny in the war. When during the next five years he was catapulted into the pages of world history, she was very conscious that the special role he played had been made possible only by small twists of fate over the years that had preserved his physical safety and kept him in the army.

With their sailing date set, President Quezon gave a luncheon on December 12 in the Eisenhowers' honor to present Ike with the Philippine Distinguished Service Cross. But Mamie was surprised and touched when the "*Presidente*" asked *her* to pin it on him. "You helped him to earn it," Quezon said. Then the Philippine president presented Mamie with a thirty-seven-piece piña luncheon set.

Before their departure for the United States, General MacArthur wrote to Ike warmly, citing his "distinguished and invaluable service" as well as his "superior professional ability, unswerving loyalty and unselfish devotion to duty...I cannot tell you how deeply I regret your leaving." The normally aloof and egocentric general, with a bottle of scotch in hand, came to the ship to say farewell, a gesture of honor he rarely if ever bestowed.

"We sure went off in a blaze of glory," Mamie wrote her parents from Hong Kong. "Seemed like all of Manila was down to bid us bon voyage. They had a band down to play us on our way." The ship sailed at 5:00, cruising out to sea as the rays of the sun dipped below the horizon. "[It was a] most wonderful sunset...planes with two of Ike's air corps buddies, Lt. Anderson & Lt. Ryder, flew out over the ship, escorted us through the breakwater and well out to sea. So many thrills & honors ... [but] I've left nothing in Manila except some good friends."

CHAPTER ELEVEN

STATESIDE ONCE MORE

he Eisenhowers' trip across the Pacific Ocean was rough and turbulent. From the time they left Manila, there were nights they "couldn't sleep for rolling out of bed." Despite this, the trip was lively, with a fancy-dress ball one evening and men's and women's bridge tournaments during the days. Mamie won the women's competition against what she termed "terrible players," but Ike couldn't find a good bridge game aboard so he was "sorta dissatisfied."

The threesome celebrated Christmas on board with champagne and a dinner table adorned with a stunning centerpiece made of pine cones, cedar, and red candles, a decoration sent to them by friends in Manila. That evening, Mamie dressed in a long, flowing gown, and Ike in black tie. "John looked like a million in his new dinner jacket. It would have made your heart swell with pride," Mamie wrote her parents. "Ike and I were overcome."

After a stop in Honolulu, there was uncertainty about where the ship would dock; it was thought they would be forced to go to Los Angeles because of a strike in San Francisco, but eventually they sailed into San Francisco as planned. Helen and Milton Eisenhower had a beautiful orchid corsage waiting for Mamie at the ramp, and they soon checked into the Drisco Hotel, where Mamie was to stay while Ike went to Camp Ord on temporary orders. There he was charged with setting up National Guard training centers under the new Selective Service program.

Mamie was thrilled to be back in the United States. "It seems too wonderful we are home, and I can talk to you whenever I please without going to the poor house." The taste of American food was so enticing, she told her parents, she was convinced that she would gain pounds in no time.

Ike's new temporary orders, however, meant that the couple would be separated for four months, which seemed an eternity after their three years in the Philippines, when they had virtually never been apart. Now Mamie fretted out loud: "Ike has been gone 7 weeks today," she wrote her parents. "Guess I won't know how to get along with him after being gone so long." Mamie also speculated that it would be hard for Ike to adjust to working for someone else, especially as he had "pretty [much] been his own boss" for eleven years. "Between us it is good discipline, tho, we are very apt to be spoiled after all we'd had." During this time, on a maneuver which included an amphibious landing on the California beaches, Ike met General Marshall for a second brief time. Marshall, referring to the luxurious lifestyle he knew army officers enjoyed in the Philippines, asked ironically, "Have you learned to tie your shoes again since coming back, Eisenhower?" Ike, stymied in his efforts to work out the complications of his current assignment, replied, "Yes sir, I am capable of that chore, anyhow."

During these months, John was sent to Tacoma, Washington, near Fort Lewis, where he stayed with his uncle Ed Eisenhower, a lawyer, and his daughter Janis, while Ike and Mamie tried to get themselves settled. After Ike's temporary assignment was completed, the two of them proceeded to Fort Lewis, fifteen miles outside Seattle. Mamie was happy to arrive finally at the post, one of the rewards of which was living in a house again.

Mamie was careful about looking after herself—especially where her health was concerned—but she did not dislike her responsibilities as a homemaker. On the contrary, she concluded that the lack of household tasks had been one of her principal problems in Manila. "If I had not been hotel-bound," she once told a reporter, "it would have been easier. [In Manila] women with household responsibilities seemed as contented as their hardworking husbands—even on days when a duck would have drowned. But there I was, cooped up in three rooms with too much time on my hands."

This was not the case at Fort Lewis. The Eisenhowers lived in a lovely four-bedroom brick house on a tree-lined avenue, and, as she had after every other move, Mamie worked hard to organize the house and unpack all their things from abroad. Many of her prized possessions had not survived the transport from the Philippines, and her early days at Fort Lewis were taken up with getting crate after crate of smashed china repaired and broken furniture restored. There were also curtains to be made and decorative touches to be added. Before this could begin, however, everything—including all the walls and windows—had to be thoroughly washed, for they were grimy, almost sooty, from the soft coal that was burned in the area. Indeed, Mamie discovered that all surfaces had to be washed down regularly throughout the year.

Under Ike's tutelage, Mamie also took up gardening, which she greatly enjoyed. She always referred to it as Ike's garden, though occasionally in letters she would, perhaps accidentally, mention "my sweet peas," or "my nasturtiums."

ℱort Lewis was a quiet place, pretty much a community unto itself. After the social years in the Philippines, Mamie thought the quiet life "would do us good." At Fort Lewis Mamie had to relearn the art of being able to entertain at no notice. More often than not Ike came home for lunch, and often with an unexpected guest. They also entertained a great deal in the evenings. Janie Howard, the wife of junior officer Edward Howard, recalled that Mamie "would have parties at the drop of a hat. I can remember she'd call up and [say], 'Well, Ike's garden's up and the peas are ripe.' So we'd have a party to celebrate that. [Once] she called and said, 'It's Ike's birthday,' and I said, 'It's five o'clock and I haven't got time to buy him a present.' 'Well,' she said, 'bring some cigarettes.' I said, 'I've only got two packs.' She said, 'That's enough,' so we went over and had the best time . . . She entertained beautifully. Everything was just perfect and she never seemed to go to any effort, she never seemed to fuss. But you knew she was behind it all."

Mamie was also busy with many post activities. She served on the committee to redecorate the Officers' Club, of which Ike was president, and she was involved in Women's Club events. She also worked regularly at the Red Cross. Janie Howard observed that Mamie was "a natural leader. She just stood out. She was herself, and that's all she had to be."

In some respects, Mamie didn't find Fort Lewis as friendly as she had remembered other army posts being. Perhaps it was because of the weather, she said; it would start raining in September and wouldn't stop until May. "People don't seem to stop by and visit like I remember they used to do [at other army posts]. Of course it rains so much, people just stay inside and there are no porches to sit on."

Despite the familiarity of everything, Mamie had her own adjustments to make again to the army ways of doing things. Although she had lived the life of army wife in most respects, in fact she had not lived on a post for well over a decade. Once again she discovered all the pleasant features of being part of a post "family," but there were, of course, disadvantages in living in a community so tightly connected with one's husband's career. As Lewis Lapham has written, "[If an army post] offers all the comfort of a small town, it also insists on the moral rectitude (or at least the appearance of moral rectitude) proper to a small town. The code is puritanical, and if a man is discovered in his wickedness he can expect the traditional punishment. No aspect of his conduct escapes judgment and he is exposed at all times to the scrutiny of his peers and the gossip of their wives."

The scrutiny was equally keen among the wives, and sometimes vicious and petty rivalries blossomed, especially among women who "adopted" their husbands' ranks and insisted on the same pecking order. The rivalries were perhaps exacerbated by the perquisites that came with rank, such as better housing and domestic help. The wives seemed more vested in their husbands' status than they were in the civilian world in which Mamie had lived in Washington, Paris, and Manila.

Perhaps as a reflection of this firmly ingrained hierarchy, many of the women referred to the top brass's wives as Mrs. "General" Joyce or Mrs. "General" Thompson. Mamie bridled at this caste system. Janie Howard recalled with amusement, "I never had enough sense to know I was a captain's wife around Mamie. She never made anyone conscious of rank, as some of them [did]. She was just fun." Mamie once said, "You know, Janie, you don't have any rank, it is your husband [who does]. You're only in the army [because of] your husband." Janie recalled, "I wanted to say, you go tell that to Mrs. Vandever . . . Mamie never made me feel she was high-ranking. [She and Ike] were just down-to-earth people."

The rivalry among officers' wives made Mamie uncomfortable, even as the years progressed and her husband rose dramatically through the ranks. She told my father that during the war she considered moving to the Thayer Hotel, at West Point, while he was a cadet, but she dismissed the idea, in part because Mrs. Omar Bradley, who was living there, "didn't like to be outranked."

Ike was thoroughly engrossed in his new work. As regimental executive of the 15th Infantry Regiment of the Third Army, he had troop duty for the first time since 1922, and this elated him. On July 1, 1940, he wrote Omar Bradley, "I'm having the time of my life. Like everyone else in the army, we're up to our necks in work and in problems, big and little. But this work is fun!"

Many men of the 15th Infantry Regiment were seasoned, active-duty troops who'd been in service in China; others were volunteers. "Although my regiment was undermanned by 400 troops, understaffed in experienced officers, underequipt in trucks, machine guns, and mortars," Ike recalled years later, "we did a thorough job of combat training over some of the most difficult terrain in the country, the 'cut-over' land of Washington State. Stumps, slashings, fallen logs, tangled brush, pitfalls, hummocks, and hills made the land a strange setting for a play in Hades." Writing to Gee Gerow, he reported, "I froze at night, never had, in any one stretch, more than 1¾ hours sleep, and at times was really fagged out—but I had a swell time." His experience convinced him that he belonged with the troops, "and with them I was always happy."

Ike's regiment and others from the Third Army infantry divisions were ready for maneuvers by midsummer 1940.

*N*ot long after their arrival, Ike's brother Ed offered to pay John's college tuition if he would agree to work with him eventually in his law firm, but John was leaning toward trying for West Point, a choice Mamie and Ike were determined that he make freely. Both of them assured John that they could afford to send him to a college if he preferred. But despite a rather grim account of the downside of an army career that Ike outlined for him, John decided to opt for West Point. To make sure John understood what he might be getting into, Ike used himself as an example: given the seniority system, the rank of colonel was likely the highest rank Ike would ever achieve. "Of course, in an emergency, anything can happen—but we're talking about a career, John, not miracles."

John was perhaps persuaded to join the army by what Ike regarded as the upside of serving in the army—a perspective John himself had seen firsthand throughout his life. As Ike later recalled:

> I said that my Army experience had been wonderfully interesting and it had brought me into contact with men of ability, honor, and a sense of high dedication to their country. I reminded John of the incident in the Philippines, when a group wanted me to leave the Army with an ironclad five-year contract at $60,000 a year. The offer had few temptations.
>
> Happy in my work and ready to face, without resentment, the bleak promotional picture, I had long ago refused to bother my head about promotion. Whenever the subject came up among the three of us at home, I said the real satisfaction was for a man who did the best he could. My ambition in the Army was to make everybody regretful when I was ordered to other duty.

With John determined to go to West Point, Mamie's chief worry concerned her mother's health. Pupah had written Mamie that Nana had "aged terribly in the last 1½ years and . . . Mikey and her troubles are mainly to blame for it all." Mike's pending divorce from Dick Gill had raised all kinds of concern within the family, who feared he might try to gain custody of their children, Richard and Michael; and Nana, ever the worrier, could not put her mind at rest about her youngest daughter's circumstances. Mike's divorce became final that summer of 1940, and when it did she told her family she intended to marry Gordon Moore, a man she had met while still married to Gill. While Mamie understood this was a highly unconventional, perhaps even scandalous, development, she remained cheerful and was determined to convince Nana to worry a little less.

Divorce, though still rare, had already become a fact of life in the family. Ike's brother Ed had one failed marriage behind him at this point, and he, too, remarried that year. As with Mike, both Mamie and Ike supported him, and Ike was best man at his brother's wedding. Bernice, his new wife, had been Ed's secretary, and Mamie wryly observed that the marriage was bound to work: since Bernice had been his "office wife," she could have few illusions.

As I have said, Mamie never abandoned those she cared so deeply about, and as she had in the past, she played the role of peacemaker between her parents and her headstrong younger sister. That summer John drove his mother to Boise, Idaho, where they met up with Ike and proceeded to Denver, where John organized and then served as best man in Mike's wedding.

John's final destination that summer was Washington, where he was enrolling in a West Point cram school run by Homer Behne Millard. Beannie Millard's objective was to make a student's year there more difficult than plebe year at West Point, and the old West Point instructor excelled at this.

Not long after John's departure, the Eisenhower household was subject to turmoil again. A letter from George Patton told Ike that two armored divisions were being created, and Patton asked Ike to serve under him as commander of a regiment. Ike was enthusiastic about this prospect and dreamed of nothing else for weeks, but then "the roof fell in." Gee Gerow, now head of War Plans, wrote to ask Ike to come to Washington to work under him. Ike was in a quandary. Above all else he wanted to be with the troops; he had had enough of staff positions, and he all but said so. The matter was further complicated in November when General Thompson, commander of the 3rd Division, requested that Ike be appointed his chief of staff.

Mamie reported on Ike's dilemma to her parents on November 27:

> Ike is so busy these days he's cuckoo. Looks like he won't get back to 15th but will get a staff job some place. He's sick about that. Gen. Thompson wants him as his Chief of Staff and Gee wants him in Washington. Waiting to see now which is which. Ike prefers to stay where we have a home. I really don't care one way or the other, but I do get a sinking spell when I think about another move.

Although Mamie tried to be scrupulously neutral during this crisis, the appeal of going to Washington must have been growing in her mind. A few days later, telling her parents that Ike had decided not to take the job in Washington, she remarked, "Needless to say I was terribly disappointed but I tried not to show it—for after all he has to do the work." Ike regretted that he was under orders to fulfill another staff job, but there were compensations. Unlike the position in Washington, D.C., at least chief of staff of the 3rd Division was *with* troops.

Resigned now to remaining at Fort Lewis, Mamie nervously eyed the troop buildup at the post and wondered how long the tranquillity of their domestic scene would last. Not long after General Kenyon Joyce, commander of the IX Army Corps, arrived at the post, Mamie worried aloud about the rumors that he wanted quarters for his aide-de-camp: "That means some poor soul will be ranked out of post. Gee I'm glad we have this house and hope that no higher-ups decide they want it."

Fort Lewis was expanding rapidly to accommodate the increasing number of troops. Mamie noted the "beehive" of activity as more than 50,000 troops flooded in. Construction crews hammered and drilled around the clock, it seemed, and Mamie could hear the constant "Hup two three four" of new recruits marching on the green. There was a substantial increase in Red Cross activity as a result. In fact, the hospital where Mamie worked was planning to expand to two thousand beds.

On March 11, 1941, Mamie conveyed some of the excitement in the air. General Joyce asked Ike to be his chief of staff. In Ike's new position, he would be responsible for all military installations in the northwestern United States.

It is a grand compliment and might give him his full colonelcy pronto. We knew a week ago when Gen. Joyce had sent a telegram to Washington and have been sitting on needles & pins. It was so very secret. It may mean we will have to move up in the circle where the General's house is. We would like to stay here tho in our little house. I am so glad for Ike. Am on my way to play Ma-Jong with Mrs. Joyce. Just wanted to let you know . . . Your Sweeten Child & Puddy.

Ike was indeed promoted to the rank of full colonel (temporary). He was thrilled. Unexpectedly he had reached the rank that he predicted would be his highest, at least a decade ahead of schedule. Congratulations poured in, but speculation about future advancement was also rife. Ike complained to John, "Damn it, as soon as you get a promotion they start talking about another one. Why can't they let a guy be happy with what he has? They take all the joy out of it."

Despite the upbeat turn of events, family concerns were never far from Mamie's mind. In February they had received news that Mike was expecting a baby, and Nana and Pupah fretted about the effect another child would have on Mike's new marriage. Mamie had pooh-poohed their worries in a revealing letter on the first of February.

I really think it's fine. If I had only had sense enough to have more children when I was young. Somehow one always manages to take care of another [child]. And what comfort and interest kids are when you get older. I hold my breath when I think of all our affection overpowering John. You should be glad over it darlings not sad. It's a blessing. Mike loves children and doesn't resent doing things for them. She is a good mother. If she didn't want this baby, then you would have something to worry about.

As spring arrived, Mamie stepped up their social activities. In one week, she invited almost fifty people to one or another event at their home, with "only . . . about 90 more people to entertain," she remarked cheerfully. Among the most interesting of her guests was Anna Roosevelt Boettiger, the president's daughter, and her husband, John, the owner and publisher of one of Seattle's leading newspapers, a man whom Ike had known since his War Department days. The Boettigers' presence on the post created quite a sensation. But despite all the social activity, Ike was spending more and more time in the field. "We hardly get to say good morning and a good nite to him," Mamie observed on April 23.

But Ike's new position was to last only three months. In July he was ordered to San Antonio to serve as chief of staff of the Third Army under General Walter Krueger. As only a few weeks elapsed between the actual orders and the day he was to report, Mamie had to fly into action, packing the house and preparing it for shipment—a great deal of work. But she must have been excited and gratified, for Ike's job was significantly bigger. More important, it would put them back in San Antonio, a city that had special meaning for them both.

*O*n July 1, the twenty-fifth anniversary of their marriage, Ike and Mamie arrived back in San Antonio. Sentimental Mamie was moved by the coincidence and Ike gave her a beautiful platinum watch, the money for which he had saved while they were in the Philippines. Coming back to San Antonio, especially at this point, was something of déjà vu. Just as it had in the period when Ike and Mamie first married, America was once again mobilizing against a foreign threat. And although the United States was not yet in the war, fewer and fewer people believed that the country could stay out of the international conflagration that had erupted on both sides of the globe.

On the very day his parents arrived in San Antonio, John and 550 "bewildered youngsters between ages seventeen and twenty-one" reported for duty at West Point. Earlier in the year, much to his parents' great pride, he had won the highest marks in a competitive exam out of a group of thirty-six hopefuls vying for a West Point appointment from Kansas. Mamie and Ike planned to visit him at Christmas, as part of a rare two-week leave. Until then, Ike would have to immerse himself in preparing for the Louisiana Maneuvers, the largest military war games in U.S. history, which were to begin in August.

Mamie also had her work cut out for her. As she had always done in the past, she disciplined herself to write thank-you notes to all the major figures at the post they'd just left, expressing her appreciation for their time together. This was no minor undertaking, because according to her own specifications each letter had to be long and individualized. "It's some chore," she remarked privately, but one she undertook without question.

In contrast to Mamie's situation when she was still a newlywed, she was also now mistress of one of the post's grander brick residences on the main, tree-lined avenue—a long way from the tiny two-room accommodations they'd shared in 1916. The five-bedroom house had spacious living quarters and several bathrooms, and it boasted a screened-in "sleeping porch," which Mamie and Ike in fact used for that purpose in the summer. Despite the grandeur, however, there were no servants, and the house itself was infested with silverfish and cockroaches in large enough quantities to prompt Mamie to have the entire place fumigated not long after their arrival.

Once again, Mamie had to unpack crate after crate of china and books, once again add decorative personal accents that would make this government-issue house feel like home. She threw herself into this project, and Nana gave her help when she and Pupah came south for their annual trip to San Antonio. By now Mamie was accustomed to the government's strict regulations about accounting for all its property after each move: if anything was missing at the end of an officer's tenure, the family was expected to pay for the replacement.

As a colonel, Ike was entitled to an executive assistant. Ernest "Tex" Lee was engaged in this post, and he kept this job throughout the war. Ike was also entitled to a striker, a "guy Friday" who would be everything from chauffeur to bartender to short-order cook. Private Mickey McKeogh, an enlisted man who had been a bellhop at the Plaza Hotel in New York, answered the ad Mamie placed for this job on the post. Hardworking and loyal, Mickey also went to London with Ike and stayed with him for the duration of the war. But in San Antonio Mickey worked primarily with Mamie in the quarters. She was a "stickler for neatness," he later recalled. "She hated to see newspapers lying around or to find Ike's cigarette butts in the fireplace, where he often threw them." Mamie later said, "[Ike] was not beyond [making a] mess himself, but he certainly didn't want it around his house or me."

In fact, Mamie had become a perfectionist in many ways. Perhaps the chaos of moving so often drove her to a preoccupation with keeping her things organized, or maybe she had finally adopted a military penchant for order. Mickey recalled that "Mrs. Ike was an easy person to get along with, as long as you did things right. If you didn't, she'd let you know, and fast." But Mamie's exacting ways brought along compensations. She took a genuine interest in the lives and welfare of those who worked for her, and years later Mickey was surprised to discover that Mamie had written his mother frequent letters during this time, telling her Mickey was well and that she shouldn't worry about him.

As Mamie got the house settled, she began active work for the Red Cross facility again. She also had time to reconnect with the many friends she still had in San Antonio—some from her days as a girl, others from her time as a newly married woman. But there were also many people on the post whom she knew from other locations, such as Camp Meade and the Philippines. She had so much company, in fact, that while Ike was absent for six weeks during the Louisiana Maneuvers, out of eighteen evenings she was at home for dinner on only two of them.

That August, Ike left for Louisiana, where General Walter Krueger's Third Army would be pitted against General Ben Lear's Second. As chief of staff of the Third Army, Ike had the central responsibility for drafting the strategy and tactics for the "Blue" side. More than a thousand planes and several armored divisions were engaged in "battle," and as many as 400,000 men would be involved.

General Marshall wanted to use this exercise to highlight the shortcomings of the U.S. Army in preparing for war. It would also be an opportunity to discover new talent and ferret out unfit officers. Most of the generals who were key during World War II— Bradley, Patton, Hodges, and many more—participated in the Louisiana Maneuvers.

Years later Ike recalled the tensions and excitement of this massive undertaking.

Old Louisiana hands warned us that ahead lay mud, malaria, and mosquitos. Their description was accurate. But they didn't add to such attractions the fact that we would also meet head-on the problems of 400,000 men moving into relatively unsettled country, where the roadnet was designed for a car or two at a time, not an army, and a climate which seemed calculated to produce exhaustion. But the work was gripping.

The lack of practical experience was particularly evident. World War I staff men of all echelons above a regiment had largely passed out of the service. The rest of us, under pressure, had to transform textbook doctrine into action. The nervous energy, technical competence, and drive required of all those present were tremendous. But those qualities alone were not enough; eternal patience was necessary, too. The commander also needed iron in his soul for one of his chief duties was to eliminate unfit officers, some of whom were good friends.

According to one account, "the Third Army following Dwight's master plan won the early engagements. Bad weather conditions threatened to turn the tide. But the Third Army column continued to close the ring and nearly captured the commander of the Second Army. Marshall was mightily impressed by Ike's performance; so was a cluster of newspapermen covering the maneuvers." As the massive exercise drew to a close, Ike was told that he had been recommended for a star. Mamie later said that Ike's achieving the rank of general was her proudest moment, but Ike took it all with characteristic modesty. "One thing is certain," he wrote a friend. "When they get clear down to my place on the list, they are passing stars out with considerable abandon."

At the end of the historic exercise, Ike and his colleagues discovered that this valuable training had nearly come to naught. While they were still in Louisiana, they got word that Congress had passed the extension of the Selective Service bill by only a single vote. Years later Ike would comment: "I still shudder to think how close we came to returning trained men home, closing down reception centers for the new draftees, reassembling a fragmentized force into its Regular Army core—all within weeks of our entry into the most colossal war of all time."

*W*ith Ike's generalcy and the flattering notices he'd received during the Louisiana Maneuvers, Mamie began to see a change in the way they were treated. In October 1941, she went to the clinic for her regular checkup and noticed the deferential treatment she was given, which she had never before experienced. Amused, she wrote her parents that "Mrs. Strong was right about having a General tacked to your name. [Today I had] especially conducted tours all thru the clinic. Ha Ha."

She also noticed that more and more people were approaching Ike for favors—a practice that made him ill at ease, though he was diplomatic and firm. One couple who called on them at their home pressed Ike for help in getting a government job for the wife. The couple overstayed their welcome and drank too much, "especially her," Mamie recounted. "Ike was disgusted, and I was a bag of nerves." As the country moved closer to war, opportunity-seekers would become commonplace; and as Ike's authority increased, he was ever more hounded. Granting special requests went against the grain of a man who made a policy of avoiding even the slightest appearance of favoritism.

By 1941 the only forces standing between the German army and victory in Europe were England and the Soviet Union; by the fall Hitler's panzer divisions were closing in on Moscow and his U-boats were threatening to choke off the lifeline between the United States and Great Britain. In the Far East, the Japanese were readying a surprise preemptive attack to open the way for their conquest of Malaya, Hong Kong, and the Philippines.

On a Sunday afternoon in early December, after a morning at the office, Ike decided to take advantage of the afternoon lull to sleep. "The nap did not last long," he later recalled. "Orders that I not be awakened under any circumstance were ignored by my aide, who wisely decided the news of the attack on Pearl Harbor was adequate reason to interrupt my rest." Mamie had just heard a report of the Japanese bombardment of the base in Hawaii when she woke Ike to say that an aide was on the phone. Like everyone else, she was stunned by the news; it had been only a short time since their stopover visit in Honolulu, and she and Ike were familiar with the naval installation there. "It just seemed like an impossible thing."

Ike dressed in his uniform and went to the office. For the next five days he dispatched Third Army units to the West Coast in case of a Japanese attack on the mainland. Patrols were also sent to guard the southern border and the coastline along the Gulf of Mexico. Then, on Friday, December 12, the War Department called to tell him that General Marshall wanted him to come to Washington immediately. Mamie quickly packed Ike a suitcase, and he headed off for the airstrip. As Mamie waved goodbye to her husband, she could not have known—nor could he—what would become of them and what the war would bring. She already knew that Ike would not be taking leave during the Christmas season as planned, and she would have to travel to West Point by herself to visit John. But who knew how long Ike would have a job where she could be near him? Like every good army wife, Mamie knew that all she could do was wait.

.   .   .

*A*fter a difficult trip—Ike's plane was grounded because of bad weather, and eventually he had to go by train—Ike arrived at Union Station in Washington, where he was met by his brother Milton, at whose Falls Church home he would stay until his own plans were clear.

From the moment Ike reported to the chief of staff on December 14, he was consumed around the clock by his new job. Given his extensive experience in the Far East—and the immediacy Pearl Harbor had created on that front—Ike was appointed head of the Philippines and Far Eastern Section of the War Plans Division. "I tried desperately to use my knowledge of the Islands and the people to come up with ideas for their relief under attack," Ike recalled. "In the tragic days of their isolation and collapsing defenses, I harked back to the review of the situation as I had seen it in 1939." At that time Ike had predicted that if the Philippine nation were in danger, it would be attacked not by huge force but by surprise, and that the keys to its security would depend on the defense of its beaches. His assessment, unfortunately, was prophetic. The Japanese did launch a surprise attack, and the beach defenses were broken and overwhelmed at nearly the outset. Despite what Ike referred to as the "heroic resistance by both Filipinos and Americans," both morale and combat capability collapsed rapidly, and the United States, he felt, bore significant responsibility for this outcome:

> For months before Pearl Harbor and Clark Field, we had been trying to fool ourselves that war was far away. When the first Japanese bombs fell on the planes parked a few miles from Manila, our ships at sea were carrying troops *away* from not *to* the city soon to be the enemy's target. Though Congress had extended the draft, it had required the discharge of all Selective Service men over twenty-four. Days before the war began, these men left Manila for San Francisco.

In Washington Ike now maintained a grueling schedule, while Mamie prepared to leave San Antonio for Christmas at West Point. Tex Lee, Ike's aide-de-camp, made first-class train reservations for Mamie and put Mickey McKeogh on the same train in coach. As Mickey later told it, "None of us knew that at Chicago, the train would split into two separate sections." After the train left Chicago, Mickey went back to the first-class section to see if Mrs. Ike wanted or needed anything. To his utter horror, there was no more train! For the next twenty hours, Mickey said, he worried about being court-martialed for losing a general's wife. When they finally reconnected in New York, Mamie was on the platform surrounded by luggage. "Where were you?" she demanded. For the next forty years the story became a running joke between them.

Mamie spent Christmas with John at West Point, where she stayed in the Thayer Hotel on campus. She found the atmosphere at West Point very different from that at Fort Sam. "Things certainly are discouraging," she observed. "Up here everything is normal. No moving of troops—a relaxation after all the turmoil of the last few weeks." She was overjoyed to see John again, but both of them were disappointed that Ike could not get away from the office for even a day. Mamie reported that when he called from Washington to say Merry Christmas, he sounded "very tired." Yet despite his crushing workload, Ike did not fail to remember his family. With the other presents he had for their Christmas celebrations, he also sent Mamie a corsage of three orchids.

Several days later, when Mamie wrote her parents about this news, she relayed that their orders were now permanent for Washington. After less than six months in the Fort Sam quarters that she had just finished decorating, she noted, "I will have to go back and pack up."

Before setting off again for Texas she went first to Washington to spend a few days with Ike "if he's not working," and to "talk things over" with him. She had been told that she could "hold quarters" for up to four months. Should they put all their possessions in storage? "We are lucky Ike is in Washington," she wrote, "instead of out in the wilds some place. Hope he stays there."

On New Year's Eve, Ike managed to get away from the office in time to get to his brother's house two hours before midnight. There, with Milton and Helen, he and Mamie celebrated the start of the new year. During their short interlude, they decided that they would stay with Helen and Milton until Mamie could find an apartment for the two of them. Their friend Harry Butcher, who "knew everyone in Washington," had been putting out feelers, and it seemed they might be able to acquire a modest apartment at the Wardman Tower that had been sealed by the estate of a recently deceased resident. It was only a one-bedroom flat, with a small living room and a kitchenette, but it would suffice.

Mamie went back to San Antonio to select a few things to make the apartment more homey, while she put the rest into storage. "Imagine me in the next week," she wrote her mother, "trying to get that big house closed. I shudder when I think of all I must do."

In addition to the careful documentation of each item, she had to crate up the Eisenhowers' valuables for storage: every piece needed special handling. China and crystal had to be individually washed, wrapped, and packed, and Mamie had more than sixty crates of china. The crystal candelabra and other knickknacks also had to be cleaned and meticulously boxed. She didn't know how long their possessions would be in storage, so even the rugs (not made from synthetic fibers in those days) had to be shampooed and moth-proofed. "I can't tell you how I hate to dismantle this lovely house you and I fixed up so lovingly," she wrote to her mother. "Every time I go onto the little porch room I could weep."

Except for the few boxes she put aside for their small apartment at the Wardman Tower, she did not see the possessions she put into storage until she and Ike bought their house in Gettysburg, Pennsylvania, in the early 1950s, more than a decade later.

By February, the boxes she had destined for the Wardman Park were on their way there by van. "I feel like a football—kicked from place to place . . . Now that the break is made, I am glad to be here," she wrote after arriving in Washington, "and poor Ike seems so pleased to have me. After two months of visiting [Milton and Helen], I'll be glad when I get our own things around us, even if it [the apartment] is small."

Fortunately, all the complicated pieces of the move fit together and she and Ike were able to settle into their own place. The first night at the Wardman Mamie and Ike had difficulty sleeping— the apartment was above a ballroom and music wafted up from below—but that was a small inconvenience. They were both so grateful to be together in their own place that such bothers were hardly noticeable. Perhaps the harder adjustment was to Ike's utterly unpredictable schedule, for he left at seven each morning with no idea of when he would return at night.

That February Ike's boss at War Plans, Gee Gerow, was assigned to troops at Camp Meade, making Ike, as Mamie put it, the "No. 1 man at War Plans." It was not an easy job. The strain of the war frayed nerves and created aggravation on the job. "Tempers are short!" Ike wrote in a diary he kept. "There are lots of amateur strategies on the job—and prima donnas everywhere. I'd give anything to be back in the field."

It must have been with some envy that Ike said his professional goodbyes to Gerow when he left to take up command of his troops at Meade. As Gerow passed Ike the baton, he assured him in so many words that his new job would be no picnic: "Well I got Pearl Harbor on the book, lost the P.I. [Philippine Islands], Singapore, Sumatra, and all the N.E.I. [Netherlands East Indies] north of the barrier. Let's see what you can do."

Now that Mamie was back in Washington, she met the new Mrs. Gerow, whom she discovered she liked. Mary Louise was "jolly and pleasant to be with," she told her parents. But Mamie, who still kept Katie's picture on her piano at home, could not put aside her feelings for her old friend. "Each time [Mary Louise] would give the charge 'Mrs. L. T. Gerow' I sorta resented it. Wonder what my reactions to seeing her with Gee will be?"

Mamie did not have long to wait. One Saturday evening a few weeks later, a few alumni of Club Eisenhower—Kate and Everett Hughes, Gee Gerow and his new wife, and Ike and Mamie—went for dinner to an Italian restaurant across from the Mayflower Hotel that had been a part of their old stamping ground. They surely spoke of old times that evening, but everyone's mind was on the future, and on the war. Now generals of the United States Army, all of them, the men would wait no more for that moment that had been, the decade before, only a part of their imagination.

If Mamie worried about what future demands would be made on her husband, she didn't discuss it. She was primarily grateful that thus far Ike was in Washington and they could be together. Ike was looking better than ever, she thought, probably because he had grown used to the long hours. Mamie, who'd get up each morning at 6:30 to cook his breakfast, conceded that the routine seemed to agree with her, too. She understood that her presence made life dramatically better for her husband while he was engaged in such important work. She was gratified that "[Ike] seems so glad that I am here & he has his own home."

By the end of February, Mamie had an inkling that General Marshall was going to ask them to move to Fort Myer. "I hate that," she confided, "but of course we couldn't refuse. T'would mean a big house again. [Marshall] seems to want to have his staff close to him." And then, with this change impending, Mamie and Ike got word that David, his father, was failing. On March 10, the old man died. Mamie wrote her parents with the news.

> Last Sunday nite we had a telegram from Roy that Father E was not expected to live through the nite. When we did not hear anything Monday we were in hopes that the old fellow would rally like he had before. Tuesday afternoon the word came of his death. One of the hardest things I had to do was telephone Ike & tell him. He is a wonder. People said he worked right on and no one could have known. Guess it was his salvation (work). Poor fellow I've felt so sorry for him. Of course with thousands of people depending on him he couldn't go home. Fortunately Milton was on the West Coast and he was there. Don't know whether Ed & Earl made it. I knew you would want to send flowers, & Lee, the Butchers, Helen & Milton, Ike & I ordered a blanket of red roses and Easter Lilies. I hope they could fill the order . . . bless his heart, he [Ike] is a fine smart man & *I* know it.

The day that Mamie had to give Ike the news of his father's death, he was working intensely on a draft message for President Roosevelt to give to Chiang Kai-shek and was to deliver it in person to the president the next day for his approval. Such pressing matters precluded leaving work, but this did not mean that Ike was unmoved by his father's passing—on the contrary. Before leaving the office that evening, he wrote in his diary:

> I have felt terribly. I should like so much to be with my mother these few days. But we're at war! And war is not soft—it has no time to indulge even the deepest and most sacred emotions. I loved my Dad. I think my Mother the finest person I've ever known. She has been the inspiration

for Dad's life and a true helpmate in every sense of the word. I am quitting work now—7:30 p.m. I haven't the heart to go on tonight.

In the coming days, he also wrote a private eulogy to his father, in a desk diary he kept close at hand.

My father was buried today. I've shut off all business and visitors for thirty minutes—to have that much time, by myself, to think of him, he had a full life. He left six boys and, most fortunately for him, Mother survives him. He was not quite 79 years old, but for the past year he had been extremely old physically. Hardened arteries, kidney trouble, etc. He was a just man well liked, well educated, a thinker. He was undemonstrative, quiet, modest, and of exemplary habits—he never used alcohol or tobacco. He was an uncomplaining person in the face of adversity, and such plaudits as were accorded him did not inflate his ego.

His finest monument is his reputation in Abilene and Dickinson County, Kansas. His word has been his bond and accepted as such; his sterling honesty, his insistence upon the immediate payment of all debts, his pride and his independence earned for him the reputation that has profited all of us boys. Because of it, all central Kansas helped me to secure an appointment to West Point in 1911, and thirty years later it did the same for my son, John. I am proud he was my father! My only regret is that it was always so difficult to let him know the great depth of my affection for him. David J. Eisenhower 1863–1942.

Perhaps his own feelings of loss prompted Ike to take a short break later that month. He'd been driving himself hard, and a weekend away promised a valuable change of scenery. Ike and Mamie went to West Point to see John, the first period of relaxation Ike had had since coming to Washington. After a few days of solid rest, they returned on the 5:30 train, and Ike slept the whole way back.

At the end of the month, Mamie and Ike were surprised and thrilled when he received his second star. General Marshall had warned him that staff officers would not be decorated in this war as they had been in 1917–18; field commanders would be given the recognition this time, he'd said. And Ike had told Marshall, assertively but impulsively, "General, I'm interested in what you say but I want you to know that I don't give a damn about your promotion plans as far as I am concerned. I came into this office from the field and I am trying to do my duty. I expect to do so as long as you want me here. If that locks me to a desk for the rest of the war, so be it!"

Embarrassed by his outburst, Ike had gone back to his desk and written in his diary an entry full of frustration about being desk-bound during the war. The next day he tore out the page and wrote: "Anger cannot win, it cannot even think clearly . . . For many years I have made it a religion never to indulge myself, but yesterday I failed."

It was only a week later when Ike learned that Marshall had petitioned President Roosevelt to give Eisenhower a second star. As his operations officer, Marshall wrote in his letter that Eisenhower was effectively his "subordinate commander." This is how it had to be, Marshall said, because his "operations office had to be able to function without constantly referring problems to him." President Roosevelt approved the nomination at noon and in the afternoon Congress confirmed it.

Apparently Tex Lee had been trying to reach Mamie to give her the news, but she did not hear of it until later that afternoon when she stopped by to look at Quarters #7, the house at Fort Myer to which they were moving. As she alighted from the car, Lee came running out of the house and planted a kiss on her cheek, saying, "Congratulations, Mrs. Major General."

"We are so thrilled [about] our Ike's second star," she wrote her parents, "because we had been led to suppose that as long as he stayed on the job he wouldn't be promoted."

On April 1, Mamie had the move to Quarters #7 completed, and she and Ike took up residence in the beautiful brick home with its panoramic view of Washington and the monuments. It was a huge house, and again there was no domestic staff that went with it. Even with Mickey and another orderly, Mamie was going to find it difficult to run. But Ike had received a jump in pay because of his new star, and that would help.

In addition to facing a daunting workload, Mamie became chairman of her group at the Soldiers, Sailors and Marines Club canteen, and she served on the committee for the Army Relief Society. Ike continued to keep erratic hours. Occasionally he would be called back to the office in the middle of the night, and as spring turned to summer, he spent almost every waking hour at the office, often missing dinner or arriving so late at a dinner party that the meal had already been served.

During that spring Ike, as chief of operations, and his staff developed a war plan, designed to facilitate a cross-channel invasion in 1943. In May, Ike went to London to try to persuade the British to support it, but he came back rather discouraged about the reception he'd received. At Marshall's behest, Ike drafted recommendations about the U.S. Army's European command, in which he suggested that General Mark Clark direct American ground forces and Major General Joseph McNarney be theater commander. Marshall appointed Eisenhower instead of McNarney.

In the midst of these crucial events in June, family tragedy struck again. Mamie was wired that Dwight's younger brother Roy had died of a stroke. "Poor Ike," Mamie recalled. "I could hardly get the courage to call him. He has so much on his mind." Once again, Ike could not go to the funeral in Kansas, and in a matter of weeks he would leave the United States for an indefinite period of time. There was much to do before taking up responsibilities at headquarters in London at the end of June.

Just before Ike's departure, John got leave from the commandant of West Point to be with his father during his last weekend in the United States. John was "mildly startled" to discover that Ike had been appointed commanding general of U.S. Army forces in Europe.

I knew that Dad enjoyed an almost unparalleled reputation in the Army and that he had been the right hand man and chief planner for the Army Chief of Staff, General George C. Marshall. But command of a theater of war—potentially the major theater—was almost too much to comprehend . . .

Dad was in a pensive mood [that weekend]. Not only was he aware of the size of the responsibilities he was about to carry; he was further sobered by the shocking news, just received, of the surrender of Tobruk in Libya. This strong point, which had survived earlier Axis offensives in the see-saw battle in the region, had become a symbol of British in-domitability.

That weekend, Mamie remembered, Ike and John were "together every possible minute," precious time that she encouraged. John found the atmosphere "sober" rather than "sad," but on Sunday Ike was running a fever, a reaction to the various shots he had been given, and that day he got out of bed only "long enough for us to take some pictures." With two days left before Ike's departure, John had to go back to West Point.

"A picture in my heart will always be their leave-taking," Mamie wrote to her parents. Ike couldn't go to the airfield to see John off, so Mamie and her friend Kitty Smith were set to ride with John out to Bolling Air Force Base. She described his departure from Quarters #7: "Picture Ike standing on the steps—John beside the car at curb. John faces his father & [gives] the snappy salute of one soldier to another. Poor old John's adams apple was sure churning up & down as we turned the corner."

In those last two days, Ike and Mamie had some private moments together. She was naturally pleased that Ike now had the opportunity to undertake the military duties for which he had been trained, John recalled, "but his leaving would place her once more in a lonely, uncertain existence."

With characteristic pluck and courage, though, Mamie put on a cheerful and optimistic face for her husband right up to the end. When it was time for Ike to leave for the air base, for Europe, and for a dangerous, unknown future, Mamie walked him to his waiting vehicle. "The last thing he did was reach out of the car and kiss my hand (saying with a broad grin), 'Goodbye, Honey.' "

Ike told his pilot that after takeoff he wanted the plane to fly back over Fort Myer "for one last look"—and Mamie had promised she would stand under the flagpole outside their quarters and wave as his plane flew over. The airfield called Mamie when Ike's plane was ready to roll, and, remembering how quick the departure from Washington could be, Mamie, with two friends who'd come to keep her company and lend support, "literally flew" across the clipped lawn to a spot beside the flagpole. But wind conditions required the plane to turn northward after it had crossed the Po-tomac, away from Fort Myer. All the same, Mamie could see the aircraft clearly as it headed away, and she and her companions yelled "Happy Landings!"

Mamie had dinner that night with friends at Fort Myer and received messages of the plane's whereabouts all evening long. Just before she went home, she got word that the plane was over the ocean and they were "really on their way."

"I'll have to admit I felt pretty low when I crawled into bed, knowing that my darling was God knew where," she wrote her parents. "I didn't cry tho a-tall."

The next morning, Mamie received a message that "the bird had landed." Not long after, she had a cable from Ike himself. It read: "BECAUSE OF YOU I'VE BEEN THE LUCKIEST MAN IN THE WORLD FOR TWENTY-SIX YEARS—LOVE IKE."

CHAPTER TWELVE

THE COMMANDER'S WIFE

he Eisenhowers had been in Quarters #7 little more than two months, but with Ike gone Mamie was given only a week to move out. "They didn't care where I went," she recalled. "They ordered Ike away; and I was ordered off the post." Not that she was particularly sorry. "I never had a house that gave me such a headache," she remarked at the time, "am glad to be shot of it except for what it stood for: Ike at home."

This was her fifth move in the two years since their return from the Philippines. She was lucky that Harry Butcher had acquired their old Wardman flat to use as a CBS corporate apartment. Butch, now a naval reserve officer, had been assigned to Ike's staff in Europe, and the plan was for Mamie to share the apartment with his wife, Ruth, and their daughter, Beverly: "Otherwise, I wouldn't have had a place to go except to Denver, and I couldn't go home to Papa and Mama." In addition to the one-bedroom apartment, the women were able to secure two other rooms at the back, one for Ruth and the other for Beverly, who was in elementary school.

Mamie had hardly settled in when she discovered that without the protection of Ike's staff, or the isolation of an army post, she was easy prey for the press, always on the lookout for any human-interest story. What the wife of the commander in chief of the European theater was doing was a new angle that would appeal to American readers. "Reporters are here every day taking up at least 2 to 3 hours of my time," she wrote her parents, "—another due here in a few minutes. Milton sees them all too but guess they like to see what kind of person I am."

To escape this problem, Mamie and a friend thought they'd make a spontaneous trip to Chicago, decided on a couple of hours' notice. Mamie figured the break would improve her morale and then she could go on to Denver to see her parents. While she was away, she heard a rumor that Ike would be returning to Washington for a few days, so she rushed back on the off chance he would be coming through. When she reached Washington, however, General Mark Clark told her he thought Ike's return was unlikely. "Naturally, I feel very low," Mamie lamented to her parents, "cause the big reason for me to stay here was the possibility of his return without warning . . . Maybe it would be worse to tell him goodbye again than not have him return."

Ike, too, was missing Mamie. The distance between them during this period of intense pressure at Allied headquarters only served to underscore the vital, if unsung, role she had played during the early days of the war. Life in London was similar to what it had been at the Operations Division of the War Department; but he complained that for all the heavy burdens he now carried, he had no home to go to "where there is incentive to forget the work part of my existence even momentarily . . . How I wish you were living here," he wrote her. "You cannot imagine how much you added to my efficiency in the hard months in Washington. Even I didn't realize it then; at least not fully—but I do now, and I'm grateful to you."

Telephone lines, which Mamie had begun to utilize a great deal before the war, were now harder to secure. That meant that communication between the two was restricted to "radios," or radiograms, and letters, which were often delivered erratically. Communication was all the more difficult because Ike was severely limited in what he could tell Mamie. Often he could give no hint of his location, of whom he was seeing, or of what was on his mind. "Even the state of the weather is secret!" he exclaimed, "*and very correctly so.*"

In an undated letter to Mamie's parents, Ike described the frustration of writing and the utter lack of privacy that was now part of his world. He was never alone, his every word and action were assessed by those around him, and for much of the war he also had a guard on duty outside his bedroom. "In one way it seems futile to write to anyone; everything I do, or see, or hear, or even think, is secret. I'm surrounded by guards & trusted subordinates all the time. I think there are 9 men constantly on guard around the two houses where my naval commander and I live." And then he added that life, as the war was progressing, was getting "tougher! If possible!"

That fall, as the planning of Operation Torch, the invasion of North Africa, intensified, Ike had little time for relaxation, or time for himself. In addition to a long working day, he had many other official duties and often he would be summoned to Winston Churchill's for a late-night supper: "Butch is a good tonic for me. I wish I could spend every evening with him & T. J. [Davis]. They keep me going . . . Spent last Sunday nite with the PM [Prime Minister] but it was no rest. We stayed up until 3:00 a.m. Tomorrow I pay my duty call on the king . . . Seems funny for a little Kansas farmer boy to be having business with world notables but, in professional affairs, I have as much confidence as anyone else . . . Well sweet— I miss you dreadfully. This job would be much easier if I had you to come home to. Don't forget me!"

In the minutes he managed to put aside for writing Mamie, his vulnerabilities often surfaced. He wrote of the longing he felt for her, his desire to be reunited, and the frustration that was caused by the uneven delivery of mail. "I do get so lonesome and anxious to hear from you both," he told her, "and though I've growled about J [regarding the irregular flow of his letters], send him my deepest affection. I'm so tied up with him it hurts." On the anniversary of Ikky's birth, he wrote poignantly, "Tomorrow, Sept. 24, Ikky would have been 25 years old. Seems rather unbelievable doesn't it? We could well have been grandparents by this time. I'm sorry we're not!"

Mamie herself was surviving with the support of the tight-knit community of army wives who had been left behind. The second floor of the Wardman Tower mirrored, in part, the American High Command in Europe. In addition to Ruth Butcher, whose husband was Ike's naval aide, the wife of Walter Bedell Smith, Ike's chief of staff, also lived there. Mamie had a regular group of women friends whom she dined and played cards with, including Kate Hughes, her friend since the Wyoming days, and Janie Howard, whom she met at Fort Lewis. "We [each] had one little ration card," Mamie later remembered. "We never got a decent meal unless we all got together and everybody put her things in."

Mamie was also plugged into the civilian community through

Helen and Milton Eisenhower and Mary and George Allen, a Washington insider who was prominent in Democratic politics (numbering among his friends Senator Harry Truman). Well-known hostess Perle Mesta, who also lived at the Wardman, regarded herself as Mamie's friend.

In addition to the social activities the wives dreamed up to keep themselves occupied—potluck suppers and mah-jongg and bridge games—Mamie also had a significant workload that demanded her attention. When she wasn't volunteering her time with the Red Cross or serving as a waitress at the canteen for the Soldiers, Sailors and Marines, she was personally answering every letter of the volumes of mail that came to her—each with a handwritten reply. Occasionally, she would attend an official dinner for a visiting dignitary or she would participate in a ceremony, as she did when she placed a wreath at the Tomb of the Unknown Soldier on Armistice Day.

Mamie was below par physically, from what she termed her "age and the strain that has been put on me in the last year," due to the countless moves. She was also suffering from digestive ailments again. These upsets were even harder to cope with in the un-air-conditioned misery of a Washington heat wave, which she said was worse than anything she'd endured in the Philippines. Many accounts have attributed her inability to "keep food down" to stress and anxiety, but the explanation may have been much simpler. In the late fall, her doctor discovered that Mamie had food allergies, a diagnosis that apparently came after discovering that she was allergic to the vitamin shots she was regularly receiving.

Despite these ups and downs, Mamie was determined to maintain her optimism, and Ike's letters helped to sustain her. She heard from him on an average of three times a week, and Tex Lee and Mickey also wrote regularly to fill her in on life with "the Boss." She was elated when many would arrive simultaneously, just as she would feel low when there had been no word for some time. Concern over Ike's safety never abated, but she filled her days as best she could, and waited.

Not long after Ike's arrival in England, he received a third star, a promotion consistent with the heavy burdens he now carried as commander of the European theater. Although many of his non-American subordinates held higher ranks in their own national services, it was Eisenhower's responsibility to forge the first truly allied coalition in modern warfare. According to Ike, in the early stages it had the tendency to act like a "bulldog meeting a tom-cat." Ike recalled,

> The whole basis of our higher organization was new. Time and time again during the summer old army friends warned me that the conception of allied unity which we took as the foundation of our command scene was impracticable and impossible; that any commander placed in my position was fore-doomed to failure and could become nothing but a scapegoat to carry the odium of defeat for the whole operation.

History would prove the pessimists wrong, but they were right that Ike would take plenty of heat. With the invasion of North Africa in November, the delicate task of dealing with the French forces there fell to Ike. It was believed that French North Africa actually favored the Allied cause—despite the Vichy government's collaboration with Germany and the capitulation of most of the French army and navy to Hitler's invading and occupying forces. A way had to be found to convert the French into supporters of this crucial operation. General Henri Giraud was spirited from a prison in the south of France and mobilized to raise volunteer forces in the region, but his influence turned out to be minimal. What happened next posed a major political gamble for Ike, and it later caused a firestorm of negative publicity.

French military leaders refused a cease-fire in North Africa without the consent of the Vichy government. Ike made a deal with Admiral Jean-François Darlan, who had been in Henri Pétain's cabinet and was captured during the campaign. Despite Darlan's ambiguous past in the Vichy regime, Ike made him the interim head of the civil government in Algeria on condition that he follow Ike's orders. "In the long run, we could defeat the local French forces," Ike said. "[But] that would also defeat our hope of making the French in Africa our allies—and would hamper a later operation in the base from which we would be attacking the Axis . . . On the other hand . . . [in dealing with Darlan] we were assured an immediate cease-fire, no more casualties, and a chance at Tunisia."

Ike knew that he might be condemned for this unpopular move. After making the decision, he told his subordinates, "I'll do my best to convince our governments, by detailed explanation, that the decision was right. If they find it necessary later to take action against this headquarters, I'll make it clear that I alone am responsible."

Despite the pressure of this crisis and the intense planning for the largest invasion yet to be mounted in military history, Ike, as at all other periods of the war, remembered Mamie's most important anniversaries. That year, he wrote her a letter on October 30, telling her not to open it until her birthday on November 14:

By the time you read this your newspapers will probably have told you where I am and you will understand why your birthday letter had to be written some time in advance. You will also realize that I have been busy—very busy . . .

I hope you won't be disturbed or worried. War inevitably carries its risks to life and limb—but the chances, in my case, are all in favor—a fact which you must always remember. Moreover—even if the worst should ever happen to me, *please* don't be too upset. In 31 years as a soldier I've been exposed to few of the risks that most have encountered. If I had been in the Theatre of Operations during World War I, I might easily have long since gone. And, while I don't mean to be fatalistic or too philosophical—I truly feel that what the U.S. and the world are facing today is so much bigger than any one of us can even comprehend, that personal sacrifice and loss must not be allowed to overwhelm any of us.

Anyway—on the day you open this letter you'll be 46. I'd like to be there to help you celebrate, and to kiss you 46 times (multiplied by any number you care to pick). I imagine Ruth will have some little party for you, or maybe Helen & Milton will try to get a hold of you. In any event I will be with you in thought and entirely aside from the usual congratulations and felicitations I will be thinking with the deepest gratitude of the many happy hours and years you've given me. I am quite aware of the fact that I'm not always easy to live with— that frequently I'm irascible and even mean—and my gratitude is all the greater when I realize how often you have put up with me in spite of such traits.

The crowning thing you've given me is our son—he has been so wonderful, unquestionably because he's so much you—that I find I live in him so very often. Your love and our son have been the greatest gifts from my life, and on your birthday I wish that my powers of expression were such as to make you understand that thoroughly—clearly and for always. I've never wanted another wife—you're mine, and for that reason I've been luckier than any other man.

I feel this war is so big—so vast—that my mind completely refuses to visualize anything beyond its possible end. But I do hope that all through it I do my duty so well, so efficiently, that regardless of what may happen to me, you and John can always be proud that we three are one family. I do *not* seek rank—I don't even seek acclaim, because it is easily possible that a commander can receive credit (and *blame*) for which he is no wise responsible. But if my own conscience tells me I've done my duty—I will always come back to you in the certainty that you'd understand any fall from the high places, and that my place in your heart would be as big as ever.

Again love and kisses on your birthday.

Mamie's friends admired her for her steady internal compass during this time. Despite the rash of criticism in the newspapers over the "Darlan deal," Mamie was savvy enough to know how to handle the press. Janie Howard recalled Mamie's "good sense" when, one afternoon, the bellhop rang the doorbell to deliver a huge box of American Beauty roses, extremely precious and hard to find during the war. There was no card. Janie said, "Oh me, isn't that wonderful!" But Mamie turned and looked at her skeptically, declaring it "bad news." "Somebody wants something," she said. "We'll find out." Mamie refused to keep the flowers and sent them to Walter Reed Army Medical Hospital.

"Sure enough," Janie said, "in about three or four days a gentleman called and announced himself from the annex office." He asked Mamie if she had received the roses, and she confirmed that she had and had sent them immediately to Walter Reed.

"Well, I want to come up and get some notes on your husband," the reporter said.

Mamie's reply was swift and firm. "You can get all the notes you want at the Pentagon. General Surles will be glad to give them to you."

Janie was stunned and said, "Why, Mamie, he sent you all those beautiful roses." But Mamie reminded her that publicity is a "two-edged sword" and that "it could cut both ways."

Ike, too, in his own playful way warned Mamie about the news media. A letter written in late November may have been his way of telling her not to believe the printed rumors she might read in the newspapers, in this case rumblings that he was due to return to Washington for a short visit.

Every once in a while Butcher tells me something about the stories that the newspaper boys publish. I never get to read them myself but you must understand that a newspaper man always has to draw on his imagination freely in order to give his stories "color." So if you read anything to the effect that I go charging across the Sahara singlehanded, with my eyebrows dripping sweat and blood—just smile! Actually I don't know what they print—but I do know that whatever it is—much of it is exaggeration.

For a brief time, Mamie had anticipated Ike's visit to the United States, for newspapers had hinted that he would probably be in Washington for consultations. In actual fact, planning for the invasion of North Africa was well in hand and there had to be a pretext for Ike's disappearance from London—hence the cover story. But Mamie had no way of knowing that it was a hoax and that her husband was in fact headed for the shores of North Africa.

"I am sorry you were so keenly disappointed about my not coming home," Ike wrote her. "For fear that you would be, I had purposely omitted all mention of such a possibility in my last letters." With the tension of the invasion mounting, he again wrote the following week, "I've never known what it was to miss anyone so much as I've missed you and John these last weeks."

Milton, as associate director of the Office of War Information, had gone to the front to see his brother during the Darlan crisis. When he returned, he must have known the invasion was imminent, but Mamie was in the dark. Then on November 8 the Allies invaded.

I was out [at] Milton's the night they went into Africa. Milton knew it, so he said, "Why don't you come out . . . I'll get a

group together and we'll have penny-ante poker." And so . . .
we went to the game room, and Milton kept fidgeting around
. . . I thought it was rather strange him playing the radio, because Milton never liked that sort of thing. He was waiting
for the announcement.

When the news came over the radio that the invasion had been
launched, they decided that Mamie should stay with Milton and
Helen for several days as a temporary sanctuary from the raft of
reporters who were waiting for her at the Wardman.

With the Allied invasion of French Morocco and Algiers on November 8, the French garrisons across North Africa were overcome
and an armistice was quickly arrived at. With Darlan now, in fact,
aiding the Allied forces, the crisis of the "deal" with him faded
from controversy. Then on Christmas Eve, Darlan was assassi-
nated. "Poor old Darlan is gone," Ike wrote Mamie. "He was a
weak character, at least nothing more than an opportunist, but so
far as I could ever find out, he played square with us here."

Ike must have felt relief that the episode was over, but the stress
and isolation of working and living alone was telling on him.

Algiers, December 30, 1942

Sometimes I get to missing you so that I simply don't know
what to do. As pressure mounts and strain increases, everyone
begins to show the weaknesses in his makeup. It is up to the
Commander to conceal his; above all to conceal doubt, fear
and distrust, especially in any subordinate, and to try to overcome the defects he finds around him. When the strain is long
continued the commander gets to feeling more and more
alone and lonesome, and his mind instinctively turns to something or someone that could help. This, of course is not well
explained—but I mean only to tell you that constantly I think
of you as someone who could provide the counterbalance for
me—and send me back to work fitter to do a good job. No
one else in the world could ever fill your place with me—and
that is the reason I need you. Maybe a simpler explanation is
merely that I LOVE YOU!! which I do, always. Never forget
that, because, except for my duty, which I try to perform cred-
itably, it is the only thing to which I can cling with confidence.

Mamie, too, needed to cling to something with confidence. With the invasion, publicity about the European High Command had increased dramatically, and the first subtle hints had come that Ike was surrounded by "temptation." A caption under one of the pictures in a *Life* magazine feature on November 9, 1942, said as much to the discerning eye. In listing General Eisenhower's personal staff—"he calls it his family"—it gave the name and job of everyone, such as "Lieutenant Commander Harry Butcher, naval aide, and 'Mickey' McKeogh, orderly, valet, and courier at large." When it came to the general's chauffeur, the caption read, "Kay Summersby, pretty Irish girl who also drives for General Eisenhower." In today's more sensitive environment, such an outrageously sexist caption would not have survived a serious editor's pen, but in 1942 it added spice that helped sell copy.

The inferences from this publication and others opened a long and painful chapter in Mamie's life, and rumors of a romance between Ike and Summersby would resurface again in her last years. Though she gave no hint to her friends that she was bothered by such innuendo about Ike's driver, her vulnerability started to show in a letter to her parents, just after the new year of 1943. "Had three letters from Ike yesterday & one from Mickey," Mamie wrote her parents. "They had a New Years Eve party—11 men & 5 women—suppose the latter were WACs—durn 'em."

The importance of the Women's Army Corps* in doing work that released male officers and enlisted men for active duty at the front was widely understood. Nevertheless, among the army wives relegated to the *home* front, there was jealousy and fear. The WACs who served in the theater of battle worked side by side with their husbands, and Mamie was well aware of the advantage proximity afforded any attractive woman. No doubt she expressed her concern. A month later, conscious of Mamie's discomfort, Ike wrote, "I love you all the time—don't go bothering your pretty head about WACS—etc etc. You just hold the thought that . . . I'm on the run to you the day the victorious army marches into Berlin!" In the "confused life we lead," he emphasized, it is easy for rumors to get started, crazy tales "without the slightest foundation in fact . . . I don't even let my people tell me what they are. My

*Established by Congress in 1942, the Women's Auxiliary Army Corps (WAAC) modified its name in 1943.

poor brain is sufficiently burdened with things that are true. So I want you to know you can smile at anything."

Defending himself against the implications suggested by yet another article, Ike exclaimed with exasperation: "So *Life* says that my old London driver came down [to North Africa]! So she did—but the big reason she wanted to serve in this theater is that she is terribly in love with a young American colonel and is to be married to him come June—assuming both are alive. I doubt that *Life* told that!"

If the presence of attractive women at the front had been at the back of her mind, it was far from being the central focus of Mamie's concern in those years. For despite the terrible pressures of Ike's work, his letters were constant, just as they were filled with love and tenderness. In fact, he remembered virtually all the important dates in her life—and for Mamie these were many, including Easter, Mother's Day, Christmas, her birthday, Valentine's Day, and the other days having sentimental associations with their courtship and marriage. As far as we know, he missed only one Mother's Day throughout the three-year European campaign.

Aside from the affectionate and thoughtful messages Ike managed to send, he was also sure to let her know how much he approved of how she was conducting herself in Washington. Early that winter General Marshall, in Algiers briefly, had obviously commented on it. Ike's penned note to Mamie said: "I do have time to tell you again that I'm prouder of you every time someone brings me news of the way you handle yourself—of the serene way that you (my mother, too, God bless her) brush off the chance to indulge in cheap publicity. You are a thorobred, and, merely incidently, I love the hell out of you."

Kate Hughes concurred that Mamie was handling herself impeccably.

She had the most extraordinary sense of the right thing to do—how and when to do it—than any woman I have ever known . . . They were difficult days when our husbands were overseas, and many people were trying to get next to her for him . . . I remember a beautiful pin that someone sent her—it was, I think, three stars [of] rubies and diamonds—and she had the good sense to send it back. One of the top milliners sent her a whole bunch beautiful hats, and she sent them back. And she loved hats and jewelry. Nobody had to tell her, she knew it [was right].

Mamie's composure was all the more commendable given her disappointment with the living arrangement she had worked out with Ruth Butcher. She was terribly fond of Ruth, but they finally decided that she and Beverly should move to a nearby apartment. Mamie had really encouraged it. Ruth had a different philosophy about how to wait out the war, and she had quite a few friends, male and female, who were not part of Mamie's trusted circle. When Ruth finally moved across the hall, Mamie was relieved that she would not have to see some of Ruth's friends, particularly one who, she complained, got "so drunk and boring at times." Milton agreed and saw that intimate associations with strangers could hurt her as well as Ike, and that Mamie could well be tarred with the same brush of rumor.

He later recalled that Mamie "drank no more than anyone did in those days—which for a 'lady' was only one. But she did think some of the others had a little too much . . . I only told her to be careful not to drink too freely in front of strangers. You could have a ginger ale in your hands and people can say whatever they want. I heard those stories, and I told her to be careful. Not about drinking too much—because she didn't—but about drinking in front of those . . . miserable gals."*

Milton's advice only confirmed for Mamie her own worry that, with a roommate, any roommate, she had little control over who visited her and what they would later say. "Everything is very friendly about the move," Mamie wrote her parents, "because I

---

*Many accounts quote Henry Jameson, an Abilene newspaper publisher, as saying that the family was worried that Mamie was drinking too much and told her to stop. Historians quote him as if he were a family intimate, but he was not; and he would have had no reliable way of knowing what the family thought. No one except John and Milton can be relied on to assess the family's attitude to Mamie's behavior during the war, and they concur. Every live witness who ever knew Mamie laughs at the thought that Mamie was then or ever had been involved in alcohol abuse. As William Ewald, a former White House aide, once pointed out, she did not have the characteristics of alcoholics—who either drink and get drunk, or don't touch a drop. Furthermore, it is absolutely certain that if Mamie had been an alcoholic, it would have utterly jeopardized her marriage to Ike.

had made up my mind to move if [Ruth] didn't." Now she would have to live on her own, no matter how difficult that might be. And although she occasionally invited a trusted friend as a guest for a night or even for days or weeks at a time, she sought to maintain her independence and flexibility. She understood that she had to protect herself, now more than ever, from becoming the object of idle gossip. However, as time would tell, many of the rumors that circulated about Mamie were politically motivated, and during those years at the Wardman, Mamie had numerous friends who were active in Democratic and Republican politics.

It is unfortunate that Mamie's proximity to a circle of frustrated and anxious wives, some of whom were not exactly temperate, should have coincided with the exacerbation of a physical problem from which she had suffered for some time. Ever since she had endured the enormous physical stress of moving household so many times after their return from the Philippines, she had been experiencing increasingly frequent spells of dizziness. This, discovered later by doctors, was due to Ménière's syndrome, a severe inner-ear disorder that is caused by pressure on a nerve and results in periodic attacks of dizziness, ringing in the ears, and vertigo. Mamie suffered mostly from lack of equilibrium, a condition that often made her unsteady on her feet. Perhaps the affliction had existed earlier: she had complained of a "pitching" sensation in the Philippines. But now the problem worsened and her doctors determined that surgery was unlikely to alleviate the symptoms.

One day, waiting on tables at the Soldiers, Sailors and Marines canteen, Mamie accidentally spilled gravy down the front of a soldier. The young man, not realizing that the waitress was the commanding general's wife, bawled, "Hey, lady, watch what you're doing!" She patted him dry and assured him that cold water would remove the stain. Increasing awareness of her own limitations may have made her question her suitability for this kind of war work.

When she was suffering an attack of Ménière's syndrome, she couldn't stand steadily for any length of time without assistance, and even the simplest tasks could become unfortunately complicated. Sometimes, she later recalled, she couldn't even hail a taxi without someone lending her an arm. Mamie didn't have a maid for most of this time period, and some mornings she would wake up and be so disabled by the dizziness that she had to crawl on her hands and knees to get to the kitchen. On those occasions, "I didn't dare walk," she recalled. "I couldn't walk." At its worst, after some attacks—they always came on unexpectedly—she would be bruised from having bumped into the furniture as she made her way around the apartment.

As time went on, Mamie found ways to function with this disability, but it stayed with her the rest of her life. Delores Moaney, who became her cook and housekeeper in 1948, remembers that the condition was often worse when Mamie first got out of bed in the morning. The pressure on the nerve in her inner ear also caused severe nightmares if she slept with her head in the wrong position.

Given her sense of privacy—and her deep desire to keep up with not only her husband but her friends, too—she never liked to dwell on her affliction. But given the lack of sensitivity in the culture of the time to handicaps of one sort or another, vicious and ambitious people used Mamie's unsteadiness as proof that the ugly and unfair rumors were true. The gossip may have been spread out of jealousy, spite, or even political fear.

Mamie was aware of the rumors that she had a drinking problem, but she knew she had not compromised what she regarded as the appropriate behavior for the wife of a commanding general. "Up to the day he died," Mamie said, "I had utter respect for everything he thought, and I would never have done anything that would have in any way changed his opinion of the woman he married."

Mamie had developed a code of conduct for herself which included an uncompromising personal policy about being seen in public. Unlike the years between the wars, when, in Ike's absence, Mamie had not hesitated about going out on the town with an escort, now she understood that the times and the circumstances were wholly different. Although Mamie had women friends or couples to her apartment, she was adamant that she would not be seen partying in public while the war was raging and her husband was having to send young men to their deaths. Ironically this principled approach may have actually played into the rumors milling around, for unkind people took her absence from the public social scene as proof that her "drinking problem" was so bad that "someone had locked her away." In a way, then, she was in a no-win situation. But her sense of duty and her strong convictions about her role guided her. "Not going out wasn't a sacrifice," Mamie asserted in her later years. "I believed in it."

Still, as Kate Hughes recalled, on many occasions Mamie's resolve cost her badly needed companionship and affection. "Gee Gerow came to town and he wanted to have his old friends down at the Mayflower, and Mamie would have loved that; it was all her old friends . . . but she wouldn't go. She said she couldn't afford to go to a party like that where there would be liquor on the table and people would say that she was out partying and drinking while her husband sent their sons to war. She never, during the whole war, went out."

With both Ike and John gone, Mamie must have felt more alone than ever.

> The only time I ever got a good night's sleep was when [one of my friends] would come over and stay all night. [Otherwise] I'd be awake until daylight. I couldn't go to sleep, I was scared to sleep. I didn't know what this awful quietness was. I wasn't used to it . . . I wasn't afraid anybody would get in, because I had double locks on everything, but I could not stand this absolute loneliness. Because even when Ike was gone other times, you see, I had a baby or I had John for company. And I tell you it was a gloomy experience.

Ike had a formula that made handling the stress of his job tolerable, and as an example of their teamwork as an army couple, Mamie's own philosophy mirrored her husband's. Ike wrote her:

> Subordinates can advise, urge, help and pray, but only one man, in his own mind and heart, can decide "Do we, or do we not." The stakes are the highest and the penalties are expressed in terms of loss of life . . . So the struggle is to do one's best; to keep the brain and the conscience clear; never be swayed by unworthy motives or inconsequential reasons but to strive to unearth the basic factors involved and then do one's duty.

Mamie, too, understood that she had to stay strong and "keep her brain and conscience clear." And just as people under Ike's command were looking to him for leadership, she too had to maintain her optimism and her good judgment as an example to the worried wives who had been left behind. To many of these women she became a "mother confessor." "She was so responsive," Ruth Butcher recalled, "that everyone felt comfortable with her." Mrs. Henry Matchett, the wife of a brigadier general, concurred. "Mamie would always sense when someone was worried." Janie Howard put it best: "Mamie was the greatest help I ever had. She had a capacity for friendship. She could know what I needed or when I was sick before I really knew it [myself] . . . I would say her greatest thing was her capacity to be a friend . . . the kind of friend who doesn't demand, doesn't ask, but [is] always there."

Mamie was ready to provide a nonjudgmental ear, but she was also ready to dispense solicited or unsolicited advice when she thought the wives of her husband's subordinates needed it. Janie remembered an incident at one of their "hen parties." The conversation about some aspect of the war prompted Janie to blurt out without thinking: "Well, Mamie, you don't have to worry, because your husband is a general." Janie's was a major at the time. Mamie didn't say a word, but later she shepherded Janie into an adjoining room where they could be alone and said firmly to her: "Nobody's safe, Janie, and Ike's got the whole burden on his shoulders. Never let me hear you complain about anything, because your husband is a professional soldier and we're the ones who have to hold up. We're the ones who can't complain."

And then she added with equal firmness: "You can't do much to help your husband, but you can do a lot to hurt him." Janie never forgot those important words.

CHAPTER THIRTEEN

"A WOMAN OF STEEL AND IMMENSE RESILIENCY"

Coping with the difficulties of residing alone—but living under the intense scrutiny of the public and the news media—Mamie and Ike each developed little ways to keep themselves "alive" for one another. They resumed many of the same habits they had shared while living together before the war. Every time Mamie so much as went out of town, even just overnight, a telegram was duly sent apprising Ike of her safe arrival. Secrecy made reciprocity on such matters impossible, but Mamie heard from or about her husband, via letter or telegram, nearly every day.

Mamie once sent Ike a phonograph record of her voice, which, he thought, had "faithfully reproduced her sound." He liked it so much he later confessed that he played it over and over again "when others were absent." She also sent him items like toothbrushes and socks and a steady supply of pulp Western novels which he read for pure escapist relaxation, as others do crossword puzzles or play solitaire. Ike often complained about the quality of the writing, though; and Beverly Butcher Byron, Ruth Butcher's daughter, recalls their constant search for novels he hadn't read.

In February 1943, Mamie wrote her parents, "The news is out about Ike and his command. The fourth star should come along in the near future—after Tunisia is taken, I think. Gen. Marshall called me as soon as he returned [from Algiers]. Said Ike didn't look nearly as tired as he'd expected. Said their house is running like clock work . . . [Ike] bought me a beautiful Algerian rug—neutral in color with brown stripes running in a diamond . . ."

When the promotion came through in mid-February, however,

Ike was puzzled that he had not heard from Mamie with some kind of reaction. (It is likely that their letters crossed in the mail.) This was a more significant promotion than it might have seemed. Ike had been a lieutenant colonel at the start of the war, only fifteen months before, and that was the rank to which he would have reverted after the hostilities—until this promotion, which, unlike the others, was a permanent rank. Ike wrote:

> So far I've received no letter from you written since I was promoted, I'm curious to learn how it struck you. It was obvious from some of your letters that you feared the big boys were preparing to give me the boot. You must not care about such things, darling. War is a hard game—it wears people out. It is quite within possibility that before this is over they will decide I'm passé—if so, why we can still get ourselves a little cottage and sit in the sun. But, of course, I'm glad that by this action the official stamp of approval seems to have been placed upon my judgement and action during the past months, I'm sure that pleases you.

With Ike's new rank came still more media attention. While he was genuinely uncomfortable with much of the fuss, it was also part of his leadership style to try to deflect from himself the endless press attention. In an undated letter to the Douds, he made his feelings very clear: "I've tried to stop much of the stuff from starting and have been able to do a lot by giving the pressmen other things to talk about, and other people to interview. One thing *I do not want* is a name as a publicity seeker, we have one of those in the army and that's more than enough!"

But Ike's desire to deflect press attention did not make reporters go away. And Mamie had no help from the army in dealing with the huge volume of congratulatory mail that came to her about her husband's promotion. Some of her close friends were scandalized, in fact, that she had been left to cope with the overwhelming quantity of letters alone, especially given the importance of maintaining public support for the war.

Kate Hughes observed, "Mamie lived a very lonely life. The way Marshall and all those people who were running the war treated her was simply outrageous. Did the wife of the commanding general of the expedition have a car? Did she have an aide?

Did she have any help at all? No. It was amazing . . . [If some] terribly big wig [came to town] and they threw all sorts of [official] parties—they just invited her—they didn't send a car for her, they didn't do anything."

Nevertheless, Mamie made a point of personally answering the letters and did as much volunteer work as her time and capability would allow. "All through this publicity storm you've been tops—sensible, considerate and modest," Ike wrote her. "You are all that any man could ask as a *partner* and a *sweetheart*." Later in the same day he wrote again: "I realize that this whirlwind of newspaper notoriety places a heavy burden on you. Every friend that has mentioned the subject to me has commented on the masterly way you've handled the matter."

Ike's mother, too, had been so inundated with mail that her companion, Naomi, wrote Ike asking for assistance. "My advice is to attempt to segregate those letters which appear genuine and sincere from those that seem to you to be just some type of bid for cheap publicity," Ike suggested. "The first kind you could bundle up occasionally and send to Mamie, in Washington, in the hopes that she might be able to hire a part-time secretary and make some answer."

John has written that Ike's promotion in 1943 was pivotally important, not just because it was a permanent one but because it was a turning point for Ike psychologically. "He had arrived in London during a period of great uncertainty. The Western allies were losing on nearly all fronts . . . and having been a lieutenant colonel only fifteen months before, Eisenhower was understandably awed by the personalities he was dealing with." He now had four stars, and "the ultimate success in the North African campaign represented a real milestone."

The genuine power Ike now commanded made everyone who ever knew him scramble to associate themselves with him. Nana was indignant that even her friends in Denver fell into that trap. Mamie dismissed the issue:

I get such a kick out of you—letting Mommie Bird [one of the Douds' neighbors] get your goat. What the heck difference does it make what she says. So many people are riding

on Ike's coattails these days one more or less doesn't matter—
even his old girls are breaking into print. An article in the
Chicago Tribune told of [Gladys Harding] going to June week
or something with him [while he was still a cadet at West
Point] and what a wonderful beau he made etc. etc. . . . The
whole thing about John and me was two lines—whom Ike
married and John being the only son and in [West Point].

Ike noted the same problem in a letter to Mamie.

The pictures I signed for you as requested were all taken
when I still wore three stars, I hope that doesn't ruin their
value for recipients, but I've found that, to some extent at
least, "popularity" (?) goes according to rank. You'd be astonished how many old friends have suddenly re-discovered their
undying affection and admiration for me. Of course they often
let me know, also, that I have a profound need for the individual concerned, particularly if a promotion could be arranged!!
    I think I must have gotten a bit cynical in that para. Ac-
tually I didn't—I just have to smile, at times, when I get
letters so incredibly naive in their presentation of the writers
self-interest as to presume, on my part, an incredible degree
of stupidity. But—maybe they're right, at that! Anyway—
Butch or Lee answers each letter and just says "I'm sorry."
    We (Butch and I) often discuss some of these things in the
privacy we have at home. We've been very proud of the way
you have reacted to it all. I know that more than one person
has probably hinted to you that a request from me might help
out a son, brother, husband etc etc. You've been a brick—
haven't even passed them on! Usually the people involved
are the ones who have spent their army careers on an "office
hour" basis. Work if the boss makes you—but don't overdo!!

Having to say no to the entreating wives cannot have been
pleasant. Mamie tried as best she could to discourage friends from
even making an effort to approach her husband. To virtually all
aspirants she relayed that it was "hard luck" but "his hands are
tied." "Ike used to say," she remembered later, " 'You know I
can take care of the men,' but he said, 'I'll be John Brown if I can

take care of the women.' " On the occasions when Ike had to relieve old friends, including one classmate, he noted that he never had any trouble with the officers themselves, but the wives were "another matter."

That May, Mamie went to Fort Sam Houston to visit her sister, Mike, and then on to Abilene to see Ike's mother. In San Antonio she received the news that King George VI had presented Ike with the Most Honourable Order of the Bath. It's "quite something," she remarked to her parents, and though she denied it, she must have gotten some pleasure from being "razzed about being Lady Mamie."

Despite this good news, Mamie was completely focused on her own family's affairs. All was not settled at the Moore household. Mamie's brother-in-law Gordon was on pins and needles waiting for his orders, and Mike was quite "undone" by the thought that Gordon would be going overseas. Mamie was understanding, if somewhat unsympathetic. After an emotional telephone call to Nana and Pupah in Denver, Mamie wrote, "We only meant to say 'hello' and let you know we were happy to be together. I could smack Mike for crying. Poor kid, it is hard, but I've seen so many other gals left behind too."

Alone herself for virtually a year by now, Mamie had indeed become tougher—and more skeptical of the motives of nearly everyone. The rumors about Kay Summersby brought much of that to light. Her closest friends, whose husbands were now subordinate to Ike, were likely to be overly sympathetic to her, but even the best-intentioned of them were not independent enough in their thinking to assess the Eisenhowers' situation as different from their own. For those who were jealous of Mamie and her husband's meteoric rise to prominence, the rumors were a convenient means to express their envy and personal disappointment.

Kevin McCann, who worked after the war as an aide to Ike, described what he thought was the "terrible isolation" Mamie had had to endure while Ike was serving in the Mediterranean and in Europe, and he was outspoken about the other wives:

Army cats of the worst sort, I know, surrounded her, each of them intent on sinking their teeth into the heart of the Commander's [and later Supreme Commander's] wife, relaying to her—in the most affectionately sympathetic manner—and enlarging viciously on it, the latest bit of scandalous gossip leaked through censorship. From Frank McCarthy, then Secretary of the General Staff, I believe . . . I have learned that only a woman of steel and immense resiliency could have retained her sanity amidst that crowd.

It is clear from her letters that Mamie believed Ike's soothing words about missing her. But I am sure a significant cause for unhappiness was that, as an object of speculation, Mamie knew that some people felt sorry for her. Prideful as always, she probably regarded this as an unnecessary side effect of the situation, and she might have wondered why Summersby was kept on staff when Ike knew that her presence bothered Mamie and probably made her life more difficult. What could be so indispensable about a driver?

What Mamie did not know—or knew only too well—was that Kay had become a valued member of Ike's staff, a tight-knit group of people who trusted and depended on one another in some of the most highly pressured circumstances Americans faced in the war.* Mamie also understood, from years past, Ike's need for female companionship. She had firsthand knowledge that when ambition, rank-pulling, and rivalry were part and parcel of the daily environment, a sympathetic and trustworthy listener was of inestimable value. From the earliest days of their marriage, Mamie herself had created a stress-free after-work environment for Ike—which included having friends in, playing cards, or "just loafing." Ike used these breathers for gaining perspective on his work and physically relaxing from the man-killing schedules he kept. Mamie had not only understood the value of such time for Ike's physical and emotional health, she had insisted on it.† Summersby's former co-workers have told me that Kay joined in such recreational

---

*My father has always likened Kay Summersby's relationship to Ike as roughly that of Mary Richards to Lou Grant.

†J. B. West, chief usher of the White House during the Eisenhower administration, quoted Ike as once saying to him, "I believe there is a point at which efficiency is best served. After you spend a certain number of hours at work, you pass your peak of efficiency. I function best at my office when I relax in the evenings."

moments far less often than accounts have suggested, for Butch and a constant flow of visitors offered much of the distraction Ike needed. Still, her presence was greatly appreciated; she was also an excellent bridge player and an able horsewoman.

If this was hard for Mamie, her difficulty stemmed from knowing that she was not able to be there and be the one on whom Ike depended. For a woman who admitted to being possessive and who knew her husband's need for such recreational breaks, there is no doubt that she felt twinges of jealousy for *everyone* associated with Ike's "official family." But whatever her feelings, she kept her own counsel. "If [Mamie] ever got depressed," Janie Howard later observed, "she would never let you know it . . . She was always optimistic. Never never did she have any sadness." Milton Eisenhower concurred. Mamie, he said at the time, is a woman of "remarkable self-control, for never by word or sign does she indicate that there is any strain for her in the separation."

It is interesting that Mamie did not confide any concerns about Kay Summersby to her friends or to her parents, to whom in times past she had confided her deepest feelings. This suggests that she was not terribly worried about the veracity of the rumors. Years later Mamie would refute any notion that Ike had had a romance with his wartime driver, saying simply, "I know Ike."

John, who has always thought that too much fuss has been made over this question, once observed to me that we have a tendency to assess relationships of earlier eras in the context of today's behavior. "Dad would have made a lousy philanderer because he was so damned Victorian and moral," he said. "Sure he was attracted to vital women, like Marian Huff in the Philippines and Kay during the war, but these were friendships, not torrid affairs." I am certain Mamie knew this, but the frustration of being unable to share her husband's life and burdens caused some resentment to spill over occasionally in her letters to him. Unable to display her vulnerabilities to the wives of lower-ranking officers and fearful of the untrustworthy intentions of other acquaintances, she sometimes lost her characteristically philosophical bearings in her letters to Ike, but these were by far and away the exception. During the course of the war, Mamie received 319 letters from Ike and fewer than a handful indicate any tension between the two.

An example of this took place in June 1943, when Mamie told Ike about some of the things she'd heard floating around Washington. His reply set forth firmly what he thought about Mamie being sucked into such negative pettiness. He would have none of it. In a letter of June 11, he laid things out.

A very strange coincidence occurred this morning. I had two letters from you (one a V mail written on May 24) and in one of them you mentioned my driver, and a story you'd heard about the former marital difficulties of her fiancé. You said it was a "not pretty" story. Your letter gave me my first intimation that there was any story whatsoever—I didn't know anything about it. In any event whatever guilt attached to him has been paid in full. At the same moment that your letter arrived I received a report that he was killed—by a mine! I knew him quite well and I liked him—he was 32 and was a full colonel of engineers, commanding a regiment. In an active theater of war when death is an every day occurrence and one is constantly receiving notice of the death of valued subordinates—and sometimes close friends—I suppose that senses of values do change—but not as to fundamentals. Decency— generosity—cooperation—assistance in trouble—devotion to duty; these are the things that are of greater value than surface appearances and customs. So what young Arnold did, I do not know. But here we considered him a valuable officer and a fine person. I'm saddened by his death. His name is added to a list that includes Andrews—Dykes—Duncan—Stewart— Vogel and others; all senior officers and good friends of mine that are no more. War is often sad . . .

Your letters often give me some hint of your loneliness, your bewilderment and your worries in carrying on your own part in this emergency. Don't think that I do not understand or that I am not truly sympathetic to the lost feeling you must so often have. Just please remember that no matter how short my notes I love you—I could never be in love with anyone else—and that you fill my thoughts and hopes for the future always. You never seem quite to comprehend how deeply I depend on you and need you. So when you're lonely, try to remember that I'd rather be by your side than anywhere else in the world.

Then only days later, on June 14, 1943, he wrote again:

These days are so crowded I meet myself at the corners—but it's the best way in times of emergency. One shouldn't have too much opportunity to think about tragedies. My worst one—so far—is separation from you. That's something I never accept gracefully in my mind. If you could be here— or wherever I'm serving—this whole thing would be easier for me.

Among the immense burdens Eisenhower carried throughout the war was his determination to be optimistic at all times—to keep his focus on others, as an inspiration to his staff, so that they could in turn do their jobs and serve him better. He was a man of iron discipline, without which he could never have maintained his stoic strength, which made it possible to keep his staff and even his wife going.* Many of his subordinates were struck by his thoughtfulness in their difficult circumstances, and in some cases a kind of hero worship resulted.

Everyone at headquarters, for instance, knew that Kay Summersby had been devastated by the death of her fiancé, Dick Arnold. She kept his picture with her at all times. Anthea Saxe, one of Kay's closest friends (Kay was her son's godmother), said: "After Dick died, Kay went into a deep depression... General Eisenhower did notice the change, and tried to help by keeping her busy so that she would have as little time to brood as possible. He gave her extra work to do, letters to write, filing, other secretarial duties. It is evident that Kay did play a part in his life. She was invaluable to the general, not as a lover, not as an object of romance, but because she was right there... He would use her as a sounding board for ideas, perhaps gripes he might have, to let off steam. He knew that Kay was completely trustworthy."

Mattie Pinette, Ike's confidential secretary, concurred: "[General Eisenhower] felt sorry for her when she lost her fiancé, and he tried to give her something to do. Most drivers, if they were

---

*Sue Sarafian (Jehl) was Kay Summersby's roommate during the war. WACs at headquarters had separate accommodations from the men. Sue Sarafian Jehl refutes the idea that there was ever a romance between Ike and Summersby. Aside from his own relationship with Mamie, she thinks that his iron discipline was also one of the reasons he didn't become romantically involved with any woman while he was overseas.

assigned to a general, [would] just sit there in the room with the other drivers and [they'd] wait, and wait and wait . . . So the general gave her correspondence to handle."

Pearlie Hargrave and Mickey McKeogh emphasized that Eisenhower took a personal interest in the welfare of every man and woman in the office. In fact, when Hargrave and McKeogh decided they wanted to marry, Ike, who highly valued their service, took the unorthodox step of hosting a wedding reception in their honor, though both were enlisted personnel.

Kay Summersby herself later analyzed the situation perhaps better than anyone else. "[Ike's] immediate staff, official family, frankly worshipped 'The Boss.' Most of our admiration stemmed from his natural thoughtfulness. When Mickey was ill, General Eisenhower ordered food sent down from the mess [and] he stopped by the hospital every other day. He did the same for Sue Sarafian, when she had a bad auto accident in Algiers; for Beetle, when he was in the hospital in England; in fact for all of us, at one time or another." Years later, she commented that General Eisenhower "was like an older brother to me, kind, thoughtful, and considerate . . . Yes, I was in love with Eisenhower, and so was everybody else who had anything to do with him."

Despite the controversy of Summersby's presence at high command, Ike wrote Mamie on July 3 indicating his reluctance to reassign her after Arnold's death: "She is a very popular person in the whole headquarters and everyone is trying to be kind. But I suspect she cannot long continue to drive—she is too sunk! Personally I think she should go back to England, but seems to want to keep on working. Her late fiancé has a young brother here in the hospital, seriously sick. She is now devoting herself to helping him."

Mamie could follow all the arguments, but they did not change one inescapable fact: before Ike had gone to Europe she had been part of his world, a helpmate who knew the lay of the land and exactly what was called for; but now Ike was leading another life, in a sphere far outside her experience. Mamie mused that the years they'd been together now seemed to be part of another space and time.

Ike responded with panic to that notion. "One of your recent letters gave me a start," he wrote on July 5, "when, in an early paragraph you referred to me as nothing more than a 'dream out of the past.' But the letter ended up O.K., so I was reassured. My lord, the reason I work so hard is so I can come home to you more quickly."

Perhaps Mamie was feeling restless. She had been cooped up in her tiny, hot, airless apartment at the Wardman for a year, and her friends were beginning to disperse. Kitty Wetzel, a guest who had stayed with her awhile, had to leave Washington to respond to a family emergency. Mamie confessed to being tired of "roommates and servant problems." That summer, as the ambitious amphibious assault on Sicily was under way, she contemplated moving up to the Thayer Hotel at West Point, but then decided against it. Perhaps it was the installation of a room air conditioner that persuaded her to stay in Washington. As a moderation against the ferocious heat and humidity of a Washington summer, the appliance was, in her view, quite literally "a lifesaver."

Ike was trying hard to maintain his sense of humor in spite of the earlier spats he'd had with Mamie by mail. In a loving, lighthearted way, he told her about a dream he had had: "Last night I dreamed you had come over here. We were having a lot of fun fixing things up the way you wanted them—particularly my house at the main headquarters. Then you found out that I was leaving at once for quite a trip; and did you give me Hail Columbia!" There had indeed been talk between them about Mamie joining Ike. Though he was probably technically capable of arranging for Mamie to wait for him in, say, London, Ike was unwilling to do so. He knew that her proximity there would do much to help them both, but "I cannot allow wives of soldiers to come into this theater. Consequently, I couldn't allow you to come, because it would be taking advantage of my own position."

That summer, to the surprise of everyone, General Henri Giraud came to visit Mamie while on a trip to Washington. Beverly Butcher Byron remembered well the excitement: "We could hear the sirens coming up Connecticut Avenue. So I ran down the steps and down a long corridor to the avenue and they said, 'You can't come through here, it's closed off.' " She made it back up the stairs again and reported to Mamie that the general had "a great big red hat on and he is nine feet tall."

The general's visit created a sensation in the building and the neighborhood for some time, and Mamie maintained *her* sense of humor. "You can imagine how my stock went up with the maids & bellboys," she joked, "to say nothing of Francis the doorman."* But Giraud's visit must have also brought home a reality that Mamie had been unwilling to face. She had thought about herself not as a public figure but, rather, as an army wife doing *her* duty. Giraud's visit gave her a kind of flash about how her life might change if her husband continued to execute his wartime responsibilities so successfully, which she says she always *knew* he would.

On July 24, Ike alluded to the heart of her concern about the effect such attention might have. "I was greatly amused by your description of Giraud's call—I can imagine the fanfare. In spite of all the publicity you are quite mistaken in saying that I no longer belong to you and Johnny."

𝒜t the end of the summer, Mamie played hostess to one of John's girlfriends while he was on leave from West Point. Although Mamie would not go out with them publicly, as part of her own personal commitment to stay out of the public eye, she arranged for them to see the town, to enjoy a dinner and theater. That September, John was again able to get away from West Point for a long weekend, surprising his mother with an unexpected knock on the door; his visit brought a shine to her eye. As Beverly Butcher Byron later recalled, when John came to visit, everything in Mamie's world stopped.

During John's visit that fall, Italy capitulated. This milestone only inflamed speculation about who would be appointed to command the long-expected cross-channel Allied invasion. If Ike were given the job, at the end of the war he would be not one more war general but the *supreme commander.* The job was a prize, and many pundits expected that Marshall would be sent to Europe to command Operation Overlord†; others said Ike would be brought back to Washington to succeed him as chief of staff.

Speculation was inevitable about who would command Overlord; so too were the rumblings about the forthcoming presidential race. No one knew whether Roosevelt would run for a fourth term,

---

*Giraud also stopped in to see John at West Point.
†The code name Operation Overlord was secret until the invasion of June 6, 1944.

but there was considerable conjecture that Douglas MacArthur, who was long said to have been interested in political office, might seek the Republican nomination. Indeed, in some popularity polls his name appeared first.

Even before the Italian capitulation in September 1943, Eisenhower had also been mentioned as a potential candidate. To Ike's great discomfort, Senator Arthur Capper from Kansas wrote him directly in Europe and asked him to run. And on September 21, the alumni of Camp Colt issued a statement that while they had "no knowledge or concern" about Ike's "political affiliations or beliefs," they urged his election to the nation's highest office on the basis of his "leadership qualities."

On August 25, Arthur Eisenhower, Ike's older brother, had written to warn him about the increasing frequency with which his name was being mentioned, even quoting a conversation he had had with his old friend Senator Truman. Arthur recommended that Ike nip the speculation in the bud.

Perhaps part of the reason Ike's name was being bandied about was due to the widespread belief that Marshall would be given the command of Overlord and that Ike would either have to take a subordinate position in Europe or return to Washington. Perhaps people imagined he might want to retire and become a political candidate instead of taking another military position. Little did they know the mind of Dwight Eisenhower.

In a reply to his brother, some two months after Arthur had written, Ike made his position plain:

I think you showed more concern in your letter of August 25 as to the danger of my name becoming mixed up in politics than the circumstances actually warrant. It is true that I have seen, here and there, a few careless and ill-considered items in the newspapers; but this happens to any man whose name appears with some frequency in the public print. Certainly, I feel no necessity, as yet, for making any statement whatsoever because to do so would, I think, merely be making myself ridiculous . . .

I live by one doctrine: All of us have now one job to do, which is winning the war. I have been given a responsible post by the President and War Department. For a soldier to turn from his war duty for any reason is to be guilty of treachery to his country and disloyalty to his superiors. The President is my Commander-in-Chief. Nothing could sway me from my purpose of carrying out faithfully his orders in whatever post he may assign me . . .

If the time should ever come when I feel it necessary to make any public statement on these matters, you may be sure that my language will leave no room for misinterpretation.

As the war progressed and Ike's popularity increased with every battlefield success, political speculation rose about Ike's interest in the presidency. The very notion made both Mamie and Ike more and more vulnerable to the promulgation of those wild and baseless rumors about her "alcoholism" and his "infidelity." What else might stop an immensely popular Ike from eventually walking onto the political stage and stealing the show?

Unlike Ike's family, worry about controversy over the presidency never crossed the Douds' minds at all. But Pupah certainly had opinions about Ike's future role in the army. He expressed hope that Ike would *not* be given the command of Overlord or the position of chief of staff. He wrote to Mamie: "He's done a fine job & has gotten his name big in history. I hope that he will soon find a chance for coming home for a little rest & visit. He has earned that."

Interestingly, despite her loneliness and deep desire to have Ike home, where *she* could again be his sounding board and his distraction from work-related worries, Mamie didn't agree with her father. Confidentially, she expressed hope that he would be given Overlord. "Don't believe all this stuff about Ike's coming home as Chief of Staff. Would be a shame to pull him out now—when he's done so well. I think the citizens would fight it because they have such confidence in him."

Mamie was sure that her husband was the man for the job, but she must not have felt that she needed to lobby for him. Just before Thanksgiving that year, Eleanor Roosevelt invited Mamie to the White House for a private informal lunch. Mamie declined with gratitude, fearing that if she stayed in Washington for the lunch, she would not make it to West Point in time for the beginning of John's Thanksgiving break.

With respect to Overlord, Mamie had to admit to herself, perhaps reluctantly, that deep down Ike needed and wanted the challenge, and that the ultimate desk job, chief of staff, would be nearly intolerable for him at this point. He would more likely want to stay in Europe in a lesser command than return to the War Department. "Big things are being decided right now," she wrote her parents.

Ike was uncertain himself about what his future job would be, and he was giving nothing away about his aspirations for future command. "But no matter what does happen—I do hope I can have a visit with you before too long. I know I'm a changed person—no one could be through what I've seen and not be different from what he was at the beginning. But in at least one way I'm certain of my reactions—I love you! I wish I could see you an hour and tell you how much!"

John remembered one of the incidents that made Mamie suspect that Ike would be given command of Overlord. She told him that she saw a newspaper photograph of Ike and thought he "looked like the cat who'd swallowed the canary." She also had her own sources in Washington who helped in deciphering what might be read between the lines. She wrote to her parents on December 15:

> I am pretty certain from gossip etc. Ike is not coming home as Chief of Staff. I knew he didn't want to come and then when he had the opportunity to talk to the President he just talked himself out of coming home. Oh, well, we didn't expect him anyway till after the war . . . Had teletypes from Ike yesterday & to-day. One yesterday wanted to know had I entered a convent as he hadn't had a letter in 21 days.

Someone may also have slipped Mamie some word. In a conspiratorial way, she wrote her parents again, obviously almost unable to contain herself.

> What he is going to do I know is exactly down his alley and he will be pleased. Nothing official has been told me & Ike has said nothing but this is what I've picked up. "Mum" is the word for you all. He might get home for a visit after the 1st of the year but I am not planning on that.

That Thanksgiving, after the Tehran conference that brought together Roosevelt, Churchill, and Stalin, Roosevelt told Eisenhower that he would be the commander of Overlord. Later, Marshall gave Ike a "tattered piece of paper" on which Roosevelt had handwritten the order.

The Christmas Eve announcement of Ike's appointment as supreme commander was made unexpectedly, and Mamie got the news while she was at the Wardman Park. Reporters from all over the city descended on the building for her reaction. Mamie had gotten a call from the management downstairs saying that journalists had overwhelmed the lobby. Unable to think of what to do, she asked them to tell the reporters that she was out. Awaiting her return, reporters camped in the lobby for more than seven hours, leaving only long after most of the residents of the building had gone to bed. Mamie felt sorry for one woman reporter who was still perched near the elevator after midnight. The next morning she was back again early, so Mamie relented and gave her an interview: "There was nothing else to do." John, home for the holiday, looked at the pandemonium around him and joked, "So this is the nice quiet Christmas leave I was going to have."

Within days, Ike set off on an inspection tour that took him from Cairo to Italy and back again. When he returned, just after Christmas, he wrote her:

> I think I've had a good case of homesickness lately. Nothing has been exactly right and everybody about me is having a tough time. I try to hang onto some shreds of a good disposition, but it does get tough at times . . . Well sweet I love you for trying so hard to make my xmas a nice one and you sent me the one thing I really wanted—a good picture of yourself. But Xmas as such always falls flat here—all days seem to be the same. I truly hope next year we'll be together; and I hope further that when we get this war won, our long partings will be at an end. All my love—always.
> Happy New Year!!!
>
> Your Ike

A week later, Mamie opened the service door of her Wardman apartment sometime after midnight, and Ike was there for a long-overdue embrace.

CHAPTER FOURTEEN

UNTIL GOD IS THROUGH WITH HIM

*J*ust before the end of the year, after Ike had been appointed supreme commander, George Marshall ordered Ike back to Washington.

> You will be under terrific strain from now on. I am interested that you are fully prepared to bear strain and I am not interested in the usual rejoinder that you can take it. It is of vast importance that you be fresh mentally and you certainly will not be if you go straight from one great problem to another. Now come on home and see your wife and trust somebody else for twenty minutes in England.

Ike may have had some reservations about making the trip to Washington. He was consumed by what he was doing and feared being pulled in all directions in the United States, by officials who wanted to confer with him and by well-meaning people who wanted to see him. He worried that he would have little time for Mamie—and for their reacquainting themselves after more than a year and a half apart. But Ike took Marshall's advice and suggested to Butcher that he come, too. With Ruth and Beverly across the hall, it would make a fine reunion.

Ike's visit had to be absolutely secret, however, and except for a few handpicked people, even his closest friends were not to know of his presence in the United States. Mamie had been told roughly when he'd arrive, but her bridge group was supposed to meet at her apartment that evening, and she was concerned that if she canceled it her companions would think something was up.

All through the game that evening she worried that Ike and Butch might walk in on the ladies. After her card partners had gone, she hurriedly tidied things up, emptying ashtrays and washing up dishes; both men arrived after midnight.

An amusing anecdote often told in our family relates to Ike's "secret visit" and an incident during his stay at Mamie's Wardman apartment. Ike and Butch had been smuggled up the freight elevator, so their presence in the building remained unknown to the service staff. According to Mamie, on the morning of trash-pickup day Ike got out of bed and, clad in pj's, answered the service-door bell with a bag of refuse in hand. The trashman's face turned gray with surprise when he opened the door. Back into bed, Ike turned to Mamie and said, "Talk yourself out of that one if you can!"

Mamie had never had a man alone with her in her apartment. "I never even went out with Ike's best friends," she said. This may have been why, according to one journalist, "rumors spread among the residents of the Wardman that [Mamie] had an unidentified lover." Because of the nature of Ike's trip, she could never confirm or deny the rumors about a man sleeping over.

During the visit, Ike and Mamie also went secretly by private railcar to see John at West Point. He invited his son to include three of his friends for dinner in the car. During the visit, John noticed, his father had gained weight since he'd last seen him. Otherwise, he "seemed the same, despite his four stars, but he was obviously rather preoccupied, impatient to get on with his new job of planning the invasion. His no-nonsense life of the past eighteen months had sharpened his manner somewhat; Mother at one time chastised him for his abruptness. He growled . . . 'Hell, I'm going back to my theater where I can do what I want.' "

Ike also flew to Kansas for a reunion with his mother and some of his brothers, and Mamie and Ike spent time relaxing in White Sulphur Springs, West Virginia, a brief interlude that gave them badly needed time and privacy. Then, the night before his departure, Ike was asked to the White House to confer with the president. Mrs. Roosevelt stopped in for a chat while he was there. But Mamie was offended that the Roosevelts had not extended the invitation to her as well. Years later the thought still riled her. "I was so provoked to think that Mr. Roosevelt, knowing I hadn't seen this man in so long, would demand that he come to the White

House and spend a whole evening, when I thought that the time belonged to me," Mamie complained. "I thought it was pretty thoughtless... We were young enough so, good heavens, [the time] meant a lot to us."

From Mamie's point of view, Ike's visit home was not exactly an unqualified success. He was "keyed up," easily distracted, and somewhat dismissive. Mamie had always insisted that Ike leave his work at the office, but preparations for D Day were not easy to put aside; he could not thoroughly relax and leave his worries about the war behind. When the dreaded moment came for his departure, according to some accounts, Mamie said very simply that it was too painful to say goodbye and that he should not come home until the war was over. When Ike was back in Europe, he wrote Mamie a loving note about their time together: "I find myself very glad I came home—even though things did seem to be a bit upsetting! I guess it was just because we'd been separated so long, and before we could really get acquainted again, I was on my way."

Ike was sure his reunion with Mamie that January had "paid dividends." A few weeks later, for Valentine's Day, he wrote:

I sent you a short Valentine message this a.m. I do hope it reaches you, it is the only observance of the day I made. I never forget that 28 years ago I brought over the West Point class ring to 1216 McCullough, proud as a peacock!! ... I'm lucky to have had you to see or send a message to every Valentine Day for 28 times. Quite a record in itself even if you were only an ordinary woman. But considering that everyone loves you—most deservedly—I wonder how my luck has held so long. Take care of yourself, my sweet—maybe on next Valentine Day I can crack your ribs instead of hurting your eyes with a scrawl like this. I love you—always.

Soon, Mamie headed off again to San Antonio for a second visit with her sister Mike. She stayed at the Officers' Club for a time, then Pupah and Nana arrived and a family council was held about buying a house for Mike. With four children, Mamie's sister was having a hard time making ends meet, and everyone agreed that their minds would be at rest if she did not have to pay rent until

Gordon, who had been sent overseas, returned. Even Ike wrote a lengthy letter on the subject.

While Mamie was having a rest in San Antonio, far from the concerns of Europe and Washington, the stress of the preinvasion period was bearing down on Ike. "He looks worn and tired," an aide commented, ". . . older now than at any time I have been with him."

In addition to the huge, even overwhelming task confronting the supreme commander, small incidents occurred that gave him no peace and fragmented whatever tranquillity he had left. Ike became furious, for example, when a newspaper reporter somehow managed to acquire some of the letters he had written his aging mother, Ida, and included them in a nationally syndicated article. A deeply private man, Ike felt violated. Mamie noted, "He seemed a little undone" by the whole affair, altogether "lonesome and low like he acted before in other times."

Ike was also under siege from people who wanted his presence at various functions, or a job or a favor, or just a photograph with a signature on it. The relentless demands sparked a sharp letter to his younger brother Earl: "So long as you want my autograph only for young children or for people that are doing their full part in helping win this war, I have no objection to sending a few signatures on to you. I merely don't like to be exploited by people who are doing nothing in this time of trial and struggle." Meanwhile, he was grateful that Mamie was holding her own. "Not long ago," Ike wrote on April 20, 1944, "a friend from the W.D. [War Department] was here—a very senior officer. He spoke to me very feelingly of the perfect way in which you have conducted yourself. You've won the admiration and respect of a lot of people that scarcely know you—but they do know some of the pitfalls you have so successfully dodged."

Despite what people regarded as Mamie's impeccable conduct, Washington gossip added significantly to her stress. After returning to the Wardman Park following her three-month stay in the family fold, Mamie was cast right back in the Washington vortex of anxiety and anticipation. Her own family in San Antonio was not without problems, but at least in Texas there were no political intrigues, no army jealousies, no demands from the press. With the massive buildup of American men and matériel in England, Washington was full of wild rumors about the immoral lifestyle enjoyed by everyone in London. Mamie had no one to talk to openly about this, and she put Ike on the defensive almost the minute she returned home.

He wrote:

May 12, 1944

This morning I received the first letter you wrote to me after returning to Washington. It was most welcome and interesting, although you finished with a dark "such tales as I've heard since returning to Washington." I know that people at home always think of an army in the field as living a life of night clubs, gayety and loose morals. So far as I can see (and admittedly my chances for seeing such things is limited) the American forces here are living cleaner and more nearly normal lives than they did in Louisiana—California—etc, when we were in large encampments. 99% of officers and men are too busy to have any time for anything else. In the largest cities, such as London, there are undoubtedly numbers of officers and men that are living loosely; but it is also true that the pictures painted by the gossips are grossly exaggerated. So far as the group around me is concerned I know that the principal concern is work—and their habits are above reproach.

Although Ike made light of it, he was at least aware of some of what was going on around him. He later complained to John that during the war one of his generals liked to brag about his sexual conquests. Ike had retorted to his old friend, "Don't tell me about your Goddamned escapades." A number of close friends of both Ike and Mamie were also engaged in romantic relationships while abroad, the "closest to home" being Harry Butcher. It was probably suspected, or already known, that Butch had found a Red Cross worker in Algiers with whom he was having an affair.

If it had not been for the gossipy atmosphere in Washington, Mamie would never have needed to be concerned, though. According to Inez Scott, one of the first WACs to join Eisenhower's "family" as a driver, Eisenhower and Bradley were two of the few officers who had "nothing to do with women" while overseas. "I had the highest respect for Ike and Mamie," she said later.

"[Throughout the war] he never forgot he was married." In any event, the tension expressed in the rumors of wild living in London was symptomatic of a greater anxiety associated with the forthcoming invasion. Everyone knew that it would have to come soon if the expeditionary forces were to take advantage of the long stretch of good weather in the summer of 1944.

Mamie herself had already hatched a plan about what she would do when word came that the invasion had started. She and Ruth Butcher were going to "run" to George and Mary Allen's apartment and hide out there. She advised her parents that when they heard the news, if they wanted they should contact her through the Allens, who would be the only people who would know her whereabouts.

As is often the case, the best-laid plans were of no use whatsoever. On June 5, Mamie, Ruth, and Beverly Butcher arrived at the Thayer Hotel at West Point to stay overnight before John's graduation the next day; Nana and Pupah arrived from Denver the same day. After an early evening, Ruth and Mamie, who were sharing a room (to save expenses), retired for the night. Before turning the lights off, they listened to the midnight news and then fell asleep.

The next morning at 7:00 Mamie was awakened by a reporter telephoning.

"What do you think about the invasion?" he asked.

"The invasion?" Mamie wondered aloud, before uttering, "No comment."

If Mamie and Ruth had wanted privacy the day the invasion was launched, they were sadly disappointed. Downstairs that morning, Mamie and John faced a bank of more than forty reporters. Throughout the day they had to be shepherded through the commencement activities in the commanding general's personal car to avoid being overrun by reporters and countless well-wishers. When John finally went up to the podium to accept his diploma, the name Eisenhower elicited a rapturous ovation.

And so it had started: the largest amphibious invasion in world history.

Mamie herself, overwhelmed as everyone was by the news from France, also had to face the fact that my father, too, would be going overseas. On May 21, Ike had written Mamie saying that he hoped she would approve "a plan" he was "cooking up." He was referring to a letter he had written General Marshall, asking permission to allow John to visit him during his three-week postgraduation leave. "I think at times I get a bit homesick," Ike had written Marshall with characteristic understatement, "and the ordinary diversions of the theater and other public places are denied me." He asked for "an opportunity to become acquainted again with my son." Marshall agreed without hesitation, and arrangements were made for John to leave that evening for England on the *Queen Mary*. He spent nearly a month with his father at headquarters in London and traveled with him on many of his trips to the front. Ike was completely absorbed in the progress of the Normandy campaign, but John's presence did much to lift his spirits.

On July 1 John returned to the United States and the beginning of his basic infantry training. Mamie was eager to have him back and to hear news of Ike firsthand, so she and George and Mary Allen excitedly met the plane at the airport. To Mamie's surprise, however, John was not the only one from headquarters to alight from the aircraft. With him were Mattie Pinette, Tex Lee, and Kay Summersby.

During Kay Summersby's stay in the United States, she was received by Mamie and a number of other army wives whose husbands she knew. In her book *Eisenhower Was My Boss*, completed after the war, she described the gathering as "a lovely afternoon," which she "enjoyed thoroughly," calling Mamie "an attractive, petite woman, her bangs the hint to a vivacious, friendly personality." Her second book, however, *Past Forgetting*, gave a rather different account of how she was received. "It was not much fun . . . No other woman was in uniform. And no other woman was being scrutinized as sharply as I was."

Though we have no direct record of how Mamie assessed Kay Summersby or whether or to what extent she regarded her as a threat, Kate Hughes (who told her husband that Kay had come to the United States with papers, asking to become a WAC) had the impression that "she was on the make." Some accounts also say that Mamie was not particularly impressed by Summersby's "presence or sagacity." One thing is certain: Mamie was annoyed that John took Kay under his wing, squiring her up to New York, where he showed her the town. Mamie had been looking forward to being with John before he went off to infantry training, and she was understandably disappointed that Kay was monopolizing his time.

Sometime during that visit, Mamie and John argued about Summersby's stay and what should have been the appropriate way to handle it. John thought that the army ladies should have done more to entertain her; the ladies, steeped in the hierarchy of the army, may have wondered why they needed to do any more than they had for a woman who was merely a chauffeur and secretary at Allied headquarters. There was a well-known social barrier between officers and their wives, on the one hand, and support staff, who were often enlisted personnel, on the other. But Summersby, a civilian at that time, was used to working closely with these women's husbands, and she did not view herself in those terms. Her assertiveness and her expectations were very possibly misinterpreted.

In the final analysis, it is doubtful that Mamie would or could have believed Kay was romantically involved with her husband. The very fact that Ike put Kay in his son's charge would surely suggest the opposite. It is inconceivable that Ike would have sent his "lover" to the United States in the care of his son. He was not the kind of person to put John in such an untenable position vis-à-vis his mother.*

Evidence that Mamie did not believe her husband was romantically attached to Kay Summersby is indicated by the letters she exchanged with Ike just after Summersby's visit. Mamie could be pointedly sharp and direct, and she would have been sure to give him a "Hail Columbia" if she had felt terribly threatened by the unexpected encounter. But the day after Kay and Ike's other staff colleagues returned to London, he thanked her for a note that Tex Lee had hand-carried back to headquarters.

> I wrote you yesterday, but last eve Lee brought me a sweet letter from you . . . so I wanted to drop a note saying how much I loved your letter; incidently you! . . . Capt. Pinette's mother died, and Lee's mother is apparently in very poor health. So it was quite a sad group that came back. God knows we have enough sadness; I lost two very good friends recently.

---

*Just before her death, Summersby confided in writer Bob Considine's wife, who asked Kay forthrightly if she had ever slept with Eisenhower. She replied, "The answer is no. Never . . . If he had asked me, beckoned a finger to me, I would have done anything he asked me to. But he never asked me."

How glad I will be when this is over. In the meantime, one simply doesn't dare to think about sacrifices and losses.

Ike's reason for sending Kay and other members of his staff to the United States was that he wanted them not only to have some leave but to tend to certain pieces of personal business. Summersby had visited Dick Arnold's mother during her visit, and she had looked into securing American citizenship (she was a British subject) and a commission in the WACs; the others had also tended to personal matters, as Ike's letter describes. Still, "Kay was upset about the reception she received in the United States from the wives," Sue Sarafian Jehl later recalled. "That's what she said when she came back from the trip. 'What did you expect?' I told her. 'If I were a wife over there, I might not have given you a welcoming reception either.' We were all very aware of what the rumors had been about the WACs and we hated it."

The tension between the two groups of women was all but inevitable under those difficult circumstances, especially in an era when a woman's future was so inextricably bound up in her husband's prospects and in the success of their marriage.

By summer, with the Normandy landing successfully completed and Allied progress in France continuing, Ike was already talking about getting permission for Mamie to live with him in Europe if he had "to stay in this region for any length of time." But as much as Mamie would have liked to imagine such a possibility, she pinned no hopes on it. She maintained her Washington pattern—working at charitable activities, hosting potluck suppers with her friends, reading mystery novels, keeping up with her voluminous mail, and occasionally traveling. In August she went to Denver to be on hand when Nana and Pupah celebrated their fiftieth wedding anniversary in September. She had a pleasant rest from journalists and well-wishers, until her presence in the city was uncovered. As Ike put it in writing to her parents, at least she had had three weeks of peace and quiet, during which she could live like anyone else. "When I come home," he joked, "I have my own disguise all figured out. I am merely going to buy a wig!"

In early September radio commentators started raising questions about Ike's apparent absence from the public scene, speculating that all was not well. A wish to get Mamie's comment on his disappearance may explain how the press had discovered her in Denver. Indeed, speculation about Ike's safety turned out to be justified. He had been in a small observation plane that had made a forced landing, and he had wrenched his knee again. For a while he had to lie prone or walk with a light cast strapped to his leg, and he hated "being cooped up." Soon, however, he was writing Mamie's parents wryly about the anniversary present he had sent them, which seemed to have brought him badly needed amusement:

> I really got a chuckle out of your problem in dividing the pen and pencil set. Actually, I pictured it up on the desk in the writing room and thought it would be sort of a household addition rather than be divided up. If you each take one item, what are you going to do with the case? Personally, I like the case better than I do either the pen or the pencil . . . My love to you both, and when you get time to write me again I don't care which of you uses the pen or the pencil—either will be satisfactory.
>
> Devotedly
> Ike

Physical ailments were not the only thing plaguing Ike during this difficult period. Field Marshal Bernard Montgomery was using his influence behind the scenes to sow discord over Ike's handling of the fall campaign, pointing out ways in which military expectations had not been met. This came with increasingly strident demands that he, Montgomery, be appointed overall land commander of Allied forces. At the same time, unbeknownst to the Allies, Hitler's troops lay coiled and ready to strike in what came to be known as the Battle of the Bulge.

These accumulated pressures elicited the "testiest" letters Mamie had from Ike during the war. She did not want to worry her parents about her concerns for John and his departure for combat duty, so, unfortunately, she allowed those worries to overcome her good judgment, expressing them instead to a husband who was facing one of the most dire moments of the war. Mamie, the outspoken, willful one whom her father had admonished decades before, came in for a sound rebuke.

Gueux, November 12, 1944

Yesterday I arrived at my advance camp, after quite a tour along the front, and found your letter, written just after Johnny had asked you to come down to see him. I fully understand your distress when contemplating his departure—I feel just as badly. But it always depresses me when you talk about "dirty tricks" I've played and what a beating you've taken apparently because of me. You've always put your own interpretation on every act, look, or word of mine, and when you've made yourself unhappy, that has, in turn, made me the same.

It's true we've now been apart for 2½ years and at a time under conditions that make separations painful and hard to bear. Because you don't have a specific war job that absorbs your time and thoughts I understand also that this distress is harder for you to bear. But you should not forget that I do miss you and love you and that the load of responsibility I carry would be intolerable unless I could have the belief that there is someone who wants me to come home—for good. Don't forget that I take a beating, every day. Entirely aside from my own problems I constantly receive letters from bereaved mothers, sisters and wives, and from others that are begging me to send their men home or, at least outside the battle zone, to a place of comparative safety.

So far as John is concerned, we can do nothing but pray. If I interfered even slightly or indirectly he would be so resentful for the remainder of his life that neither I (nor you if he thought you had anything to do with it) could be comfortable with him. It's all so terrible, so awful, that I constantly wonder how "civilization" can stand war at all. But, God how I do hope and pray that all will be well with him.

Now sweet, don't get me wrong in this letter. I'm not "fussing" at you, But please try to see me in something besides a despicable light and at least let me be *certain* of my welcome home when this mess is finished.

I truly love you and I do know that when you blow off steam you don't really think of me as such a black hearted creature as your language implies. I'd rather you didn't mention any of this again.

Two weeks later, Ike added: "I'm truly sorry if I've let my letters lately reflect any impatience with your messages. I really do know how upset and ill you have been ... Anyway I love you heaps."

Mamie's anxiety about John's safety and about Ike's leg coincided with the fact that SHAEF (Supreme Headquarters, Allied Expeditionary Force) intelligence had picked up reports that the Nazis had organized a small group of English-speaking Germans, dressed them in American uniforms, and assigned them the mission to assassinate Eisenhower. A group of about sixty men were said to have passed through the lines heading for Paris, where they were to meet a contingent of German sympathizers who would furnish them with details about Eisenhower's living arrangements and habitual movements. The band, under the command of Otto Skorzeny, were reported to be "completely ruthless [and] prepared to sacrifice their lives." For security reasons Ike had become a virtual prisoner at Versailles, where SHAEF headquarters were located, and he could no longer make the visits to the front that had afforded him such satisfaction and emotional release.

Mamie was with John at Fort Benning over the Christmas holiday, staying as a guest of Brigadier General William Hobson. Midday on Christmas Eve, while they were gathered at the post commander's residence, Hobson received a call from a newspaper reporter who had found out that Mamie was there and wanted to know if she would respond to reports that her husband had been shot. "No comment on that one," said Hobson, hanging up. The general turned to an aide who was standing beside him: "See to it that Mrs. Eisenhower doesn't listen to the radio while I do some checking."

Mamie wrote Ike about the incident and he responded, "I am distressed that rumors get about that can disturb you so much. It was fine of Bunny Hobson to protect you so well."

This incident was a turning point for Mamie. The futility of living in a state of perpetual anxiety about her husband's safety came sharply into focus, and she knew at that moment that things couldn't go on as they had been.

I worried like all the rest of the wives and stewed and fretted and everything, and finally, I thought, Well this is absolutely ridiculous; there's nothing I can do about it ... I had to build a philosophy, which was that nothing was going to happen to

[Ike] until God was through with what he had put him on this earth to do. Now, I wasn't quite so sure about John, but I thought Ike had a great responsibility and it had come so unexpectedly in lots of ways. He must have chosen this man for something ... [especially given the] many times [Ike] came near death—God did have something else for him to do.

Ike got his fifth star during those tense weeks, and the Allies finally prevailed in the terrible Battle of the Bulge that Christmas and New Year's. With the subsequent breakthrough, Allied forces continued their drive for the heart of Germany.

*M*amie was in Florida when the news came that the Allies had accepted Germany's unconditional surrender. She had gone south for a vacation and not many knew that she was in residence at the Hollywood Beach Hotel, near Fort Lauderdale. When the news of Germany's surrender came across the airwaves, word traveled fast. To her own shock, and that of the hotel management, a crowd of people and reporters spontaneously formed, so overwhelmingly large that police had to be called in to cordon off the area, and only passing the strictest identification procedures allowed one to enter the hotel. Mamie's old friends "Bootsie" and Sam White, who had faithfully attended her after her accident in the mountains of Baguio in the Philippines and who later helped her move from Fort Sam Houston to Washington just after Pearl Harbor, were coincidentally in the area. Though they had difficulty getting their cards presented upstairs, when Mamie heard they were in the building she was thrilled that she would have old friends with whom to share the day of joyful news.

Mamie obviously felt enormous relief at the outcome of events in which her husband had played such a large part; but while the world was celebrating the end of hostilities, nothing about her life was at all settled. She had no illusions about the probability of Ike's permanent return to the States. When it was announced that he would be given the command of the occupation forces in Germany, she wasn't surprised. "It was just what I expected," she wrote her parents, "because there isn't any job in the U.S. for anyone [of] his rank. Till Marshall leaves as Chief of Staff. Which he will not do until V-J Day."

Nevertheless, as mentioned so many times in his letters, Ike was determined to get permission to bring Mamie to Europe after his orders came through, and she was anxious to go. Ike suspected that some overall policy might have to be arranged, but even if it couldn't, he told her, "I'd be willing to risk the cry of 'favoritism' to have you here." Ike asked a number of the other generals how they would feel about bringing their wives to Europe, now that they all had semipermanent or permanent postwar positions. On June 4, 1945, Ike wrote Mamie: "The only other general officer who is most desirous of getting his wife over here is Bradley. Most think the wives would be so uncomfortable and lonely as to be miserable. So far as I'm concerned I'd like to see you try it anyway." On the same day, Ike wrote Marshall asking for permission to bring Mamie to Europe. "I will admit that the last six weeks have been my hardest of the war," he wrote Marshall. "My trouble is that I just plain miss my family." Ike outlined some of Mamie's medical problems and concluded, "I would feel far more comfortable about her if she could be with me." Then he added:

> My real feeling is that most people would understand that after three years of continued separation at my age, and with no opportunity to engage, except on extraordinary occasions, in normal social activities, they would be sympathetic about it. I should very much like to have your frank reaction because while I am perfectly willing to carry on in this assignment as long as the War Department may decide I should do so, I really would like to make it a bit easier on myself from a personal viewpoint.

Marshall, confronted with the necessity of taking a position, deferred the matter to President Truman, who turned down the request. Truman's refusal must have been a blow. Of all the officers with five stars—Marshall, MacArthur, and [Admiral] Arnold—only Eisenhower had spent the three war years without his wife. Even MacArthur, commanding his troops in the Far East, had Jean with him at headquarters—and everyone knew that MacArthur had not asked anyone for permission.

That summer, Ike came to the United States to participate in a number of victory parades, after many such events in Europe. He had given his speech at the Guildhall in London, which set the tone for his tumultuous return to America. As he received the citizenship of the City of London, he declared: "Humility must always be the portion of any man who receives acclaim earned in the blood of his followers and sacrifices of his friends." He had written that speech himself, dictating and revising every word. To his wife he wrote:

I assume that when I get home for a visit I'll have to go through some formalities at various places. (Please say or hint nothing about such a possibility.) The question is whether you'll be killed off, in the hot weather, trotting along with me! It's something we don't have to decide just yet, but it may come up soon. But keep it very secret just now.

Life magazine was at the airport in Washington when Ike arrived from Europe. The caption it published under a photograph of the two Eisenhowers says, "Mrs. Eisenhower greets the general as he steps from his plane at Washington's airport. Photographers missed the long kiss Eisenhower gave his wife. He refused to pose for another."

Ike's schedule during his short stay was grueling, and they had to content themselves with fleeting moments together during an overburdened travel schedule, except for a week together at the Greenbrier in White Sulphur Springs, West Virginia, which he termed "the nicest thing that happened to me during the war."

*V*ictory parades were held in New York, Washington, West Point, Kansas City, and Abilene. New York, a normally sophisticated and, some would say, rather cynical city, hosted one of the biggest parades in history for the returning general. On June 19, the New York *World-Telegram* declared in headlines an inch and a half high, "6,000,000 SALUTE EISENHOWER; The City Roars Out Its Mightiest Welcome." The lead read: "New York and its idolizing millions today showered an epic ovation upon a soldier of epic deed, Gen. of Army Dwight D. Eisenhower." According to the paper, the Big Apple's celebration overshadowed the "riotous receptions he'd received in London, in Paris and in Washington."

It's hard to imagine what Mamie's reaction would have been, beyond amusement, to an associated story at the bottom of the front page headlined: "Shy Mrs. Eisenhower Shares City's Acclaim."

> Mrs. Mamie Eisenhower, a good-natured little housewife from Abilene, Kansas, today shared New York's tumultuous acclaim for the homecoming commander of the Allied Forces. But Gen. Ike's lady was retiringly modest and tried to keep in the background.

Some of Mamie's other friends, however, did not have such joyful reunions with their husbands. All the years of anxious worry and concern had been, for some, unfortunately justified. After the victory parade in Washington, Butch asked Ruth for a divorce so that he could marry the Red Cross worker, Molly Ford, with whom he had been romantically involved. Mamie's "heart bled" for her former flat mate and friend, and Butch's decision to abandon Ruth was one of the factors that led to a parting of the ways between him and Ike. His wartime memoirs made the fissure complete.

Beverly Butcher Byron remembers that Mamie was adamant and outspoken about Butch's decision to pursue this divorce, especially before he and Ruth tried to work things out between them. Years later, even after Ike was elected president, "Mamie did not care to see [Butch and Molly] in the White House—even though Daddy managed part of the California campaign during the election," Beverly recalled. This was not a matter of moral prudery— Mamie's sister had made a similar choice and she had stood with her. It is simply that Mamie remained deeply loyal to her friend Ruth for the rest of her life and hated to see the pain that her friend had been forced to endure.

After Ike's visit to the United States, and his return to Europe, Mamie confessed that she was "back in the dumps." The letdown was great, and Ike's tenure in Europe was still open-ended. Ike sympathized with her mood, "I don't see how you could help it in Washington, from what I was able to see . . . If you'd just once understand how exclusively I love you and long for you then you'd realize how much the week at White Sulphur meant. Please don't forget that I love you only—loyal friends and helpers are not involved in the wonderful feelings I have for you."

Demands that Ike participate in victory parades and ceremonial occasions continued unabated in Europe. Mamie, showing her insecurity and perhaps jealousy, wished that it would all simply be over. Losing her patience, as she could, she confronted Ike about an official trip he took to Ireland, and she was only too aware that Kay Summersby had been born there. In a final spat via transatlantic mail, Ike retorted,

> What could you have meant by my being "highly interested in Ireland" is beyond me. Jimmy, Sgt. Farr and I got there one evening, carried out a schedule for the next 24 hours that would kill a horse . . . I didn't stay in Ireland a second longer than I expected and only ⅓ as long as the dignitaries desired.

With the war over, it was as if all those waiting for the return of their loved ones had developed a collective case of exhaustion, like runners in a marathon who collapse just before the finish line. Mamie was no exception. She was deeply affected by Ruth Butcher's situation, which she found tragic. "Ruth and Bev are leaving Sat. for Miami," Mamie wrote her parents, "where Ruth is going to establish a residence. She only weighs 114 lbs.—poor kid."

Mamie tried to stay busy by joining a Spanish class that was being hosted by Bess Truman at the White House, and the demands placed on her by well-wishers increased significantly. But she was not the only one struggling with the aftermath and letdown of the war's end. Ike himself was in need of family. With the end of the war in Japan, Ike prevailed on John to spend more time with him in Europe. "He realize[s] I am lonely and need him," he explained to Mamie.

Mamie's own low-grade loneliness also persisted. She told her parents that it seemed like "it" would never be over. "I really will never believe Ike is coming home till I see the orders. Seems so long and I've gotten so pessimistic over the C of S job. New York papers this am say they need him in Europe, so that's that."

But Ike would not allow himself to sink into pessimism. He was already thinking about life after his return home, which he knew would bring challenges of another sort. He wrote to Mamie:

> Of course we've changed. How could two people go through what we have, each in his own way . . . and still believe they could be exactly as they were. The rule of nature is constant change. But it seems to me the thing to do is to retain our sense of humor, and try to make an interesting game of getting acquainted again. After all, there is no "problem" separating us—it is merely distance, and that can some day be eliminated.

Three months after V-J Day, that distance was indeed eliminated at long last. In November, Ike was called home for temporary consultations at the War Department; soon thereafter an upper-respiratory infection he developed turned into pneumonia. His recuperation coincided with General Marshall's retirement, and Ike was ordered to take over as chief of staff of the army. Mamie and Ike's long years of separation were over.

The struggle to maintain faith and constancy in the belief that this day would arrive had taxed them both. But the good Lord had been kind, and they were together again. The time and the circumstances that had shaped their worlds for three years had created a gulf that would now have to be bridged. Both of them knew that there would be adjustments ahead; as Mamie later told her friend Perle Mesta, "Neither of us really knew what the other [had been] through."

CHAPTER FIFTEEN

QUARTERS #1

*W*hen Ike became chief of staff of the army and George Marshall went into his long-awaited retirement, a light-hearted moment enlivened a dinner honoring General Marshall. According to *Life* magazine:

> At a Washington banquet for General George Marshall, ex-Ambassador to Japan Joseph C. Grew served as toastmaster [and] said in a loud voice that Marshall wanted nothing more than to retire to Leesburg with Mrs. Eisenhower. While the guests roared, Grew squirmed unhappily and murmured, "My apologies to the general." Mamie piped up, "Which general?"

The story was told and retold many times, especially as America began to evaluate Mamie, who was now a potential First Lady. Her ready wit surprised many, and as her public visibility grew, she had many other occasions on which to display her ability to respond publicly, with forthrightness and humor.

From the moment Ike had stepped off that plane, he was a potential presidential candidate in the eyes of many Americans. But far more important to him than any amount of opportunity and adulation, the end of the war closed a difficult chapter in his relationship with Mamie. Their life together since 1916 had been marked by long separations, loneliness, and tragedy, just as it had been punctuated by periods of great contentment and joy. From 1945 onward, Mamie rarely left Ike's side except for short periods, and this proximity brought a kind of closure to their lives of hardship, just as it gave them peace of mind. Most of the issues in their early relationship had been essentially settled. Mamie would no longer have to summon the courage and pluck to board a ship for faraway posts; no longer would they be separated for months or even years at a time; and with Ike's permanent rank, they would also be afforded a comfortable if not extravagant retirement.

Despite the return to some semblance of normal life, postwar adjustment for the Eisenhowers, as for many people, would prove to be a challenge of another kind. Mamie noticed that Ike had "changed terrifically." He was used to issuing orders to his staff, and the occasional abruptness she had observed during his secret visit in January 1944 now also included impatience with anything that smacked of frivolity or stupidity. The endurance of slaughter and destruction, not to mention the countless life-and-death choices he personally had had to make, had understandably hardened him. He had lost much of the whimsical ease he had shown on their trip through the Alps in the 1920s. He was now more serious and, though not a church-goer, much more spiritually inclined.

Also, Ike now came back to the United States with a retinue. During the war he had become reliant on the services of a valet who catered to his every personal need, and there were other staff members on whom he depended. "Ike's staff tended to freeze Mamie out," my mother recalled. "They managed his time and obligations. Mamie could feel herself being nudged to the periphery, and she had to fight for her place." Things as simple as those cherished moments before the war, when Mamie had risen before dawn to cook his breakfast, were gone forever.

As John also observed, Ike, whose singular welfare had been of crucial importance to everyone during the hostilities, could, after the war, be "almost blind" sometimes in setting his own priorities over those of others. Furthermore, he showed a resolute stubbornness about how Mamie or others regarded a whole host of issues concerning his life during the war years. On the topic of Kay Summersby, for instance, "[Ike] never apologized for her presence on his staff, not one bit. He expected everyone to accept his version of events," my father told me.

But most of all, Ike's intense loneliness during those three years away had made him self-reliant emotionally in a way he had never been before—and that meant he was less dependent on Mamie. But the same could be said of her. No matter how determined Mamie was to jump back into married life, it was not that easy. In

Ike's absence she had become accustomed to making her own living, social, and financial decisions. She would have to relinquish many of her personal ways of doing things to allow Ike to resume his position as head of the household, and for a headstrong woman like Mamie, the difficulty of adjusting to this cannot be underestimated. Despite some spats and what my mother would later observe as a tendency "to talk at cross-purposes," both dominating personalities set about melding themselves into a married couple again, this time more set in their ways and more certain of their views.

Though Ike may have become more self-confident and authoritative, he retained a genuine modesty about himself and his work during the war. He also never lost his demonstrative nature, which, if anything, went in a new and creative direction after he took up oil painting in 1946. A portrait of Mamie was the first of many paintings he undertook, and presents he gave her on her special days were often ones he designed himself.

Ike's letters during the war had powerfully articulated how much he had wanted to come home to Mamie. He knew he never had to question Mamie's loyalty or motives in any of her dealings with him. Unlike virtually everyone else, she had no agenda, ambition, or ulterior motive that disfigured her relationship with him. She had been there for him from the very beginning, and she had shown unshakable faith in his capabilities long before there was an external reason to know that her unwavering belief in him wasn't misplaced. Thirty years of shared marital history now stood them in good stead.

In the coming years, personal disappointments regarding many of Ike's closest wartime colleagues became difficult for both of them. Jealousy, pettiness, and vanity left many generals scrambling to fashion a more flattering or prominent place for themselves in history. Barbs were published; sniping was common. Ike was hurt and bewildered by much of this. Even harder for him to understand were the efforts people made to exploit both the war and their own relationship with him for money and notoriety, especially people who had been members of his "official wartime family," in whom he had invested so much of his goodwill and idealism. My father's childhood friend and the family's lawyer, George "Bo" Horkan, observed, "Ike had been a military man

[who] wasn't fully acclimated to the use that people were going to make of him."

Ike had a genuine disdain for anything that might smack of publicity-seeking. During the last year of the war, for instance, Metro-Goldwyn-Mayer asked for his consent to produce a feature film about his life. Ike toyed with the idea and finally agreed, but stipulated that the war be over first, that neither he nor any other member of the Eisenhower family receive money of any kind from the project, and that this latter condition be made public. He also demanded that MGM assign a significant percentage of the proceeds to an endowment fund at Kansas State University, where his brother Milton was serving as president. Ike's proposal turned a potentially lucrative deal into one so uncommercial that the project was dropped.

From 1945 onward, a growing number of his most trusted aides started writing books about their years in his service, which miffed and often troubled Ike. The first to do so was Harry Butcher, who began before the war was even over. *My Three Years with Eisenhower* was to be based on the diary that Eisenhower had asked Butcher to keep on life at headquarters. (When Mamie heard about the title, she joked that she could write a book called *My Three Years Without Eisenhower*.) Ike had envisioned that the diary would someday be sent to a war college or be used by academic historians, rather like the volume he himself wrote in the 1920s, but Butcher had ideas of his own and took the material instead to Simon and Schuster. He often wrote Ike about the progress of his project, including one in which he boasted that serialization alone from *The Saturday Evening Post* promised to bring as much as $175,000. "Simon and Schuster are convinced this thing will be a best-seller," Butch wrote Ike in early August of 1945. "Jack Goodman startled me with his glowing predictions of world-wide circulation."

A month later Butch enthusiastically declared in a letter to Ike that "Dick Simon, one of the partners [of Simon and Schuster], told me that an infallible rule of merchandizing is to wrap a low-brow article in a high-class package." Ike was more than ambivalent about the project. He didn't begrudge Butch the money, but he did worry about how he would use the highly personal material. He tried to persuade Butch to use the diary only as a way to refresh his memory in recounting his own personal experiences. A direct

238 | *M*RS. IKE

narrative, Ike worried, might somehow be seen as an official or semiofficial view of the war, especially as Butch had sought Eisenhower's public endorsement of the project. His former naval aide's own background was in public relations, not military strategy, and Ike felt that Butch was in no position to provide an adequate analysis of the tactical and strategic considerations that had influenced the development of the war plans. As the project developed, his concern only grew.

Butcher raised Ike's ire even more when it became clear that he was planning to include in the book the eulogy Ike wrote about his father at the time of his death, a notation which Butch had found among Ike's papers. ("I did not know that anyone had ever seen the notes I jotted down at the time of my Dad's death," Ike grimly wrote him.) But by far and away the most serious breaking point on the project came at the end of 1945. On official stationery of the chief of staff of the army, Ike wrote Butch about his concerns regarding Butch's portrayal of some of the most important figures with whom Eisenhower had worked intimately during the war. The first installment appeared in the December 15, 1945, issue of *The Saturday Evening Post*, and after reading the section containing Butcher's account of Ike's impressions of Winston Churchill, Eisenhower implored his former naval aide to review everything else that was about to go into print.

> I hope you will give equal attention to anything involving any other foreign official . . . where the promotion of bad feeling would be to defeat the very purposes that I strove so hard to advance during the war. My feeling is that you were admitted into a circle where every individual had a right to believe that matters discussed were to remain secret.

Ike reminded Butcher that it was he who had brought Butcher into that circle. He had no problem with Butch's project, he reiterated

> [except] where because of the mention of personalities or other equally delicate subjects I or any other participants in the discussion had the right to believe that the matter had died at the instant it was born. There is no possibility of my giving you any line of demarcation, but you know how re-

pugnant it would be to me ever to appear in the position of having violated good faith.

After the *Post* article was published, Ike had the painful experience of receiving Churchill's response to it.

I have skimmed over the Butcher article and I must say I think you have been ill used by your confidential aide . . . Great events and personalities are all made small when passed through the medium of this small mind . . . I am not vexed myself at anything he has said, though, I really do feel so very sorry to have kept you up so late on many occasions. It is a fault I have . . . It is rather late at my age to reform, but I'll try my best.

At the same time, Ike's valet, Mickey McKeogh, who'd been with the Eisenhowers since their posting to Fort Sam Houston at the outbreak of the war, was also busily engaged in a book project. By September 7, only a month after V-J Day, Mickey had already found a ghostwriter and had begun looking for a publisher. The book, which would be titled *General Ike and Sergeant Mickey*, was another personal reminiscence about service to the supreme commander. Ike would have preferred that Mickey not write the story, but he wished him success.

Ike disliked books by his staff members, as much because of the potential for embarrassing flattery as for any loss of privacy. This was an era when self-promotion was still regarded with great disdain, but, most important, Ike had believed in the most idealistic of terms about the great crusade that had been waged against Nazi Germany. In this epic war he had viewed himself simply as a soldier who had done his duty, in the highest sense of the word, and he abhorred the possibility that commercialism might cheapen what they'd been through together. Ike's letters to Mamie made it clear that he had especially admired her avoiding every opportunity to seek publicity for herself or for him. His "official family" also knew those were his views.*

---

*In fact, Sue Sarafian Jehl, who remained with him throughout the chief-of-staff period, told me that General Eisenhower had said to her that he hoped she was not planning to write a book, a desire she has respected to this day.

These considerations must have accounted for his shock and disappointment when Kay Summersby wrote to tell him of a book she had contracted to write, which would eventually be titled *Eisenhower Was My Boss*. "I was somewhat astonished to learn that you were in New York working on a book," he wrote. "I thought that you had gone back to the WACs some months ago and assumed that you were somewhere on a military station." Ike was also surprised and rather offended to be dragged into discussions about the title of her book, which had been tentatively called *Ike's Girl Friday*. Ike wrote: "The suggestion they made seemed to be a bit out of line and I informed them to this effect. You know, of course, I wish you the best of luck in this publishing venture; but since these people asked me for my honest opinion, I had to give it to them."*

Eisenhower's correspondence with Summersby had been cordial, even friendly, until then, but this was a turning point. His concern was not what she would say in her memoir but his disbelief that she had left her hard-sought military position to write a personal account of working with him—and would follow it with an extensive publicity and lecture tour. My father later suggested that Ike also understood that he had "overestimated Kay's loyalty to him."

Ike's doubts about Kay Summersby had not come out of the blue. He had had an increasing number of occasions to question Kay's judgment. John, who had spent considerable time at Allied headquarters after the end of the war, recalls that even before Ike returned home in November, he was already "on to her," conscious that Kay was something of an opportunist. She had relied on her relationship with Eisenhower and high-ranking officials to forgive her occasional lapses, such as the time she had failed to order cars to meet Ike on his return flight to Cannes (to his annoyance). After his reprimand, she had cursed him in front of friends later in the evening after he'd retired to bed. According to my father, she had become rather spoiled by her familiarity with the top brass.

More important, she had become an obvious offender of a practice that Ike detested: using favoritism for one's own personal ad-

---

*Ike would have held Butcher and Summersby, as officers, to a higher standard on such matters than he did noncom McKeogh.

vancement. In 1944 she had asked to be commissioned in the WACs and to obtain American citizenship, a special request that created very difficult problems for the high command. Before agreeing to help her with her oft-repeated request, Ike solicited a memorandum about procedures for a British subject becoming a commissioned officer or an enlisted person in the WACs.

In response, Major General M. G. White, assistant chief of staff, set out the complexities of both getting Summersby a commission in the WACs and securing her American citizenship under current circumstances. When Eisenhower read that to make such an appointment the army would be "giving a non-citizen, not a member of the Corps, treatment that we have steadfastly refused to equally deserving women in the Corps," Ike declined to support Summersby's aspirations. On July 16, 1944, he sent White a message:

> Have read your memorandum to me of July 8 on the subject of WAC Commission and now understand difficulties and possible embarrassments which I formerly did not realize. Please drop the matter. Thank you sincerely for your consideration and trouble. Eisenhower.

Summersby persisted anyway, and got her commission some months later, on October 14, 1944. Contrary to accounts suggesting that Ike secured the commission for her as part of some romantic scheme for them to stay together, it was not Eisenhower who arranged it.* Nor, indeed, had Ike been the one to suggest that Kay serve as his aide. Sue Sarafian Jehl remembers that after Summersby received her commission in the WACs, she asked Sue what insignia she should request. Sue replied that she should ask General Eisenhower for the aide-de-camp position, because it would bring fifteen dollars more per month.

Ike's orders to assume the position of army chief of staff ended Kay's tenure as his personal assistant. She was ineligible for any job at the Pentagon because of her nationality—a bitter blow for her. Although Ike had been deeply grateful for her valued service

---

*Most likely it was President Roosevelt, who admired Kay and had hinted in Algiers that it was something he could arrange for her. (The source for this can be found in both of Summersby's books, and Sue Sarafian Jehl confirmed it to me.)

and personal loyalty during the war, by that time he felt sorry for her, knowing how alone she felt when the "official family" dispersed. Nevertheless, Eisenhower was flabbergasted when he discovered that after all the controversy surrounding her commission, by 1946 she was requesting "separation," or discharge, from the WACs and that instead of resigning her commission in Europe, she wanted to do so in the United States, a procedure requiring special permission, which was extended only in exceptional circumstances. (For foreign officers, any kind of discharge usually had to take place near their homes.)

Then, a year later, Kay asked Stuart Symington, secretary of the air force, to write Eisenhower, as chief of staff of the army, to see about reinstating her in the WACs. "As a general rule WACs are not recalled to active duty," a memorandum said. But before Ike's office could respond, Summersby had changed her mind once more.

In a diary entry Ike made on December 2, 1947, written before Kay Summersby signed up with a publisher to write her memoir, he noted:

Heard today, through a mutual friend, that my wartime secretary (rather personal aide and receptionist) is in dire straits. A clear-cut case of a fine person going to pieces over the death of a loved one, in this instance the man she was all set to marry. Will do what I can to help, but it would seem hopeless . . . I trust she pulls herself together but she is Irish and tragic.

As Summersby made requests for special treatment during the postwar years, Ike's letters to her became progressively more terse. Later, popular mythologists would tantalize millions by suggesting that Eisenhower abandoned Summersby as part of his duty to his wife and the army. But the truth of the matter was that through her own actions, Summersby, like Harry Butcher, had removed herself from Ike's circle of trusted former colleagues.

Ike's new job as chief of staff was "as bad as I always thought it would be," he wrote in his diary. "I'm astounded and appalled at the size and scope of plans the staff sees as necessary to maintain our security position now and in the future. The cost is terrific

... Of course the number-one problem is demobilization, and due to a bundle of misunderstandings I'll have to go before Congress personally and give them the facts of life."

The job brought with it many uncomfortable occasions. *Life* reported that while testifying on Capitol Hill about the draft one day, Ike was overrun by a group of wives who "wanted their husbands home." He "beat a strategic retreat into Representative Andrew May's office, but the women broke through and drove him into a corner. Tight-faced, the general explained patiently that there was little he could do to help. Later he admitted the engagement left him 'emotionally upset.' "

While Ike tackled the unpleasant tasks of demobilization and the development of new security concepts, Mamie settled into life at Quarters #1 at Fort Myer, the chief of staff's residence. As on so many occasions throughout their lives together, Mamie again had the job of moving in, personalizing a government house as quickly as possible, decorating on short notice, and setting up an apparatus for entertaining, now at the very highest levels.

That September, Field Marshal Montgomery arrived in Washington for a visit, with plans to dine as guest of honor at Quarters #1. The day of the dinner, Ike received word that his mother had died in her sleep. She had given no indication of her passing other than making a "faint rustle and a sigh," and her companion, who had been in the room, reported that Ida had died quietly "with almost a smile on her face." In the evening Mamie stood in the receiving line for Montgomery, in place of her husband, who, grief-stricken, remained in their bedroom upstairs.

For both, a rigorous travel schedule was the hallmark of the Quarters #1 years. In early 1946, Ike went to Hawaii, Guam, the Philippines, Japan, Korea, and China. Mamie joined him for some of these trips around the United States and abroad, including one to Latin America, where she and Ike together were decorated by the Brazilian government.

During a trip to Europe Ike and Mamie were met by John, and the three visited many of Ike's wartime colleagues and were invited to be guests of the royal family at Balmoral Castle in Scotland. Mamie must have taken great pleasure in sending her mother a letter from the castle on Balmoral stationery. She reported that they had tea with the king and queen and their two daughters, Elizabeth and Margaret Rose; then at dinner, served promptly at 8:30, Mamie was seated to the right of the king; afterward the guests repaired to the ballroom for Scottish reel dancing, which Mamie joined in. "They could not have been more hospitable or informal," she reported to her mother.

John, by now a company commander in the 16th Infantry, was attached to the Vienna Area Command in the army of occupation in Austria. Life in Austria in the immediate aftermath of the war was grim, and that winter, the worst in many decades, people were dying from starvation. The army worked under very difficult circumstances. Despite this, John managed to keep his perspective.

> Our chain of command was working beautifully last week. My company keeps some stairs clean that a battalion uses, and those stairs are the biggest worry I have. The other day the Colonel went up the stairs and noticed a footprint on the wall, where someone no doubt tied a shoe. He blew his top and got on the Lt Col executive officer, who called me up and got on me, who barreled out in the next room and got on the first sergeant, after having gone down the steps to the scene of the crime to make a complete investigation. The first sergeant sent a messenger into the supply room, where a detail was working. One man was detached from the detail and sent down the steps with a rag, one each, to wipe it off. Twenty minutes later, going down the steps, I was elated to see the footprint gone. Six links of the chain were used to tell one man to wipe off the footprint. I calculate that that cost the government four dollars, and my trouble calculating it cost another fifty cents. If the taxpayers only knew!

John had been dating a number of women whose army fathers were also stationed there. One of them, tall brunette Barbara Thompson, the daughter of Colonel Percy Thompson, caught his eye. She and her family "lived in one of the comfortable houses" in the American sector of Vienna. John and five other officers lived in a bachelor officers' billet in the "quaint" section of Vienna called Grinzing, on the upper floors of a handsome house that belonged to Countess Alice Vediano. Here and at the American residences, they spent many evenings playing bridge, celebrating birthdays, and giving dinner parties for each other. "Other nights," Barbara recalled, "we frequented the 16th Infantry Club on Maria Hilferstrasse and the nightclub at the Bristol Hotel, which was under American control."

The first indication that Ike and Mamie had of John's intention to marry came in a cable he sent in January 1947 which read: "I'M ENGAGED STOP SEND MINIATURE STOP JOHN." Later that month, Ike wrote Pupah about the impending nuptials. "By this time you know that Johnnie is now planning on getting married when he comes home this year, specifically during the month of June. This is a reversal of his original plan, which was to be married in April in Europe, a scheme that had Mamie almost frantic because of her disappointment in missing his wedding."

That May, in anticipation of their marriage, John and Barbara traveled by Liberty ship from Europe to the United States. My mother met her future parents-in-law for the first time at Quarters #1. Barbara, whose father's career had sent him to some of the more remote posts in the United States, was overwhelmed by Quarters #1, set in a park of huge oak and maple trees. "Mrs. Eisenhower's touch was everywhere," she said in describing the fully staffed quarters. Oriental rugs covered the floors, family pictures crowded the grand piano, rich gold damask draperies hung at large windows, filtering the afternoon sun, and fresh flowers were displayed throughout. A long, handsome mahogany table dominated the dining room, and it was set with fine crystal and china. The pleasant sounds of dinner preparation could be heard faintly in the background, and sprinklers on the lawn added a note of stability to the atmosphere of luxury, order, and peace.

"General Eisenhower had come home early to meet us," Barbara remembered. "He was dressed in his immaculate uniform, which was devoid of medals except for the Distinguished Service Medal and the Order of Merit. On his shoulder gleamed the five stars that denoted his rank. He smiled broadly and motioned us to chairs. His good spirits and magnetic personality filled the room. Mrs. Eisenhower, petite and very pretty, was at his side. Her large blue eyes twinkled as she asked us about our trip. She thanked me for postponing the wedding so all the family could be there, and soon we were happily sipping Cokes and chatting like old friends."

Barbara found Mamie gracious and cordial, but she was startled some days later by her directness. Mamie had said that she would like to see some of my mother's New York purchases and anything else from her trousseau, but she chided her for leaving her clothes in disarray in the guest room, noting that she'd been embarrassed that her ladies' maid had had to straighten up. "This was followed by a lecture on the hallmarks of slovenly housewifery. Even more horrifying, she told me that tired bedroom slippers and runover heels were a sure way to lose a husband, whether one realized it or not. I took this to include my well-weathered saddle shoes and tired penny loafers . . . Later I came to realize these lectures were reserved for those she cared about. [But] at the time I felt she considered me a hopeless choice as a future daughter-in-law."

Yet that had not been the case. Mamie told many family members how pleased she was with John's fiancée, and to one acquaintance she recalled, "We were very grateful that John had chosen such a wonderful girl as Barbie, with such a fine family background . . . We had never met the Thompsons . . . but we knew that she had to be a mighty nice girl to come from a good army family."

Despite Mamie's endorsement, it took time for Barbara to gain the confidence she needed to deal not only with her new mother-in-law, who could be painfully forthright, but also with the high-visibility social scene which she had been thrust into. However, Barbara soon discovered that Mamie would come to invest great loyalty and affection in the daughter she never had.

John and Barbara were married on June 10, 1947, at Fort Monroe. It had been a difficult wedding to plan because of the intense social and media interest in it. The question of whom to include on the guest list was a problem Ike and Mamie solved by inviting none of their friends. Mamie and Ike's immediate families were in attendance, though, and the Douds came to Washington a month in advance. Age was beginning to tell on them both. Pupah by now was literally deaf, and at the wedding Nana fell off a low porch and broke her arm, which meant that Mamie, who took her to the hospital, had to miss almost all the reception.

Much as his father had done, John took his bride on a short honeymoon that included a few nights away and then a visit to his many relatives out West.

．　　．　　．

*B*arbie and John's wedding came in the midst of one of the transitional periods in Mamie's and Ike's lives. Retirement loomed on the horizon. The question was, What would Ike do next?

"The commercial offers I could decline out of hand," Ike recalled many years later. "I did not think it fitting for me, a man who had been honored by his government with military responsibilities, to profit financially for no other reason other than that my name was widely known. Offers from the educational field were something else. I looked at those long and hard."

Ike eventually accepted the offer from the trustees of Columbia University to become its president. But he was only too aware that there was another option—the possibility of running for president. By 1948 polls of both Democrats and Republicans placed Eisenhower as their first choice for the White House. Truman was even said to have sent an emissary to offer Ike the top spot on the ticket, keeping the vice-presidential spot for himself.

One account suggests the following scenario: "Coyly [Mamie] approach[ed] Ike with the growing speculation. 'You could probably be president if you wanted to.' He tersely responded, 'I don't.' "

Under continued pressure throughout 1947 and early 1948, Ike finally went public, making available a letter he had sent to Leonard Finder, publisher of the *Manchester Evening Leader*, who'd offered him a committed slate of New Hampshire delegates. Eisenhower wrote of his wariness about a military man seeking the presidency, and concluded, "I am not available and could not accept nomination to a high political office."

He later recalled, "Naturally there were journalists who believed I was a candidate for public office. All journalists know that political life can be rugged, yet each assumed, automatically, that every man who has the chance wants to get into political life and that anyone who denies such ambition is a liar." Speculation only increased when Ike formally stepped down as chief of staff of the army.

On February 7, 1948, after more than thirty-three years in the service of his country, Dwight Eisenhower retired from active military duty. Before walking across the hall to the noontime swearing-in ceremony of Omar Bradley, he dictated a brief final message "To the American Soldier." He spoke of his years of service and the pride and sense of accomplishment he had felt in his career. He ended by saying: "I cannot let this day pass without telling fighting men—those who have left the ranks and those of you who still wear the uniform—that my fondest boast shall always be: I was their fellow-soldier."

In Secretary of the Army Kenneth Royall's office Ike administered the oath of office to Omar Bradley. Then President Truman pinned an oak-leaf cluster on Ike, his third Distinguished Service Medal. In the emotion of the moment, Truman almost forgot to give Ike a silver cigarette case he had brought as a gift. The ceremony lasted no more than five minutes.

It had been previously arranged that Mamie and Ike would stay at Quarters #1 until going to Columbia in May. In the intervening months—Ike's accumulated leave—he wrote his wartime memoirs, *Crusade in Europe*, dictating five thousand words a day and keeping two secretaries and a researcher busy full-time. While Ike worked away furiously on his book, Mamie was engrossed in preparation for their departure from army life to Columbia, a change which entailed a complicated three-way move. She would be sending their personal effects to New York; most of their furniture would join everything else they already had in storage; and a few items were to go to John and Barbara in Highland Falls, New York, where my father was a West Point instructor.

Mamie chose the New York interior designer Elisabeth Draper to decorate the president's house at Columbia, and while Ike worked on his memoirs, she pored over countless books of wallpaper and fabric samples. By May, Quarters #1 was filled with packing boxes. With the help of her devoted staff—Rosie Woods, her personal maid; Sergeant Leonard Dry and Sergeant John Moaney, who'd been with Ike during the war; and Delores, the cook and Sergeant Moaney's wife—the Eisenhowers left Washington and began a new, now civilian, life in New York City. Before their departure, however, the army offered a last farewell.

One might have thought that there would have been a sizable military parade for the general who had commanded the successful Allied forces in Europe, but Ike had sent out the word to "play it down." He and Mamie wanted to slip away without fuss. Mamie recalled that they rose early the last morning and breakfasted with

General Frank Caffey and his wife, Louise, with whom they were staying at Fort Myer. The day was cloudy, and there was a chill in the air. As the time drew near for them to take their leave, Mamie stood just inside the door and Rosie checked to make sure her stocking seams were straight, taking a clothes brush to make sure that the impression Mrs. Eisenhower conveyed would be perfect.

Ike, clad in battle jacket, stepped from the quarters, as an army band sounded a salute and a small detachment of troops snapped to attention. A soldier stepped forward and presented Mamie with a large bouquet of yellow roses.

Old friends and acquaintances had lined the wide veranda and spread out across the sweeping lawn. Mamie and Ike said goodbye and waved to these friends and well-wishers who'd come to send them off. People lined the route all the way to the gates of Fort Myer.

After they left the post, Mamie and Ike transferred to their own car, which they had only just purchased for civilian life—a nine-passenger Chrysler Imperial, more than enough to accommodate the Eisenhowers and Sergeant Dry, who stayed on as their chauffeur. After they settled back into the plush seats and the car sped away, a silence descended over the two of them. They were both consumed by nostalgic thoughts about their more than thirty years of army life. Perhaps there was also a tinge of sadness that it was all finally over. Mamie recalled later that suddenly Ike turned to her. "Leaning over, he said, with his terrific grin . . . 'Mamie, do you realize that after thirty-three years in the army we are riding away in our only asset?' "

"Well," she said, "that broke the ice and we both had to laugh."

CHAPTER SIXTEEN

ON THE ROAD AGAIN

*M*amie once said: "I am an army wife . . . the other things were interims." The "other things" were, of course, wife of the president of Columbia University and, later, First Lady of the United States. She thoroughly enjoyed their years at Columbia and revered and respected all that the White House represented—"I never drove up to the south portico without a lump coming to my throat," she recalled in 1974. But Quarters #1 had been the pinnacle of all she and Ike had worked for.

Ike's position as president of Columbia was a departure from all the other responsibilities he had undertaken in the past, and he looked forward to the challenge. Moreover, for the first time in their lives, they would have no financial worries: Ike would receive both army retirement pay and a Columbia salary; also *Crusade in Europe* would hit the best-seller list.

Before taking up his duties at Columbia on June 7, 1948, Ike set out the terms of his agreement: "The Trustees understood thoroughly two considerations I've laid down. I must convince myself, within a year, that I can be of real service. [And] I must have more recreation time than my average of the past twenty-five years. If either of these two conditions is not met, I'll quit." Ike meant what he said: he had lived a life of killing stress, especially over the last decade. In the eight years between 1938 and 1946, he had had no more than five days of real vacation. With those conditions agreed to, Ike was looking forward to Columbia even though his appointment to the university had met with controversy, most notably from some on the faculty who were disappointed that a long-standing academic had not been given the position.

On October 12, 1948, Eisenhower was officially inaugurated president of Columbia University. More than 19,000 spectators showed up that day, including the presidents of two hundred U.S. colleges and universities and thirty-five foreign educational institutions, as well as delegates from 150 more. It was a regal occasion with enough pomp and circumstance to rival any ceremony Ike had ever attended, even in connection with the war. Just weeks after Ike's investiture, Harry Truman stunned the country—indeed, the world—with his upset victory over Republican candidate Thomas Dewey.

Ike had refused to throw his hat into the presidential ring that year, but his presence at Columbia only enhanced his attractiveness to many of his supporters for the next race, in four years. This pressure would increase, as he came into contact with people entirely new to him—industrialists, newspaper publishers, and philanthropists.

In spite of renewed political speculation, Ike settled into his new job and new life at one of the oldest and most distinguished universities in the country. Columbia was a major institution, with 27,000 students, 8,200 faculty members, and a 3,000-member maintenance staff. Within six months, Ike had concluded, "Columbia is the place I THINK I can do the most good for all—even if that amount is rather pitiful."

Meanwhile, Mamie's life at Columbia seemed serenely similar to her responsibilities at Quarters #1. After renovating and decorating the four-story neo-Georgian mansion, she took responsibility, as in times past, for Ike's official, and their own unofficial, entertaining, seeing that Ike got the relaxation he needed. The president's residence at 60 Morningside Drive, perched on the edge of Morningside Park and overlooking Harlem, became one of Mamie's favorite dwellings. It was beautifully laid out for entertaining, and, with some modifications on the third floor for family living, it could be homey too.

Their first year, life at Columbia fell into a pleasant, if hectic, pattern. They entertained frequently and attended small dinner parties in the homes of moguls such as Tom Watson of IBM and Henry Ford. Those evenings were more in the way of official business than simple pleasure; part of Ike's job was to work with the Columbia trustees and scour the country for potential donors.

As in the past, Mamie did some volunteer work. Her favorite project was one she undertook with David Rockefeller at the Manhattan Mission, where they raised money for a recreation center for underprivileged children to use after school. She also attended and presided over official university functions. Like her predecessor, Mrs. Nicholas Murray Butler, she too gave teas for faculty wives or for large donors, but there were complaints among the faculty wives that she never did enough. Some of them thought Mamie was aloof, and speculated that she kept her distance because she was "intimidated" by them. But they clearly did not know Mamie Eisenhower. If she seemed to be of another world, she was—and unapologetically so. She and the faculty wives had little in common except as figures within a hierarchical structure. Mamie likened what she saw of the academic community to the world of an army post. At the highest echelons "you did the same type of entertaining, only on a larger scale," she once said. "The deans and the professors and so forth . . . were in a class by themselves, just like captains or majors or colonels in the army."

Not surprisingly, it was still within army circles that Mamie found her greatest friendship and companionship. In their unofficial hours, Ike and Mamie liked to entertain old army friends, who enjoyed and appreciated the intimate hospitality at 60 Morningside. General Alfred Gruenther, one of Ike's closest wartime friends, expressed his delight about one gathering.

Mamie my love,
You are the most wonderful hostess in the world. I still marvel at the smooth way your household ran with that horde of Mongolians eating every three hours and generally messing up the house. Through it all, you never allowed even one frown to develop on your pretty face. In other words, sweet Mamie, I think you're tops. Why you even made us believe that you were sad to see us go.

Ike had brought a number of his military colleagues with him to his new assignment, including Robert Shultz and Craig Cannon, who were assigned to him in his capacity as a retired five-star general. General Howard Snyder, the Eisenhowers' personal physician, was also part of their permanent entourage.

For the wives of the men who worked for her husband, Mamie was counselor, mother-protector, and mentor. My mother recalled, "Their roles appeared to be as ladies-in-waiting, but because of the personality of my mother-in-law, they willingly performed small duties with love and affection." Mamie also had a broader group of friends in New York, some of whom had lived in Washington with her during the war. One such person was Perle Mesta, who taught Mamie how to play a new game called canasta. During the afternoon card parties, canasta and its refinement, bolivia, soon replaced mah-jongg as Mamie's favorite games. Mamie was very much like Ike when it came to playing cards: she took her canasta and bolivia every bit as seriously as he did bridge—so seriously, in fact, that they could not play together, lest they quarrel.

"To me, canasta seemed like a game of luck," Barbara observed, "but played at that level, it was one of skill." Even though the women played for small change, Mamie kept meticulous records of her winnings and losses, and she was usually in the black. Nevertheless, she kept a special wallet into which she put her winnings, as a reserve for "financing the game."

*I*ke's wartime stature and the unsolicited speculation about his possible presidential aspirations kept him and Mamie both in the public eye. Ike received as many as two hundred requests a day for appearances, and Mamie, less known by the press and public, was also exposed to a heightened level of scrutiny. Not long after arriving at Columbia, she received a number of letters, some of which were anonymous, about her hair. In one, she was urged strenuously to cut her bangs and change her style to something "more becoming." The writer confessed that she did not want to sign her name, because she was a faculty wife and would undoubtedly come into contact with Mamie, and then she enclosed a list of good New York hairdressers.

"Mamie was completely unswayed and unshaken by the controversy," my mother has recalled. "Later it extended to newspapers and magazines. 'I like my bangs and I don't intend to change them for anyone' was her attitude and comment to me."*

---

*Later, in Paris, Mamie decided to wear the bangs slightly differently, curling

During the 1952 presidential campaign, headquarters received so many letters about Mamie's hair that they had a special form letter to answer them. But Mamie refused to change her style; she was not there to be made over.

On the rare occasions when Mamie and Ike went out in public in New York, they were often mobbed by well-wishers. Once, at the opening of *South Pacific*, they were so overwhelmed that after the show the management was forced to darken the houselights and lead them out the back door, but the crowd awaiting them outside frightened Mamie even more. She recalled that the enthusiastic throng drove her back into the theater.

For Mamie the greatest joy of being at Columbia—aside from a highly competent housekeeper who helped her run the mansion like clockwork—was that she was in close proximity to my parents. My father had taken a graduate degree at Columbia and then gone back to teach at West Point, a relatively short drive up the Hudson. With my brother David's birth on March 31, 1948 (while Ike was still chief of staff), Mamie had become a grandmother, a new role she relished. She was elated when, fourteen months later, my sister Barbara Anne made her entry into the world.

Ike and Mamie were at a luncheon at Mrs. Cornelius Vanderbilt's home in New York when they were given the message that the baby's birth was imminent; they left and drove immediately to West Point. My mother recalls their arriving just as she was being wheeled out of the delivery room. "I saw Johnnie, Dad, and Mamie through the mists of the anesthesia and waved. When they were informed that the baby was a girl, Dad and Johnnie voiced their disappointment loudly. Mamie whirled on them and said, 'Ike and John, quit talking that way, why God will strike you dead! The baby is healthy and beautiful. Shame on you!'" Barbara figured John and Ike had probably had a football team in mind and a baby girl "had not been part of the plan," but in typical Mamie style she had spoken up loudly for the female gender.

Mamie enjoyed going up to Highland Falls to visit the young Eisenhower family for the afternoon, and my mother always ap-

---

them so they'd stay higher on her forehead. Nana had seen a picture in the newspaper and had written to ask what had happened to her hair. Mamie responded, "Nobody has made me change my bangs. I like them curled."

preciated these visits, though she regarded them with at least some trepidation. When Mamie came she always brought Rosie, her personal maid, and Sergeant Dry would drive them up. Mrs. Caroline Lent, the house manager at 60 Morningside, would call when they left to give Barbara their estimated time of arrival. When the limousine rolled up in front of their small West Point quarters, Mamie would alight, come in, remove her gloves, and deposit all the presents she invariably brought near the front door. After hugging and kissing everyone, she would call Dry in and ask him to get his tool kit.

"She could spot a needed repair from a mile away," my mother recalled. "I always wished that just once I could get everything in the house perfect so we could really have a visit instead of this comic-opera routine. It became a challenge, and whenever I got the word Mamie was on her way, I knew I had two hours. I would work extra hard to have everything in order, but my idea of perfection was far short of hers, and it was years before she could sit and sip a Coke and not be moved to take action on some obvious chore that needed doing."

Mamie thought she was being helpful. She was the first to recognize that her daughter-in-law, now the mother of two children, should have assistance with her housekeeping and mothering chores. She wrote Nana, estimating the young family's expenses, and then said, "... the kids are broke, bless their hearts. [But] they try so hard and are so cheerful ... John looks better than I've ever seen him—Barbara never complains, but I know she is tired and uncomfortable ..." One day not long after, Barbara opened the mail and to her utter surprise found a handsome check from Mamie—money intended to pay for a maid. Obviously recognizing the lifesaver Pupah's checks had been to her, Mamie wanted to be sure that her daughter-in-law would have the same help.

*I*ke enjoyed his job as president of Columbia, but he was under immense pressure from both the academic community and President Truman, who relied heavily on him in the discussions then going on about how to unify the armed services. Ike served in an advisory capacity at the Department of Defense, and his duties in Washington took him away from Columbia a good deal, much to the unhappiness of some on the Columbia campus.

On July 21, 1949, the Senate voted to ratify the North Atlantic Treaty Organization, and two days later President Truman requested an appropriation of $1.5 billion to underwrite the first year of expenses for NATO. There were opponents to the measure and to the funding, but the voices raised against NATO were all but quelled when, that September, the Soviet Union exploded its first atomic device. Less than a year later, the Korean War broke out.

Ike was granted an indefinite leave from Columbia when President Truman recalled him into military service. He had genuinely enjoyed his tenure at Columbia and had managed his role with some success. Critics never much mentioned it, but he had brought international attention to the university and managed to raise nearly $500,000 for Columbia, "from men who had to be told where Columbia was located." But service to the president of the United States would always come first.

The call came one evening as Ike and Mamie were riding by train to Denver, where they would be spending Christmas with Nana and Pupah. It was snowing heavily that night when the train stopped at a station en route. Eisenhower was asked to leave his car to take a call. As Ike stood in a freight house at a lonely station in Heidelberg, Ohio, the president requested that he assume command of NATO.

After Christmas, Ike, accompanied by Mamie, spoke to reporters before his departure for Europe. When *Newsweek* asked Mamie about the assignment, she sounded a philosophical note. " 'Naturally there will be tears,' she said, speaking as an Army wife of 34 years experience. 'We're all human. But it's something we have to do if we're going to have a country. Something we have to do for our children and grandchildren, so we might as well do it with all our hearts and souls.' "

But after they left Denver and the reality of Ike's new assignment sunk in, Mamie wrote her mother: "I am really in a dream. It doesn't seem possible I am going again to a new place to live. It seems so crazy at our age that we can't seem to settle down." Her mother knew that Mamie cherished the role of grandmother. "Mamie will go all to pieces when she leaves the children. She is too attached to them if that is possible," Nana wrote Pupah.

The move to Europe also meant that Mamie and Ike would have to defer the renovation of the farm they had bought in Gettysburg, Pennsylvania. After an extensive search of Connecticut, the Hudson Valley, and the Virginia hunt country, both had been attracted to the area for nostalgic reasons, and during the war Mamie had toured the Gettysburg battlefield and had become entranced with the "romance of the place."

Gettysburg was also near Washington, and their friends George and Mary Allen had a country retreat nearby. The property they found was a pre–Civil War farm that had served as a dressing station for Confederate forces during the Battle of Gettysburg. To the east was pastureland, to the west a panoramic view of the distant mountains. Mamie was enchanted with the location, the quaint old farmhouse, and the huge ash trees that stood majestically near it. "[The farm] had three of the most wonderful trees in front and a great pine kitchen with a rocking chair and geraniums in the window. Being a city girl, this all appealed to me," Mamie recalled. "I just loved that place."

The house needed a complete overhaul, but Mamie was excited by the prospect of overseeing it. The whole idea of owning a house, for the first time in their marriage, far outweighed whatever work would be required to make it habitable. Little did they know at the time that everything but part of an old staircase and the remains of an old Dutch oven would have to be rebuilt.

Ike confirmed that the acquisition of the farm in 1950 was "a reflection of our confidence that the balance of my working years would be spent at Columbia, followed by retirement at Gettysburg." But now, with his new assignment overseas, such plans had to be scrubbed or deferred. In early 1951, Ike left for Europe on a preliminary six-capital tour, trying to win support for NATO. On his return he addressed Congress, on February 2. While he was gone, Mamie faced the bewildering task of trying to figure out what to take with them on their new assignment.

Within a few weeks, Ike and Mamie sailed for Europe aboard the *Queen Elizabeth* for what appeared to be an indefinite period of time. There was much work for both of them to do. NATO was in its infancy and the new commander would have to exert considerable energy to establish it firmly. Mamie had to worry about where they would live, as no official residence had yet been found, though she was given the choice of a number of villas. After some controversy, she selected the Villa Saint-Pierre, ten miles west of Paris, a lovely residence that had been used by Napoléon III and later occupied by Louis Pasteur. Mamie remembered,

"They showed these different places to Ike, then they showed them to me, and I chose this one at Marnes-la-Coquette. Ike started to laugh and said, 'I told them this was the *last* place you would choose ... '" Mamie had selected Villa Saint-Pierre because the estate had "beautiful grounds and great possibilities, which I could see, having had to fix a lot of houses all over the world."

My mother remembers that it was "the most livable and least elaborate of all the villas Mamie had to choose from." The white fourteen-room mansion with Tuscan columns looked (in the words of *Better Homes and Gardens*) "curiously like the White House," though it boasted a small pond that was well stocked with fish. Later Mamie and Ike put in a vegetable garden, which included family specialties like corn.

Mamie and Ike lived in a six-room suite at the Trianon Palace Hotel while they waited for workmen to finish a badly needed modernization of the villa's kitchen and bathrooms. When they finally did move in, Mamie had the pick of any antique furniture she wanted from French government warehouses; the French, in their enthusiasm to provide properly for the NATO commander and his wife, assigned as many as eight decorators to the project, each with a different idea of how the villa should look. Mamie was sent crates full of antiques for her approval, and she slowly put together a showcase that boasted a dining room that could seat forty. She favored a traditional interpretation for the house, utilizing such priceless pieces as an ancient French tapestry for the dining room and Napoléon's bed from Fontainebleau for one of the guest rooms.

There was only one room about which Mamie's mind was resolutely decided—their bedroom. She had painted all their bedrooms the same color scheme for decades, wherever they lived, and she now insisted on her keynote hues, which she kept on a color board she carried from home to home: light moss-green walls with gladioli-pink curtains and bedspread and chairs in flowered chintz. Maintaining these colors in their bedroom throughout the years had given them both a sense of stability and a sense of place, an illusion that they had essentially been more settled than they ever really were.

.   .   .

*M*ore than once Mamie must have reflected on how different life was now compared with what it had been during their earlier tour in France. Both periods coincided with the aftermath of great wars, but the times were vastly different in 1950–52 from what they had been in the 1920s, when she and Ike had been so carefree. Mamie was now a public figure who had to entertain at the highest official levels, and she was expected to run one of the great houses of France. She was far more confident now, with a firm sense of her own likes and dislikes, yet she remained unimpressed by the social hierarchy she moved in, reporting to her parents, "the place teems with Princesses and Countesses but [I] can never remember their names."

Similarly, Mamie was unwilling to succumb to the pressure exerted by the world of high fashion. Although she purchased a few dresses and gowns in Paris, she had bought most of her wardrobe in New York before their departure. When she was criticized in the French press for preferring to wear American clothes, she tossed it off, saying, "Imagine paying $800 or $900 for a dress! I'm perfectly happy with those little $17.95 numbers I order from New York newspaper ads."

*T*hat summer, while Mamie and Ike were still at the Trianon Palace Hotel, my father got leave and my parents, along with David and Anne, accompanied Nana to France for a summer visit. Pupah had been ill off and on for some time, but Nana thought he was well enough so that she could go to France for a "change of scenery" after her own bout with pneumonia.

Excitement about the trip was high. John wrote his parents, "David is now so exultant over having finished his last [immunization shots for the trip] . . . he is making quite a spectacle of himself. He stops bums on the street and confronts them with "IhadmyshotandnowiamgettingonabiiiairplaneandgoingtoParistoseeMimiIkeRosieMoaneyand—Sergeant Dry!!!' We hear this routing some umpteen-dozen times a day."

Sergeant Dry picked up the group at Orly Field and drove them thirty miles through the rural countryside to Versailles. My mother remembers their shock at passing through many small villages that had "Ike Go Home" painted on the sides of buildings. Indeed, there had been riots in Paris, staged by the French Communists protesting the advent of NATO. Because of a constant threat of terrorists, both Mamie and Ike had round-the-clock security. Mamie's bodyguard was a man named "Monsieur" Meechem, an Irish cop who was assigned to the Central Intelligence Division of the U.S. Army. John recalls, "he used to terrify Mother by looking up the flue of the fireplace for bombs. When the folks would go to restaurants he would hover, hand menacingly in pocket, glaring at the other customers while they ate." When Mamie, Nana, and Barbara went into Paris to shop, Meechem was ever present, always on the lookout for would-be assassins.

One day, Mamie told my mother that she wanted to take her into the city to buy her an evening dress. "Every woman needs a Paris gown," she said with conviction. Nana, Barbara, and Mamie climbed into Mamie's limousine, bound for the rue Saint-Honoré. "When it came to shopping, Mamie, who had limited stamina, could outlast us all," my mother remembered. The three of them visited all the couture houses: Schiaparelli, Lanvin, Dior, and many more. Barbara fell in love with a multilayered gown of light melon-colored organdy by Jacques Griffe. She was astonished that the dress cost five hundred dollars, but Mamie did not blink—she knew all too well the importance of both saving your pennies and spending them. Visiting the design houses was an awe-inspiring experience for my mother, and later when she had to go back alone for the fittings, Mamie arranged for Perle Mesta, ambassador to Luxembourg, to accompany her. "You will never be able to stand up to the *vendeuse* [saleswoman]," Mamie had said. My mother later reflected, "Neither Mamie nor I ever dreamed that she was buying me the dress I would wear to Ike's Inaugural Ball."

That evening when the women returned to the hotel, Ike was waiting for them as they stepped off the elevator. He put his arms around Mamie and Nana and broke the news: word had just arrived from Denver of Pupah's death. Plans were hastily made for Mamie, Nana, John, and Rosie to leave for Denver and the funeral. With time being short, they would have to fly. "[Pupah] has been in precarious health for many years," Ike wrote in his diary in those days. "When I met him in 1915 he had blood pressure of 240 and weighed that many pounds, but as always in such cases the finality of death came as a shock."

Pupah had apparently died at his writing table—possibly using either the pen or the pencil from the set Ike had given him and

Nana for their fiftieth wedding anniversary. Mike had managed to get to Denver before his death, but that did little to comfort Nana, who was consumed with grief and guilt. Pupah had warned her that he would die when she was on one of her trips away, and now he had "made good on his promise."

After a two-day trip, the tired group from Europe arrived at 750 Lafayette Street. Pupah's casket was already set on a bier next to the fireplace in the music room. Consistent with family tradition, the family members rotated shifts of staying up with the body. Nana and Mamie, exhausted from their journey, left that task to John and his cousins.

Nana was filled with remorse, and it lasted till the day she died. She could not forgive herself for being away in her husband's last hours. Nana may have felt a sense of unfinished business, and grieved that she had lost the chance to talk to Pupah about their lives together in a way that might have brought closure to the private problems they had shielded so successfully from the rest of the family. Her feeling of desolation persisted. Nine months after Pupah was buried with "our darlings" at Fairmount Cemetery, Mamie was prompted to write: "Mother, now you stop saying you're no good anymore. We've still got lots to do and you are going to be on your feet shouting. This you *must* do for me."

*I*nevitably Mamie spent considerable time sorting out the chaotic family situation in the aftermath of Pupah's death. But she also traveled around Europe with Ike, who was received by royal families and the political leadership of each country. Mamie became friendly with many of Europe's monarchs, but she was fondest of the British royal family, most especially Queen Elizabeth (now the queen mother) and the dowager Queen Mary. In addition, she and Ike entertained visitors from the United States, many of whom wanted to discuss the political situation back home. Nearly all of them carried one message: "The country needs you, Ike; come back and run for president."

CHAPTER SEVENTEEN

A CALL TO DUTY

*S*ince 1948, and the Republicans' astounding defeat, it was widely believed that the GOP had finally understood that it could no longer "afford to take another licking." As the *Washington Post* and *Times-Herald* publisher Eugene Meyer wrote to a friend, "Ike is the sure thing, and I do not think Truman would run against him."

Simultaneous with the discussion about a Republican bid by Eisenhower, a Draft Eisenhower movement developed within the Democratic party. It was under discussion by everybody but Eisenhower himself. In an article in *Life*, Sydney Olson described a series of secret meetings held among the Democratic kingmakers, who acknowledged the need for a change. "Top-ranking Democrats all over the U.S. are going to raise funds and try to pack their state delegates solidly with Draft Eisenhower men. The plan is to continue this . . . right up to the convention. The strategists even hope to persuade President Truman himself to place Eisenhower's name in nomination as he sings his own swan song . . . Harry Truman must see the light . . . But he will be presented with only two alternatives: *retire with honor or be retired by force*."

With pressure growing for an Eisenhower candidacy, Harry Truman sent a handwritten letter to Paris, unbeknownst to everyone but Ike, and possibly Mamie:

December 18, 1951

Dear Ike:
The columnists, the slick magazines and all the political peo-

ple who like to speculate are saying many things about what is to happen in 1952.

As I told you in 1948 and at our luncheon in 1951, do what you think best for the country. My own position is in the balance. If I do what I want to do, I'll go back to Missouri and *maybe* run for the Senate. If you decide to finish the European job (and I don't know who else can) I must keep the isolationists out of the White House. I wish you would let me know what you intend to do. It will be between us and no one else.

I have the utmost confidence in your judgement and your patriotism.

My best to you and Mrs. Ike for a happy holiday season.

Most sincerely,
Harry Truman

As the calendar moved into the holiday season, Mamie wrote her mother that they were overwhelmed by two thousand Christmas cards. For the holiday celebrations, they were joined by a number of friends, including a wartime associate, Sir James ("Jimmy") Gault, and his wife, Peggy, Bill Robinson, of *The New York Herald Tribune*, and Cliff Roberts, a New York financier. Mamie recounted a raucous scene before Christmas dinner, when Bill and Cliff arrived in their dinner jackets sporting "I Like Ike" ties and "I Like Ike" caps and buttons. When Ike saw them, Mamie confided, "his face turned red, but we had to laugh because they looked so silly . . . Poor Ike, they really put it on him and he doesn't know which way to turn."

A minor distraction in the midst of all this was news of my birth on December 31, 1951. When my grandparents heard of it, on January 2, Granddad painted, on the message side of a French postcard that said "*Heureux Anniversaire*" (Happy Birthday), a small landscape of the view from their villa. Then he sent the exquisite little "daub" to the United States to welcome me into the world. Mamie was so captivated by the small painting that she asked Ike to paint a larger version for her, which he did. It hung over the headboard of their bed at the White House and later at Gettysburg.

The far-off event of my birth may have made the idea of returning to the States even more attractive for Mamie, but such considerations were purely political and firmly in Ike's domain. On January 14, 1952, John wrote his father with his own assessment of the situation.

> My feeling is that this country is absolutely desperate for leadership—not dictatorship—but leadership. There is the gloomy possibility of the American people's having to choose in November between Taft and Truman or his successor. I think they deserve a better break. I, therefore, recognizing the back-room nature of conventions feel you should perhaps unbend a little and give Lodge & Co. a little more help than you are doing. I think you can make your stand on what issues they wish known and get yourself squared away with the public without stooping to real campaigning, attacking opponents etc. In other words it seems to me that you can give them a little help. Your word for this is probably "conniving." Maybe so. But it is a worthy cause.
>
> In many ways I feel remarkably aloof about it all. If I could think of a couple of men the country could choose between that I felt were really good choices, I would probably wish you bad political luck on the basis of the complications that your election would cause for us all. But I don't see any alternatives on the scene and feel that it is almost a duty for you to give your supporters at least the minimum help they feel is necessary to get you nominated. Of course, not knowing their demands [I] might be asking a little too much on this.

Ike's brother Milton was in complete agreement. If the presidential nominees were to be Truman and Taft, then, he thought, "any personal sacrifice on the part of any honest American citizen is wholly justified."

Ike had always said that if he had a clear call from the American people, he'd give consideration to running for president. And it was that very message that Jacqueline Cochran, a noted aviator and businesswoman, was determined to give him when she arrived in Paris in mid-February. Cochran was an admirer with a simple philosophy about an Eisenhower presidency. "No one can be that popular and not be president," she said.

Cochran's assignment was to bring a film of a huge Eisenhower for President rally that she and other Eisenhower backers, such as John Hay Whitney and Tex McCrary, had staged at Madison Square Garden on February 11, immediately after a prizefight one evening around midnight. Trainloads of people had come from as far away as Texas in behalf of the Ike for President movement. The Garden had a capacity of 16,000 people, and, according to Cochran, as many as 25,000 to 50,000 people had jammed inside the building. When the announcer asked all those who had not been invited to leave, Cochran recalled, "they refused to. 'We want Ike too,' they shouted." The boisterous crowd had stayed until 5:00 a.m. and "nearly every policeman and fire fighter were called out to handle the crowd . . . This is no exaggeration."

The Madison Square Garden rally had been a resounding success. The problem was, as Cochran remembered, "[we had] a fighting campaign without a candidate." The organizers of the event asked her to fly to Paris with the film and show it to the General and Mrs. Eisenhower. In the steady stream of Democrats and Republicans who came to Paris to encourage Ike to run, no presentation had a bigger effect on Ike, she recalled. The general was "flabbergasted by what he saw."

After watching it, Ike, visibly shaken, asked her if she would like a drink. When it was served, she raised her glass and said, " 'To the President of the United States.' I was the first person to ever say this to him and he burst into tears . . . he was so overwhelmed and overcome with the public demonstration."

During the long discussion that ensued, Ike spoke emotionally about his parents and the future of the country, and Mamie "sat there and never said one word, [but] she never missed a word that was said. I've never seen a human being so interested." According to Cochran, Ike asked her to keep the whole meeting confidential but told her she could go back and tell Bill Robinson, "I'm going to run."

Ike wrote in his diary that "viewing [the film] finally developed into a real emotional experience for Mamie and me. I've not been so upset in years." The next day, he wrote a letter to an old friend from Abilene, Swede Hazlett. The film, he told Hazlett, "brought home to me for the first time something of the depth of the longing in America today for a change . . . I can't tell you what an emotional upset it is for one to realize suddenly that he himself may become the symbol of that longing and hope."

Mamie, too, had been stunned by what she saw. As she put it years later, the film had "frightened" her. Seeing it made her realize that "things had gone farther in the U.S." than they could have known, living in Europe.

Despite the pressure on Ike to declare himself a candidate, the work at NATO continued. During this period, as in earlier times, Mamie and Ike took many opportunities to travel. Perhaps one of their most difficult trips occurred not long after Jacqueline Cochran's visit, when they were summoned to London for the funeral of King George VI. "We were saddened by the King's death," Ike later wrote, "we liked him very much; and he was a real force for decency and good."

Directly after the funeral, Mamie and Ike were off to Ankara and Istanbul. Although Mamie always professed to hate flying, even *she* was intrigued by their flight over the Bosporus. "It was really thrilling," she wrote Nana. "Afterward we flew to Salonika for a huge military review, also to a Greek church on the highest peak where Paul used to preach. Then to Athens. What a day . . ." That night they dined with King Paul and Queen Frederika, as well as the ex-queen Helen of Romania, and then journeyed on to Naples. "Well, your child made the grade," Mamie added.

But many of Mamie's challenges were still to come, and this kind of official visit, so much a part of her responsibilities while in Europe, was the prelude to becoming First Lady, a life that would soon be hers for eight years.

In March 1952 Ike won the New Hampshire primary with an impressive 50 percent of the vote, which gave him all fourteen of the state's delegates. He was "very moved" and "deeply touched" by the results, Ike told reporters in France, even though he had written to a group of Republican lawmakers a week earlier saying there was no impending return in his "immediate future." Then, in Minnesota a week later, Ike received 108,692 write-in votes, even though his name was not on the ballot, while favorite son Harold Stassen, whose name was on the ballot, got 129,076. The "miracle of Minnesota" was too strong a showing of support to ignore. On March 20, in Rocquencourt, Eisenhower announced he would leave for the United States to run for the presidency. Nine days later, Truman, whom Estes Kefauver had defeated in the New Hampshire primary, unexpectedly proclaimed at a Jefferson-Jackson Day dinner that he would not seek reelection.

Throughout these trying months, Ike had undoubtedly talked with Mamie about the prospects for a presidential run, but she maintained her characteristic unwillingness to intervene in his decision-making process. Perhaps no clear signal from Mamie heightened the ambivalence from which he still seemed to suffer. Even though he'd made the announcement, had this really been a "clear call to duty"? One historian summarized Ike's dilemma: "World War II had brought [him] a world following. He wished to ensure that it was used in a great cause and not hijacked by self-seeking politicians." In sharp disagreement with both the Truman budget deficit of $14 billion submitted earlier in the year and Taft's commitment to bring the troops home from Europe, Ike could never "avoid the burden of worry over the country's future course," as Bill Robinson observed. "[And] there would be fewer frustrations for the leader than there would be for the commentator," he had said to Ike.

Nevertheless, the prospect brought with it more than a little dread. Already, while in Paris, Ike had become embroiled in a political controversy over Texas claims to disputed tidelands set out specifically in a U.S.–Texas treaty. Ike supported Texas on the basis that the treaty had settled the matter. When warned about the negative response his position would have in the Northeast, Ike replied sharply, "I am compelled to remark that I believe what I believe," adding that he would not tailor his "opinions and convictions to the one single measure of net vote appeal."

The presidential election promised more such controversy, and attacks from the Taft people had already begun, prompting Ike to write Cliff Roberts on May 19, just before their departure, "I really dread—for the first time in my life—the prospect of coming back to my own country."

Mamie, too, felt much of the pressure, but she was nostalgic about leaving France. It had been an exciting time for her. She had visited some of the most beautiful and exotic places in Europe, and she had also finally ironed out all the details concerned with running the *petit château*. Now she would have to send all their possessions home (by ship and not by air). "I'm in a mental tizzy with all the packing and planning," she wrote her mother, adding wistfully, "Never did this house or grounds look more beautiful."

In Mamie's last letter to her mother from Villa Saint-Pierre, Marnes-la-Coquette, she described the glorious farewell ceremony at Les Invalides, where Napoléon is buried and where Ike was decorated with France's highest military honor, the Médaille Militaire—which was pinned on his uniform by Premier Antoine Pinay. Twenty-three years before, she and Ike had brought John and his friend Bo to Les Invalides as sightseers. "Yesterday at Les Invalides was so beautiful and touching," Mamie wrote Nana. "How I wish one of my family could have seen it all. Such a terrific honor—such a perfect day."

Mamie's own role did not go unacknowledged before she left France. When Ike received the Grand Cross of the Order of Malta, Mamie was awarded the Cross of Merit for her "unselfish service to mankind." She told a reporter later, "It was more wonderful than anything I expected or deserved; I came away from France with a new strength of purpose."

Still, there were daunting challenges ahead—the uncertainty of civilian life, the demands of a political campaign. "Boy, how I dread all the hoopla we will need to go thru," she confided to her mother.

With Ike's agreement to run for the presidency, he and Mamie would now be wrenched once more from the relatively protected environment of the army. Even in its most difficult moments, army life could not compare with the complexity, dynamism, and ugliness that were part and parcel of American political life.

The Republican primary season was bitter, and the most vicious partisans in the whole process were the right-wing Taftites—a group that "failed to yield easily." They "regarded Ike as an alien interloper, an emissary from an 'un-American Paris–London–New York dominated axis.'" One leading New York intellectual even acknowledged that a group of men in the Republican party would "rather wreck the party than lose control."

During the primary campaign in New Hampshire, for example, a cropped photograph was circulated that showed General Eisenhower with Marshal Georgy Zhukov; its caption read: "Zhukov,

Communist general, decorates drinking partner Eisenhower, at Frankfurt, Germany." Other rumors said that Ike was a Jew, a Soviet agent, or that he had been "baptized by the Pope." Some even said that he might have some "mysterious disease that made his election too risky." Many of the crazy accusations emanated from Wichita, Kansas, and the poison pen of one Joseph P. Kamp, and in a number of states rumors that this pamphleteer started found their way into the Taft campaign's advertisements.

In no time at all, Ike's political adversaries also dredged up old rumors about him and Kay Summersby. Others gossiped about Mamie having a drinking problem. Though Mamie brushed the stories off as "campaign talk," she was conscious of them, especially those related to her supposed alcoholism. Once during the campaign, while she was drinking a glass of water, she noticed that a photographer was lifting his camera to take a shot. Knowing full well what would be made of the picture, she asked the cameraman to destroy the film, and he did. "All those stories [about Mamie's alcoholism] . . . were pure politics," Kate Hughes later recounted with disgust, remembering when the rumor of Mamie's alcoholism had "started in earnest."

It had been a large gathering at one of the embassies in Washington. Ike said to Mamie's dinner partner, "Please take Mamie by the arm, she's unsteady on her feet." From that, Mrs. Hughes said, the rumor was spread all over Washington that Mamie had been "tight" and had to be taken in to dinner:

> One of the women who was there at the time came up to me to ask about Mamie. "Well," I said, "yes, she's unsteady on her feet because she has that inner ear problem." . . . But [those who spread the gossip] were bound and determined that Taft should have [the nomination] . . . They couldn't do anything to Ike, he was too much of a hero, so they took it out on Mamie, and from then on they hammered her . . . They were so hell-bent on destroying her and destroying Ike through her that they made up all these stories.

In 1955 the Democrats raised the topic again, by speculating on Mamie's health—and the probability that the "personal situation in the Eisenhower household" would preclude Ike's running for a second term. The implication enraged Ike and prompted him to exclaim: "Boy, politics is really a lousy business. This is about as low as it can come."

Nevertheless, Mamie was then, as later, philosophical about such lies. At the end of her life, she was pressed on nationwide television to answer these allegations of alcoholism. She told Barbara Walters, "It never bothered me if people thought that. I lived with myself, I know it wasn't so. And my friends knew I was not [an alcoholic]." She recounted a story about her Irish maid of sixteen years. One time in Newport, Rosie's friends teased her by saying, "Well, I hear your Madam is a great drinker." Mamie related, "Rosie rose up in her elegant splendor and she said, 'I want to assure you that she does not; otherwise I would not be with her.' That solved that in a hurry."

Yet Mamie was not completely thick-skinned during the campaign. She could rise above the attacks against her, but according to her brother-in-law Milton Eisenhower, what really upset her was the ludicrous accusation that Ike was anti-Semitic. "That really shocked her, a thing so completely untrue," Milton said.

Baseless rumors aside, Ike won the nomination at the convention that summer in Chicago—though it seemed at times to be touch and go. Neither he nor Mamie could have missed the irony of Robert Taft's expectation that General Douglas MacArthur would be his running mate and that they would make "quite a team." On the eve of the convention, Taft was within seventy-five votes of clinching the nomination; one poll predicted he could claim 530 delegates to Eisenhower's 427. But Henry Cabot Lodge, Ike's convention manager, cleverly proposed and won passage of a "Fair Play Amendment" that made it possible to seat Eisenhower delegates who had previously been excluded by convention rules. It was enough to secure the nomination for Eisenhower on the first ballot.

Even amid these most public days, private matters were on Mamie's mind. A war in Korea had been raging since the North Koreans stormed the 38th parallel in an unprovoked attack on the South two years earlier. Since that fateful day of June 25, 1950, nearly 21,000 men had lost their lives, 91,000 more had been wounded, and 13,000 were missing. John, serving in the 15th Infantry—indeed, in the same battalion that his father had commanded as a lieutenant colonel twelve years before—received orders to go to the front.

Before leaving Chicago, Ike and Mamie had to say goodbye to John. His appointment had created concern in many circles, raising fears that he might be captured, a possibility that could compromise his father's presidential candidacy. But Ike, sensitive to his son's career aspirations, supported his desire to go into combat. However, John later recalled that in the private moments they had before his departure, "Dad gave me the admonition, Never get captured. [If] I ever found myself surrounded by Chinese or North Koreans, I had every intention of keeping my promise and using my .45 pistol, taking, I hope[d], some of them with me."

Mindful of the seriousness of the family situation and the danger in which John would soon find himself, Mamie said:

Ike and I said good-bye to Johnnie surrounded by dozens of reporters and cameramen. It was just as much of a strain on [Ike] as it was on me—maybe more so; he knew the awfulness of war. All the three of us could do was stand and stare until it was time for me to kiss Johnnie. Anything we might have said would have been news, the reporters all had their notebooks open. Even after Johnnie boarded the plane and Ike and I choked back our feelings while waiting for the take-off, flash bulbs went off. I don't blame the photographers or reporters, they had jobs to do; it was just that we would have liked to keep our private grief to ourselves.

Mamie would soon find other threats to the way of life they had established for themselves. As the campaign started, Mamie realized that she would have to struggle to keep from being pushed away from her husband by well-meaning, if overly assertive, campaign aides. During the first campaign stop in Philadelphia, Ike's campaign manager, Governor Sherman Adams of New Hampshire, made it plain that he would take the hotel suite next to the candidate's so that they could confer at any hour of the day or night, while the candidate's wife was relegated to another floor. Mamie nixed that idea when she "uncompromisingly ensconced" herself in the connecting suite.

The campaign would entail an extensive tour. The nineteen-car

Pullman that served as Eisenhower's campaign train and a propeller plane would make it possible to cover 51,276 miles, visiting forty-five states and 232 towns. It did not take Ike's campaign aides long to discover that Mamie was a valuable asset. Because Ike's opponent, Governor Adlai Stevenson, was a divorced man who had not remarried, Eisenhower's campaign could capitalize on Mamie's appeal to women. "She is a better campaigner than I am," Ike said.

And indeed, Mamie had a real rapport with the crowds and was a good sport with the news media. On one early-morning campaign stop, reporters discovered, she appeared in a bathrobe at the back of the train with Ike: they got her to restage the appearance so it could be photographed. Giving up to ten interviews a day, Mamie sounded more like a woman of common sense than a politician's wife, an image that had great appeal. Once she was asked if, as an army wife, she would worry about her son going to Korea. "That's a strange question to ask a mother," she responded. "Soldier's wife or not, I'm still very much a mother." And when Hedda Hopper grilled her about her bangs, asking her if she thought every American woman should wear her hair Mamie-style, she replied: "Certainly not."

Wherever Mamie was interviewed, or when she met people on the campaign trail, she never failed to use her firsthand local knowledge of the region; and as an army wife, she'd lived in many of them. As had been her habit for years, she also carried on her extensive correspondence with the American public right from the campaign train. She personally dictated more than seventy-five letters a day, replying to at least some of the thousands that poured in—all of which would eventually be acknowledged. And for each, Mamie had a special touch. In September, after the campaign train had left Indiana, for instance, she wrote to Ruby Norman Lucier, one of Ike's old girlfriends from Abilene, to thank her for her support.

"Aboard Eisenhower Campaign Special"

Dear Ruby,
What a delightful surprise to meet my husband's old girl friend! but I do think our meeting was ever so much more pleasant than the movies have led us to expect from this clas-

sic situation. I am so glad you were able to board the train . . .
it was wonderful meeting you, one of our very strong supporters. The spirit and enthusiasm of our welcome in Indiana
make me more confident that we shall win through to victory
in November. I hope that we can get together again for a more
leisurely chat. It was grand seeing you.*

The campaign was exhausting, but Mamie held up extraordi-
narily well: "To look at those faces just did something to me,"
she said later. "I'd be so tired and so worn out, and you'd look at
those hopeful faces and it would give you new impetus to go on."
Mamie was aware of the immensely positive contribution she
was making to the campaign, a contribution recognized in two
campaign songs, "Mamie" and "I Want Mamie," the first such
tunes to be written for a candidate's wife.† During the race, she
also helped Ike to refine his message in ways that would work
with audiences. Once, when he read her part of a speech he was
about to give, she advised him to drop some of the statistics and
talk directly to his audience. On another occasion, she was much
blunter: "Ike," she said, "that doesn't sound like you . . . You can't
say that, it's not in character."
Typical of Mamie, she brought to her political work her own
brand of stubborn independence—a freewheeling approach that
may have annoyed some of her husband's aides. For instance, once
when they were campaigning in Denver, Mamie told her mother's
African-American cook, Jerusha, that she would be happy to speak
to her Black Republican Club; she did so without clearing the
scheduling with any of the campaign managers, and remained un-
repentant when fury erupted among the more exclusive white
clubs that had been turned down for appearances. The Republican
stalwart Harold Stassen recalled that by the end of the campaign,
Mamie confessed that she had liked it and "would miss the great
camaraderie of 'all our gang' at the finish. She marveled at her own
transformation in just four months from a person who never once
did a single thing or uttered a word with the slightest political

*Throughout his career all the way into the presidency, Mamie and Ike kept in
touch with many of Ike's childhood friends. When Ruby Norman Lucier died in
1955, Mamie and Ike sent flowers and a long letter of condolence.
†In the 1956 campaign, "Sweetheart of the GOP" was composed for her.

meaning into a 'campaigner' who felt as strongly about the need for her husband to win the election as did he and all those around him."

Mamie's "connection" with crowds all over the country became legendary, immortalized by the slogan, "I Like Ike, But I LOVE MAMIE." One journalist described her rapport: "Between the instant when the crowd first sees Mrs. Eisenhower and the instant of explosion there is a brilliant flash of communication, an exchange of emotion between the woman on this platform and the people below ... This feeling, however illogical, is an extremely important political fact, no one can say precisely how important, but the *New York Times* top political reporter, James ('Scotty') Reston, having watched her in action for some time, made a reasoned estimate a fortnight ago. 'Mamie,' he wrote, 'must be worth at least 50 electoral votes.' "

That November Ike and Mamie waited for the election results at the Commodore Hotel in New York. The landslide victory was sweet: Ike carried thirty-nine states; and 55.1 percent of the voters had cast their ballots for him.

On Inauguration Day, that cold, windswept January 20, 1953, Ike was only too ready to acknowledge publicly the vital role that Mamie had played during the campaign. After Chief Justice Frederick Vinson finished administering the oath of office, for the first time in the history of the nation the new president spontaneously turned to his First Lady and kissed her for all to see, on this, the most widely covered event that had ever been broadcast on television.*

The president of the United States broke precedent again by starting his inaugural address with a prayer he had written himself. For a Kansas farm boy raised with deep spiritual beliefs—ones forged anew amid the slaughter and destruction of war—it was natural that he should assume the world's most powerful position by beseeching the Almighty for help.

---

*It was also traditional for the new president to ride back to the White House with his vice president; Ike abandoned the practice to ride back with Mamie.

CHAPTER EIGHTEEN

A NEIGHBOR IN THE WHITE HOUSE

*A*lthough there may still be some debate in the historical community, I know from my own personal sense of my grandfather that there can be no doubt that the motivating factor in his decision to run for the presidency *twice* was his profound sense of duty. The Republican party had been out of power for twenty years, and many were convinced—especially in the light of corruption in Washington—that returning the Republicans to the White House would strengthen the two-party system so essential for the future of democracy in America. This was a critical factor in his decision; for neither of my grandparents needed the White House for reasons of status or for fulfillment of ambition. Every dream they might ever have had, even those beyond their most improbable expectations, had been theirs already in the postwar years, both in Europe and at home. Indeed, had they returned to Columbia after the NATO years rather than running for the presidency, they would have regained the privacy they had both cherished so much—rather than see it painfully exploited in the coming years.

So for Ike and Mamie, the White House was the final destination of duty. And for Mamie it was a place she would use to touch people's lives.

Army life proved to be outstanding preparation for being First Lady. Many of the tricks Mamie had used to ease their earlier moves from one place to another worked well under these new circumstances. As with every other home she had settled in, she made it her first act in the White House to secure their bedroom as the bulwark of family stability. When she was shown the layout of the second-floor family accommodations, she was horrified that the last few occupants had arranged things so that the president's wife's bedroom was a small room off a larger one that had been used as a sitting room. She declared that the inhospitable small space would now be used as a dressing room, and she and Ike would share the larger one next to it. According to J. B. West, deputy chief usher, who would later fill the top job, "There would be no separate bedrooms for the Eisenhowers." When a full-size double bed was finally put in place, he remembered, Mamie signaled her satisfaction by declaring, "I've had the first good night's sleep I've had since we've been in the White House. Our new bed finally got here, and now I can reach over and pat Ike on his old bald head anytime I want to!"

For Mamie, the White House years were contented ones. She enjoyed having Ike so near: "I have my man right where I want him," she'd often quip. Their eight years in the Executive Mansion were the longest period they had ever spent in one place.

"As a couple," West remembered, "the Eisenhowers were openly affectionate . . . he always knew the right sentimental touch, the proper number of carnations to send . . . It was perfectly natural for President Eisenhower to reach over and put his arm around Mrs. Ike as he called her. Having shared their home with staff for many of their married years, they didn't seem to mind if we observed them holding hands or exchanging a goodbye kiss. They simply ignored us." At Easter that first year, Ike sent Mamie a huge bouquet of flowers and wrote on the card, "To remind you that 37 years ago we went to church—you in violets and roses— me in a blue uniform. Always your lover. Ike."

Mamie had very clear ideas about what her role as First Lady should be. The "people of the United States didn't elect me, they elected Ike," she said firmly. But she took on the job of managing a domestic staff of eighty and running the 132-room Executive Mansion with the same sure hand she had used to run Quarters #1 and the Villa Saint-Pierre. West recalled, "She needed no period of adjustment to learn White House routines, no slow introduction to her role as First Lady . . . For Mamie Eisenhower the White House was a snap."

"As wife of an army officer," he went on, "she understood the hierarchy of a large establishment, the division of responsibilities, and how to direct a staff. She knew exactly what she wanted every moment, and exactly how it should be done. And she could give orders, staccato-crisp, detailed and final, as if it were she who had been a five-star general. She established her White House command immediately."

If Mamie was the family's domestic five-star general, then her command headquarters, where she met with members of her staff, was the bedroom she shared with Ike. Persistent circulatory trouble made her feet and ankles swell, and her inner-ear disorder could often catch her unawares; so she'd sit in bed wearing a bedjacket, with a writing tray over her lap, to go over business of the day with her administrative staff: at first, Chief Usher Howell Crim, and, later, J. B. West; Mabel Walker, the White House housekeeper; and Mary Jane McCafree, her personal secretary. She adopted this unorthodox approach as a way to conserve her energy and to stay off her feet.

In addition to overseeing social and household matters, Mamie managed both the White House entertainment budget and their own personal accounts. All of the staff were acutely aware of Mamie's frugality; she had "infinite ways" of cutting corners. "Every morning, she perused the newspapers, looking for bargains in foods and household items," West remembered. "Shopping by telephone from those newspapers, she always called the head of the department store, who must certainly have been startled to take an order from the First Lady of the land."

In all issues related to the management of the Executive Mansion, there was a clear dividing line between Mamie's work and Ike's, a division of labor similar to that which they had developed during their army years. Mamie insisted on being consulted on all proposed activities to be scheduled in the mansion itself, reserving the right to veto conflicting events. She also insisted on approving all menus, even for Ike's stag luncheons and dinners. Conversely, in the eight years the Eisenhowers lived in the White House, she went to the Oval Office only four times, and each time, she said, by invitation.

It soon became known that there was tension between Ike's secretary, Ann Whitman, and Mamie. My father recalls that Mrs. Whitman was a "dragon secretary" who could be very "possessive" with information. "Mother liked to think that she ran the home. But Ann would plead exigency to avoid telling Mamie what was going on . . . She did nothing to spare Mother's feelings."

As he'd done during the war, Ike was not about to make personnel changes to please his wife. According to John, "he was dependent on his staff" and he regarded its business as pertaining to the West Wing only; Mamie would simply have to bite her tongue—however begrudgingly at times—and adjust. While she managed an uneasy peace and developed a functional working relationship with Mrs. Whitman, Mamie was never fully comfortable or happy with the staff interference that had become part of the Eisenhowers' lives after World War II.

Mamie was studiously careful about keeping the personal and the White House accounts separate—training she'd learned in the army. "Don't run it on the Eagle" was her battle cry, my mother remembers. The White House was not an institution to be exploited. When her friends came by in the afternoons to play canasta or bolivia, there would be no White House cars to ferry them there. They'd have to find their own way, usually by taxi. Even Nana, who lived off and on in the White House during her widowhood, was expected to bring and use her own Chrysler limousine rather than a car from the government pool.

Nana spent a great deal of time with Ike and Mamie at the White House, and though she had her own room, she did not move in entirely. She still maintained her home at 750 Lafayette Street in Denver, which was sometimes used as the summer White House. It's hard to imagine a summer White House today that would necessitate the president of the United States sharing a bathroom with at least one other woman who wasn't his wife, but both my grandparents were fond of visiting Denver, where they had many friends and where Ike could slip into the mountains for hunting or fishing outings. Mamie and Ike also frequented the Augusta National Golf Course in Georgia, where "Mamie's Cabin" boasted more space.

Pupah's death only underscored the responsibility Mamie felt for her mother, but still they acted more like friends than mother and daughter. Kate Hughes had always noted how Mamie and her mother were just like "two old gals together," and J. B. West confirmed it. Both women would stay in bed till late in the morning, he recalled, Mamie working, her mother reading or watching T.V. Sometimes during staff meetings in Mamie's room, the phone would ring and she would pick it up, joking, "Excuse me, I have a long-distance call from Mother"—who was just across the hallway.

In the mornings, Mamie also dictated her correspondence to Mary Jane McCafree, responding to or acknowledging the seven hundred to one thousand letters she received every month. As this was well before the age of the computer or the auto-pen, the work was a major undertaking. But Mamie believed that someone who took the time to write deserved a proper answer. Mamie's letter writing was so legendary that Senator Stuart Symington was prompted to tell her, "You always write as if you meant it. I suppose that is one of the reasons you have the country in the palm of your hand."

In addition to answering her mail, Mamie often passed on many requests from the public for help—on everything from public housing and pensions to civil-service complaints. She saw this not as interference in policy but merely as acts of good neighborliness. But Mamie's intervention sometimes made a material difference to those who wrote her, and Mamie knew it. For instance, once a blind musician sent Mamie an original composition he'd written, and as a result Mamie facilitated an audition for him with the National Symphony Orchestra.

Mamie's propensity to work from bed created the impression, fostered by Ike's critics, that she was inactive or incapacitated. Once when a little girl was visiting the White House, she looked up at the First Lady and said forthrightly, "Why don't you work around here?" Mamie was startled by the question. "Oh honey, but I do," she replied. "Who told you I didn't?"

The impression of inactivity her critics promulgated was far from the reality. At the end of the administration, the White House Social Office records contained half a million letters, revealing "the extent of Mamie's correspondence with the general public." And in 1956, *Newsweek* reported that during the first term alone Mamie "[shook] hands with 100,000 persons and . . . launched as many as five charity drives a week." In one three-day period she shook hands with as many as 5,500 people—a task made more arduous because of the special attention she placed on each encounter.

Whenever women came through a receiving line, Mamie always had personal comments on what they were wearing, where they had come from, or what they planned to do. West remembered, "If there were a thousand people going through the line, she'd have a thousand little items of small talk for them. In fact, she could charm the socks off of anybody she met."

An article that appeared in 1954 offered another insight into her own distinctive social style. "One of the veteran hostesses of Washington recently paid [the First Lady] perhaps the greatest compliment that one woman can pay another," the journalist noted. "She said: 'Mamie is different in more ways than one. She never gossips even at the smallest and most intimate parties. If she can not say something positive and nice about a person she doesn't say anything. And yet you never feel she's a prig. Somehow she changes the atmosphere and you find yourself beginning to appreciate people instead of just picking them apart.' This is a compliment in any city, but in Washington it is a superlative."

Perhaps her secret was that she adopted a very non-Washington approach. "In our entertaining," she explained, "neither religion nor political party played any part, for when I had the Senate wives for luncheon or for a Congressional tea, I never knew whether one was a Republican or a Democrat . . . I didn't want to know. I liked that person for what they were—my guest."

Mamie's natural nonpolitical approach had its effect. After a luncheon for Senate wives, Jacqueline Kennedy, married to Senator John F. Kennedy, wrote to her, "I think it is so wonderful the way you make everyone feel so much at home. Thank you so much for having made such a memorable occasion possible—I will never forget it."

Sometimes Mamie's pace could take an exacting toll, however. Reverend Edward Elson, pastor of the Washington Presbyterian Church, which she and Ike attended, recalled visiting her one day. Mamie asked if he would mind if she continued to recline on a daybed as they chatted. "Her entire forearm and hand, as well as her ankles and feet, were swollen, the result of shaking hands with hundreds of people at a White House ceremony the day before. But she had uncomplainingly carried on," he remembered.

Mamie and Ike also engaged in a very busy official entertaining schedule. During the two terms, the Eisenhowers entertained more heads of state (seventy) in the White House than any other presidential couple before them. Perhaps this was because they were the first (and only) presidential couple to have lived abroad so extensively. And many of the heads of state and government figures were their "old friends" from the war years, like Queen

Elizabeth and Prince Philip, Charles de Gaulle, and Winston Churchill. But Ike and Mamie also had an unprecedented sensitivity to the developing Third World, due, perhaps, to their tours in Panama and the Philippines. The administration hosted many leaders from Africa, Latin America, and Asia.

Of all the guests they had at the White House during those years, Mamie's favorite, surprisingly perhaps, was Field Marshal Montgomery: "He didn't demand anything," she recalled. But if Ike's irascible old comrade-in-arms was capable of treading slightly out of line, Mamie could gently put him back in his place. After his arrival, she remembered, Monty looked around the main floor of the mansion and declared, "Well, it isn't Buckingham Palace." To which Mamie replied, "Well, thank goodness for that!"

West recalled that "Mamie Eisenhower as a hostess was spectacular. In her diamonds and décolleté gowns, she fairly sparkled. She and the General brought more spit and polish, more pomp and circumstance, to their lavish, formal entertaining than any other President and First Lady in my White House existence [which lasted through the Kennedy Administration]."

$\mathcal{E}$very year Mamie was First Lady she was voted onto the New York Dress Institute's list of the world's twelve best-dressed women, along with the famously fashionable Babe Paley and the Duchess of Windsor. "Mrs. Eisenhower brings a new viewpoint on clothes to the White House," said the designer Molly Parnis. "She's proving that a grandmother needn't be an old lady. She's making maturity glamorous."

But Mamie was not without her critics, including Mrs. Parnis herself, who found her charm bracelets, for instance, hopelessly sentimental, complaining that Mamie's choice of accessories was based more on personal preference than on any established principles of style. As one fashion analyst explained, Mamie's way of dressing, "adorning basic style with marks of familial success and individuality . . . subordinating dress to ensemble, and ensemble to personality, was not a look calculated to advertise a designer's product." But the critics who decried what became known as the " 'Mamie-look' . . . fazed her not at all." As she had demonstrated many times before, she abhorred the pretensions so common in fashion-conscious circles. Once, after she'd "hit the list," she was complimented on her hat—assumed to be a Paris original—and with a twinkle in her eye, "Mamie cut through the gush: 'I got it by mail order . . . $9.95.' " Another time at a diplomatic reception, Mamie noticed a mortified woman wearing the same dress as she and trying desperately to cover it with her coat. That prompted Mamie to exclaim: "Don't hide it. I think it's pretty."

Although the First Lady did nothing to conceal her love of a good bargain hunt, she also appreciated and wore dresses made by well-known American designers. Her inaugural gown was designed by Nettie Rosenstein; she wore Molly Parnis day dresses; she favored Sally Victor hats; and many of the gowns she wore for important state dinners, like the ones for Nikita Khrushchev and Charles de Gaulle, were designed by Arnold Scaasi. Scaasi later recalled their first meeting and confesses that he was utterly "surprised at how pretty Mrs. Eisenhower was. Photographs did not capture her exquisite coloring, her wonderful skin, or the remarkable figure she had for a woman in her early sixties," he said. "She was not photogenic. Her bangs sometimes looked rather strange in photographs," Scaasi recalled, "but in person they were very attractive and looked normal and perfectly right. She had a very high forehead and she wore her hair in the most flattering way [she could]. Mrs. Eisenhower loved pretty clothes—colorful clothes. They weren't 'hard chic.' She liked clothes that moved well, and she liked to show off her waist and bosom; the dresses always had to have a lot of movement."

Mamie also had an excellent eye for classical design in garments from which she would get good wear. She was not about to bow to the pressure of what the fashion industry deemed in vogue. For instance, when Dior raised hemlines in the spring of 1953, Mamie refused to do so herself. "As a soldier's wife," she said, "I learned early in life that pride in personal appearance is not a superficial thing." Mamie knew that the way one looked said much about one's self-esteem and respect for others, and that people would judge you by it. But without a limitless budget, she had come to know during army life how to tell "fashion from fad," a training that had helped her "shop intelligently."

A big disappointment for Mamie during this period came with the discovery that redoing the White House would be impossible.

On the heels of the Truman restoration of the Executive Mansion, there was only $375 left in the decorating account, and Ike refused to ask Congress for a new appropriation. Mamie, who later richly decorated much of their own house at Gettysburg, had to make do with the B. Altman furniture acquired during the Truman years. Nevertheless, that didn't mean she didn't try to make some changes. Startled that there were so few authentic presidential furnishings, she launched an effort to solicit donations of antiques and china, and many of her friends made such gifts, including the exquisite vermilion collection given by Margaret Biddle.

Without congressionally allocated funds, Mamie still tried to make the Executive Mansion more attractive and livable. The third floor, for instance, badly needed curtains, so she went to Fort Myer and bought parachute silk for ten cents a yard and had the White House seamstress Lillian Parks make them up. Lillian recalled that the finished draperies looked lovely, but she had had a "devil of a time" working with the fabric. "The President had a budget he wanted to balance, but he was going to balance it on my head!"

Aside from her official duties, Mamie always found time for her family and her friends. I remember well many of those friends, but perhaps one of the most colorful was George Allen. Whenever he and his wife, Mary, were around, you could always count on a good time. Allen was a big man—he probably weighed about 250 pounds—who was always making bets with Ike about his weight, wagering on the number of pounds he would lose by a certain date. My mother, Barbara, was the one to "hold the money," and when Ike won because Allen failed to meet his goal she would get the sum—once "enough to buy virtually a whole spring wardrobe," she recalled.

Mamie's many years in Washington ensured that she was surrounded by old friends, like the Allens, whom Mamie and Ike had met before the war. Some—like the Nevinses and the Gruenthers—they'd known since the Philippines, or before. And Mike, Mamie's sister, also lived in Washington, making get-togethers possible whenever the spirit moved them. As in years past, the two sisters were "inseparable," and though they still "fussed and fought" with each other, they were fiercely loyal to one another.

Mike's proximity to Mamie during these years was a lifesaver for her; Mike often did shopping and ran errands that Mamie could not, because of her own public visibility. At the same time, Mamie watched Mike's four children grow to adulthood, taking a special interest in each of them, and giving a debutante ball at the White House for her two nieces Ellen and Mamie, her namesake. Sue Gill, the wife of her nephew Richard Gill, remembers the loyal tenacity the First Lady invested even in this newest member of the family. "Unlike other members of the Doud family, she accepted me from the start and she *always* stood up for me."

One tragic personal event in the early White House years was the untimely death of Helen Eisenhower, Milton's wife. Mamie had been close to Helen when they had both lived in Washington in the 1930s and during the war years when Ike had been away. After Ike became president, he used Milton as a sounding board for his policies and gave him a number of "at-large assignments." In 1953, for example, Helen and Milton undertook a fact-finding trip across Latin America; in five grueling weeks of travel, Helen served as the official hostess for the American delegation. She was remembered as "smiling or otherwise being the very model of a gracious hostess"—even though a biopsy the previous year had indicated she had a cancerous tumor. In the spring of 1954 a second tumor was found, and on July 20, 1955, Helen died in her bedroom from a sudden blood clot that had moved into her heart. She was not yet fifty.

Helen's death came as a blow to Milton. And Mamie, Ike, and everyone who knew and loved Helen grieved. She was "fine, brave, generous, [and] utterly selfless in her devotion to others," the writer Kenneth Davis said. Like the terrible loss Mamie had felt with the death of Katie Gerow, a passing which Mamie continued to mark even decades after her death by sending flowers to Arlington National Cemetery, Helen's death again underscored for Mamie the transitory nature of life. This is one of the reasons she made it an article of faith never to take anyone for granted. On redoubling her efforts, she conveyed that commitment not only to her friends but to strangers as well.

𝒟uring the campaign and after she'd gone to the White House, when she would often be presented with beautiful bouquets, Mamie would always send them to a nearby hospital or nursing home and then promptly acknowledge the flowers with a thank-you note. She also sent the flowers that had been used for state dinners to local hospitals, so they could be enjoyed by patients in the Washington community.

Mamie's old friend Janie Howard remembered that when Janie was ill and had gone to Walter Reed Hospital, Mamie sent flowers and later, when she had recovered enough to go out, invited her to the White House and served her favorite meal ("Imagine remembering that!"). That evening Janie told Mamie about the other women she had met in her ward, and Mamie said, "Well, send me their names." The First Lady sent each of these unknown women a little bouquet and a card. "It made them so happy," Janie recalled. "They were all terminal cases."

For those asking the First Lady to sponsor charitable events, where possible she would make small donations, even if only a nominal amount. "I like to spread my money about," she'd say. She understood then that the charities could at least say that the president and Mrs. Eisenhower had personally contributed to their cause. And "when I was offered free tickets to charity benefits," Mamie recalled, "I always told them . . . I pay my own way." I myself remember that years later, after Granddad died, "Mimi" took me along to a fund-raising dinner for Eisenhower College, paying the thousand-dollar-a-plate cost for herself and for me.

Perhaps the most striking quality about Mamie as First Lady was the way she treated people who worked for her at the White House, or anywhere along the way. Kate Hughes recalled: "She thanked [everyone]—but you never felt she was doing it for effect. She thanked every brakeman, every conductor, everybody who did anything for her." Only occasionally she'd react if she felt that someone was abusing his or her proximity to the White House. Rank brought with it a certain level of deference, which the rigid hierarchy of the army had accustomed her to, and she could bristle at those who failed to respect the position of First Lady.

But as had been the case during her army years, "family for her was more than blood relatives," recalled Reverend Elson. "In a very real sense . . . [her] 'family' encompassed the whole household—staff and aides, housekeepers, orderlies, drivers, Secret Service men and their families." Mamie did indeed take a great interest in the personal lives of her domestic employees. As West observed, "drawing them into lengthy discussions about their activities, their families, their homes, their state of health, she seemed, for a First Lady, to bestow an unusual amount of concern. When anybody got sick, she always sent flowers from the bouquet room; even if she heard our relatives were ill, she sent flowers too." Mamie celebrated the birthday of everyone who worked for her with a cake and a present, no matter how low in the pecking order. At Christmas she personally selected and wrapped presents for the entire staff; she'd invite small groups up to the second floor, and give each person a Christmas gift. West recalls that she even had presents for his wife and daughter.

Just as important, Mamie's care and concern knew no racial lines. Every year she gave a sterling-silver place setting to Delores Moaney, the Eisenhowers' cook and the wife of Sergeant John Moaney, Granddad's valet; eventually Delores collected a full set of elegant silverware in this way. After the White House years Mamie also gave her a mink jacket, and at Christmas gave presents to all her children and grandchildren. Delores later told me that her granddaughter often received the same gift that Mamie gave my sisters and me.

In fact, Delores has always been perplexed and upset by the notion, conveyed by some, that Ike and Mamie were racist. She recalls with great emotion that whenever Ike would see her, he would always take off his hat to her in respect. "He always treated me like a lady," she asserts, and she remembers the Eisenhowers would decline invitations if Delores and Moaney were not given proper accommodations or treated equitably with their white counterparts. And neither of them would tolerate the expression of racism in their presence. Once, at the White House, a guest used a pejorative word for Negro, and Ike jumped from his seat with an angry retort: "You will not talk that way in my house again!"

Preston Bruce, another African American, who served as a doorman at the White House, recalled how the president and First Lady helped his family when his son was in a car accident. Later, on the birth of his first grandchild, Mamie sent his daughter Elaine two dozen Mamie Eisenhower carnations. "Welcome, William Bruce Pryor, to this wonderful world," Mamie wrote. Ten years later, after Ike died, Mamie invited three generations of the Bruce family to Gettysburg, and every year until her death Preston Bruce came to visit her at the farm.

. . .

$\mathcal{M}$amie was determined that before the end of Ike's first term the house at the Gettysburg farm would be renovated. Ike had wanted to delay work on it until after 1956, on the probability that he would not run for a second term, but Mamie cajoled and carried on "the way every woman does when she wants to get her way," she'd laughingly tell us.

It was a massive undertaking, complicated by the fact that union labor was brought in from cities as far away as Washington and Baltimore. Many of the blueprint plans were also changed by Mamie at the last minute to accommodate important afterthoughts. Aside from central air-conditioning, one such alteration was an enlargement of the windows facing east in Mamie and Ike's bedroom: Mamie insisted that she be able to see out of them from bed.

Mamie had not laid eyes on her own furniture for more than ten years, and she was desperate to put together the pieces of her first home—an instinct that was probably intensified because there was no money for decoration of the White House. A reporter from the *New York Herald Tribune* recounted: "The First Lady told me how she hopes to move family treasures, gathered over 38 years of marriage, to the farm from storage in Washington. 'I'm so excited, I can hardly bear it,' she had said."

The Gettysburg project was completed in 1955, and to celebrate both the housewarming and Mamie and Ike's wedding anniversary, the two gave a party at the farm for the White House domestic staff. Never before had a president of the United States and his wife recognized the contributions of housemaids, butlers, plumbers, carpenters, and telephone operators as they did. Since one shift had to remain in Washington to maintain the smooth running of the Executive Mansion, they actually threw two parties so that everyone could be included.

For some, it might have seemed odd that the opening of this famous couple's first house—the only one that truly belonged to them—would have been an occasion to entertain butlers, maids, and telephone operators. But for Mamie it was perfectly natural for her to share this joyful moment with the people who surrounded her, members of *her* official family. None of them could have any doubt about what they meant to Mamie Doud Eisenhower.

CHAPTER NINETEEN

"FOR NEVER FAILING HELP"

wo months after the staff party at Gettysburg, my grandparents decided to go to Denver for a vacation. There, in Nana's house, in the wee hours of September 24, 1955, Ike awoke around two o'clock complaining of chest and body discomfort. He had had two heavy meals that day: steak and Bermuda onions for lunch, leg of lamb for dinner. The presumption was that he had indigestion. Mamie gave him some milk of magnesia and called their personal physician, General Howard Snyder.

When Snyder arrived, he decided that his patient had had a heart attack. He gave Eisenhower a number of medications designed to thin the blood, reduce pain, and promote rest. The president apparently rejected an oxygen mask and "incoherently" asked for "other forms of relief." Finally Dr. Snyder called in Sergeant Moaney to massage Eisenhower with warm rubbing alcohol, while they circled his body with hot water bottles. Despite these ministrations, the president went into shock. Snyder told Mamie to slip into bed with her husband and wrap herself around him to see if this would bring up his body temperature and quiet him. Mamie held her stricken husband in her enveloping embrace, calmly soothing him. Her presence had the desired effect. Before long he settled down and slowly drifted off to sleep.

The next morning Ike was rushed to Fitzsimmons Army Medical Hospital, and it was confirmed that he had had a heart attack. Mamie's own role in the drama was said to have saved his life. Years later, she remarked on the fact that this heart attack had occurred on the anniversary of Ikky's birth.

. . .

 ohn was told about his father's condition just as he was completing a round of golf near our home in Fort Belvoir, Virginia. Heart attacks were more serious in those days than they are today, when we have the benefit of many advances in medical technology; so when John heard the news, he assumed "it was all over." He made arrangements to go to Denver as quickly as possible.

When he arrived, Mamie told John that as they were taking Ike off to the hospital, all he could think about was that his billfold was left behind somewhere in the bedroom at Nana's house: in it were the winnings of a bet he had made with George Allen, money he had been intending to use to buy my mother, Barbara, a present. Then Mamie shook her head, in deep concern: "I just can't believe that Ike's work is finished," she told my father.

Nonetheless, Mamie put on the cheerful and optimistic face she had worn so often in periods of great crisis. She had a miraculous way of rising to these grave occasions, and she never let on the depths of her worries about Ike's health and future.

"Mamie, above all others, never accepted the assumption that I had incurred a disabling illness," Ike recalled later. "While solicitous above all for my health and welfare, she perhaps more than any other retained the conviction that my job as president was not finished."

Ike and Mamie stayed in Denver for seven weeks. As his convalescence progressed, Ike was able, increasingly, to confer with cabinet members and White House staff. Nevertheless, he was being carefully watched, and Mamie stayed by his side, personally responding to every one of the eleven thousand get-well letters and cards that arrived. On November 11, as he left the *Columbine* (Air Force One) at National Airport, he said to waiting reporters, "I've been told I have a reprieve if not a pardon." Doctors took his medical condition—and his temperament—very seriously: after his heart attack, he was not allowed to watch the Army-Navy football game on television again. For the same reason, he was not told about the riots at Columbia during the spring of 1968 until after they had been settled.

After a brief visit to Washington, they went up to the newly renovated house at Gettysburg, where Ike could fully recuperate.

As is common with many people who have just had a heart attack, Ike seemed frustrated and depressed. Furthermore, he was faced with one of the most important personal decisions of his life: whether or not he would seek a second presidential term. The doctors, in analyzing his condition, concluded that he had ten more productive years ahead of him. Pleased by the positive prognosis and grateful to be in their new home, on their first evening they celebrated Mamie's fifty-ninth birthday with six friends.

Since the completion of the house, Mamie had wanted to have it blessed. Now, perhaps with the convergence of all these events, she felt even more strongly about it. This prompted Ike to ask Reverend Elson if he would perform a small ceremony.

> Dear Dr. Elson,
> Mrs. Eisenhower may have mentioned something to you yesterday concerning her hope that you and Mrs. Elson might come up to Gettysburg for luncheon on the day following Thanksgiving, and at that time have the little "house blessing" ceremony of which we have sometimes spoken. Of course something may happen to upset that program, but I am sure at present this is what she is contemplating, if such would meet with your convenience.

The brief service took place in their living room, where so many of Mamie's treasures were now assembled. Over the fireplace was a marble mantelpiece which had once graced the White House but which had been sold at auction in the mid-nineteenth century and later purchased as a gift for the Eisenhowers from their staffs. Also in the room with its gold-and-burnt-umber silk draperies and damask upholstery was the piano Mamie had saved the money to purchase during the Depression. Across the hall, in the red-and-gray dining room, was the tea service that Ike had saved his pennies to buy, piece by piece, for their wedding anniversaries in the 1930s.

At the appointed hour, Dr. Elson prayed, saying: Bless this house, "that it may henceforth be a place of health and healing, a haven of tranquillity, an abode of love, and a sanctuary of worship. Bless all who call it home, and all the loved ones and friends who are encompassed by it in abiding love and devotion to Thee."

After Ike's recuperation and their return to Washington, in gratitude for the unflagging support Mamie had given him during those terrible September days and in the weeks and months that followed, Ike designed a gold medallion for Mamie, to be worn as a pendant; he had it struck at Tiffany's. The inscription read: "For never failing help, since 1916, in calm and in crisis, in dark days and in bright. Love, Ike."

*O*ne month after my grandparents' return to the East Coast, my youngest sister, Mary Jean, was born at Walter Reed Hospital. What a joy her arrival must have been against the backdrop of those other events that troubling fall.

Mamie reveled in the arrival of her newest grandchild. She had already accommodated the third floor of the White House for our frequent visits: she had made over one of the larger rooms as a playroom, and the solarium at the very top of the Executive Mansion was a sitting and dining room for us when we visited. Mamie kept three birds there for our enjoyment, a canary and two parakeets: Gabby, High Glory, and Pete. When Pete died, she allowed us to give him a solemn burial on the edge of what is now the Rose Garden.

She kept bicycles and an electric miniature of a Thunderbird car for us to ride up and down the ground-floor hallways when the morning tours were over. She also welcomed us into her room after her staff meetings, and we would rummage through the knick-knacks she kept for us on her side table. She could be a captivating grandmother; her shimmering blue eyes held you in their enchanting grip while she imparted secrets and planned conspiracies.

But even as very young children, we knew that the rules in Mimi's house were to be strictly obeyed. No running up and down corridors, no sliding down banisters, no greasy fingers on the woodwork, no getting down from the table before the meal was over. All of us were strictly schooled in manners, and Mamie even taught us to use finger bowls properly by the time we were three years old. We would receive admonitions about drying our hair after swimming in the White House pool, and lectures about wearing warm clothing when we went out to play—scolding about wet heads and inadequate clothing coming, perhaps, from her reflexive fear about our health and well-being. And though unknown to us at the time, whenever the Secret Service drove us somewhere, she would always make a point of telling them to drive very carefully. "Let's have no more tragedies," she would say.

Being in the White House had not been without its concerns in that regard. During their first term, especially, internal turmoil over the McCarthy accusations and genuine fear of Communist infiltration of high-security projects called into question even our own personal safety. (During the course of 1953 to 1954, there had been 8,008 cases of security risks identified by "properly appointed boards.") After my father left for Korea, Mamie and Ike extended their protective wings over my mother and the three of us. Not long after the Rosenbergs were executed on spying charges, my father had written Ike confidentially from Korea:

> As to the added protection, I agree with that also. I am afraid that it is completely impossible for the Secret Service people to hide from Barbara that they are doubling the guard, but I think it is a good move. In that connection, I have instructed Barbara that she is not to move back to Highland Falls until I get home. She can visit either set of grandparents, but if there have been unusual quantities of threatening letters, I want her in a place where the house can be more easily watched. She may give some muzzle blast on this subject, but I am sure she will comply.

Our close association with the president drew us together as a family, physically and in every other way. My grandparents were very family-oriented, and they tried, often without success, to find a balance between ordinary family life and the extraordinary pressures that the presidency puts on those close to him. The "long arm of the White House," as my father would call it, made that balance all but impossible.

Although Mamie was a stickler for getting even the smallest details right in most other things, "she was very uncritical of how the kids [her grandchildren] were raised," my mother recalls. In fact, when I became a mother myself, Mimi would often hold Barbara up as an example of what a good mother really is. "We have seen quite a bit of Barbara and the children," Mamie had written an acquaintance after John had left for Korea. "We love her dearly and would really do anything in the world to make up to her for the lack of her husband and the Father of her babies.

For a young girl of twenty-six she is a wonderful Mother, and the children just worship her, as we do."

To help out, my mother remembers, after my father returned from Korea "Mimi made a special effort to take the kids off our hands occasionally, so we could have a rest. When she went to Maine Chance, a health spa, or when she went to visit her mother, she would encourage us to move into the White House to keep Ike company—but it was really a rest for us, and we appreciated it." On other occasions when the presidential couple were traveling, Mamie would send Delores down to help my mother for a few weeks—a virtual lifesaver in a house with four tireless children.

Mamie was always conscious of the importance of keeping romance alive in a marriage. She no doubt believed these little breaks would help give my parents the breathers she and Ike had had decades earlier when my father went to Denver for the summers. My parents were then the same age she and Ike had been when they lived at the Wyoming, and Mamie would often talk about those years. "I had the impression that they were very close in those days and that they confided in one another," my mother recalls. "Mamie would tell me about how they would love to talk and have a cigarette together. She made [their relationship] sound so cozy. 'These are your best years,' she'd tell me."

Ike, too, was mindful of the stresses and strains of raising four growing children, and he had admired, since his youth, the unselfish roles women play in providing the glue that keep families together. After my younger sister was born, he wrote my mother some encouraging words, in long hand, from the White House:

Dearest Barbie:
Yesterday, from Johnny's conversation, I gathered that life has been somewhat complicated for you recently. What with preparing to go to Florida, attending PTA's and related school meetings, seeing that the children are on time for birthday parties, Cub meetings and Sunday School—to say nothing of assorted dusting, cooking, washing and being beautiful for the morning callers—you are getting *tired*. Under such conditions the world goes sour—nerves get on edge and things go generally to pot that some need is indicated for a psychiatrist's couch! (There may be some danger in that.)

In any event, under such indications I have a simple pre-scription. Other well known specialists in "young matrons' troubles" may disagree, but I still firmly hold to the cure of the new dress! Of course I am flexible, and a hat or hats—shoes—or even frilly unmentionables may do the trick! But one indispensable part of the cure is that the hat, dress or etc or etc *must* be unexpected. Herewith I enclose one! It's a secret—and I've forgotten it. This must be or others might find out about my techniques, and I'd lose all my practice.

Along with the cure itself, some frills are sometimes useful. Hence the flowers. I hope they help.

Always devotedly
Dad

Ike must have learned such secrets from Mamie, who knew well the therapeutic value of a new hat. Mamie also was a great believer in always dressing up for her husband, never allowing him to see her when she wasn't looking her best. She would even change for dinner in the evenings—either into a cocktail dress or, if they were being more informal, into a long flowing caftan or tea gown.

One oft-told story, which I cannot verify but which sounds like Mamie, if not Ike, tells of an evening during the White House years when Mamie kept Ike waiting. When she emerged finally, Ike is said to have snapped, "You have kept the president of the United States waiting!" To which she retorted, "Oh, I thought I was dressing for my husband."

*M*any accounts suggest that Mamie's deepest wish was to have Ike retire to Gettysburg after his first term in office, but as in the period before Operation Overlord, Mamie understood that Ike still had work to do, and she wanted to see him fully engaged to the very extent of his capability, even if it meant sacrifices on her part. She "thought idleness would be fatal for my temperament," Ike put it later. "Consequently she argued that I should listen to all my most trusted advisors, and then make my own decision. She said she was ready to accept and support me in that decision, no matter what its nature."

On January 13, 1956, Ike hosted a stag dinner at the White House to discuss the matter. So secret were both the meeting and the guest list that Ike himself put the place cards on the table. Milton and my father opposed Ike's running for a second term. But the consensus of the others at that dinner was that he should: they believed that the Eisenhower administration was among the most competent Executive Branch teams ever assembled, and, true or not, they worried that other candidates would not share their commitment to shepherding the United States through this delicate postwar period, which required defense preparedness and a sound fiscal policy. Ike was also all too aware that another Republican in his place might not win, and he was concerned that efforts to bring his party toward the center continue. "The Republican party must be known as a progressive organization or it is sunk," Ike wrote.

Perhaps it was Mamie who, in the end, presented the most convincing argument of all. She "could not reconcile herself to the idea that efforts on behalf of what I believe in had come to an end," Ike recalled. On February 29, 1956, Ike announced that he would again seek the Republican nomination for president of the United States.

*E*ven though one of the most important decisions affecting their lives was finally made, worries still remained. On June 6, Ike suffered an ileitis attack. At Walter Reed Hospital, ten eminent surgeons pondered whether they should operate, given the president's recent heart attack; they were unable to reach unanimity.

"One doctor held out against surgery. The rest balked at going ahead without a unanimous opinion," my father remembered. "Sometime after midnight Dr. Walter Tkach, who'd been keeping me informed, came up and said, 'If we don't move soon, we are going to lose our patient.' . . . Finally the dissenting doctor agreed, but Mother, who clung to the belief that it was unnecessary, refused to sign the permission papers. I did so in her place."

Mamie could not bear the strain of making the wrong, perhaps life-ending, decision. Believing, as she did, that we all live according to our fate, perhaps she was unwilling to play God. To her immense relief, however, Ike recovered from the operation and made steady physical progress. Weeks later, on July 1, he reiterated his candidacy for a second term.

That summer the Democrats again nominated Adlai Stevenson to run against Eisenhower. With the increased usage of television, the second campaign was not nearly so physically demanding as the first had been, but the question about the president's health was an inevitable issue in the race. When the votes were tabulated, however, it was clear that while the electorate may have been concerned about his condition, they were confident of his ability to carry out his responsibilities, duties he had continued to execute with a deft hand. On election day, with the Suez crisis as a backdrop, the voters returned Ike to office with the largest plurality in American history, with 9.5 million votes. He won 457 electoral votes and carried forty-one states.

The following week, Mamie celebrated her sixtieth birthday, and Ike wrote her:

Darling
Happy Birthday—in a "quilted" bedjacket—which I hope you will like. The tea Kettle came to mind because, in the late campaign, you were the hottest thing *we* had . . . Loads of love. And the sixties aren't so bad, I've already had six of them so I know.

As ever your Ike

The start of a new presidential term did not mean the end of the health problems that had plagued Ike since September 1955. During a very stressful autumn in 1957, he dispatched federal troops to Little Rock, Arkansas, which Mamie thought was absolutely the right thing to do. "Those folks have got to get an education too," she had remarked of the black students attempting to attend a segregated white school there. With continued instability in the Middle East and the Soviet launch of Sputnik, Ike again fell ill. On November 25, he suffered a slight stroke, serious enough to make it impossible for him to attend a White House state dinner in honor of Muhammad V of Morocco. There was some debate about whether or not the dinner should be canceled, but when Ike said that he was going to dress and go himself, it was quickly decided that Mamie would ask Vice President Nixon, with his wife, Pat, to help her host the affair.

"It was a ghostly white Mamie Eisenhower who descended the elevator with Vice President and Mrs. Nixon that night," West

remembered. "When dinner was over, she went upstairs immediately, passing on a complaint, which was most unusual for a
woman who often lavishly praised her staff. 'The State dining
room looked so dull tonight. Those red carnations were much too
dark'—indicating the flowers she had chosen for the banquet table. It seemed to me that the room may have seemed dull because
the light of her life lay ill upstairs."

Serving as hostess that evening "was perhaps the most difficult
assignment she ever undertook in the White House," Nixon later
said. "That night, a very troubled First Lady greeted her guests
with superb poise and charm."

Everyone was amazed at Ike's recuperative powers after his mild
stroke. "Three days [later]," my father recalled, "he was able to
attend Thanksgiving services. By the end of the week, he was
determined to go to the Heads of Government meeting of the
NATO conference two weeks hence."

This was the last major health crisis of Eisenhower's presidency,
but Mamie would spend the rest of her years with Ike on the
lookout, lest circumstances overtax him. The three illnesses so
close together made Mamie wonder if, as Nixon remembered,
"[the presidency] really is too much for any one man to bear."

Now constantly under his doctors' eagle eye, Ike didn't like the
restrictive orders they often gave him, which he frequently ignored. "Doc" Snyder bore the brunt of his annoyance, though the
president could also show some humor on the subject. In October
1958, Snyder noted in his diary, "Mamie was present when I took
the President's blood pressure . . . She made a wry face. The President remarked, 'If it was any lower than that, I would forget my
swear words,' and then he laughed."*

.   .   .

*Many historical accounts, quoting Snyder's diary, paint Ike as crotchety, almost
rude. But by this time in his career, Snyder was an elderly man himself; his hand
shook so much that even I, as a child, noticed it, watching it with riveted fascination. Apparently Ike was unhappy that Snyder would not let other doctors treat
him routinely, and he found it "painful" when Snyder, with his unsteady hand,
gave him injections. But he couldn't bring himself to fire Snyder, an old family
friend, and often hoped that he would get the hint and leave. This, no doubt,
accounts for Ike's demeanor around him, which always seemed to be one of some
irritation.

ℬefore the second term was out, Mamie herself would undergo surgery. While the administration was unprecedentedly open about the president's health, Mamie's condition was regarded as a private matter. Her hysterectomy was described merely as an operation "typical of women her age."

Even though Mamie had access to the best medical care in the country, she faced this major surgery with the same trepidation she had experienced in the past. On White House stationery, Ike penned her a note of reassurance:

Darling—
As you suggested this a.m. I shall not come to have dinner with you tonight. But my thoughts will be with you—I shall pray that the Good Lord will relieve your mind of apprehension and give you confidence that all will be well.

I shall, of course, keep in close touch and as soon as I hear that the operation has been completed I will take the first opportunity to come to you.

Always your devoted
Ike

P.S. All my love.

In 1959, before leaving office, Ike planned three major "goodwill tours" abroad, the first of their kind. He hoped they would, as he said, "raise the morale of struggling and underprivileged peoples, to enhance confidence in the value of friendship with the United States, and to give them assurance of their own security and chances for progress." The first, which evolved over a number of planning sessions, encompassed eleven nations, including Iran, India, Pakistan, Morocco, and Afghanistan. The trip would cover 22,000 miles in nine days.

Mamie herself decided against going on this trip, given the strain that flying and the intensive schedule would place on her. Instead, my mother, who was accompanying my father, would serve where necessary as the "ranking woman" in her place. "I was absolutely astonished when I was invited to go," my mother remembers. "This was not Mamie's way to relinquish her position—even though I would be traveling as John's wife and not the

First Lady's representative. I felt complimented that she would agree."

Mamie was surely wistful to see the threesome set off, for though she did not say so specifically, she was concerned that Ike might not have enough stamina to withstand the demands of such a trip. She followed Ike's progress closely, and with relief and excitement was there to greet the presidential delegation on their return. With only days before Christmas, Mamie had festively decorated the White House, and a huge crowd had gathered near Lafayette Square to welcome the party home with a candlelight vigil.

"Now that he is safely back for Christmas," the journalist Marvin Arrowsmith wrote Mamie, "perhaps you would like to know how well he seemed to stand up during the grueling three-continent journey that sometimes had us reporters on the ropes. In short his performance from a physical standpoint amazed us. At 69 years of age, he wore us younger fellows to a frazzle."

The trip had been an unquestioned success, and the American president was uproariously received in parts of the world no U.S. chief executive had ever seen. The images of Eisenhower in front of assembled millions in Karachi, New Delhi, and Kabul prompted Queen Elizabeth to send him a handwritten letter: "We have followed with intense interest and much admiration your tremendous journey to so many countries, and feel we shall never again be able to claim that *we* are being made to do too much on our future tours!"

In late February 1960, Ike made another two-week, thirteen-stop trip, this time to Latin America, a tour that included meeting with four presidents and making thirty-seven speeches. And in May, he went to Europe for a summit conference with Soviet premier Nikita Khrushchev. Two weeks after the U-2 aerial reconnaissance flight went down in Soviet airspace, Khrushchev walked out of the talks, cutting the conference short. Ike wired Mamie from Paris:

Tonight prospects are for an earlier return to the United States than we had previously predicted. I will not try to expand on what you must have read in your papers. No matter what happens, I shall be glad to be home once more. Love, Ike

Then a month later, on June 12, my mother and father again accompanied Ike on the last major goodwill effort of his administration. An eight-stop, two-week tour took them to Anchorage, Wake, Manila, Taipei, Naha, Seoul, back to Wake, and Honolulu—the stops in Anchorage and Honolulu to welcome Alaska and Hawaii, just signed into law as new states of the union.

Both my parents recall that they were deeply concerned when the party reached Manila. The overwhelmingly enthusiastic greeting extended by the Philippine people was gratefully received, but Ike was showing signs of deep fatigue.

Although many accounts say that after this trip Mamie made overt efforts to discourage the Nixon campaign from using Ike in appearances that summer, family members are divided on how much influence Mamie really had, and whether her concerns stopped Nixon from asking Ike for assistance. It was known at the time that a powerful contingent within the Nixon campaign wanted their candidate to win the election "on his own," without Ike's help. Certainly if Ike had been asked, he would have overridden Mamie's worries and campaigned for his vice president.

With the White House years drawing to a close, Mamie put special effort into making Christmas memorable that year. All of us joined together for our last major holiday at the Executive Mansion. She had decorated the White House as never before, with a towering Christmas tree, pine boughs and holly everywhere, as well as a number of exquisitely made crèches of the Nativity story. Presents were piled high under the magnificent tree and stretched for yards into the East Room.

Mamie had always set particular store by Christmas—but this year, there were more than the usual reasons to want to draw the family close to her. Nana, who had been bedridden with a stroke for more than a year, had died that September, and this Christmas would also be the last the Eisenhowers would spend in government service; with Ike just seventy and Mamie in her mid-sixties, they would at last retire to private life.

To add festivity and joy to those days, my mother worked tirelessly to help my siblings and me perform a Nativity play on the second floor of the White House. Our Christmas story was presented on the finely polished floors of the wide corridor that separated the family quarters from the Queen's Room and the Lincoln Bedroom; we used the Monroe Room (now the Treaty Room) as our dressing room.

As there were only four of us, we had many roles to play. Fortunately, no scene required more than four actors: Mary, Joseph, Baby Jesus, and donkey; Three Kings and Baby Jesus, etc. My mother had gone to considerable trouble crafting the costumes, making sure that as angels we had white lights crowning our halos and that as Kings we wore the brocades and silks she'd acquired in the Middle East on the goodwill tour the previous year. The festivities were a high point for Mamie. In her last year in the White House, the spirit of Christmas had truly been captured.

For Mamie the White House had been a period of accomplishment and fulfillment. She had relished "living over the shop" and being her husband's partner in this new challenge. She had opened up the White House to an unprecedented number of Americans from all walks of life. Aside from the women's clubs and associations she received and sponsored, as well as her considerable charitable work in promoting the American Heart Association—an involvement that had "stimulated public support" and under Mamie's patronage had seen its most "fruitful" years—her touch was felt in many small ways, too.

In reinstituting the traditional White House Easter Egg Roll, discontinued in 1940, she made sure that it was racially integrated for the first time. She had also held a special first-ever White House reception for the National Council of Negro Women, an organization of which she was an honorary member. She had supported the idea of having Marian Anderson sing the national anthem at Ike's swearing-in ceremony, and had invited Lucille Ball to the White House while she was still on Senator Joseph McCarthy's list of suspected Communists. She had even campaigned for a woman congressional candidate, Ellen Harris, with the words, "Ladies, I hope you'll vote for her. We women have to have a voice in things."

These were not, nor were they ever intended to be, acts of political activism. They were simply commonsense courtesies that expressed the sympathy she had for the lives of ordinary people, for the lives of her American neighbors.

Mamie was right for the 1950s. She was a glamorous grandmother in an era when the postwar nation was busily engaged in raising its children and rebuilding the strongest free country in the world. While today some might scoff at her legacy—that she had only been a homemaker—she typified the good things about what it meant to have and be a family, to celebrate loved ones, and to grow old gracefully without ever really giving in to it. She will be remembered for being a good neighbor.

*A*s the second term of the Eisenhower administration drew to an end, Ike, too, reflected on his last eventful years in office. Sputnik, the U-2 incident, and the failed Paris summit had all been disappointments, though progress had been made with the Soviets during the administration. From the "Atoms for Peace" speech, the General Exchanges Agreement of 1958, and the initiation of negotiations on a nuclear test ban to Khrushchev's unprecedented two-week visit, Eisenhower did not leave office a broken man, as some have suggested. In the last year of his term he fought and won one of the hardest political battles of his presidency: a Democratic Congress passed his balanced budget, one of three during his presidency, amid increased calls for more defense spending to overcome an alleged missile gap. Securing this balanced budget had not been a minor achievement.

Nixon's defeat in the 1960 election had indeed been disappointing, and Ike worried that it would result in a future repudiation of his past fiscal policies. But despite these frustrations, Eisenhower left a solid record as he departed the White House. Among the achievements he thought were his most important: during his eight years in office, not one American was killed in combat after the Korean War ended; Communism had been contained—no territory had been lost to a Communist regime in his eight years; his administration had instituted the first civil-rights legislation since 1875 and had begun the desegregation of schools (Little Rock), U.S. government agencies, the army, and the District of Columbia. Eisenhower had also worked out an unusually effective relationship with Congress: 87 percent of his "most important" proposed legislation had passed, though Democrats had controlled Congress during most of his administration; he had expanded Social Security, so that 90 percent of the population was under its coverage by 1960; he had built an interstate highway system; and he had maintained a sound economy with the virtual elimination of inflation (less than 3 percent). To his successor, John F. Kennedy, he left a country at peace, its prestige among the nations of the world at its zenith, with a 1961 "budget in balance."

Mamie, her tenure as First Lady at an end, began the difficult and time-consuming business of packing up once again, this time to Gettysburg, for the last move of their lives. Not long before their departure, Ellis Slater, a close family friend, found Mamie in her room one day, balancing her checkbook. When she heard Slater in the doorway, she looked up and said wistfully—surveying all that had been her home for eight years—"Don't things look bare?"

On Ike's last day in office, he said his goodbyes and at 5:00 p.m. left the Oval Office. That evening he and Mamie dined alone.

Heavy snow fell overnight and temperatures dropped. Forces from some of the local army posts were called in to help the desperate District authorities clear away the snow in time for the Inauguration, as well as the parade and the balls that would follow. After John F. Kennedy was sworn in to office, Ike and Mamie tried to slip out quietly to the car awaiting them. As they had so many times before, they took their familiar route through Frederick and Emmitsburg to Gettysburg. Occasionally they would encounter groups along the way, standing in the deep snow clapping and offering greetings to the newly retired president and First Lady. (In Gettysburg the next evening, locals would turn out for an enthusiastic "welcome home" rally in the town square.)

Finally, after a long, tiring day, Mamie and Ike arrived at the farm. In just hours, so much had already changed. The Secret Service men were gone, the countless aides and assistants had departed, and the focus of the nation had already shifted—the mantle of power had been passed to a new president.

After forty-six years of service to his country, Ike got out of the car and, walking carefully to avoid the snowdrifts, for the first time opened the gate to the farm himself. My father, who was behind the wheel, drove the car through and Ike climbed in again. Then together with Mamie, they rode up the long, snowy lane.

CHAPTER TWENTY

HOME AT LAST

When I find myself contemplating a post-war existence, I always picture a little place away from the cities (but with someone near enough for occasional bridge) and the two of us just getting brown in the sun, (and possibly thick in the middle). A dozen cats and dogs, with a horse or two, maybe a place to fish (not too strenuously) and a field in which to shoot a few birds once in a while—I think that's roughly my idea of a good life.

It took fifteen years for Ike and Mamie to realize that vision of retirement which Granddad had outlined to her during the war. It had been a circuitous route getting here, through Columbia, NATO, and the White House. But now on the Gettysburg farm, in the only home which they'd ever owned, they would spend the rest of their lives.

The heart of the house was a "casual and comfortable" sunporch, "not much larger than a modest living room, where we spent hours from early breakfast to late evening. Facing east, with the morning sun brightening it and in shadow through the heat of a summer day . . . it was an oasis of relaxation," Ike remembered. In one corner he had his easel set up, and not far away was a card table where Mamie would play solitaire while he worked away on his latest daub.

Ike, the gentleman farmer, ran the 190-acre estate—440 in total with other parcels he ran with his partners. It was a sizable operation, with nine farmhands to work the fields of corn and soybeans and a herd of more than thirty choice Aberdeen Angus.

In anticipation of my grandparents' retirement, my family had moved to a home adjacent to the farm which had been refashioned from a one-room rural schoolhouse; the land was eventually connected to my grandparents' property by a gravel road. My father took a leave of absence from the army and prepared to serve as an editorial assistant to Granddad while he worked on his White House memoirs.

When Ike and Mamie weren't traveling, life at the farm took on a predictable pattern. Granddad would go the office in Gettysburg every morning, come home for lunch, and return to work until six o'clock. He would often wedge in a game of golf at some point in the day. Mamie recalled that he carried on work exactly as he'd done all through the years. "I still ran my house. We had many friends [come to visit]. Life went on very much the same. In fact I think it was a little bit better, because we were home and our own people were around us," she said.

Mamie enjoyed entertaining at the farm and answering her correspondence, but she also took in her afternoon soap operas, earlier and tamer than what we have today. She had been a fan of the daytime dramas ever since they hit the airwaves in the 1950s. Beverly Butcher Byron laughingly recalled that it was not unusual for Mamie to call her mother, Ruth, and joke, "Well, what are we going to wear to the wedding today?" referring to a soap-opera ceremony to be aired that afternoon. Mamie thought that the soap operas she watched were "very true to life," though she later admitted that she would not watch any of the hospital shows after Ike had had his heart attack.

Ike and Mamie's retirement was typical enough for people of their age and economic status. But one of the most significant features of their new life was the total and utter change in circumstances. Ike had been so accustomed to the trappings of power, one aide remembers, that "he thought you still picked up the receiver and asked for 'Central.' " He also had to get a driver's license, putting him behind the wheel for the first time since 1935.

Unlike former presidents and their wives today, my grandparents had no Secret Service protection until more than four years after leaving office, when President Lyndon Johnson signed the provision into law in 1965. At the farm, it was not unusual to find tourists who had been out on the battlefield drive up the lane and knock on my grandparents' front door just to say hello. My father recalls that even more disconcerting were the more than half-dozen "deranged" people who "found their way into our unprotected domain. Two were openly dangerous."

"Only a couple of months after our settling in Gettysburg," he remembers, "I found myself loading a souvenir M-14 rifle to cover the Boss's departure from his office in town to his car. I had good reason: a disturbed former sergeant, who had verbally threatened the Boss's life, was on the loose in Gettysburg and no state police were in sight."

*S*ome friends wondered how Ike would get his new book completed, since he had received so many speaking requests and invitations. According to Ellis Slater, much of the pressure came from people who wanted Ike and Mamie to get involved in various charitable programs and political activities. "[Ike] said, 'Well, I don't mind as long as I can be helpful, because I figure that when the time comes that a person can't do some good, he might as well die.' " Years after Ike had left office, the pace continued unabated. In one thirty-day period, his office processed over 7,500 pieces of mail and answered two-thirds of it within the month. "What retirement?" Slater reflected.

As *Life* observed, although "Ike's days are no longer filled with the awesome power and decisions of a General of the Army or a U.S. President—nor is his way smoothed by a retinue of aides"— he is able to fulfill his long-awaited role "as elder statesman free from all partisan pettiness, in a position, he once said, 'to advise or influence people for the sake of the whole country.' "

Ike was called upon to counsel the Kennedy administration on foreign-policy dilemmas, such as the Cuban missile crisis, but he also spoke out against the new administration's position on fiscal issues. Not long after leaving office, he told a group of Republicans that he took sharp issue with the current leadership. "I am sick and tired of hearing alleged leaders scoff at a balanced budget . . . Is it so wicked to show some respect for the pioneer qualities of thrift and energy?"

Mamie, too, was actively engaged in many projects, helping the American Heart Association, making appearances for the New York Cancer Committee, and supporting the activities of the local Presbyterian church. The new First Lady, Jacqueline Kennedy, also asked her to be the fund-raising co-chair of the National Cultural Center in Washington, which had been authorized by Eisen-hower when he signed the bill for it on September 2, 1958 (after Kennedy's assassination, it was renamed the Kennedy Center for the Performing Arts). To mark Mamie's participation in the proj-ect, Mrs. Kennedy held a tea in her honor at the White House on June 22, 1962.

When my grandparents weren't in Gettysburg or traveling to see friends or giving speeches, they spent their time at Augusta Na-tional Golf Club in Augusta, Georgia, or at the Eldorado Golf Club in Palm Desert, California. They would usually leave for the West Coast after celebrating Christmas with us at the farm. But twice my family joined them in Palm Desert for the holiday. We swam in the club's pools and took golf lessons, and Granddad took us all to Disneyland.

In a birthday letter to me in 1961, Granddad wrote:

Dear Susie,
Do you know something? Just by being here at Eldorado with your grandmother and me, *you* are giving *us* a wonderful birth-day present. It's a little mixed-up but true.

Have a happy birthday darling, we will all try to make it so. And know that I love you always.

Affectionately,
Granddad

Even though many of their demands were purely recreational, Mamie had to maintain a high level of organization. In 1962 she and Ike took my brother, David, and sister Anne to Europe with them, along with friends from California, Freeman and Jane Gos-den and their son Craig. They toured the European capitals and visited many of the heads of state Ike and Mamie regarded as personal friends. Just to get this trip organized required packing more than fifty suitcases and steamer trunks; they traveled with everything: pillows, enough linens for daily changes, medicines for every conceivable ailment, countless items of clothing, with all the accessories, and presents for everyone they visited.

My sister Anne, who was Mamie's roommate during the trip, marveled at her organizational ability. Evening bags each had a perfect little comb and mirror and were vacuumed clean to remove any strands of cigarette tobacco; every hat was packed so it wouldn't crush; and the standing hair dryer had to be included, complete with electric converters. When they boarded the *Queen Elizabeth*, Mamie realized to her consternation that she had forgotten to pack toilet paper. So before the ship left port, someone was dispatched to buy and pack a supply that would last them for the duration of the trip.

Many indelible memories remain of my grandparents' retirement years. My mother, thinking about what kind of birthday present we could give Granddad, came up with the idea of putting on little shows, like the pageant at that last White House Christmas. These productions were orchestrated with a limited cast, and occasionally some of our school friends would play certain parts. Elaborate costumes were put together and homemade sets devised, and the songs of the three musicals we produced—*Young Abe Lincoln*, *The Music Man*, and *The Sound of Music*—were lip-synched from the phonograph record, discreetly hidden offstage.

Despite my sisters' and brother's early interest, I ended up as the family horsewoman, riding Granddad's horses and taking them to local shows. At the height of the farm's productivity, there were between five and seven horses in the stables. The family still enjoys telling the story about the day I became distracted and the horses grazing in the field broke through the gate and ran out, eventually trampling Granddad's golf green. My grandparents and parents were on the porch at the time. Granddad, overlooking the damage to his prized green, declared that the running horses made a "beautiful sight"; Mimi was the one who was shaken. Not knowing what the reaction had been, I dreaded going into the house after we had finally rounded up the horses. But the general good spirit and understanding I found there was really much more than I deserved.*

Perhaps Christmastime reflected the high point of family feeling. As in the past, Mamie made the holiday memorable, with a magnificent tree in the living room and presents reaching well into the middle of the room. Barbecues at the teahouse and evenings

---

*After the horses trampled the green, it developed a rare disease and never really recovered. It was completely replaced years later by the National Park Service.

in front of the T.V. were also happy, if much quieter, times than either of my grandparents had experienced for decades.

We grandchildren found some amusement in my grandparents' interaction. More often than not they would be serenely engaged in some pursuit, in quiet companionship on the porch. But all of us knew that they never played cards together, since Ike was impatient with Mimi's skills and logic. "Why did you play that card?" he could snap. Petulantly she would respond with what one friend called a "whim of iron." "Because I felt like it," she'd say without apology. Aside from the occasional clash of powerful male and female personalities, they never left any doubt about their commitment and abiding devotion to one another.

Perhaps an inevitable part of Ike's retirement was that for the first time since leaving the Philippines, he had the leisure for prolonged thought and reflection. There can be no doubt that there were adjustments to make after more than twenty years in positions of immense authority. He admitted that he missed making decisions that he knew would have central importance to the conduct of policy and the quality of life for the American people. John recalls that his father was often pensive during those years, and as new memoirs of some of his wartime colleagues were published, he was sometimes bothered by new interpretations of events he'd known so well. At the same time the Democrats found it politically expedient to cast a negative and often unfair light on the Eisenhower administration's eight years—years Ike had been proud of. With the assassination of the Kennedy brothers and the murder of Martin Luther King, Jr., as well as widespread campus riots and antiwar demonstrations, those last years of Ike's life saw huge changes; and many of the values that my grandparents had spent their lives advancing—"Duty, Honor, Country"—were increasingly ridiculed as outdated or irrelevant.

Mamie and John could never have known the full depth of Ike's feelings about those comrades-in-arms and political figures who attacked his public service; about the apparent domestic instability in the country; or about the personal disappointments he'd faced, like the loss of Ikky. "If I have one instinctive passion in my dealings with others," Ike had once written Nana, "it is the right of every individual to his or her privacy in heart and mind. Humans are more emotional and sentimental beings than they are logical and intellectual. When, therefore, they are shocked or hurt in their deepest selves, others who love them should, as I see it, stand by but refrain from probing, advising, or even—in a verbal sense—sympathizing."

*I*n November 1965, ten years after his first heart attack, Granddad was stricken with another coronary in Augusta, Georgia. After that, my father recalled, "Dad showed signs of being aware that another attack might be his last. He began to simplify his estate by such matters as dispersing his magnificent herd of Angus cattle, and the doctors restricted his golfing, a real passion of his life. Dad showed no signs of outward worry, especially for himself . . . but isolated incidents disclosed [that] the recognition of mortality existed beneath the surface."

As part of putting his affairs in order, Ike and Mamie gave the Gettysburg farm to the Department of the Interior for its eventual use as a museum. And Ike was relieved that the Johnson administration, in the aftermath of Kennedy's assassination, assigned Secret Service men not only to former presidents but also to their wives—an assurance that Mamie would be protected. Many of the same agents who had served on their security detail during the presidential years returned. As soon as they had established their new command post in a small office attached to the barn, they gave Ike the code name Scoreboard; Mamie was called Springtime.

A year or so after Ike's heart attack, he made a pilgrimage alone (but for the Secret Service men) to Fairmount Cemetery in Denver, where he had Ikky's coffin removed for reburial in Abilene; he accompanied the coffin to the Chapel of Meditation at the Eisenhower Museum and childhood home, and watched as the small casket was interred there, next to the spot where he and Mamie would eventually be buried. In the most profound way, he was preparing for his own death.

Not long after, at a family gathering at the farm during the Thanksgiving of 1967, my brother, David, announced that he and Julie Nixon, Richard Nixon's second daughter, wanted to marry. Ike, worried about his namesake's future and the effect early marriage would have on his educational and professional career, was cautious. In contrast, Mamie, ever the romantic, was thrilled with the news and immediately disappeared and returned to the table with Nana's engagement ring, which she suggested David now give to Julie. When David called Julie on the phone that weekend, she asked him what it looked like. "Like a silver dollar," he told her. Julie was delighted that the sizable diamond, in an antique platinum setting, fit her finger perfectly.

Within weeks of that important family gathering, Mamie and Ike and their retinue set off for Palm Desert by train. En route, they stopped in Abilene to visit the Chapel of Meditation. My father recalls that Mamie told him later that Ike "had left, upset, an emotion brought on not by concern for himself but the sight of the tiny plaque on the floor where my older brother had been placed." When they got to California, Ike went to bed with some kind of an ailment, with "his spirits low."

Only months later, in March 1968, Ike had a third heart attack. For the last year of his life he was confined to Walter Reed Army Medical Center, and Mamie seldom left his side. He stayed alert and abreast of developments in the 1968 presidential race, however. For the first time, he decided to break with his earlier precedent and endorse a candidate before the convention, throwing his support behind his former vice president, Richard Nixon, and that August he agreed to address the Republican National Convention. As Julie later observed, "His decision proved to be a fateful one. Mamie knew, even before the television cameras were set up in the living room of Ward Eight at Walter Reed, how much effort, how much emotion, this speech represented for Ike."

The next morning Granddad suffered another heart attack. For days, it seemed he would not pull through. His heart, after the infarct, tended to "flutter" without pumping blood—a situation that could lead to death if not brought under control. All of us rushed to Washington from various parts of the country, convinced these days were his last. I vividly remember that after we all gathered in the waiting room of Ward 8 and received an update on Granddad's condition, one of the doctors told us that two men, independently of one another, had volunteered to donate their hearts to Granddad for a transplant. I was deeply moved by these gestures: America at its impossibly generous best.

Despite the severity of Granddad's situation, he maintained his fighting spirit. Once, when we were at his bedside during the height of the crisis, a doctor told us that we had to leave, that we had visited with the general long enough. From the depths of what we thought was his deathbed, Granddad roared, "And how many stars do you have?"

"Three," the army doctor answered.

"Well, I have five, and I tell you they are going to stay!"

From the August crisis onward, Mamie watched Ike like a hawk, rarely leaving his side except to go to her own room next to his, where she worked on answering letters. She carefully monitored his activity, restricting his visitors to two at a time. "On Mrs. Eisenhower's orders, time is up," the nurses would say.

For Granddad's birthday that year I made a special cake for him. Sodium had been restricted in his diet, so I baked my cake with only approved ingredients and carried it by train from Wilmington, Delaware, where my boarding school was located. Granddad was elated that I had come and even more touched that I had gone to the trouble of baking him a cake from scratch, even if the layers were askew and the icing applied unevenly. He sent me a long thank-you note, dictated from his bed.

After Granddad's heart attack in August, he seemed to rally and then stabilize. As the weeks turned into months, Mamie occasionally left the hospital for a very short while, but only if he was having a good day. My sister Anne married that November, and Mamie made a rare appearance at the wedding in Valley Forge, Pennsylvania.

With Richard Nixon's successful election in November, my brother, David, and his fiancée, Julie, decided to marry in December, before the inauguration would change the private nature of their wedding. Given Ike's health, he and Mamie stayed at the hospital and did not attend the ceremony, but by arrangement they were able to watch it on closed-circuit television from his hospital room.

Despite signs of improvement, and always with the hope that he might soon be going home, Ike gave Mamie a handwritten letter expressing his appreciation that she and the hospital staff had made "one more Merry Christmas" possible. "When I read those words," Mamie remembered, "I realized that Ike knew this was our last Christmas together. Later I shed a few tears and put that brave letter away with my most treasured possessions."

The family did not spend Christmas or New Year's with my grandparents that year. Mimi herself came down with a severe respiratory illness and was still sick when my father visited the hospital again after the holidays. "She seemed in no condition for me to break the news of my forthcoming appointment as ambassador to Belgium, even though Brussels was only a few hours' flying time away," my father recalled. "[But] I had no compunctions about telling Dad. As it turns out, he had known about the possibility for some time and was enthusiastic. 'Don't worry,' he assured me, 'I won't tell Mamie.' "

Granddad seemed to improve, and General Robert Shultz, his longtime aide, was looking into the possibility of installing an elevator at the Gettysburg office in anticipation of his return. After Mamie recovered, she regained her optimism and never allowed herself to imagine that Ike might not get better. "He was a very strong character," she later reflected. "He never let me know for a minute that he wasn't getting well, because he knew what it would do to me. I was the one he worried about."

In March, the doctors had to perform an emergency operation on Ike to alleviate an intestinal blockage, caused by twisted scar tissue from his earlier ileitis operation. Even with his weakened heart, Ike pulled through. On March 3, Mimi wrote me, filling me in on the news. Now knowing about my father's impending appointment as ambassador to Belgium, she also gave me advice about my own plans for the coming year.

> Dear Sue,
> Your Grandad [sic] enjoyed your letter that I had to read him. We are all so grateful he came through his last operation. I am sure it was the prayers because that [which] could be done humanly was done. Today he has eaten a bit which will help as he really was starved. David and Julie were here . . . to see him and you know how much he loves you all and what a tonic you are. Your mother was here this a.m. and your Dad tonight.
> You must go to Belgium for tis an opportunity for you. Marvelous schools there and prestige of being in school abroad. I will stay here in the hospital until Ike is well.
> Lots of love honey and we hope to see you soon.
>
> Mimi

Three weeks later, while my younger sister and I were in South America visiting my sister Anne, my grandfather suffered a major setback: fluid filled his lungs, and he was becoming increasingly weak. He psychologically made preparations for the end. In his last days, he discussed spiritual matters with Billy Graham and left some last-minute instructions for my father. "Be good to Mamie," he said.

Except to catch some occasional sleep, Mamie never left his side. Sometime in the last hours of his life, Granddad said aloud, "I have always loved my wife, I have always loved my children, I have always loved my grandchildren, and I have always loved my country."

My father and brother were with Mamie when the end came. As his final gesture, Ike suddenly ordered my father and one of the doctors to lower the shades and pull him up. "Two big men," he growled. "Higher!" Then he said, "I want to go, God take me."

John recalled that his father said this softly and then seemed to relax. A doctor gave him a sedative, and he never regained consciousness. Everyone left but Mamie, who remained by Ike's side, holding his hand. Sometime later my brother, David, and my father, John, returned to the room. As they stood at either end of Ike's bed, they saw the signal on the electrocardiogram machine "flutter and even out."

Ike's long fight was over. "Mother, David, and I began filing out of the room," my father recalled. "[But] something told me to go back. I stopped in the doorway and returned to the foot of the bed. On the machine the heart showed a final beat. General [Leonard] Heaton and I looked at our watches together. It was 12:35 p.m. March 28, 1969. Almost instantly bells began to toll all over the city."

*M*amie said that watching her husband die was the hardest thing she'd ever done in her life. "When he was dying out there at Walter Reed, I thought, 'Well I don't know how you stood the responsibilities' . . . I often wondered how in the world he could ever go to sleep at night with all those horrors that he had seen [during the war] years, those awful camps, and the responsibility of so many lives . . . One night [many years before] I heard him say, very quietly, 'God, I've done the best that I could today,' and I think that was the theory he went on . . . But Ike had a good life. He had a wonderful life. He lived eight years longer than the Bible said . . . and he was a modest man, that's why my heart and pride rest with him."

Others—those who knew him well—would evoke Carl Sandburg in summing up Ike's qualities, "steel and velvet . . . as hard as a rock and soft as a drifting fog." William Bragg Ewald, an aide, put it another way: Eisenhower was "one who held in his heart and mind the paradox of terrible storm and peace unspeakable and perfect."

A quiet family funeral for my grandfather, as a five-star general and a two-term former president, was not possible. During his illness, he and my father had planned his own state funeral, stipulating, for instance, what music was to be played, what passages should be read. Ike had made it clear that he wanted to be buried in a sixty-dollar G.I. coffin, a wish that was carried out.

Mamie bore up in those days magnificently. Leaders from around the world descended on Washington, and she graciously received them in a suite at the Washington Hilton, just next to the Wyoming. President Charles de Gaulle, the shah of Iran, European royalty, the president of the Philippines—these and countless others came to call.

The body lay in state in the Capitol rotunda. Unsteady and uncertain of her step, Mamie was not able to follow the casket up the long stairs; she reached the rotunda via elevator and rejoined the assemblage for a moving and poignant service.* Richard Nixon gave a stirring eulogy, but, issued later, Lyndon Johnson's words, in all their simplicity, might have pleased Ike even more.

America will be a lonely land without him. But America will always be a better nation—stronger, safer, more conscious of its heritage, more certain of its destiny—because Ike was with us when America needed him.

---

*Along with many distinguished people, like General Omar Bradley and General Lauris Norstad, Granddad had stipulated that his beloved Sergeant Moaney, his valet since the North African campaign, serve as one of the honorary pallbearers, probably the first black man to be given the honor of attending an American president's casket.

After the public had the opportunity to pay its last respects, a funeral service was held at the National Cathedral, after which the casket was put on a train bound for Abilene. Mamie insisted that an American flag be draped over the car in which the casket was carried. She wanted to let the thousands who stood along the train route know where her husband actually lay.

As the train began its somber journey, all of us were overwhelmed by the reaction of the American people to Granddad's death. Affection was evident at every station stop. On every platform, crowds of townspeople would be waiting silently to pay their last respects. I was struck by the diversity of these groups: young and old, black and white—it seemed that all of America was there to send the old soldier home.

Our first evening on the train coincided with my brother's twenty-first birthday. Mamie ordered a birthday cake and champagne so that we could help David celebrate. It was a bittersweet party. As we raised our glasses and sang "Happy Birthday," all of us were conscious that we were shepherding Granddad's body to his final resting place. As the train swayed to and fro Mamie held Mike's arm, her china-blue eyes shimmering from joy but also from an unreachable sadness.

That evening after everyone retired, I was unable to sleep. I opened the tightly drawn curtains of my sleeping compartment and watched the Midwestern countryside streak past—perhaps it was three o'clock in the morning. I was still numbly looking out the window, mesmerized by the landscape and the moon shadows playing tricks on my eyes, when all of a sudden I noticed a solitary figure, standing erect on top of a small slope, just coming into view. As we got closer I could see a man, perhaps in his late fifties, dressed in civilian clothes. Bathed by the clear moonlit sky, he raised his hand in salute as the train passed. He remained at attention until we had gone.

Mamie also stayed awake these nights, watching the many thousands of people who lined the train route home. She, too, was sustained by the individual and collective outpourings. On April 2, my grandfather was interred at the Chapel of Meditation, next to Ikky and not far from his boyhood home.

Later that day we solemnly boarded the train for Washington. Soon, Mamie would have to face one of the greatest challenges of her seventy-two years—a life without her Ike.

CHAPTER TWENTY-ONE

THE YEARS ALONE

$\mathcal{A}$lmost immediately after Granddad's death, Mamie joined my father in Belgium, where he had taken up his responsibilities as ambassador. She arrived in Europe, escorted by Ike's brother Milton and her regular Secret Service contingent, with a volume of baggage so "awesome" that my father quipped, it had to be the "second invasion of Normandy."

While my mother stayed in the United States to pack up our household, Mamie served as John's hostess; my father remembers that all of Belgium treated her like a queen.

But Mamie soon tired of being away from home and decided to return to the United States and settle all the details remaining after Ike's death. With my parents in Belgium, my siblings and I spent many weekends at the Gettysburg house, keeping her company that year. For all of us then, we always had the feeling that we'd encounter Granddad coming around the corner. His spirit was everywhere—as if he had just stepped out for the afternoon to go to the office. While Ike was still alive, Mamie used to say that when he was not around, the "house seemed to sag." But it took years after his death for that feeling to finally and permanently pervade their cherished farmhouse. In the last years of Mamie's life, even though she made her residence there, the house would eventually begin to feel hollow and strangely empty.

$\mathcal{I}$n the early years of her widowhood, Mamie kept herself busy with activities in Ike's memory. She christened the CVN *Eisen-*

hower, a nuclear-powered aircraft carrier. She helped to open the Eisenhower Medical Center in California and Eisenhower Hall at West Point. Like Granddad, who had put his secretary's daughter through college with the Social Security payments he received (and couldn't manage to get stopped), Mamie too continued to sponsor an underprivileged child at camp every summer. "I used to send a boy and a girl to summer camp every year," she told an interviewer. "Now I can just afford to send one child. I'm like a retired person. I can't get raises because I'm living on a fixed income." Nevertheless, she managed her finances with care, caution, and sometimes deep concern. But she contributed, developed, and maintained an abiding interest in the newly founded Eisenhower College, located in Seneca Falls, New York. In an increasingly radicalized political climate in the country, Mamie came to admire and respect the kind of students who enrolled there. She saw them as serious young people, focused on learning and good citizenship, and she wanted desperately for the fledgling college to survive. "I would do just about anything to help them [Eisenhower College]. I think the students up there are terrific. They really help put the heart back in me."

To help ease the school's fiscal problems, Mamie sold her Chrysler limousine, sending the proceeds to the college, and attended a number of fund-raising dinners in its behalf. The students and faculty seemed to project optimism about America in a bewildering period of our nation's history.

Mamie, like Ike, was deeply concerned about the changes taking place in the country. She couldn't imagine the reasons for the cynicism expressed by so many. She had always had an unwavering conviction that her life had been exceptional because she had been born an American. As the 1970s wore on, no matter what she was wearing or whom she'd be seeing, she kept a rhinestone American-flag brooch pinned to her dress. Perhaps it was a talisman to ward off the negativism infecting the United States, but I had the feeling it made her feel better to make such a glittering statement. She was the last First Lady born in the nineteenth century and the first one to preside over the space age. Her own lifetime reflected the vast opportunity that had existed in the United States, and she wanted no one to forget it.

As real flags were being burned on the steps of the Capitol, along with draft cards and Selective Service applications, Mamie would remind me that in the United States "anything was possible," anything could be achieved. When she'd say that, she wasn't just referring to what her country had done to catapult a Kansas farm boy into the command of armies and ultimately to the White House; she was thinking of her own family, too, and all that Pupah and his ancestors had achieved. She remained, to the end, deeply proud of being an American, of being an Eisenhower, of being a Doud.

When she wasn't attending a fund-raising event for the college or a dinner for one of her causes, she spent her time at Gettysburg, broken by visits to "Mamie's Cabin" at Augusta National Golf Club, or she would make her annual pilgrimage to Boone to see Uncle Joel, and to Abilene, where she would visit the Chapel of Meditation. When my parents were in Belgium, many of her holidays were also spent with the Nixons at the White House.

She was buoyed by her friends in those years, staying in touch with those she cared about with long, newsy conversations by phone. She also maintained a staggeringly large correspondence not only with her friends and family but with many others who wrote her from around the country. She took her writing to such lengths that I often received thank-you notes for an Easter card or even thank-you notes for thank-you notes.

Though she nearly always sounded upbeat on the phone, in her down moments she would confess she now had an appreciation for the plight of widows in a way she had never had before. She knew all too well the feeling of being what she called "on the shelf." And she could poignantly articulate the sheer loneliness of her situation. "Only had about two hours of sleep last night, so I feel like a rag and bone today." On another occasion she wrote, "Things are going along as usual, [but] we had one of our famous electrical storms this morning, whereupon I hid on the back stairs in the dark."

Though seemingly unable to get over Granddad's death, she understood how quickly people tire of complaining widows. "Death is inevitable," she told a longtime acquaintance, "there's nothing you can do about it. Till then one must get out and stay cheerful."

. . .

*A*s each of us married—I was the third of my siblings to do so, at a ceremony in Gettysburg and a reception on the farm—our family became scattered, and the central focus of family life, which had been so real during Granddad's life, was dissipated. David and Julie were in California, Anne was in Colombia, I was in London, and my sister Mary eventually moved from Washington to Columbus, Georgia. "The thing we must realize, is that we older folks have already had our day and we must manage to take care of ourselves," Mamie wrote to my mother. "As all of the birds have left the nest and are starting out on their own, I know how Nana felt those years in the White House when we all had our husbands and our own problems to keep us busy. So, as I told John when he was here, I am going ahead and leading my own life, doing what I want to do."

Now more alone than ever, she too had more time to think than she had ever had before. During our frequent visits and phone calls, she liked to take the opportunity to impart some of the wisdom she had acquired during "her day." Sometimes, in her frustration, she could be quite critical of us, making what my father would call "personal remarks." But this was the perfectionist in Mamie coming out, molded by a lifetime of association with the army, where spit and polish was the order of the day; she had made much of that discipline her own. The thing I remember most about Mamie was not the little details she could be difficult about but her amazing ability to cope with the big problems life presented.

Not only did Mimi convey unflagging support to those she loved, she could be astonishingly open about the mistakes she had made in her own life. She would never have left Ike's side in Panama or the Philippines, she'd tell me, and she seemed deeply concerned that her grandchildren, by now all married, might take the "easy way out" and assume "the line of least resistance."

"Your father is the only son I ever had," she'd say, as if thinking of it that way made it easier to reconcile Ikky's passing. She told me she felt tremendous, almost overpowering, love for my father, John, and she regretted that, for his sake, she had not had more children. She always thought there was time, she said, but with all their moves the right moment never seemed to present itself.

I had two babies eighteen months apart, and the decision to have a second child so soon was one that met with her whole-hearted approval. "I was glad to receive your letter telling me about the new baby you are expecting," she wrote. "I think you are very wise to have the second child so soon, for you might as well stay home with two as one. No joking, Caroline will be happy to have a playmate."

As the years progressed, she increasingly relied on reminiscences for sustenance, remarking in another letter:

> You children were all more like Ike's and my children than our grandchildren and have meant so much to us all through the years. I was thankful when Ike finally died that he had the opportunity of knowing each one of you but sorry he did not know his great-grandchildren . . . The farm never looked prettier and you could have a field day here at the present time.
>
> I often look at your wedding pictures and live over the night that you were married, the supper party here, and the things that went on which were really quite humorous in afterthought. This house has known many happy times like your wedding supper, along with other sorrows. In other words—it is home.

With Ike gone, much of the energy she had focused on him was now directed toward us. Concerns about Watergate consumed much of her thoughts, and she fretted about the outcome. "Nixon is our heartbreaking worry here," she wrote me on March 21, 1974. "Feel so sorry for the family." Keeping a slower schedule at the time because of her health, she added, "Guess the holidays were too much for my 78 years. I thought I was twenty."

For all her worries, however, one of the happiest events of her widowhood came eighteen months later, at her eightieth-birthday party on November 14, 1976. She had always placed special value on birthdays and anniversaries, and, like her fiftieth wedding anniversary, eighty years marked a major milestone. There was an unavoidable contrast between the two occasions, ten years apart.

On their fiftieth wedding anniversary she and Ike had celebrated at a black-tie family reunion given by my parents. It was a day of immense sentimental importance to Mamie, and she had worn a stunning gold-and-white organdy gown that had beautifully set off the radiance in her still smooth and lineless face. Now, a decade later, Mamie looked much the same except for the twenty pounds she had shed and a glint of sadness that never really left her eyes.

On her birthday we gathered at the farm for our dinner celebration. My mother, searching for ways of finding a meaningful gift, put together a little book of remembrances, a collection to which we all contributed. In my father's message, he chose to remind his mother of vignettes, memories that were mostly "theirs alone": "The leg aches you used to rub in the middle of the night; the frightening foghorns moaning through the mists of San Francisco Bay in 1936; graduation from West Point on June 6, 1944, the two of us facing banks of photographers . . ."

My mother wrote Mimi, "Remember all our visits and vacations with you when the children were small . . . I will never forget the fun we had. They were sorely needed breaks in the business of child rearing. In that department you gave me constant support and help."

My sister Anne reminded Mamie about being her roommate on the trip to Europe in 1962; and I recalled "the magic of a White House Christmas, the birds Gabby, High Glory, and Pete; the Thunderbird on the ground floor; sledding at Camp David. Do you remember the day the horses trampled the golf green?" My sister Mary wrote a poem to her "friend and confidant."

But it was my brother David's contribution that made Mimi roar with laughter:

Mimi is one person who has retained everything over the years. Today, she is every bit as much feminine, saucy, wise, sharp, loyal, vigilant and idealistic as she ever has been. We should add helpful, too.

Where else can David get consistently reliable "fashion tips" on the length of men's hair styles? Or on the "look" in men's clothing? Where else can David get accurate readings of how much "Eisenhower" is in him? Mamie keeps Julie up to date on these things, too.

Our checkered record of following Mamie's advice is not

discouraging—she is forever mindful of the famous adage: "To err is human, to forgive is divine."

We have listened when it counts. Mimi's enthusiasm was vital in getting us together at a time when even the "optimists" of the family foresaw several years of college in our way. The "gradualists" predicted that the young couple would complete college, then graduate school, get jobs, achieve salaries of $65,000 per year, and pay off the mortgage before settling down. Not Mamie. She insisted that the two act at once, that Julie call her "Mimi" and that David move swiftly lest his opportunity be lost.

That and much more we owe you, Mimi. You are a friend, confidant and support . . . [and] you never grow old . . .

$\mathcal{M}$amie always said, "I want to think about the good times," and our party that evening was certainly a celebration of them. Regrettably, in that same year, Kay Summersby's *Past Forgetting: My Love Affair with Dwight Eisenhower* was published. It all started in early 1973, when Harry Truman had given a series of interviews to reporter Merle Miller that were eventually made into a book, in which he claimed that Ike had written to Chief of Staff George Marshall asking for a divorce so that he could marry Kay Summersby. Marshall, according to Truman, had told Ike that if he even came close to doing such a thing he would "not only bust him out of the Army, he'd see to it that never for the rest of his life would he be able to draw a peaceful breath . . . he'd see to it that the rest of his life was a living hell."

On hearing that, Robert Taft supporters were supposedly planning to use the letters "all over the country," Truman said. "I don't like Eisenhower; you know I never have . . . [but] one of the last things I did as President, I got those letters from his file in the Pentagon and destroyed them."

As many scholars have pointed out, the story doesn't make sense. Why would Truman tear up the letters if they might have helped put his fellow Democrat Adlai Stevenson, for whom he was campaigning, into the White House?

Nevertheless, a controversy raged for some time about whether or not the letters existed or whether they had been destroyed, saved, or sent to Marshall. Some suggested that the highly partisan Truman was suffering from a faulty memory, and others, from spiteful pique; still others continued to look. No letter was ever found, though a thorough search of Marshall's papers did indeed reveal a personal letter from Ike: he had written the chief of staff asking for permission to bring Mamie to Europe.

When Summersby was asked about the comments in the Truman interview, she was more surprised than anyone. But several years later, dying of cancer and hard up for money, she was persuaded to write another book. She never saw a word of the manuscript, however. She died within a month of signing the contract on the lucrative deal.

One of Summersby's close friends, journalist Bob Considine, said the ghostwriter gave the book "a racy flavor that corresponded roughly to what by then had become an accepted belief that she and Ike were lovers." Like Considine, all of Summersby's friends agreed that ghostwriters had "invented" the book, basing it on *Eisenhower Was My Boss*. Sue Sarafian Jehl complained that the book "didn't sound at all like Kay." Other people who knew her decried the book as "a complete myth."

"In fact, this last dreadful book was only written after her death. She never saw a word of it . . . The whole thing was made up. Absolutely . . ." said Anthea Saxe, her closest friend. "The book is so unlike Kay, it was ridiculous."

Those closest to Mamie thought she seemed to take the controversy in great stride. In fact, her attitude amazed all of us. Her simple response to the firestorm Truman had started on the publication of *Plain Speaking* was simple: "Mr. Truman knew better," she said. Of Ike's relationship with Summersby, she told Barbara Walters, "Ike told me all about her when he came home from the war. There was no romance. He couldn't have had anything to do with her or he wouldn't have come home to me. And he came home just as he did before he went away."

Long before this controversy had erupted—sometime in 1972, during one of my father's visits to the farm—Mamie had, in his words, "pointed to a box in the corner of her bedroom at Gettysburg and informed me that it contained all of the 319 letters my father had written her while overseas during World War II. She indicated she wanted me to use them as I desired. Like a dutiful son I removed the box, took it home to Valley Forge, and promptly forgot about it," he recalled. "A year later I got around to taking a serious look at the contents."

In the summer of 1976 John decided "the time had come to edit them for publication," hence the volume *Letters to Mamie*, which all but laid to rest the rumors. The book, not surprisingly, generated considerable mail. One letter prompted my father to send it on to his mother.

May 28, 1978

Dear Mr. Eisenhower,

... You may recall meeting me at Telegraph Cottage late in June 1944. I was wearing a Red Cross uniform, was introduced to you as Peg Chase, and had been transferred from Italy back to London (where I had met Ike in October 1942). Thanks to my friendship with "Tex" Lee, I had been with Kay and your father frequently until the end of the war. Never did I have the feeling that your father "loved" Mrs. Summersby. She played a sharp game of bridge, rode a horse fearlessly, and was a great help in providing the opportunity for rare moments of recreation. Your father was truly a lonely man, isolated in his commanding position. But he never wavered in his loyalty and love for his wife. Kay mistook or imagined his many kindnesses to her (and to the uniformed women who knew him) for something beyond affection. How she could write such a stupid book is beyond my understanding!

In 1953, when the Republican party was eager to nominate your father for president, there was some concern about the gossip about the relationship between Kay and Ike. Several prominent gentlemen from So. California questioned me closely about the allegations. I was able to convince them that there was no truth to the gossip ... With my best wishes to you and your dear mother.

Sincerely,
Margaret Camajani
(Mrs. Giovanni Camajani)

Despite the pain of those years, "Mamie never played the injured wife," family friend and lawyer George "Bo" Horkan recalled. "If you ever wanted to make an evaluation of what kind of woman Mamie was, it was how she comported herself throughout that entire episode, without a word of complaint, but it hurt her. It hurt her."

With Nixon's resignation in 1974, the eventual closing of Eisenhower College, and the renewed controversy over Kay Summersby, Mamie withdrew more and more from the world—often pushing away those she loved. She spent an increasing amount of time in her room, no longer going down to the sunporch to take her meals. She became less and less willing to spend money on herself, and her mostly unfounded anxiety about living on a fixed income made her fret that inflation had made "prices as high as a cat's back."

From her bed, she could look out the windows facing east. In the lofty branches of the huge ash tree, just outside the window, she would watch with riveted interest the lives of the robins that had built a nest there. When we came to visit, she would tell us about the antics of the birds and the squirrels that were now so much a part of her life.

"I think she wanted to be alone with her memories," my sister Mary hypothesized. "And she was tired. Tired of being cheerful, tired of being diplomatic. Just tired."

In many ways Mamie increasingly relied on the Secret Service men, who provided protection and, on trips, a measure of companionship. "Mamie was fond of her Secret Service men," my mother recalled. "The ones that had been with her for years had a special place. They sometimes carried up her tray, fastened her beads, or took her for rides." They told her that headquarters had sent out a directive that they were only to guard and protect her, but a few who had been with her longest would often still "help"—calling Mamie "Mom." The new agents stood by the letter of the directive and this infuriated her; she was often angry at them all.

With the Secret Service headquarters in an office attached to the barn, some distance from the house, Mamie was essentially alone in the midst of many. Her devoted Sergeant Moaney and his wife, Delores, had retired, and Mamie made do with a number of women who came in to work part-time. She often did the cooking for herself on a hot plate—or munched on something directly from the refrigerator. Once she fell down, and was not discovered until a new shift of Secret Service men had taken over.

Her respect for the family order of things further isolated her. Like the war period, when she refused to go out as a matter of principle, during the holiday seasons she began to take a similar position. She often declined to attend family gatherings, saying that she had to remain at Gettysburg so that the Secret Service men could be with their families. "I am on [their] wives' side," she would say.

Mimi would gratefully receive our Sunday phone calls and revel in our visits, always insisting things were fine with her—anxious to emphasize the importance of what we were doing in our own lives. My sister Mary observed that she would say, " 'You should lead your own lives,' but deep down she probably hoped that no one would listen." Though Mamie was verbally critical about how her sister Mike had managed to keep all of her kids attached to her "apron strings," we probably should have guessed that she longed for the kind of relationship Mike had with her children and she had had with her own parents.

To add to the increasingly incomprehensible nature of contemporary life, in Mamie's last years many young people she knew were getting a divorce. My sister and I were among them. Always good "on the big things," she tried hard to understand what women of my generation wanted, and tried to be supportive. But she couldn't grasp why, for instance, I had left a perfectly decent man, my husband of six years, to start a new life alone with our two children. She had always had a deep affinity for other women, glorying in their good luck and sympathizing with their disappointments and loneliness. But the new pressures on me as a single parent were quite beyond her experience, leaving us to converse about it in uncomfortable confusion. I would come and visit and tell her about my new life, and she would hold in her remarks, listening stiffly to my chronicles of the new challenges, expressing her greatest doubts only to other family members long after I'd gone.

*M*amie thought a good deal about leaving Gettysburg in those years. She looked into going back to the Wyoming; she even spent some time in a suite at the Sheraton Park, next to the Wardman Towers. Consideration was also given to moving to the army distaff home in Washington, but she hesitated because the accommodations were too confining. Besides, John would later point out, "she had no intention of living by their rules." Nevertheless, her situation at Gettysburg, according to her doctors, jeopardized her health and safety, as did the annual pilgrimages she insisted on taking to the places that had meant so much to her and Ike. After one physical her doctor wrote: "Equally important in the management of Mrs. Eisenhower's problems [is that they] relate to her failure to make firm decisions about leaving Gettysburg and her failure to appreciate her present state of health and the practice of accepting obligations without seeking advice. Her recent long train trip to Palm Springs is an example . . . [She] should not accept those requests from 'her public' without seeking medical advice . . . When the 'public' knows the facts, they will not demand her participation."

*P*erhaps the final blow was the resurfacing again of the Summersby controversy, six months before her death. In the spring of 1979, a television network miniseries, based on *Past Forgetting*, was aired, and a paperback novel, written from the show, was released simultaneously.

While Mamie maintained an upbeat attitude throughout, others did not. Merrill Mueller, a correspondent during World War II who had covered the high command, was hired to be a technical adviser on the series. "The first couple of drafts," Mueller said, "kicked history out of the window. There were torrid love scenes . . . It was laughable, ridiculous. They asked me to edit it. I said, 'No way. It needs a rewrite top to bottom.'" Mueller left the project at that stage, stipulating that "no technical advisory credit be listed."

Mickey McKeogh's biggest problem with the program, he said, was that the producers "could not have researched it much, if at all." Eighty-five percent of the show, he said, was "pure baloney." Mickey was never contacted about any aspect of the project, despite his closeness to the general during the war.

When the miniseries aired, we were all conscious that Mimi might have felt a bit defenseless, but she would never have admitted it. According to McKeogh, she watched every one of the segments. "Every night, after an episode ended, we would call each other," he said. At the time, he worried that some scenes might upset her, but Mamie's response was: "Mickey, it doesn't bother me one way or the other. We both know it isn't true."

Mickey remembered the only thing she said she was offended by was the notion that Ike had called her Kay during his secret visit in January 1944. "Ike never called me Kay or anything else but Mamie," she told him firmly.

Beatrice Markle, a local woman who did some cleaning for my grandmother, recalled that Mrs. Eisenhower asked her to watch the episodes with her. Mamie did not seem to be angry with the contents of the program, nor did she give any indication that it depressed her, Mrs. Markle noted, but Mamie did comment on how unattractively she thought she had been portrayed: "Oh, how ugly I've been made to look, but then they have to."

Whatever Mamie may have thought of the show, she was not able to contemplate it in peace. Mail flooded in from all over the country. "The only thing that really disturbed her," my father said, "was receiving sympathy letters. Nobody likes getting sympathy letters."

Many of Ike's intimate wartime family—the daily eyewitnesses to Ike's relationship with Kay Summersby—spoke out against the program. Sir James Gault was deeply offended by the controversy and wrote a letter to the London *Times*. General Mark Clark and many others were also incensed. "In all the years I was in Europe and Africa living with or near the general," Clark said later, "I never noted anything but friendship between him and Kay. I deeply resent such talk. For people to write or say what they have about this imaginary attachment is deplorable—an offense to Mamie and Ike's memory." To me, the show, based on a historically dubious, fictionalized "memoir," only sadly underscored the vast changes that had taken place in Mamie's own lifetime—indeed since World War II. In a democracy, rewriting history is worrisome enough, but, sadly, respect and tradition were also under siege, as the nation's "heroes" were being pulled down everywhere. With the advent of these docudramas, the entertainment industry now profited handsomely from exploiting this national trend.

I often wondered why, after fifty years of unselfish national service, Mimi didn't feel betrayed by a culture that seemed all too ready to believe and almost revel in this unproven gossip. But she gave not a hint of bitterness. In fact, my sister Mary remembers that Mamie commented to her that she had been married to Ike for fifty-three years and "she was comfortable with all that implied."

All the same, Mrs. Markle concluded: "I think it got to her more than she'd like us to know."

*M*amie admitted that she could feel herself slowing down. On August 20, 1979, she wrote me that she had just about decided to spend next winter in Clearwater, Florida, not far from her sister Mike, with whom she remained close. She thought that she would stay at the Old Biltmore Estate, which she admitted was "horribly expensive, but as old age is with me now, I might as well spend my money."

Only weeks later she wrote again, telling me that she was just about to go to Walter Reed Army Hospital for her three-month checkup. "There are many new symptoms of old age we have to iron out at this time," she wrote. And then she added, "Mary Allen's death last Friday was a great shock to me for we had been close friends for years—unexpected too as she was at least 15 years younger than I. Leaves me the only one of the Bolivia group."

Mamie had always been articulate about the difference between the way she felt physically and the way she felt inside. "Even though I'm old on the outside," she would tell me, "I still feel like a young girl." That May she had written her childhood friend Eileen Archibold, "I'm still that little girl skating up and down the sidewalk."

Regardless of how she felt within herself, Mamie had begun to fail physically. According to her medical reports, she had suffered several minor strokes, although they had not been detected earlier. Mimi must have known that she was nearing the end of her life: she kept a packed bag in her dressing room that would be ready if she had to be rushed to the hospital for any reason. What we didn't know until later is that she also had a hanging bag prepared, and in it was the dress she wanted to be buried in, the gown she had worn to celebrate her fiftieth wedding anniversary.

On September 25, sometime after 10:00 in the morning, Mamie was rushed to Walter Reed Hospital suffering from a stroke. Just after the attack, though, she had the presence of mind to see that her burial gown came with her.

My sister Mary recalled that she got the news of Mimi's stroke when, ironically, the television network interrupted *The Guiding Light*, a daytime drama, to show her being wheeled to Ward 8, her head askew, her mouth gaping open. Mary knew Mimi would have been profoundly upset if she had ever had any idea that the news media had filmed her at such an undignified moment.

For one month at Walter Reed, Mimi battled with the impaired use of one leg, paralysis on one side of her mouth, and a frustrating inability to speak coherently, though her mind worked perfectly well. I visited her frequently, as did other family members, but no one but my sister Mary was able to decipher more than the occasional word. Mary, who spent considerable time with her at the hospital, eventually began to understand her gibberish, and was often surprised by what she had to say, such as: "You act like you understand me. But I had parents who had strokes and I also pretended to understand them." Mary reassured her and gained Mimi's confidence.

Mary remembers that during those last weeks our grandmother spoke mostly about her childhood and her parents, mindful that there was little else she could tell any of us about her life with Granddad.

My mother visited her at the hospital and pinned her get-well cards on the curtains so Mamie could see them. Among the bags full of letters was one from Jean MacArthur:

My dear Mamie,
I had dinner with our lovely mutual friend, Mildred Hilson, and of course we talked about you. I have thought of you so much since reading of your hospitalization. I do hope by now you are improving & can soon be home again.

As we grow older I think we go back often in our memory to "long ago happy days." Certainly Manila with you & Ike are always a very special part of those memories.
                         Much love, my dear, & God bless you—
                         Jean

On October 31, Mary visited Mimi in the morning, before returning to her home in Columbus, Georgia. "Mary Jean," Mimi said in her strange language, "I'm glad you came to see me this morning." Perhaps Mimi had forgotten that she had been there regularly for some three weeks, Mary thought, but that was not the case.

"I'm going to die tomorrow," Mimi said with finality.

Delores Moaney and Mamie's sister Mike visited her that day too, but the last family member to see her alive was my father, John. He recalled that he spent two hours with her and left, "feeling low." As he turned to leave that evening, he glanced at his mother one more time, and he remembered that she "looked as if she was going to weep."

On November 1, 1979, at 1:35 a.m., Mamie Doud Eisenhower died in her sleep. Without family members around her, without a room full of physicians, she died as she had lived so many times of her life, peacefully but alone.

𝓘mmediate family members were widely dispersed when the news came of Mimi's death. Despite this, in keeping with family tradition the Gill and Moore cousins, who lived in Washington, stayed up with the body at the funeral home.

From all over the country the family rushed to Washington, and a few days later a service was held at Fort Myer. Many dignitaries attended, led by President and Mrs. Jimmy Carter. Then, courtesy of the president, the body was carried to Abilene, along with family members, aboard Air Force One. Among her family and a crowd of friends, Mamie was at last laid to rest next to her Ike and young son Ikky.

"There are very few originals in this world," wrote one journalist of her passing. "And when one leaves it there is a void. Mamie Eisenhower was an original. She had the courage to define herself rather than have outsiders tell her what she was and what she should be . . . She wore her dignity like a mantle. She set an image for the role of the classic wife, the classic mother, the classic non-political President's wife. She had the guts to be her classic self. She was *Mamie*."

The day of her death, an interview she had given Barbara Walters three weeks before her stroke was broadcast. It *was* classic Mamie. When Miss Walters asked her if her marriage had ever been in jeopardy, Mamie looked at her strangely and said, "All marriages are in jeopardy. That's where your good sense comes in." Did she ever worry about another woman? "Heavens no," Mamie exclaimed. "I wouldn't have stayed with him five minutes if I hadn't had the greatest respect in the world for him, and I never lost my respect."

But when Miss Walters asked her how she wanted to be remembered, Mamie was utterly startled by the question. "Humh, I hadn't even thought about such a thing," she said. And then waving her hand, as if to pass it off as nothing, she added, "Just a good friend."

EPILOGUE

*W*ithout my knowing it fully then, Mamie's death left me with an odd feeling of isolation, a loss of moorings. She had, after all, been my link to a set of values that had survived for centuries and defined womanhood as it was known to all who came before me. Her death to me felt like one more proof that the old order—a way of life—had permanently passed from the scene. Even so, I understood that day, as many people do now, that not everything we call progress has been for the better. Though enormous gains have been made for women especially, a great deal has been lost for us all. The focus on family and friendship that had once been of paramount importance has taken second place in our busy and harried lives. This has been one of our country's greatest losses. As the historian Garry Wills wrote at the time, "Mamie Eisenhower's death seems like the end of an older, in some ways simpler, in some ways nobler America."

After Mamie's death, all of us made trips back to the farm at Gettysburg, if not to settle Mamie's affairs then at least to sit in the silence of the empty house and think about her passing and what was, for us, the end of an era.

My sister Mary was among the first to return and was surprised to find a small photograph album on a chair to the right of the curio cabinet where Mimi stored records and pictures. Picking it up, she discovered that it contained the photographs taken on our grandparents' fiftieth wedding anniversary. When Mary asked one of the park rangers why the album was out, he said they had moved nothing, that it had been sitting on the chair when they reported for duty.

Knowing how fastidious Mamie was about putting things away, Mary guessed that she must have been looking at the photographs not long before she had her stroke. Perhaps she was reviewing her life, which was quite likely, as the anniversary of Ikky's birth, a date Mamie always remembered, occurred the day before she was rushed to Walter Reed.

The house she left behind was in very neat order. As she had all her life, she meticulously cared for "her things." My sister Anne always felt that Mamie was possessive of objects because they had always been in storage and she'd never had her own home until Gettysburg. After Mimi's death, Anne found that every object was documented, with a history of the piece and Mimi's own instructions on whom she wanted to leave it to. Anne remembers that Mimi had wanted her to have a pair of opera glasses that Madame Chiang Kai-shek had given her. In the case with the glasses, Mimi had kept the letter to her from Madame Chiang, as well as her own note to Anne. We discovered that virtually all the major pieces of the house were documented in this way.*

My mother, whose job it was to go through Mamie's most personal effects, found the task an emotionally demanding experience. After working for the better part of a day, thinking about Mamie as she sorted through her lingerie, her evening bags, her hats and accessories of every description, she finished her work and decided to walk around the house one last time before leaving. She wandered out onto the sunporch and drew the curtains back to look at the view that had meant so much to both Mamie and Ike. To her stunned surprise, the three big ash trees that Mamie so loved were gone. It looked almost as if the whole front of the house had been denuded. Anxious inquiries revealed that the trees had begun to die and the park service had cut them down, planning to replace them with other young ash trees.

For my mother this incident, more than any other, underscored Mamie's departure both physically and in some senses spiritually from the property. "It was no longer their home," my mother recalled. "Suddenly it was a museum ready to open."

*After the renovation of the Gettysburg farm, Mamie kept a detailed list of everything in the house, to ensure that any controversy about a gift could easily be resolved. She gave all that material to my father for safekeeping.

But I never really felt that way. I could never separate those rooms from what had happened in them. I went back to the house and on the sunporch I could not help but relive the times we had spent there. It was as if I could hear the faint sounds of laughter and the call "Deal again!" It was at that cast-iron card table that we had played her favorite game of poker—my brother impishly delighted to collect his winnings from her. It was there that she and I had played quiet games of two-handed solitaire. And it was also at that very spot she and I had exchanged the first argumentative words of our relationship, sometime in the midst of my divorce. When I had exclaimed, "Mimi, you make me so mad!" she sat at the table, looking at me with her glittering bright blue eyes. And smiling, she said, "You mean angry, honey, mad means you've lost your mind!" And we both laughed.

She was a friend to so many, but also to us. Her philosophy, honed over years of hardship, was something we kept with us, that stays with us still. When someone passed on gossip about one of her friends, she'd dismiss it by saying, "Oh I don't believe that." If told that a friend of hers was using her, she'd reply gaily, "And I'm using her! She makes me laugh." If things bothered us or brought us low, she'd exclaim, "Just throw it over your shoulder." But most of all, she defended those she loved, and she loved fiercely.

Thinking about his mother later, my father told me that Mamie had lived her life haunted by fears of death and of personal inadequacy. He thought that they had overcome her after Ikky's death. If Mamie Eisenhower had indeed lived with such fears, she spent a lifetime masking them—courageously putting on a bright face to the future, with so many challenges to face. She had a kind of bravery, and Ike played a big part in evoking it.

"I always felt stronger because I knew Ike was there," she once said. "If we had a bad lightning storm, and I'm frightened to death of lightning, if I could hold his hand or get my head under his shoulder, I felt perfectly safe."

She, too, had added to his life immeasurably. Standing back, putting herself behind him, she had given him wings to pursue his career, to fulfill his duty. She had, in a sense, given the nation her husband, a devoted public servant, a world leader. As Kate Hughes once said, "She does the best job of being Mrs. Eisenhower that anyone could possibly do."

After her death Mamie was both eulogized and dismissed. But perhaps the words of Reverend Edward Elson seemed most appropriate in describing the vital essence of her role in the Eisenhower partnership. "Some women achieve distinction as club leaders or teachers. Others reach great heights in the professions or the arts. But to be a mate of a man . . . to complete his incompleteness, to make a strong man stronger—that too is the essence of greatness."

Years later, while my grandparents' personal effects were still being sorted out, I came across a letter resting somewhere on top of a pile of papers, but I recognized my grandfather's handwriting immediately. I was surprised, as this was long after *Letters to Mamie* had been published, and one letter had apparently become separated from the others. On the outside of the envelope, addressed to Mrs. Dwight D. Eisenhower, Wardman Park, there was a simple line: "censored by"—and Granddad had signed his own name.

Written during the war, it was to be opened only in case of his demise. I wondered how it had been delivered to Mimi, and if she had ever read it.

I savored the letter for a moment. The paper had become a bit brown, the corners a little curled. Written on short bond paper, with no letterhead or any special markings, it would not have been clear who had written it, if not for the envelope.

July 1, 1943

Darling Girl—
I hope you never have to read this note—because it's kept in an envelope that is to be opened only in case of accident to me. But if such should happen you will receive, this way, at least one more assurance that I love you only—that I have been the most fortunate of men in having you for my wife, and that I'm proud of our son. I love him so much that I follow every word he writes to me with curious intensity. He is what he is, only because he had you for a mother. So do not grieve—if I go out in this war, I hope I will have left a name of which you need not be ashamed, and that it will be uni-

versally acknowledged that I did my duty to the best of my ability.

Spend no time in mourning—you can still make a number of people happy in this world—and that's the surest road to your own happiness. With all my love always—Your Lover, for all these years.

NOTES

ABBREVIATIONS

ABE   Arthur B. Eisenhower
BTE   Barbara Thompson Eisenhower
BTEF   Barbara Thompson Eisenhower Foltz
DDE   Dwight David Eisenhower
DDEL   Dwight David Eisenhower Library
ED   Eleanor Doud
EMD   Elvira Mathilde Doud (Nana)
EWC   Eda Wilhemina Carlson (Auntie)
GCM   George C. Marshall
HB   Harry Butcher
HST   Harry S Truman
ISE   Ida Stover Eisenhower
JC   Joel Carlson
JFM   Jean Faircloth MacArthur
JNE   Julie Nixon Eisenhower
JSD   John S. Doud
JSDE   John S. D. Eisenhower
KG   Katie Geron
KS   Kay Summersby
MD   Mamie Doud
MDE   Mamie Doud Eisenhower
OH   Oral History
RNL   Ruby Norman Lucier
SE   Susan Eisenhower

FOREWORD

xviii "clichés to guard their privacy": Barbara T. Eisenhower (Foltz)'s unpublished manuscript (hereafter BTE manuscript) based on tapes and interviews she conducted with her mother-in-law, Mamie Eisenhower; private collection.

CHAPTER ONE

3 "You have to use the gifts you have": Author interview with Mary Jane McCafree Monroe, March 17, 1995. The interviewee was Mamie Eisenhower's secretary during the campaigns and the White House years.

4 "I hate old-lady clothes": Karal Ann Marling, *As Seen on T.V.* (Cambridge, Mass.: Harvard University Press, 1994), p. 24.

6 "wowed the sovereigns and shopgirls": Ruth Montgomery, "Mamie: An Intimate Portrait of Our Vivacious First Lady after One Year in the White House," *Look*, February 23, 1954, p. 31.

6 "I've *never* had any social ambitions": John Wickman interview with MDE, August 16, 1972, OH #12, DDEL.

6 For background on the early years of John S. Doud, see Alden Hatch, *Red Carpet for Mamie Eisenhower* (New York: Popular Library, 1954), p. 18.

7 For background on the early Carlsons, see George Feltner, "Eisenhower's Mother-in-Law," *American Swedish Monthly*, October 1952; and Boone County Historical Society, bulletin 6, June/July 1971.

8 "Oh my God, it was worth a whole sermon": Author interview with JSDE, August 23, 1994.

8 On Nana as a tomboy: Author interview with JSDE, August 24, 1994.

8 On speaking Swedish at home, and other early details: BTE manuscript.

8 "Carl is capable and kind": The family has photocopies of this and other letters in Swedish. They were also published in "Swedish Letters Read in the White House," *American Swedish Monthly*, May 1960.

9 she looked like "a little picked chicken": JNE, *Special People* (New York: Simon and Schuster, 1977), p. 212.

9 Cedar Rapids was only a short train ride away from Boone: From MDE's handwritten biographical notes, written during the first presidential campaign; private collection.

10 Mamie also spent part of her summer vacations: From handwritten notes made by MDE, July 25, 1963, private collection.

10 "On Sundays, we'd visit Boone": BTE 1979 taped interview with MDE, private collection.

10 he already had a fortune: Dorothy Brandon, *Mamie Doud Eisenhower: Portrait of a First Lady* (New York: Charles Scribner's Sons, 1954), p. 49.

10 "Eleanor could ride in a carriage": BTE undated taped interview with Mamie; BTE manuscript, private collection.

10 To alleviate water retention: BTE to MDE, last tape, September 16, 1979, private collection.

11 At the turn of the century: See Hatch, *Red Carpet*, p. 36, for this and other background on Denver in those years.

11 Care about appearances: The Douds as "appearance conscious" was always a source of amusement in our family. Many stories abounded. See JSDE, *Strictly Personal* (Garden City, N.Y.: Doubleday and Company, 1974), p. 13.

11 "Auntie got the short end": Author interview with JSDE, August 23, 1994.

12 Regarding the pride Mamie attached to their modern "rec" room: Author interview with JSDE, August 23, 1994. Also see Wickman (and Maclyn Burg) interview with MDE, July 20, 1972, OH #12, DDEL.

12 In 1904, while the family still lived: Lester David and Irene David, *Ike and Mamie: The Story of the General and His Lady* (New York: G. P. Putnam's Sons, 1981), pp. 26–27.

12 "Our whole life was centered around [our] family...": BTE 1979 interview with MDE, private collection.

13 "My Dear Little Eleanor": JSD to ED, February 20, 1911, private collection.

13 And in those early years, Mamie asked for and received jewelry: BTE 1979 interview with MDE, private collection.

13 "It was a girl family": BTE 1979 interview with MDE, private collection.

14 But perhaps the biggest dates in the year were the birthdays: BTE 1979 interview with MDE, private collection.

14 "Dear Papa": MDE to JSD, November 15, 1911, private collection.

14 "[Mama] leaned on him": BTE 1979 interview with MDE, private collection.

14 Even after his daughters had married: BTE 1979 interview with MDE, private collection.

15 "The women of the house beat him down": Author interview with JSDE, August 24, 1994.

15 Once, he punished her for some wrongdoing: BTE 1979 interview with MDE, private collection.

15 when Pupah was on the road: JSDE, *Strictly Personal*, p. 12.

16 "Beloved Parents, Brothers and Sister": Among photocopies in Ei-

senhower family possession. It is my understanding that the originals are in the Swedish Museum in Philadelphia, but I do not have that confirmed.

17 All the town, it seemed: See Hatch, *Red Carpet*, p. 47.

17 Nana was so distraught: BTE 1979 interview with MDE, private collection.

18 wrong for parents to make young children focus on death so much: BTE 1979 interview with MDE, private collection.

18 Mamie would make a special effort to minimize sadness: BTE interview with Kate Hughes, undated, private collection.

19 "My Dear Little Puddy": JSD to MDE, June 3, 1912, private collection.

20 On Mamie's attendence at Corona Street School, see Hatch, *Red Carpet*, pp. 39–48.

20 On the Douds' attitude regarding formal education: BTE 1979 interview with MDE, private collection.

20 For the school year 1914–15: Hatch, *Red Carpet*, p. 52.

21 regarded as one of Denver's most captivating belles: Hatch, *Red Carpet*, p. 57.

21 she was utterly feminine: "The President's Lady" (cover story), *Time*, January 19, 1953, p. 17.

CHAPTER TWO

22 Some Eisenhower historians say: Steve Neal, *The Eisenhowers: Reluctant Dynasty* (Garden City, N.Y.: Doubleday and Company 1978), p. 4.

22 But recent scholarship suggests: Walter Petto, "Notes on the Origins of Dwight D. Eisenhower" (Saarbrucken, Germany), *The Palatine Immigrant*, vol. 17, no. 2 (September 1992), pp. 160–75.

23 After a thorough medical examination: Neal, *Eisenhowers: Reluctant Dynasty*, p. 3.

23 Jacob, Dwight's grandfather: Stephen E. Ambrose, *Eisenhower: Soldier, General of the Army, President-Elect* (New York: Simon and Schuster, 1983), p. 14.

23 Although the pacifist teachings: Ibid.

24 Abilene's infamous Texas Street: DDE, *At Ease: Stories I Tell to Friends* (Garden City, N.Y.: Doubleday and Company, 1967), p. 65.

24 the Union Army, under General Sheridan: DDE, *At Ease*, p. 77.

25 The campaign had rivaled Sherman's march: Ibid.

25 "a man of few words": Bela Kornitzer, "The Story of Ike and His Four Brothers," *U.S. News and World Report*, July 1, 1955, p. 116.

26 The disaster meant that the Eisenhowers lost everything: Michael

R. Beschloss, *Eisenhower: A Centennial Life* (New York: HarperCollins, 1990), p. 17.

26 Because they had no money for a crib: Ibid., p. 18.

26 "when Roy was born": Kornitzer, "The Story of Ike and His Four Brothers," p. 114.

27 Fifty years later: Beschloss, *Eisenhower: A Centennial Life*, p. 18.

27 David, as his son Arthur later recalled: Kornitzer, "The Story of Ike and His Four Brothers," p. 116.

27 Edgar once said: Ibid., p. 117.

28 "To me this was distressing": Ibid., p. 122.

28 "We were a cheerful and vital family": DDE, *At Ease*, p. 74.

28 "her sincerity, her open smile": Ibid., p. 76.

28 Dwight, for example, was befriended: Ibid., p. 89.

29 According to Arthur, Edgar and Dwight "were so tough": Kornitzer, "The Story of Ike and His Four Brothers," p. 124.

29 But by 1905: DDE, *At Ease*, p. 95.

29 "History was always Dwight's passion": Neal, *Eisenhowers: Reluctant Dynasty*, p. 17.

29 "This had the desired effect": DDE, *In Review: Pictures I've Kept* (Garden City, N.Y.: Doubleday, 1969), p. 5.

29 "It was not difficult to persuade me": Ibid., p. 9.

30 Securing the West Point appointment: DDE, *At Ease*, pp. 105–6.

30 Milton, who was with them on the day: Ibid., p. 108.

31 Dwight had difficulties adjusting: DDE, *In Review*, p. 12.

31 "From here on in": Ibid., p. 13.

31 Although he was lean: Ibid., p. 14.

31 "I was almost despondent": DDE, *At Ease*, p. 16.

31 "I sure hate to be so helpless": Box 1, Ruby Norman Lucier Papers, DDEL.

31 Eisenhower's disciplinary record: DDE, *In Review*, p. 15.

32 Eisenhower is said to have replied sarcastically: Author interview with JSDE, December 13, 1995.

32 As the days wore on: See Beschloss, *Eisenhower: A Centennial Life*, pp. 21 and 24.

CHAPTER THREE

33 "always had an itchy foot": BTE 1979 interview with MDE, private collection.

34 Story of the meeting of MD and DDE: BTE 1979 interview with MDE, private collection.

34 "If she had been intrigued": DDE, *At Ease: Stories I Tell to Friends* (Garden City, N.Y.: Doubleday and Company, 1967), p. 113.

34 As he told a journalist: Virgil Pinkley and James F. Scheer, *Eisenhower Declassified* (Old Tappan, N.J.; Flemming H. Revell Company, 1979), p. 72.

34 " 'Now Miss Doud' ": Mamie Eisenhower, "My Memories of Ike," *Reader's Digest*, February 1970, p. 71.

34 Captivated by Mamie's flirtatious charm: BTE 1979 interview with MDE, private collection.

35 "stop her flighty nonsense": Dorothy Brandon, *Mamie Doud Eisenhower: Portrait of a First Lady* (New York: Charles Scribner's Sons, 1954), p. 51.

35 "My Dear Little Girl": JSD to MDE, December 6, 1915, private collection.

36 "Dearest Ruby": DDE to RNL, Box 1, Ruby Norman Lucier Papers, DDEL.

37 There was never really a formal proposal: BTE manuscript, private collection.

37 "We took it for granted": BTE 1979 interview with MDE, private collection.

38 Her father finally conceded: Brandon, *Mamie Eisenhower: Portrait of a First Lady*, p. 59.

39 "After looking at the matter": DDE, *At Ease*, p. 118.

39 "The diamond": BTE manuscript, private collection.

39 "As a symbol of my new seriousness": DDE, *At Ease*, pp. 117–18.

40 "I was worried I would lose him": BTE 1979 interview with MDE, private collection.

40 When Mamie told her parents: BTE manuscript, private collection.

41 As the lights of Denver: John Wickman, interview with MDE, July 20, 1972, OH #12, DDEL.

42 Then they caught a glimpse: Ibid.

42 "they were completely different": BTE manuscript, private collection.

42 she would hang out of the upstairs window: Denis Medina, curator of the Eisenhower Museum at the Eisenhower Center, to author.

43 "The Eisenhowers were so": Author interview with JSDE, August 24, 1994.

43 Mamie, too, had her theories: Wickman interview with MDE, July 20, 1972, OH #12, DDEL.

CHAPTER FOUR

45 "squeeze a dollar": Dorothy Brandon, *Mamie Doud Eisenhower: Portrait of a First Lady* (New York: Charles Scribner's Sons, 1954) p. 48.

45 "Shortly after we were married": MDE, "My Memories of Ike," *Reader's Digest*, February 1970, p. 71.

45 "In our family": BTE manuscript, private collection.

46 "the role of peacemaker": JSDE, *Strictly Personal* (Garden City, N.Y.: Doubleday, 1974), p. 14.

46 "untrained soldiers": For this anecdote, see DDE, *At Ease: Stories I Tell to Friends* (Garden City, N.Y.: Doubleday and Company, 1967), pp. 124–25.

46 "When she stepped out of line": Author interview with Mary Jane McCafree Monroe, March 17, 1995.

47 The "old army": See Russell Weigly, *The History of the American Army* (Bloomington: Indiana University Press, 1984); Marvin Fletcher, *The Peacetime Army: A Research Guide* (Burlington: Greenwood Press, 1988), p. 10.

48 On post, the tradition of calling: BTE manuscript, private collection.

49 "Dearest Santa Claus": MDE to JSD, December 15, 1916, private collection.

50 "Our car sat idly": BTE manuscript, private collection.

50 "Ike, jump on": DDE, *At Ease*, p. 128.

51 "It was no place": This account is based on BTE 1979 interview with MDE, private collection.

52 Mamie refused: BTE 1979 interview with MDE, private collection.

52 "you either came through": MDE to BTE, September 19, 1979, their last taped interview, private collection.

52 "I seemed embedded": DDE, *At Ease*, p. 136.

52 Ike's pleas: Steve Neal, *The Eisenhowers: Reluctant Dynasty* (Garden City, N.Y.: Doubleday and Company, 1978), p. 43.

52 "Our new Captain Eisenhower": Ibid., p. 143.

53 Mamie's excitement: The account of how they settled in in Gettysburg is based on BTE manuscript, private collection.

54 "It *was* a very difficult time": John Wickman interview with MDE, July 20, 1972, OH #12, DDEL.

54 That July: BTE manuscript, private collection.

55 "The week was a nightmare": DDE, *At Ease*, p. 150.

56 "My Own Dearest Mother": DDE to EMD, November 9, 1918, private collection.

56 With Ike's departure for Europe: The facts pertaining to this section were found in BTE manuscript, private collection.

CHAPTER FIVE

58 Since Mamie was gone: BTE manuscript, private collection.

58 Only the highest-ranking officers had quarters: DDE, *At Ease: Stories I Tell to Friends* (Garden City, N.Y.: Doubleday and Company, 1967), p. 155.

58 The convoy was given: *Trail Tales*, Boone Historical Society, April 1990; DDE, *At Ease*, pp. 158–59.

59 "Dearest": DDE to MDE, June 18, 1919, private collection.

59 "I can't say too much": *Trail Tales*, p. 6.

59 With the convoy: BTE manuscript, private collection.

60 Leaving Laurel: BTE manuscript, private collection.

61 "Dearest Mother": DDE to EMD, November 16, 1919, private collection.

62 "When we left Fort Sam": BTE 1979 interview with MDE, private collection.

62 Now they had to make do: John Wickman interview with MDE, July 20, 1972, OH #12, DDEL.

62 Perhaps that was one of the things Mamie liked best about it: Ibid.

63 Once, when Patton: Author interview with JSDE, August 24, 1994.

63 Once, both Patton and Eisenhower: DDE, *At Ease*, p. 171.

63 "our career": Wickman interview with MDE, August 16, 1972, OH #12, DDEL.

63 "bought into the partnership idea": Author interview with JSDE, August 23, 1994.

64 Though social faux pas were rare: This anecdote was told by Mamie in BTE 1979 interviews with MDE, though it has appeared in many other accounts.

65 Ike, too, recalled those happy times: DDE, *At Ease*, p. 180.

65 "Dearest Folksies": MDE to Douds, undated, Box 4, family letters, 1920, BTE Papers, DDEL.

66 That fall, with only Eda and Mike remaining: EWC to JC, September 17, 1920, Box 1, BTE Papers, DDEL.

66 The next month: EWC to JC, undated, Box 1, BTE Papers, DDEL.

67 "Nana was taking care of Ikky": BTE last interview with MDE, September 16, 1979, private collection.

68 "Dearest Folksies": MDE to Douds, undated, Box 1, BTE Papers, DDEL.

69 "Our first week at home": DDE to Douds, January 29, 1921, private collection.

70 "I haven't received the statements": DDE to Douds, January 29, 1921, private collection.

70 "Dearest Folksies": MDE to Douds, January 31, 1921, Box 1, BTE Papers, DDEL.

71 "we are in the midst": DDE to Douds, dated only "Tuesday," private collection.

71 "Dear Mrs. Doud": A. M. Sheets to EMD, private collection.

72 "no matter what activities": DDE, *At Ease*, pp. 181–82.

CHAPTER SIX

73 "Giving up a baby": *Better Homes and Gardens*, August 1960, p. 49.

73 Ikky's death "closed a chapter": JNE, *Special People* (New York: Simon and Schuster, 1977), p. 198.

73 Every year on the anniversary: BTE last interview with MDE, September 16, 1979, private collection.

74 "ragged edges of a breakdown": Michael R. Beschloss, *Eisenhower: A Centennial Life* (New York: HarperCollins, 1990), p. 28; and Lester David and Irene David, *Ike and Mamie: The Story of the General and His Lady* (New York: G. P. Putnam's Sons, 1981), p. 81.

74 Even though Mamie already knew she was pregnant: BTE 1979 tapes with MDE, private collection.

74 "handsome silver vase inscribed": DDE, *At Ease: Stories I Tell to Friends* (Garden City, N.Y.: Doubleday and Company, 1967), p. 182.

75 Since attempts to construct a canal: Bob Considine, *The Panama Canal* (New York: Random House, 1951), p. 103.

75 "Yellow fever, malaria and cold feet": Ibid.

75 with one of the worst cases of seasickness: BTE manuscript, private collection. This account, based on BTE's interviews, differs from DDE's (see *At Ease*, p. 183). Most probably, Mamie held up pretty well during the journey until that one big storm.

76 "proper grooming": Dorothy Brandon, *Mamie Doud Eisenhower: Portrait of a First Lady* (New York: Charles Scribner's Sons, 1954), p. 24.

76 "For Mamie": DDE, *At Ease*, p. 184.

76 No one could say: David McCullough, *The Path Between the Seas: The Creation of the Panama Canal* (New York: Simon and Schuster, 1977), p. 55. Also see DDE, *At Ease*, p. 185.

76 Ike and Mamie were assigned: Details of their accommodations were found in BTE manuscript, private collection.

77 bedbugs were also a concern: John Wickman interview with MDE, July 20, 1972, OH #12, DDEL.

77 "Mrs. Conner thought": Wickman interview with MDE, July 10, 1972, OH #12, DDEL.

77 achieved an "uneasy peace with her surroundings": BTE manuscript, private collection.

77 On cutting her hair: Brandon, *Portrait of a First Lady*, pp. 136–37.

78 No funds were forthcoming: BTE manuscript, unpublished, private collection.

78 "You're going to Denver": Wickman interview with MDE, July 20, 1972, OH #12, DDEL.

78 "My Sweetgirl": DDE to MDE, June 3 (1922), private collection.

80 On the night the baby was born: BTE manuscript, private collection.

80 "did much to fill the gap": DDE, *At Ease*, p. 194.

81 "Dear Folksies": MDE to Douds, undated, Box 4, BTE Papers, DDEL.

81 "One of the profound beliefs": DDE, *At Ease*, p. 195.

82 but her possessiveness: BTE last interview with MDE, September 16, 1979, private collection.

82 "Dearest Daddy": MDE to JSD, undated letter, Box 4, BTE Papers, DDEL.

83 "I was down to skin and bones": BTE 1979 interviews with MDE, private collection.

83 But as Mamie began to feel better: BTE manuscript, private collection.

84 "Dearest Folksies": MDE to Douds, "Thursday," Box 4, BTE Papers, DDEL.

85 "I knew almost from the day I married Ike": Brandon, *Portrait of a First Lady*, p. 77.

CHAPTER SEVEN

87 "necessary stop": Marvin Fletcher, *The Peacetime Army: A Research Guide* (Burlington: Greenwood Press, 1988), p. 8.

87 "No matter what orders": DDE, *At Ease: Stories I Tell to Friends* (Garden City, N.Y.: Doubleday and Company, 1967), p. 199.

87 "I was ready to fly": Ibid. p. 200.

87 facing his well-prepared competition: See Stephen E. Ambrose, *Eisenhower: Soldier, General of the Army, President-Elect* (New York: Simon and Schuster, 1983), p. 79, on the whole process.

88 "the night I invaded Dad's attic study": JSDE, *Strictly Personal* (Garden City, N.Y.: Doubleday and Company, 1974), pp. 1–2.

89 Katie did much to teach Mamie the ropes: Author interview with BTEF, December 13, 1995.

90 "They took a guy who'd graduated number one in his class": Author interview with JSDE, August 24, 1994.

90 "full of zip and rebellion": See JSDE, *Strictly Personal*, p. 14. This was also confirmed in numerous telephone interviews.

91 "John would be no difficulty": MDE interview with John Wickman, July 20, 1972, OH #2, DDEL.

91 "[Eisenhower] has shown superior ability": Eisenhower Efficiency Reports, Dwight David Eisenhower Museum.

91 "apply the knowledge": See Ira L. Reeves, *Military Education in the United States* (Free Press, 1914).

91 "A major never had been": Wickman interview with MDE, July 20, 1972, OH #12, DDEL.

92 Because of weather delays: Dorothy Brandon, *Mamie Doud Eisenhower: Portrait of a First Lady* (New York: Charles Scribner's Sons, 1954), p. 164.

93 "Dearest Folksies": MDE to Douds, December 25, 1928, Box 1, BTE Papers, DDEL.

94 Mamie also found it hard: Wickman interview with MDE, July 20, 1972, OH #12, DDEL.

94 "Dear Dad, Mother, and All": DDE to Douds, February 11, 1929, private collection.

95 "Ike says he's dying by inches": MDE to Douds, March 13, 1929, Box 1, BTE Papers, DDEL.

95 "Two hundred miles": MDE to Douds, April 6, 1929, Box 1, BTE Papers, DDEL.

96 "Dearest Folksies": MDE to Douds, April 17, 1929, Box 1, BTE Papers, DDEL.

97 "Aren't we seeing the country, tho": MDE to Douds, May 13, 1929, Box 1, BTE Papers, DDEL.

97 My father vividly remembers: JSDE, *Strictly Personal*, p. 3.

97 "I wish you could hear": MDE to Douds, May 13, 1929, Box 1, BTE Papers, DDEL.

98 "talked about Ikky a lot": Author interview with JSDE, July 27, 1995.

98 "The weather is marvelous now": MDE to Douds, June 10, 1929, Box 1, BTE Papers, DDEL.

98 "kicking up their heels": BTE last taped interview with MDE, September 16, 1979, private collection.

98 Their outings on the town: These news clippings were enclosed in MDE to Douds, May 13, 1929, BTE Papers, DDEL.

98 "on their own steam": DDE to Douds, April 26, 1929, private collection.

98 some months before the guidebook: MDE to JSD, June 10, 1929, Box 1, BTE Papers, DDEL.

98 Ike checked himself into the American Hospital: MDE to Douds, June 17, 1929, Box 1, BTE Papers, DDEL.

99 Mamie was enraptured with the Riviera: This description can be found in MDE to Douds, July 15, 1929, Box 1, BTE Papers, DDEL.

100 "Ike is just in his glory after breakfast": MDE to Douds, July 15, 1929, Box 1, BTE Papers, DDEL.

100 "Last night we sat in the garden": MDE to Douds, July 15, 1929, Box 1, BTE Papers, DDEL.

101 "Wednesday—August 28": The following passages in this chapter are excerpts from what is called the Gruber Diary (though the passages quoted were written by Ike), box 1, William R. Gruber Papers, DDEL.

107 "pour tout [sic] la commission": MDE to Douds, September 22, 1929, Box 1, BTE Papers, DDEL.

CHAPTER EIGHT

109 "It was a long, irksome job": DDE, *At Ease: Stories I Tell to Friends* (Garden City, N.Y.: Doubleday and Company, 1967), pp. 211–12.

110 Club Eisenhower reassembled: There is a reference to this in one of Mamie's letters to her parents, dated September 24, 1930, Box 1, BTE Papers, DDEL.

110 "Mamie always seemed like a sort of helpless little creature": BTE undated interview with Kate Hughes, private collection.

110 "She was there for Johnny": Ibid.

110 "violent leg aches": JSDE, *Strictly Personal* (Garden City, N.Y.: Doubleday and Company, 1974), p. 10.

111 "Like any other youngster": Ibid., p. 11.

111 "He's marble-crazy right now": MDE to Douds, November 10, 1930, Box 1, BTE Papers, DDEL.

111 regale her parents with purchasing victories: MDE to Douds, January 20, 1931, Box 1, BTE Papers, DDEL.

111 "I got a beautiful": MDE to Douds, September 2, 1933, Box 1, BTE Papers, DDEL.

111 Pupah paid for a maid for Mamie: John Wickman interview with MDE, July 20, 1972, OH #12, DDEL.

112 "Johnnie & I are giving": DDE to Douds, November 12, 1931, private collection.

112 "The day Ike gave me": Dorothy Brandon, *Mamie Doud Eisenhower: Portrait of a First Lady* (New York: Charles Scribner's Sons, 1954), p. 173.

112 "Darling, July 1": DDE Pre-presidential Papers, DDEL.

113 "This week will be a busy one": MDE to Douds, November 13, 1930, Box 1, BTE Papers, DDEL.

113 Once, she and Ike invited: See Steve Neal, *The Eisenhowers: Reluctant Dynasty* (Garden City, N.Y.: Doubleday, 1978), p. 78; and Brandon, *Portrait of a First Lady*, p. 173.

113 "The party flowers": Ibid.

114 "I looked grand last night": MDE to Douds, November 12, 1931, Box 1, BTE Papers, DDEL.

114 "It was a safe society": Author interview with JSDE, August 23, 1994.

114 "I remember admiring": Author interview with JSDE, August 24, 1994.

115 "I am thrilled over": MDE to Douds, July 13, 1932, Box 1, BTE Papers, DDEL.

115 "I pictured you two going": MDE to Douds, June 3, 1935, Box 2, BTE Papers, DDEL.

115 "It was hard-going for a ten- or eleven-year-old": Author interview with JSDE, August 24, 1994.

115 "I remember gushing": Author interview with JSDE, August 23, 1994.

116 "We are getting along fine": MDE to Douds, July 4, 1932, Box 1, BTE Papers, DDEL.

116 "I walked six holes": MDE to Douds, June 23, 1932, Box 1, BTE Papers, DDEL.

116 "You enjoyed going to the Senate": DDE to Douds, February 5, 1931, private collection.

117 "Am terribly sorry about Auntie": MDE to Douds, October 1, 1931, Box 1, BTE Papers, DDEL.

117 "Yesterday I spent the morning": MDE to Douds, undated, Box 4, BTE Papers, DDEL.

118 "You don't have to do a thing": KG to MDE, December 30, 1931, private collection.

118 "it is my only parlour trick": MDE to Douds, March 31, 1932, Box 1, BTE Papers, DDEL.

118 On the effects of the Depression, see Robert Goldston, *The Road Between the Wars* (New York: Fawcett Crest, 1978).

118 "deferred bonus was identical": DDE, *At Ease*, p. 215.

119 "animated by the essence": Neal, *Eisenhowers: Reluctant Dynasty*, p. 86.

119 "The presence of Federal troops in some number": Letter to President Hoover from L. H. Reichelderfer, July 28, 1932, folder "Bonus March," Box 129, DDE Pre-presidential Papers, 1916–52, DDEL.

119 "I told him that the matter": DDE, *At Ease*, p. 216.

119 "Dad kept his clothes": From a memo written by JSDE, a remembrance of apartment #302, private collection.

120 "The veterans, whether or not": DDE, *At Ease*, p. 217.

120 "I have never seen greater relief": Transcript of the MacArthur press conference, July 28, 1932, 11:00 p.m., folder "Bonus March," Box 129, DDE Pre-presidential Papers, 1916–1952, DDEL.

121 "Dearest Folks . . . *Well* if we didn't have excitement": MDE to Douds, July 30, 1932, Box 1, BTE Papers, DDEL. The author has reversed the order of two paragraphs to make it easier to read.

122 "Dearest Daddy": Ibid.

123 "Dearest Mamie": KG to MDE, dated August 9, private collection.

124 "We had thot [sic] of asking": MDE to Douds, October 27, 1932, Box 1, BTE Papers, DDEL.

124 "Everyone expects to do very little": MDE to Douds, August 18, 1932, Box 1, BTE Papers, DDEL.

124 "There is an order out": MDE to Douds, October 8, 1932, Box 2, BTE Papers, DDEL.

CHAPTER NINE

126 "We have been moving": MDE to Douds, August 12, 1933, Box 1, BTE Papers, DDEL.

126 "Too bad": MDE to Douds, July 26, 1933, Box 1, BTE Papers, DDEL.

127 "Ike's back": MDE to Douds, November 6, 1933, Box 1, BTE Papers, DDEL.

127 Ike's civilian doctor was so intrigued: MDE to Douds, November 11, 1933, Box 1, BTE Papers, DDEL.

127 "We have a good, warm home": MDE to Douds, November 28, 1933, Box 1, BTE Papers, DDEL.

127 "Dad and I rose about the same time": JSDE, *Strictly Personal* (Garden City, N.Y.: Doubleday and Company, 1974), p. 6.

128 On becoming blood brothers: Ibid. pp. 7–8.

129 While Mamie may have had some flashes of conscience: MDE to Douds, September 22, 1933, Box 1, BTE Papers, DDEL.

129 "My parents": Author interview with JSDE, August 24, 1994; JSDE memo of reminiscences of #302 Wyoming apartments.

129 Other Sundays: See JSDE, *Strictly Personal*, p. 8.

130 "Ike just follows": MDE to Douds, September 18, 1934, Box 2, BTE Papers, DDEL.

130 "I am sorry you worry": MDE to Douds, October 29, 1934, Box 2, BTE Papers, DDEL.

130 During this time: Steve Neal, *The Eisenhowers: Reluctant Dynasty* (Garden City, N.Y.: Doubleday, 1978), p. 94.

130 "Well, Ike," she said: John Wickman interview with MDE, July 20, 1972, OH #12, DDEL.

131 "Well what a birthday": MDE to Douds, November 16, 1934, Box 2, BTE Papers, DDEL.

131 When Ike hesitated: Neal, *Eisenhowers: Reluctant Dynasty*, p. 95.

132 "As you probably know": DDE to Col. Daniel Van Voorhis, Chief of Staff, Hawaiian Department, Fort Shafter, June 5, 1935, Box 118, DDEL.

132 "It's heartbreaking": MDE to Douds, May 18, 1935; MDE to Douds, June 3, 1935, Box 2, BTE Papers, DDEL.

132 "Poor little girl": MDE to Douds, June 17, 1935, Box 2, BTE Papers, DDEL.

133 "I've had a terrible time": MDE to Douds, June 25, 1935, Box 2, BTE Papers, DDEL.

133 "[He] seems terribly low": MDE to Douds, July 10, 1935, Box 2, BTE Papers, DDEL.

134 "... I deeply appreciate": DDE to Douds, undated, private collection.

135 Miserable at being separated: MDE to Douds, November 15, 1935, Box 2, BTE Papers, DDEL.

135 "He was terribly lonesome": Ibid.

135 "Once in a while": DDE to JSDE, November 27, 1935, private collection.

136 For Christmas 1935: MDE to Douds, January 4, 1936, Box 2, BTE Papers, DDEL.

137 "I'm having a pretty hard time": MDE to Douds, February 13, 1936, Box 2, BTE Papers, DDEL.

137 "I still don't know what Ike's plans are": MDE to Douds, February 13, 1936, Box 2, BTE Papers, DDEL.

137 "far from cheerful": MDE to Douds, March 31, 1936, Box 2, BTE Papers, DDEL.

138 "Gee says": MDE to Douds, April 26, 1936, Box 2, BTE Papers, DDEL.

138 "[It's] hard to realize": MDE to Douds, May 18, 1936, Box 2, BTE Papers, DDEL.

138 "So Tues.": MDE to Douds, July 26, 1936, Box 2, BTE Papers, DDEL.

139 "Poor fellow": Ibid.

139 "Kate and Everett are fine friends": MDE to Douds, July 21, 1936, Box 2, BTE Papers, DDEL.

CHAPTER TEN

140 For the establishment of the Philippines, see Robert Goldston, *The Road Between the Wars* (New York: Fawcett Crest, 1978), p. 141.

141 When MacArthur informed Ike: Steve Neal, *The Eisenhowers: Reluctant Dynasty* (Garden City, N.Y.: Doubleday, 1978), p. 102.

142 "One had to react alertly": DDE, *At Ease* (Garden City, N.Y.: Doubleday and Company, 1967), p. 226.

143 "I gather I have grounds": Author interview with JSDE, August 24, 1994.

143 General MacArthur . . . had requested: John Wickman interview with MDE, August 15, 1972, OH #12, DDEL.

143 At night the hotel staff: Dorothy Brandon, *Mamie Doud Eisenhower: Portrait of a First Lady* (New York: Charles Scribner's Sons: 1954), p. 185.

144 Coping with the heat: MDE to Douds, April 28, 1938, Box 2, BTE Papers, DDEL.

144 the evening the quake took place: MDE to Douds, August 27, 1937, Box 2, BTE Papers, DDEL; see also JSDE, *Strictly Personal* (Garden City, N.Y.: Doubleday and Company, 1974), p. 23. On reactions to other quakes: MDE to Douds, February 25, 1938, and May 27, 1938, Box 2, BTE Papers, DDEL.

144 On the Philippines' paternalistic culture: MDE to Douds, March 21, 1938, Box 2, BTE Papers, DDEL.

144 Perhaps the most unsettling discovery: Author interview with JSDE, August 24, 1994.

145 On the road to Baguio: MDE to Douds, February 17, 1938, and June 27, 1938, Box 2, BTE Papers, DDEL.

145 Regarding the account of the accident and Mamie's subsequent illness: Author interview with JSDE, August 24, 1994.

146 The incident regarding Oswald: see JSDE, *Strictly Personal*, p. 23.

147 "He'd done right well for himself": MDE to Douds, May 7, 1937, Box 2, BTE Papers, DDEL.

147 the winds of war: Goldston, *The Road Between the Wars*, pp. 189–90, 202.

147 On December 12: See JSDE, *Strictly Personal*, p. 24.

148 "the famous Chinese Pier": MDE to Douds, January 17, 1938, Box 2, BTE Papers, DDEL.

148 "I am rotten": Ibid.

148 With the birth of the general's first child: MDE to Douds, February 25, 1938, Box 2, BTE Papers, DDEL.

148 The exotic charm of it: MDE to Douds, January 21, 1938, Box 2, BTE Papers, DDEL.

149 On his last Sunday there: DDE, *At Ease*, p. 227.

149 "It was a terrific shock": MDE to Douds, February 9, 1938, Box 2, BTE Papers, DDEL.

150 "The accident has made me realize": MDE to Douds, February 8, 1938, Box 2, BTE Papers, DDEL.

150 "not only a congenial fellow": DDE, *At Ease*, p. 227.

151 Mamie could tell: MDE to Douds, February 25, 1938, Box 2, BTE Papers, DDEL.

151 "You know I am pretty level-headed": MDE to Douds, dated Easter Sunday 1938 (a more specific date obscured), Box 2, BTE Papers, DDEL.

151 "I told him": MDE to Douds, April 4, 1938, Box 2, BTE Papers, DDEL.

151 "I know it is going to be a blow to you": MDE to Douds, March 9, 1938, Box 2, BTE Papers, DDEL.

152 "It must be for the best": Ibid.

152 She bought a pair of golf shoes: MDE to Douds, March 21, 1938, Box 2, BTE Papers, DDEL.

152 Ike, she noticed: MDE to Douds, April 4, 1938, Box 2, BTE Papers, DDEL.

152 "I wish I wasn't such a sissy": MDE to Douds, March 21, 1938, Box 2, BTE Papers, DDEL.

152 the progress of the MacArthurs' baby: MDE to Douds, May 27, 1938, Box 2, BTE Papers, DDEL.

153 "Wasn't it slick": MDE to Douds, October 3, 1940, Box 3, BTE Papers, DDEL.

153 a huge dinner party in the Palm Court: MDE to Douds, April 6, 1938, Box 2, BTE Papers, DDEL.

153 After the affair was over: MDE to Douds, May 13, 1938, Box 2, BTE Papers, DDEL.

154 The Manila social season was coming to a close: MDE to Douds, June 3, 1938, Box 2, BTE Papers, DDEL.

154 "It was a grand send-off": MDE to Douds, June 29, 1938, Box 2, BTE Papers, DDEL.

155 For the account of their trip to Yokohama, see JSDE, *Strictly Personal*, p. 25.

156 "Two nights out of Victoria": MDE to Douds, November 9, 1938, Box 2, BTE Papers, DDEL.

156 "I am sure I will be a different person": Ibid.

156 "come out this way": MDE to Douds, May 29, 1939, Box 2, BTE Papers, DDEL.

156 "[I] used to lie in my bed": Wickman interview with MDE, August 15, 1972, OH #12, DDEL.

156 "Ike is grand": MDE to Douds, April 17, 1939, and April 21, 1939, Box 2, BTE Papers, DDEL.

157 "My Valentine": Note card sent to Mamie from DDE, private collection.

157 On the Marshall appointment: MDE to Douds, May 3, 1939, Box 2, BTE Papers, DDEL.

157 he "still can't see why": MDE to Douds, June 6, 1939, Box 2, BTE Papers, DDEL.

158 "Yes, Ike and I talked about Ikky": MDE to Douds, October 9, 1939, Box 2, BTE Papers, DDEL.

158 For an account of the luncheon, see also MDE to Douds, December 15, 1939, Box 2, BTE Papers, DDEL; and Alden Hatch, *Red Carpet for Mamie Eisenhower* (New York: Popular Library, 1954), p. 136.

159 For an account of MacArthur's reaction to their departure, see Stephen E. Ambrose, *Eisenhower; Soldier, General of the Army, President-Elect* (New York: Simon and Schuster, 1983), p. 117.

159 "We sure went off in a blaze of glory": MDE to Douds, December 15, 1939, Box 2, BTE Papers, DDEL.

CHAPTER ELEVEN

160 On the passage home: MDE to Douds, January 1, 1940, Box 3, BTE Papers, DDEL.

160 Mamie was thrilled to be back in the United States: MDE to Douds, January 8, 1940, Box 3, BTE Papers, DDEL.

161 Now Mamie fretted out loud: MDE to Douds, April 5, 1940, Box 3, BTE Papers, DDEL.

161 "pretty [much] been his own boss": MDE to Douds, January 15, 1940, Box 3, BTE Papers, DDEL.

161 Marshall, referring to the luxurious lifestyle: DDE, *At Ease: Stories I Tell to Friends* (Garden City, N.Y.: Doubleday and Company, 1967), p. 236.

161 "If I had not been hotel-bound": Dorothy Brandon, *Mamie Doud Eisenhower: Portrait of a First Lady* (New York: Charles Scribner's Sons, 1954), p. 192.

162 "would have parties at the drop of a hat" and "a natural leader": BTE undated interview with Janie Howard, private collection.

163 "People don't seem": MDE to Douds, February 20, 1940, Box 3, BTE Papers, DDEL.

163 Mamie bridled at this caste system: BTE interview with Janie Howard, private collection.

164 "didn't like to be outranked": Author interview with JSDE, November 1, 1995.

164 Ike was thoroughly engrossed: Stephen E. Ambrose, *Eisenhower: Soldier, General of the Army, President-Elect* (New York: Simon and Schuster, 1983), p. 120.

164 "Although my regiment": DDE, *At Ease*, p. 237.

164 His experience convinced him: Ambrose, *Soldier, General of the Army*, p. 120.

164 Ike used himself as an example: DDE, *At Ease*, p. 241.

165 "I said that my Army experience": Ibid.

166 Beannie Millard's objective: JSDE, *Strictly Personal* (Garden City, N.Y.: Doubleday and Company, 1974), p. 30.

166 "Ike is so busy": MDE to Douds, November 27, 1940, Box 3, BTE Papers, DDEL.

167 "That means some poor soul": MDE to Douds, October 9, 1940, Box 3, BTE Papers, DDEL.

167 "It is a grand compliment": MDE to Douds, March 11, 1941, Box 3, BTE Papers, DDEL.

167 Ike complained to John: Ambrose, *Soldier, General of the Army*, p. 127.

168 "I really think it's fine": MDE to Douds, February 1, 1941, Box 3, BTE Papers, DDEL.

168 Mamie stepped up their social activities: See MDE to Douds, April 23, 1941, Box 3, BTE Papers, DDEL.

168 "We hardly get to say": MDE to Douds, April 23, 1941, Box 3, BTE Papers, DDEL.

169 "bewildered youngsters": JSDE, *Strictly Personal*, p. 35.

169 Mamie also had her work: MDE to Douds, July 19, 1941, Box 3, BTE Papers, DDEL.

170 "She hated to see newspapers lying around": Lester David and Irene David, *Ike and Mamie: The Story of the General and His Lady* (New York: G. P. Putnam's Sons, 1981), p. 104.

170 "[Ike] was not beyond [making a] mess himself": Wickman interview with MDE, August 15, 1972, OH #12, DDEL.

170 Mickey was surprised: Lester David and Irene David, *Ike and Mamie*, p. 104.

171 while Ike was absent: MDE to Douds, July 19, 1941, Box 3, BTE Papers, DDEL.

171 "Old Louisiana hands": DDE, *At Ease*, p. 242.

172 "the Third Army": Steve Neal, *The Eisenhowers: Reluctant Dynasty* (Garden City, N.Y.: Doubleday, 1978), p. 113.

172 "One thing is certain": DDE, *At Ease*, p. 244.

172 "I still shudder": Ibid.

172 "Mrs. Strong was right": MDE to Douds, October 22, 1941, Box 3, BTE Papers, DDEL.

173 "The nap": DDE, *At Ease*, p. 245.

173 Mamie had just heard a report: John Wickman interview with MDE, August 15, 1972, OH #12, DDEL.

174 "I tried desperately": DDE, *At Ease*, p. 246.

174 "For months before Pearl Harbor": Ibid., pp. 246–47.

175 For the account of the separated train, see Lester David and Irene David, *Ike and Mamie*, pp. 102–3.

175 Mamie spent Christmas with John at West Point: MDE to Douds, December 27, 1941, Box 3, BTE Papers, DDEL.

176 "Imagine me in the next week": MDE to Douds, early January 1942, Box 3, BTE Papers, DDEL.

176 "I can't tell you": MDE to Douds, January 15, 1942, Box 3, BTE Papers, DDEL.

176 "I feel like a football": MDE to Douds, February 7, 1942, Box 3, BTE Papers, DDEL.

177 "No. 1 man": Ibid.

177 "Tempers are short!": See Neal, *Eisenhowers: Reluctant Dynasty*, p. 120.

177 "Well I got Pearl Harbor": Ibid., p. 122.

177 On reaction to the new Mrs. Gerow: MDE to Douds, February 7, 1942, Box 3, BTE Papers, DDEL.

177 She understood that her presence: MDE to Douds, February 19, 1942, Box 3, BTE Papers, DDEL.

178 "I hate that": MDE to Douds, February 19, 1942, Box 3, BTE Papers, DDEL.

178 "Last Sunday nite": MDE to Douds, March 13, 1942, Box 3, BTE Papers, DDEL.

178 "I have felt terribly": DDE, *At Ease*, p. 305.

179 "My father was buried today": Ibid., p. 304.

179 Ike slept the whole way back: MDE to Douds, March 31, 1942, Box 3, BTE Papers, DDEL.

180 "General, I'm interested": Ambrose, *Soldier, General of the Army*, p. 143.

180 It was only a week later: DDE, *At Ease*, p. 250.

180 As she alighted from the car: MDE to Douds, March 31, 1942, Box 3, BTE Papers, DDEL.

181 "I knew that Dad enjoyed": JSDE, *Letters to Mamie* (Garden City, N.Y.: Doubleday and Company, 1978), p. 20.

182 "A picture in my heart": For the account of their last days together, see MDE to Douds, July 5, 1942, Box 3, BTE Papers, DDEL.

182 "but his leaving": JSDE, *Letters*, p. 20.

182 "The last thing he did": MDE to Douds, July 5, 1942, Box 3, BTE Papers, DDEL.

183 "the bird had landed": Ibid.

CHAPTER TWELVE

184 Mamie was given only a week: John Wickman interview with MDE, August 15, 1972, OH #12, DDEL.

184 "I never had a house": MDE to Douds, July 4, 1942, Box 3, BTE Papers, DDEL.

184 "Otherwise, I wouldn't have had a place to go": Wickman interview with MDE, August 15, 1972, OH #12, DDEL.

184 "Reporters are here every day": MDE to Douds, July 25, 1942, Box 3, BTE Papers, DDEL.

185 "Naturally, I feel very low": MDE to Douds, September 1942, Box 3, BTE Papers, DDEL.

185 "where there is incentive": DDE to MDE, August 12, 1942, JSDE, *Letters to Mamie* (Garden City, N.Y.: Doubleday and Company, 1978), p. 32.

185 "Even the state of the weather": DDE to MDE, August 9, 1942, JSDE, *Letters*, p. 35.

185 "In one way it seems futile": DDE to Douds, undated, private collection.

186 "Butch is a good tonic for me": DDE to MDE, undated letter, photocopy in private collection.

186 "I do get so lonesome": DDE to MDE, August 9, 1942, JSDE, *Letters*, p. 35.

186 "Tomorrow, Sept. 24, Ikky": DDE to MDE, September 23, 1942, JSDE, *Letters*, p. 44.

186 "We [each] had one little ration card": Wickman interview with MDE, August 15, 1972, OH #12, DDEL.

188 a "bulldog meeting a tomcat": DDE, *In Review: Pictures I've Kept* (Garden City, N.Y.: Doubleday, 1969), p. 46.

188 "In the long run": Michael R. Beschloss, *Eisenhower: A Centennial Life* (New York: HarperCollins, 1990), p. 42.

188 "I'll do my best": DDE, *At Ease: Stories I Tell to Friends* (Garden City, N.Y.: Doubleday and Company, 1967), p. 256.

189 "By the time you read this": DDE to MDE, October 30, 1942, JSDE, *Letters*, p. 50.

190 Janie Howard's story about the roses came from BTE undated interview with Janie Howard, private collection.

191 "Every once in a while": DDE to MDE, November 17, 1942, JSDE, *Letters*, p. 63.

191 "I am sorry": DDE to MDE, November 24, 1942, JSDE, *Letters*, p. 65.

191 "I've never known": DDE to MDE, December 5, 1942, JSDE, *Letters*, p. 68.

191 "I was out [at] Milton's": Wickman interview with MDE, August 15, 1972, OH #12, DDEL.

192 "Poor old Darlan": DDE to MDE, December 30, 1942, JSDE, *Letters*, p. 75.

192 "Sometimes I get to missing you": Ibid.

193 "Had three letters from Ike": MDE to Douds, January 21, 1943, Box 3, BTE Papers, DDEL.

193 "I love you all the time": DDE to MDE, February 26, 1943, JSDE, *Letters*, p. 98.

193 "confused life we lead": DDE to MDE, February 28, 1943, JSDE, *Letters*, p. 99.

194 "So *Life* says": DDE to MDE, March 2, 1943, JSDE, *Letters*, pp. 104–5.

194 "I do have time to tell you": DDE to MDE, January 26, 1943, JSDE, *Letters*, p. 68.

194 "She had the most extraordinary": BTE undated interview with Kate Hughes, private collection.

195 Mamie was relieved: MDE to Douds, July 15, 1943, BTE Papers, Box 3, DDEL.

195 "drank no more": Carl Anthony, *First Ladies: The Saga of the Presidents' Wives and Their Power* (New York: William Morrow, 1990), p. 504.

195 "Everything is very friendly": MDE to Douds, January 28, 1943, Box 3, BTE Papers, DDEL.

196 " 'Hey lady . . . ' ": Lester David and Irene David, *Ike and Mamie: The Story of the General and His Lady* (New York: G. P. Putnam's Sons, 1981), p. 115.

196 On Mamie's affliction with Ménière's syndrome, see Wickman interview with MDE, August 15, 1972, OH #12, pp. 92–93, DDEL.

197 "Up to the day he died": BTE last interview with MDE, September 16, 1979, private collection.

197 "someone had locked her away": Author interview with Beverly Butcher Byron, January 19, 1995.

198 "Gee Gerow came to town": BTE undated interview with Kate Hughes, private collection.

198 "The only time I ever got a good night's sleep": Wickman interview with MDE, August 15, 1972, OH #12, DDEL.

198 "Subordinates can advise": DDE to MDE, February 15, 1943, JSDE, *Letters*, p. 95.

199 Quotations for Butcher and Matchett, see Lester David and Irene David, *Ike and Mamie*, p. 114.

199 "Mamie was the greatest help": BTE undated interview with Janie Howard, private collection.

199 Account of the incident at the "hen party": Ibid.

CHAPTER THIRTEEN

200 Ike often complained: Author interview with Beverly Butcher Byron, January 19, 1995.

200 "The news is out": MDE to Douds, February 10, 1943, Box 4, BTE Papers, DDEL.

201 "So far": DDE to MDE, February 26, 1943, JSDE, *Letters to Mamie* (Garden City, N.Y.: Doubleday and Company, 1978), p. 98.

201 "I've tried to stop": DDE to Douds, private collection.

201 "Mamie lived a very lonely life": BTE undated interview with Kate Hughes, private collection.

202 "All through this publicity": DDE to MDE, March 2, 1943, JSDE, *Letters*, pp. 104–5.

202 "My advice is": DDE to Naomi Engle, April 3, 1943, Pre-presidential Papers, 1916–1952, DDEL.

202 "He had arrived in London": JSDE, *Letters*, p. 9.

202 "I get such a kick out of you": MDE to Douds, June 17, 1943, Box 4, BTE Papers, DDEL.

203 "The pictures I signed": DDE to MDE, March 15, 1943, JSDE, *Letters*, p. 110.

203 "hard luck": MDE to Douds, July 15, 1943, Box 4, BTE Papers, DDEL.

203 "Ike used to say": John Wickman interview with MDE, August 15, 1972, OH #12, DDEL.

204 It's "quite something": MDE to Douds, May 30, 1943, Box 4, BTE Papers, DDEL.

204 "We only meant": MDE to Douds, undated letter written during this visit, Box 4, BTE Papers, DDEL.

204 "Army cats": Kevin McCann, March 1, 1974, private collection.

205 "I believe there is a point": J. B. West, *Upstairs at the White House: My Life with the First Ladies* (New York: Coward, McCann, and Geoghegan, 1973), p. 137.

206 "If [Mamie] ever got depressed": BTE undated interview with Janie Howard, private collection.

206 a woman of "remarkable self-control": Carl Anthony, *First Ladies: The Saga of the Presidents' Wives and Their Power* (New York: William Morrow, 1990), p. 503.

206 "Dad would have made": Author interview with JSDE, August 24, 1994.

207 "A very strange coincidence": DDE to MDE, June 11, 1943, JSDE, *Letters*, pp. 127–28.

208 "These days are so crowded": DDE to MDE, June 14, 1943, JSDE, *Letters*, p. 129.

208 "After Dick died": Lester David and Irene David, *Ike and Mamie: The Story of the General and His Lady* (New York: G. P. Putnam's Sons, 1981), pp. 146–47. The Davids' book has many firsthand accounts regarding Ike's relationship with Kay Summersby. Every member of his "official family" was of the same view that no romance had occurred. See "Kay—The 'Romance,' " pp. 142–57.

208 "[General Eisenhower] felt sorry for her": Ibid., p. 154.

209 Eisenhower took a personal interest: Ibid., p. 155.

209 "[Ike's] immediate staff": Kay Summersby, *Eisenhower Was My Boss*, (New York: Prentice Hall, 1948), p. 287.

209 Years later, she commented: *Kansas City Star*, AP story, February 10, 1974.

209 "She is a very popular person": DDE to MDE, July 3, 1943, JSDE, *Letters*, p. 132.

209 "One of your recent letters": DDE to MDE, July 5, 1943, JSDE, *Letters*, pp. 133–34.

210 friends were beginning to disperse: MDE to Douds, July 6, 1943, Box 4, BTE Papers, DDEL.

210 "Last night I dreamed": DDE to MDE, July 18, 1943, JSDE, *Letters*, p. 136.

210 "I cannot allow": DDE to MDE, September 8, 1943, JSDE, *Letters*, p. 146.

210 "We could hear the sirens": Author interview with Beverly Butcher Byron, January 19, 1995.

211 "I was greatly amused": DDE to MDE, July 24, 1943, JSDE, *Letters*, p. 137.

212 Even before the Italian capitulation: Michael R. Beschloss, *Eisenhower: A Centennial Life* (New York: HarperCollins, 1990), p. 61.

212 the alumni of Camp Colt: Steve Neal, *The Eisenhowers: Reluctant Dynasty* (Garden City, N.Y.: Doubleday and Company, 1978), p. 46.

212 "I think you showed more concern": ABE to DDE, August 25, 1943; DDE to ABE, October 20, 1943, Pre-presidential Papers, DDEL.

213 "He's done a fine job": JSD to MDE, October 1943, private collection.

213 "Don't believe all this stuff": MDE to Douds, November 16, 1943, Box 4, BTE Papers, DDEL.

214 "Big things are being decided": MDE to Douds, November 22, 1943, Box 4, BTE Papers, DDEL.

214 "But no matter what does happen": DDE to MDE, December 14, 1943, JSDE, *Letters*, p. 158.

214 "I am pretty certain": MDE to Douds, December 15, 1943, Box 4, BTE Papers, DDEL.

214 "What he is going to do": MDE to Douds, December 18, 1943, Box 4, BTE Papers, DDEL.

215 "There was nothing else to do": MDE to Douds, December 30, 1943, Box 4, BTE Papers, DDEL.

215 "I think I've had a good case": DDE to MDE, December 26, 1943, JSDE, *Letters*, p. 159.

CHAPTER FOURTEEN

216 "You will be under terrific strain": Stephen E. Ambrose, *Soldier, General of the Army, President-Elect* (New York: Simon and Schuster, 1983), p. 276.

217 An amusing anecdote: John Wickman interview with MDE, August 15, 1972, OH #12, DDEL.

217 "rumors spread among the residents": Carl Anthony, *First Ladies: The Saga of the Presidents' Wives and Their Power* (New York: William Morrow, 1990), p. 507.

217 Otherwise, he "seemed the same": JSDE, *Strictly Personal* (Garden City, N.Y.: Doubleday and Company, 1974), p. 51.

217 "I was so provoked": John Wickman interview with MDE, August 15, 1972, OH #12, DDEL.

218 "I find myself very glad": DDE to MDE, January 20, 1944, JSDE, *Letters to Mamie* (Garden City, N.Y.: Doubleday and Company, 1978), p. 164.

218 "paid dividends": DDE to MDE, January 24, 1944, JSDE, *Letters*, p. 165.

218 "I sent you a short Valentine": DDE to MDE, February 14, 1944, JSDE, *Letters*, p. 168.

219 "He looks worn": Steve Neal, *The Eisenhowers: Reluctant Dynasty* (Garden City, N.Y.: Doubleday and Company, 1978), p. 184.

219 "He seemed a little undone": MDE to Douds, March 21, 1944, Box 4, BTE Papers, DDEL.

219 "So long as you want": Neal, *Eisenhowers: Reluctant Dynasty*, p. 184.

219 "Not long ago": DDE to MDE, April 20, 1944, JSDE, *Letters*, pp. 176–77.

220 "This morning I received": DDE to MDE, May 12, 1944, JSDE, *Letters*, p. 179.

220 "Don't tell me about": Author interview with JSDE, November 1, 1995.

220 Eisenhower and Bradley were two: Leverett Richards, "Ex WAC to Present Historic License Plate," National WAC Veterans Association publication, April 1974.

222 "I think at times I get a bit homesick": Neal, *Eisenhowers: Reluctant Dynasty*, p. 184.

222 "a lovely afternoon": Summersby, *Eisenhower Was My Boss* (New York: Prentice-Hall, 1948), pp. 156–57.

222 "It was not much fun": Kay Summersby, *Past Forgetting* (New York: Simon and Schuster, 1976), p. 226.

222 Kate Hughes . . . had the impression: BTE undated interview with Kate Hughes, private collection.

222 "presence or sagacity": These remarks, attributed to Mrs. Robert Littlejohn, wife of Eisenhower's quartermaster general, are in David John Caldwell Irving, *The War Between the Generals* (New York: Langdon and Lattes, 1981), pp. 192–93.

223 "I wrote you yesterday": DDE to MDE, July 16, 1944, JSDE, *Letters*, p. 196.

223 "The answer is no": Bob Considine, "Kay Summersby Victim of Character Assassination," *Boston Herald American*, January 24, 1975.

224 "Kay was upset": Author interview with Sue Sarafian Jehl, August 26, 1995.

224 "When I come home": DDE to Douds, September 14, 1944, private collection.

225 "I really got a chuckle": Ibid.

226 "Yesterday I arrived": DDE to MDE, November 12, 1944, JSDE, *Letters*, p. 219.

227 "I'm truly sorry": DDE to MDE, November 28, 1944, JSDE, *Letters*, p. 222.

227 For the account of the assassination concern, see: JSDE, *The Bitter Woods* (New York: G. P. Putnam's Sons, 1969), pp. 33 and 281.

227 "I am distressed": DDE to MDE, January 18, 1945, JSDE, *Letters*, p. 232.

227 "I worried": John Wickman interview with MDE, August 15, 1972, OH #12, DDEL.

228 Mamie's old friends "Bootsie" and Sam White: Dorothy Brandon, *Mamie Doud Eisenhower: Portrait of a First Lady* (New York: Charles Scribner's Sons, 1954), p. 228.

228 "It was just what I expected": MDE to Douds, May 14, 1945, Box 4, BTE Papers, DDEL.

229 "The only other general officer": DDE to MDE, June 4, 1945, JSDE, *Letters*, pp. 257–58.

229 "My real feeling": DDE to GCM, June 4, 1945, Eisenhower Papers, Johns Hopkins University.

229 Marshall, confronted with the necessity: Stephen E. Ambrose, *Soldier, General of the Army, President-Elect* (New York: Simon and Schuster, 1983), p. 415.

230 "I assume that when I get home": DDE to MDE, May 18, 1945, JSDE, *Letters*, p. 255.

230 "Mrs. Eisenhower greets": *Life*, July 2, 1945.

230 "the nicest thing": DDE to MDE, July 12, 1945, JSDE, *Letters*, p. 263.

231 "Mrs. Mamie Eisenhower": New York *World-Telegram*, June 19, 1945, p. 1.

231 On Mamie's reaction to the Butcher divorce: Author interview with Beverly Butcher Byron, January 19, 1995, private collection.

231 "I don't see how you could help it": DDE to MDE, July 23, 1945, JSDE, *Letters*, p. 265.

231 "If you'd just once": DDE to MDE, July 13 or 14, 1945, JSDE, *Letters*, pp. 263–64.

232 "What could you have meant": DDE to MDE, September 4, 1945, JSDE, *Letters*, p. 270.

232 "Ruth and Bev are leaving": MDE to Douds, September 27, 1945, Box 4, BTE Papers, DDEL.

232 "He realize[s] I am lonely": DDE to MDE, June 9, 1945, JSDE, *Letters*, p. 259.

232 "I really will never believe": MDE to Douds, October 7, 1945, Box 4, BTE Papers, DDEL.

233 "Of course we've changed": DDE to MDE, September 25, 1944, JSDE, *Letters*, p. 211.

233 "Neither of us really knew": Anthony, *First Ladies*, p. 504.

CHAPTER FIFTEEN

234 "At a Washington banquet": Robert Wallace, article in *Life*, October 13, 1952, p. 158.

235 Mamie noticed that Ike: Author interview with JSDE, October 17, 1995.

235 "Ike's staff tended to freeze Mamie out": BTE manuscript, private collection.

235 "[Ike] never apologized": Author interview with JSDE, October 17, 1995.

236 "Ike had been a military man": Author interview with George A. Horkan, Jr., August 7, 1994.

237 "Simon and Schuster are convinced": HB Papers, August 2, 1945, DDEL.

237 "an infallible rule of merchandizing": See HB to DDE, September 7, 1945, HB Papers, DDEL.

238 "I did not know that anyone had ever seen": Regarding the use of his notes at the time of his father's death, see DDE to HB, July 31, 1945, DDEL.

238 "I hope you will give equal attention": DDE to HB, December 26, 1945, DDEL; see also Merle Miller, *Ike the Soldier: As They Knew Him* (New York: G. P. Putnam's Sons, 1987), pp. 380–81.

239 "I have skimmed over": Ibid.

239 Ike disliked books by his staff members: DDE to HB, October 12, 1945, DDEL. In that letter he says: "The embarrassment that comes out of the thing is that, naturally, I know that the book will paint me in flattering strokes. Consequently any indication that I was aware of what went in it would put me in a most silly light. If you were cursing me all the way through the book I would have no objection to being thought a collaborator, but you know my horror of self-praise."

240 "I was somewhat astonished": DDE to KS, June 1, 1948, Box 112, Pre-presidential Papers, 1916–1952, DDEL.

240 "The suggestion they made": DDE to KS, July 28, 1948, Box 112, Pre-presidential Papers, 1916–1952, DDEL.

240 "overestimated Kay's loyalty": Author interview with JSDE, October 17, 1995.

240 After his reprimand: JSDE interview with the author, August 24, 1994.

241 "Have read your memorandum to me": July 16, 1944, Summersby file, Box 112, Pre-presidential Papers, 1916–1952, DDEL.

241 Nor, indeed, had Ike been the one to suggest: Author interview with Sue Sarafian Jehl, August 25, 1995.

242 "Heard today": DDE diary, December 2, 1947; Robert H. Ferrell, *The Eisenhower Diaries* (New York: W. W. Norton and Company, 1981), p. 145.

242 "as bad as I always thought": Michael R. Beschloss, *Eisenhower: A Centennial Life* (New York: HarperCollins, 1990), p. 87.

243 He "beat a strategic retreat": *Life*, February 4, 1946, p. 24.

243 She had given no indication of her passing: DDE, *At Ease: Stories I Tell to Friends* (Garden City, N.Y.: Doubleday and Company, 1967), pp. 306–7.

243 remained in their bedroom upstairs: BTE manuscript, private collection.

243 Regarding their visit to Balmoral: MDE to Douds, October 10, 1946, Box 4, BTE Papers, DDEL.

244 "Our chain of command": JSDE to DDE and MDE, November 3, 1946, private collection.

244 She and her family: BTE manuscript, private collection.

245 "By this time": DDE to JSD, January 31, 1947, Pre-presidential Papers, 1916–1952, DDEL.

245 Regarding the description of Quarters #1 and BTE's first meeting with the Eisenhowers: BTE manuscript, private collection.

246 Barbara found Mamie gracious and cordial: Ibid.

246 "We were very grateful": John Wickman interview with MDE, August 16, 1972, OH #12, DDEL.

247 "The commercial offers I could decline": DDE, *At Ease*, p. 334.

247 By 1948: Beschloss, *Eisenhower: A Centennial Life*, p. 94.

247 "Coyly [Mamie] approach[ed]": Carl Anthony, *First Ladies: The Saga of the Presidents' Wives and Their Power* (New York: William Morrow, 1990), p. 534.

247 "I am not available": BTE manuscript, private collection.

247 "Naturally there were journalists": DDE, *At Ease*, p. 333.

248 "I cannot let this day pass . . .": Stephen E. Ambrose, *Eisenhower: Soldier, General of the Army, President-Elect* (New York: Simon and Schuster, 1983), p. 473.

248 For the description of the last days in the army: BTE manuscript, private collection.

CHAPTER SIXTEEN

250 "I am an army wife": John Wickman interview with MDE, August 15, 1972, OH #12, DDEL.

250 "I never drove up to the south portico": Steve Neal, *The Eisenhowers: Reluctant Dynasty* (Garden City, N.Y.: Doubleday and Company, 1978), p. 400.

250 On terms at Columbia and vacation time, see Michael R. Beschloss, *Eisenhower: A Centennial Life* (New York: HarperCollins, 1990), p. 91.

251 For details regarding the Columbia inauguration and institutional details, see *Life*, October 25, 1948, p. 42.

251 "Columbia is the place": Ibid.

252 Her favorite project: Wickman interview with MDE, August 16, 1972, OH #12, DDEL.

252 "The deans and the professors": Wickman interview with MDE, August 16, 1972, OH #12, DDEL.

252 "Mamie my love": Alfred Gruenther to MDE, July 7, 1949, private collection.

253 Regarding Mamie's relationship with the wives of her husband's aides; the game of canasta: BTE manuscript, private collection.

253 "Mamie was completely unswayed": Ibid.

254 "Nobody has made me change": MDE to EMD, April 3, 1952, Box 4, BTE Papers, DDEL.

254 On campaign form letter: Abbott Washburn, former Eisenhower for President staffer, to the author.

254 Regarding the throng at *South Pacific*: BTE manuscript; Wickman interview with MDE, August 16, 1972, OH #12, DDEL.

254 "I saw Johnnie, Dad, and Mamie": Author interview with BTE, November 1, 1995, BTE manuscript, private collection.

255 "She could spot a needed repair": Ibid.

255 ". . . the kids are broke": MDE to Douds, dated only Tuesday (1948), private collection.

255 found a handsome check: Author interview with BTEF, December 13, 1995.

256 "from men who had to be told": Stephen E. Ambrose, *Soldier, General of the Army, President-Elect* (New York: Simon and Schuster, 1983), p. 485.

256 "Naturally there will be tears": *Newsweek*, January 1, 1951, p. 14.

256 "I am really in a dream": MDE to Douds, January 1951, Box 4, BTE Papers, DDEL.

256 "Mamie will go all to pieces": EMD to JSD, January 1, 1951, private collection.

257 entranced with the "romance of the place": MDE to Douds, October 18, 1943, Box 3, BTE Papers, DDEL.

257 "[The farm] had three of the most": BTE manuscript, private collection.

257 Ike confirmed: DDE, *At Ease: Stories I Tell to Friends* (Garden City, N.Y.: Doubleday and Company, 1967), p. 361.

258 On the selection process for the Paris house, see Wickman interview with MDE, August 16, 1972, pp. 135–37; Dorothy Brandon, *Mamie Doud Eisenhower: Portrait of a First Lady* (New York: Charles Scribner's Sons, 1954), p. 267.

258 "the most livable and least elaborate": Author interview with BTEF, December 13, 1995.

258 "curiously like the White House": "Why Mamie Will Be Glad to Leave the White House," *Better Homes and Gardens*, August 1960, p. 48.

258 On decorating: see Brandon, *Mamie Doud Eisenhower*, p. 268.

259 "the place teems with": MDE to Douds, March 18, 1951, Box 4, BTE Papers, DDEL.

259 "Imagine paying": *Look*, February 25, 1954, p. 31.

259 "David is now so exultant": JSDE to DDE and MDE, June 8, 1951, private collection.

260 "he used to terrify": Author interview with JSDE, February 8, 1996.

260 "When it came to shopping, Mamie": Author interview with BTEF, December 13, 1995.

260 "Neither Mamie nor I": BTE manuscript, private collection.

260 "[Pupah] has been in precarious health": Robert H. Ferrell, *Eisenhower Diaries* (New York: W. W. Norton and Company, 1981), p. 196.

261 he had "made good on his promise": Author interview with JSDE, August 24, 1994.

261 "Mother, now you stop saying": MDE to EMD, March 3, 1952, Box 4, BTE Papers, DDEL.

CHAPTER SEVENTEEN

262 could no longer "afford to take another licking": See Herbert S. Parmet, *Eisenhower and the American Crusades* (New York: Macmillan, 1972), pp. 30–41.

262 "Top-ranking Democrats": Sidney Olson, "The Democratic Plan to Draft Eisenhower, *Life*, April 12, 1950, p. 50.

262 "Dear Ike: The columnists, the slick": HST to DDE, December 18, 1951, Truman Library; DDEL.

263 For the holiday celebrations: MDE to EMD, December 27, 1951, Box 4, BTE Papers, DDEL.

264 "My feeling is that": JSDE to DDE, January 14, 1952, private collection.

264 "any personal sacrifice": Michael R. Beschloss, *Eisenhower: A Centennial Life* (New York: HarperCollins, 1990), p. 103.

264 "No one can be that popular": Jacqueline Cochran interview, OH #42, DDEL.

264 Cochran's assignment was to bring: Ibid.

265 Ike, visibly shaken: Ibid.

265 Mamie "sat there": Ibid.

265 "viewing [the film]": Robert H. Ferrell, *Eisenhower Diaries* (New York: W. W. Norton and Company, 1981), p. 314.

265 "brought home to me": Stephen E. Ambrose, *Soldier, General of the Army, President-Elect* (New York: Simon and Schuster, 1983), p. 524.

266 "things had gone farther": John Wickman interview with MDE, August 16, 1972, OH #12, DDEL.

266 "We were saddened by the King's death": DDE to EMD, February 13, 1952, private collection.

266 "It was really thrilling": MDE to EMD, March 10, 1952, Box 4, BTE Papers, DDEL.

267 "clear call to duty": Parmet, *Crusades*, pp. 55–56.

267 "World War II had brought": Beschloss, *Eisenhower: A Centennial Life*, p. 93.

267 "avoid the burden": Ambrose, *Soldier, General of the Army*, p. 528.

267 "I am compelled to remark": Ibid., p. 527.

267 "I really dread": Ibid.

267 "I'm in a mental tizzy": MDE to EMD, April 24, 1952, Box 4, BTE Papers, DDEL.

268 "Yesterday at Les Invalides": MDE to EMD, May 22, 1952, Box 4, BTE Papers, DDEL.

268 "It was more wonderful": Dorothy Brandon, *Mamie Doud Eisenhower: Portrait of a First Lady* (New York: Charles Scribner's Sons, 1954), pp. 277–78.

268 "Boy, how I dread": MDE to EMD, May 22, 1952, Box 4, BTE Papers, DDEL.

268 "failed to yield easily": Parmet, *Crusades*, p. 59.

268 "rather wreck": Ibid., p. 44. Remarks attributed to Paul Hoffman, director of the Ford Foundation.

268 During the primary campaign: Parmet, *Crusades*, p. 60.

269 Once during the campaign: Carl Anthony, *First Ladies: The Saga of the Presidents' Wives and Their Power* (New York: William Morrow, 1990), p. 548.

269 "One of the women who was there": BTE undated interview with Kate Hughes, private collection.

269 "personal situation in the Eisenhower household": See *Newsweek*, March 21, 1955, p. 28, and *Time*, March 21, 1955, p. 15.

270 "Boy, politics is really": *The Diaries of James C. Hagerty*, ed. Robert H. Ferrell (Bloomington: Indiana University Press, 1983), p. 207.

270 Mamie was not completely thick-skinned: Anthony, *First Ladies*, p. 548.

271 "Dad gave me the admonition": JSDE, *Strictly Personal* (Garden City, N.Y.: Doubleday and Company, 1974), p. 134.

271 "Ike and I said goodbye to Johnnie": Brandon, *Mamie Doud Eisenhower*, pp. 291–92.

271 Mamie nixed that idea: Anthony, *First Ladies*, p. 547.

272 "She is a better campaigner": Ibid., p. 548.

272 Once she was asked: *Life*, July 21, 1952.

272 "Dear Ruby": MDE to RNL, September 15, 1952, Box 1, Pre-presidential Papers, 1916–1952, DDEL.

273 "To look at those faces": Wickman interview with MDE, August 16, 1972, OH #12, DDEL.

273 "Ike . . . that doesn't sound like you": There are many accounts of this. See Anthony, *First Ladies*, p. 547.

273 once when they were campaigning in Denver: Anthony, *First Ladies*, p. 547.

273 "would miss the great camaraderie": Harold E. Stassen, *Eisenhower: Turning the World Toward Peace* (St. Paul: Merrill/Magnus, 1990), pp. 79–80.

274 "Between the instant": Robert Wallace, "And Folks, Here's My Mamie," *Life*, October 13, 1952.

CHAPTER EIGHTEEN

276 "There would be no separate bedrooms": J. B. West, *Upstairs at the White House: My Life with the First Ladies* (New York: Coward, McCann, and Geoghegan, 1973), p. 130.

276 "As a couple": Ibid., p. 136.

276 "To remind you": DDE to MDE, private collection.

276 "people of the United States": BTE last interview with Mamie, September 16, 1979, private collection.

276 "She needed no period of adjustment": West, *Upstairs*, p. 132.

276 "As wife of an army officer": Ibid., p. 131.

277 On MDE's relationship with DDE's secretary, Mrs. Whitman: Author interview with JSDE, January 12, 1996.

278 "Don't run it on the Eagle": Author interview with BTEF, December 13, 1995.

278 "two old gals together": BTE undated interview with Kate Hughes, private collection; West, *Upstairs*, p. 141.

279 "You always write as if you meant it": Carl Anthony, *First Ladies: The Saga of the Presidents' Wives and Their Power* (New York: William Morrow, 1990), p. 556.

279 Regarding Mamie passing on requests: Ibid.

279 "Why don't you work": Anthony, *First Ladies*, p. 557.

279 On the extent of her correspondence, see Martin M. Teasley, "Ike Was Her Career: The Papers of Mamie Doud Eisenhower," *Prologue*, vol. 19, no. 2 (Summer 1987), pp. 106–15.

279 during the first term alone: *Newsweek*, May 28, 1956, p. 31; Anthony, *First Ladies*, p. 557.

279 "If there were a thousand": West, *Upstairs*, p. 135.

280 "One of the veteran hostesses": E. Heskell Smith, "First Lady," *The Queen*, April 21, 1954.

280 "In our entertaining": John Wickman interview with MDE, August 16, 1972, OH #12, DDEL.

280 "I think it is so wonderful": Anthony, *First Ladies*, p. 575.

280 "Her entire forearm": Memorial tribute to Mamie Eisenhower, November 6, 1979, Reverend Edward L. R. Elson, Chaplain of the United States Senate.

281 "He didn't demand anything": Wickman interview with MDE, August 16, 1972, OH #12, DDEL.

281 "Mamie Eisenhower as a hostess": West, *Upstairs*, p. 135.

281 On best-dressed women: Karal Ann Marling, *As Seen on T.V.* (Cambridge, Mass.: Harvard University Press, 1994), p. 36.

281 "Mrs. Eisenhower brings a new viewpoint": Ibid., p. 26.

281 "adorning basic style": Ibid.

282 "Mamie cut through the gush": Anthony, *First Ladies*, p. 553.

282 "Don't hide it": Marling, *As Seen on T.V.*, p. 36.

282 "surprised at how pretty": Author interview with Arnold Scaasi, December 8, 1995.

282 On Dior's hemlines: Marling, *As Seen on T.V.*, p. 26.

282 "As a soldier's wife": Anthony, *First Ladies*, p. 552.

283 "The President had a budget he wanted to balance": Author interview with Lillian Parks, August 21, 1995.

283 Aside from her official duties: Author interview with BTEF, December 13, 1995.

283 "inseparable": Michael Doud Gill to the author.

284 "Unlike other members": Author interview with Sue Gill, May 28, 1996; based on a letter to her parents, November 6, 1979.

284 "smiling or otherwise": Stephen Ambrose and Richard Immerman, *Milton S. Eisenhower, Educational Statesman* (Baltimore and London: Johns Hopkins Press, 1983), pp. 163–64.

284 "fine, brave, generous": Ibid., p. 163.

285 On letters and flowers: "Inside the White House," *National Geographic*, January 1961, p. 16; Teasley, "Ike Was Her Career," p. 111.

285 "Imagine remembering that!": BTE undated interview with Janie Howard, private collection.

285 "I like to spread my money about": Author interview with Mary Jane McCafree Monroe, March 17, 1995.

285 "when I was offered": Steve Neal, *The Eisenhowers: Reluctant Dynasty* (Garden City, N.Y.: Doubleday and Company, 1978), p. 401.

285 "She thanked [everyone]": BTE undated interview with Kate Hughes, private collection.

285 "family for her": Edward L. R. Elson, memorial service for MDE, November 6, 1979.

285 On concern for employees' families: See West, *Upstairs*, p. 155.

286 Ike jumped from his seat: Interview with Delores Moaney, January 5 and 17, 1996.

286 Regarding the Bruce family relationship with MDE and DDE, see Preston Bruce, *From the Door of the White House* (New York: Lothrop, Lee & Shepard Books, 1984), pp. 56, 68, 69.

287 "The First Lady told me": *New York Herald Tribune*, May 26, 1954.

287 For details of the housewarming party, see West, *Upstairs*, p. 167.

CHAPTER NINETEEN

288 Regarding Ike's heart attack: Michael R. Beschloss, *Eisenhower: A Centennial Life* (New York: HarperCollins, 1990), p. 135.

289 "I just can't believe": JSDE, *Strictly Personal* (Garden City, N.Y.: Doubleday and Company, 1974), p. 181.

289 "Mamie, above all others": DDE, *Mandate for Change* (Garden City, N.Y.: Doubleday and Company, 1963), p. 542.

289 "I've been told I have a reprieve": Author interview with JSDE, October 17, 1995.

290 "Dear Dr. Elson": Elson's funeral eulogy, Memorial Service for Mamie Eisenhower, November 6, 1979.

290 "that it may henceforth": Ibid.

291 "For never failing help": Both the design and the medal are in the author's possession.

292 Figures on security breaches: DDE, *In Review: Pictures I've Kept* (Garden City, N.Y.: Doubleday and Company, 1969), p. 139.

292 "As to the added protection": JSDE to DDE, undated, private collection.

292 "We have seen quite a lot of Barbara": MDE to Frances Dolan, December 10, 1952, private collection.

293 "Mimi made a special effort": Author interview with BTEF, December 13, 1995.

293 "These are your best years": Ibid.

293 "Dearest Barbie": DDE to BTE, undated, private collection.

294 "Consequently she argued": DDE, *Mandate for Change*, p. 571.

295 "The Republican party must be known": Beschloss, *Centennial Life*, p. 138.

295 She "could not reconcile": DDE, *Mandate for Change*, p. 542.

295 "One doctor held out against surgery": JSDE, *Strictly Personal*, p. 186.

296 "Darling": November 14, 1956, private collection.

296 "It was a ghostly white": J. B. West, *Upstairs at the White House: My Life with the First Ladies* (New York: Coward, McCann and Geoghegan, 1973), p. 184.

297 "was perhaps the most difficult assignment": Richard M. Nixon, *My Six Crises* (Garden City, N.Y.: Doubleday and Company, 1962), p. 171.

297 "Three days [later]": JSDE, *Strictly Personal*, p. 197.

297 "[the presidency] really is too much": Nixon, *Six Crises*, p. 172.

297 "Mamie was present": Beschloss, *Centennial Life*, p. 153.

298 "Darling— As you suggested": DDE to MDE, undated, private collection.

298 "raise the morale of struggling": DDE, *In Review*, p. 212.

298 "This was not Mamie's way": Author interview with BTEF, December 29, 1995.

299 "Now that he is safely back for Christmas": D. L. Kimball, *I Remember Mamie* (Fayette, Iowa: Trends and Events, Inc., 1981), p. 201.

299 "We have followed with intense interest": Elizabeth R to DDE, January 24, 1960. The full text of the handwritten letter is as follows. It was significant that the queen sent the recipe for drop scones to Ike and not to Mamie.

January 24, 1960

Dear Mr. President,

Seeing a picture of you in today's newspaper standing in front of a barbecue grilling quail, reminded me that I had never sent you the recipe of the drop scones, which I provided you at Balmoral.

I now hasten to do so, and I hope you will find them successful.

Though the quantities are for 16 people, where there are fewer, I generally put in less flour and milk, but use the other ingredients as stated.

I have also tried using golden syrup or treacle instead of only sugar and that can be very good, too.

I think the mixture needs a great deal of beating while making, and shouldn't stand about too long before cooking.

We have followed with intense interest and much admiration your tremendous journey to so many countries, and feel we shall never again be able to claim that *we* are being made to do too much on our future tours!

We remember with such pleasure your visit to Balmoral, and I hope the photograph will be a reminder of the very happy day you spent with us.

With all good wishes to you and Mrs. Eisenhower.

> Yours sincerely
> Elizabeth R

299 "Tonight prospects are for an earlier return": DDE to MDE, private collection.

301 On Mamie's involvement with the Heart Association and other groups, see Carl Anthony, *First Ladies: The Saga of the Presidents' Wives and Their Power* (New York: William Morrow, 1990), p. 586.

301 In reinstituting: Ibid., pp. 581, 560.

301 "Ladies, I hope you'll vote": *Time*, October 18, 1954. On the Eisenhower administration's record, see Virgil Pinkley and James F.

Scheer, *Eisenhower Declassified* (Old Tappan, N.J.: Flemming H. Revell Company, 1979), pp. 351–59; and Herbert S. Parmet, *Eisenhower and the American Crusades* (New York: Macmillan, 1972), pp. 573–78.

303 "Don't things look bare?": Ellis D. Slater, *The Ike I Knew* (Ellis D. Slater Trust, 1980), p. 106.

303 Ike got out of the car: Author interview with JSDE, October 17, 1995.

CHAPTER TWENTY

304 "When I find myself contemplating": DDE to MDE, December 2, 1943, JSDE, *Letters to Mamie* (Garden City, N.Y.: Doubleday and Company, 1978), p. 157.

304 The heart of the house: DDE, *At Ease: Stories I Tell to Friends* (Garden City, N.Y.: Doubleday and Company, 1967), p. 360.

305 "I still ran my house": John Wickman interview with MDE, August 16, 1972, p. 174.

305 "Well, what are we": Author interview with Beverly Butcher Byron.

305 "he thought you still": William B. Ewald, *Eisenhower the President: Crucial Days, 1951–1960* (Englewood Cliffs, N.J.: Prentice-Hall, 1981), p. 7.

306 "deranged" people who "found their way": JSDE, *Strictly Personal* (Garden City, N.Y.: Doubleday and Company, 1974), pp. 294–95.

306 "[Ike] said, 'Well I don't mind' ": Ellis D. Slater, *The Ike I Knew* (Ellis D. Slater Trust, 1980), diary entry of September 25, 1961, p. 248.

306 "What retirement": Ibid., diary entry of November 1964, p. 259.

306 "Ike's days are no longer filled": *Life*, July 7, 1961, pp. 61, 65.

306 "I am sick and tired": Ibid.

307 "Dear Susie": DDE to SE, December 27, 1961, private collection.

307 On trip to Europe: Author interview with Anne Eisenhower, December 12, 1995.

309 "If I have one instinctive": DDE to EMD, January 19, 1952, private collection.

310 "Dad showed signs": JSDE, *Strictly Personal*, p. 328.

311 "Like a silver dollar": Author interview with JNE, January 4, 1996.

311 Ike "had left, upset": JSDE, *Strictly Personal*, pp. 328–29; and author interview with JSDE, August 24, 1994.

311 "His decision": JNE, *Special People* (New York: Simon and Schuster, 1977), p. 190.

312 Ike gave Mamie a handwritten letter: MDE, "My Memories of Ike," *Reader's Digest*, February 1970, p. 74.

312 "She seemed in no condition": JSDE, *Strictly Personal*, p. 333.

313 "He was a very strong character": Wickman interview with MDE, August 15, 1972, OH #12, DDEL.

313 "Dear Sue": MDE to SE, private collection.

314 "Be good to Mamie": JSDE, *Strictly Personal*, p. 335.

314 "Mother, David, and I": Ibid.

314 "When he was dying out there at Walter Reed": Wickman interviews with MDE, OH #12, DDEL.

315 Others—those who knew him well": Ralph E. Becker, *Miracle on the Potomac* (Silver Spring, Md.; Bartleby Press, 1990), p. 2.

315 "America will be a lonely land": Neal, *Reluctant Dynasty*, p. 448.

CHAPTER TWENTY-ONE

317 with a volume of baggage: JSDE, *Strictly Personal* (Garden City, N.Y.: Doubleday and Company, 1974), p. 350.

318 Mamie too continued to sponsor: Steve Neal, *The Eisenhowers: Reluctant Dynasty* (Garden City, N.Y.: Doubleday and Company, 1978), p. 462.

318 "I would do just about anything": Ibid.

319 "Only had about two hours": MDE to BTE, August 20, 1971, and June 28, 1971, Box 4, BTE Papers, DDEL.

319 "Death is inevitable": John Wickman interview with MDE, August 16, 1972, OH #12, DDEL.

320 "The thing we must realize": MDE to BTE, January 28, 1971, Box 4, BTE Papers, DDEL.

321 "I was glad to receive your letter": MDE to SE, March 27, 1973, private collection.

321 "You children were": MDE to SE, June 16, 1974, private collection.

321 "Nixon is our heartbreaking worry here": MDE to SE, March 21, 1974, private collection.

322 Excerpts from Mamie's eightieth-birthday book of reminiscences: private collection.

323 On the alleged letter: Lester David and Irene David, *Ike and Mamie: The Story of the General and His Lady* (New York: G. P. Putnam's Sons, 1981), p. 130. See Merle Miller, *Plain Speaking: An Oral Biography of Harry S Truman* (New York: Berkeley Publishing Corporation, 1974); Merle Miller, *Ike the Soldier: As They Knew Him* (New York: Putnam's Sons, 1987).

323 "I don't like Eisenhower": Introduction to Sotheby's sale of Summersby memorabilia; Miller; *Plain Speaking*, pp. 339–40.

324 The ghostwriter gave [the book] a racy flavor": Bob Considine, January 24, 1975, *Boston Herald American*.

324 "In fact, this last dreadful book": Miller, *Ike the Soldier*, p. 653.

324 "Mr. Truman knew better": JNE, *Special People* (New York: Simon and Schuster, 1977), p. 213.

324 "Ike told me all about her": Barbara Walters, *20/20*, November 1, 1979.

325 "the time had come": JSDE, *Letters to Mamie* (Garden City, N.Y.: Doubleday and Company, 1978), editor's note, p. 7.

325 "Mamie never played": Author interview with George A. Horkan, Jr., August 7, 1994.

326 "I think she wanted": Author interview with Mary Eisenhower Atwater, January 4, 1996.

326 "Mamie was fond": Notes for BTE manuscript.

327 "You should lead your own lives": Author interview with Mary Eisenhower Atwater, January 4, 1996.

328 "she had no intention": Author interview with JSDE, October 17, 1995.

328 Annual physical and other medical information on MDE: Thomas Mattingly Health Record of MDE, Box 4, cited entry: May 5, 1978.

328 "The first couple of drafts": "Ike, Summersby Had No Affair," *Syracuse Herald Journal*, May 7, 1979.

328 Mickey McKeogh's biggest problem: "Focus," *The Bowie Blade*, May 31, 1979.

329 "Every night, after an episode ended": Lester David and Irene David, *Ike and Mamie*, pp. 257–58.

329 "Oh, how ugly": James Patterson, "Mamie Remembered," *Gettysburg Times*, wire story, November 11, 1979.

329 "The only thing that really disturbed her": Neal, *Reluctant Dynasty*, p. 460.

329 "In all the years": Virgil Pinkley and James F. Scheer, *Eisenhower Declassified* (Old Tappan, N.J.: Flemming H. Revell Company, 1979), p. 364.

330 "she was comfortable with all that implied": Author interview with Mary Eisenhower Atwater, January 4, 1996.

330 "horribly expensive": MDE to SE, August 20, 1979, private collection.

330 "Mary Allen's death": MDE to SE, September 3, 1979, private collection.

330 Letter to Eileen Archibold: Lester David and Irene David, *Ike and Mamie: The Story of the General and His Lady* (New York: G. P. Putnam's Sons, 1981), pp. 268–69.

331 "You act like you understand me": Author interview of Mary Eisenhower Atwater, January 4, 1996.

331 "My dear Mamie": Jean Faircloth MacArthur to MDE, private collection.

332 "There are very few originals": Marian Christy, "Recalling a Departed Original: First and Always Mamie," *Boston Globe*, November 5, 1979.

EPILOGUE

335 "Mamie Eisenhower's death": Taken from an unmarked newspaper clipping found among Eisenhower family papers.

337 "I always felt stronger": John Wickman interview with MDE, August 15, 1972, OH #12, DDEL.

338 "Some women achieve distinction": Elson eulogy, MDE Funeral Service, November 6, 1979.

338 "Darling Girl": DDE to MDE, July 1, 1943, private collection.

QUESTIONS TO PONDER

1. Mamie and Ike had many differences in their backgrounds and upbringing. How did these contrasts affect their marriage? Did it fuel their attraction to each other, or did it hamper their ability to communicate with one another?

2. Mamie found Army life exacting and difficult. Would modern women feel that way?

3. The death of the Eisenhowers' son, Doud Dwight, was a shattering event for Ike and Mamie. What impact do you think it had on their marriage? Do you think they could have handled it better?

4. Mamie was pregnant when she and Ike were sent to Panama. Given the recent death of their son, do you think Mamie should or should not have subjected herself to this dangerous assignment?

5. What impact do you think the Panama posting played on their lives together?

6. Ike wasn't sure that he wanted the posting in Europe in the late twenties, yet Mamie persuaded him to go. What role, if any, do you think that assignment played in Ike's later career?

7. How do you think Mamie felt about leaving the Wyoming Apartments when Ike went to the Philippines? Was she right to stay behind for a year while John was finishing school, or do you think she and John should have gone with Ike to Manila at the outset?

8. During the Wyoming days, Mamie's friend Katie Gerow died. How did Mamie react to her death and what effect did this and other deaths have on Mamie's life and outlook?

9. The Philippines were hardship years again. Was Mamie unadventurous, or do you think living in such a country would be fun, exciting?

10. Was Mamie prepared emotionally and by training for the role of wife of the Commander of Allied Forces Europe? If no, why not? If so, why?

11. Do you think Mamie's principled position to stay out of the public eye during the war made her life unnecessarily difficult?

12. How would you feel if you had to move your home four times in a year?

13. How do you think Mamie handled the loneliness of being left at the home front?

14. What impression do you have of Ike's letters to Mamie during the war?

15. Do you think living in the public eye during the war required special skills and fortitude?

16. After the war, Mamie and Ike lived in Quarters One at Fort Meyer, the President's Mansion at Columbia University, the Villa Saint-Pierre outside of Paris, and the White House. Which of these assignments do you think Mamie found most challenging? Which do you think she liked best?

17. Mamie was certainly well qualified to be First Lady. What special qualities do you think she brought to the job, and how was her tenure at the White House influenced by her years as an Army wife?

18. During their lifetimes, the Eisenhowers were intensely loyal to their friends. What do you think contributed to these attachments?

19. What impact, if any, do you think Ike's powerful positions and his immense popularity had on his relationship with Mamie?

20. Do you think Ike was domineering or deferential to Mamie

during their lives together? Detached or sentimental? Attentive or distracted? Romantic or disinterested?

21. What role do you think respect played in their regard for one another?

22. Do you think Ike had any regrets at the end of his life?

23. Do you think Mamie had any regrets at the end of her life?

24. After more than fifty years together, in sum, what kind of marriage do you think Ike and Mamie had?

25. Did this story make you feel happy or sad?

26. Do you think that the military demands too much of its members and their families?

27. How have times changed since Ike and Mamie died? Is America a better place to live now than during the period in which they lived, or has it lost special values that people miss?

28. Why do you think that as a First Lady Mamie is not very well known?

29. What legacy do you think they have left for their grandchildren? For the United States?

INDEX

ABOUT THE AUTHOR

Susan Eisenhower is president of the Eisenhower Institute. Formerly chairman and co-founder of the Center for Political and Strategic Studies (CPSS), she joined the Institute as president when the two organizations combined programs in the fall of 2000.

Ms. Eisenhower has spent fifteen years of her career on foreign policy issues, though she came to the field from the business community. A onetime consultant to IBM, American Express, and Loral Space Systems, she is best known for her work on US-Russian relations and international security issues. In 1997, Ms. Eisenhower testified before the Senate Armed Services and Senate Budget Committees on NATO expansion and in 1998 she was appointed to the National Academy of Sciences' standing Committee on International Security and Arms Control (CISAC). She was appointed to a second term. During the fall semester of 1998, she lectured on the topic "Russia and the West" at the Kennedy School of Government's Institute of Politics at Harvard University. Two years later, while still chairing CPSS, she held the position of Distinguished Visiting Fellow, with a focus on security issues, at the Nixon Center. She has spoken at many universities and World Affairs Councils and to professional audiences such as the one assembled at the Army War College, where she gave the 1998 Commandant's Lecture.

In the spring of 2000, Ms. Eisenhower was appointed by the secretary of energy to a blue ribbon task force to evaluate U.S. funded nuclear non-proliferation programs in Russia, and she currently sits as an advisor on another DOE study of this issue. In the summer of 2001, she was appointed to serve on the International

Space Station Management and Cost Evaluation Task Force, which analyzed ISS management and cost overruns. She also serves as an Academic Fellow of the International Peace and Security program of Carnegie Corporation of New York, and she is a director of the Carnegie Endowment for International Peace, and the Nuclear Threat Initiative. She has also served on the National Advisory Council of NASA.

Ms. Eisenhower has authored three books, two of which—*Breaking Free* and *Mrs. Ike*—have appeared on bestseller lists. She has also edited three collected volumes, *NATO at Fifty* and two on Central Asia, including the most recent, *Islam and Central Asia: An Enduring Legacy or an Evolving Threat?* She has also penned hundreds of op-eds and articles for publications, such as the *Washington Post*, the *LA Times*, *USA Today*, the Naval Institute's *Proceedings*, and the London *Spectator*. Frequently, she has provided analysis for NPR, television networks, and television programs, including: CNN, CNN International, MSNBC, *Nightline, This Week, The CBS Evening News with Dan Rather, ABC Evening News with Peter Jennings, The News Hour with Jim Lehrer, Fox News with Brit Hume,* and *"Hardball with Chris Matthews."*

Mamie's dressing table at the Gettysburg house BOB SACHA

Mamie's grandparents, Mari and Carl Carlson PRIVATE COLLECTION

Mamie's mother, Elvira (or Nana, as she was called), not long after her marriage to John Doud PRIVATE COLLECTION

Mamie with her teddy bear, Colorado Springs, 1905 PRIVATE COLLECTION

The Doud family at Cheyenne Canyon, Colorado, with friends: *(from left)* Mamie, Nana, Joel and Mari Carlson; *(last two on right)* Buster Doud, Eda Carlson DWIGHT D. EISENHOWER LIBRARY

The young Doud family: *(from left)* Mike, Pupah, Buster, Eleanor, Nana, and Mamie EISENHOWER NATIONAL HISTORIC SITE

Mamie *(front)* with neighbors in Denver. Her hair had been cut off as punishment for willful behavior
DWIGHT D. EISENHOWER LIBRARY

Mamie at the Des Moines River
PRIVATE COLLECTION

The Douds' home in Cedar Rapids, Iowa

Nana and Pupah in their Winton in front of 750 Lafayette Street, Denver, in 1906. On the porch are Mamie holding a bunny *(right)*, Eleanor *(seated)*, nurse with Buster, and cook with Mike   NATIONAL PARK SERVICE

Mamie, in 1911, at the age of fifteen   PRIVATE COLLECTION

Mamie in her debutante year, 1914–15

David J. Eisenhower and Ida Stover on their wedding day, September 23, 1885
NATIONAL PARK SERVICE

Ike in fifth grade *(in front, second from left)*. His upbringing was in stark contrast with Mamie's   U.S. ARMY

David and Ida Eisenhower and their six sons in 1902: *(from left)* Ike, Ed, Earl, Arthur, Roy, and *(front center)* Milton   DWIGHT D. EISENHOWER LIBRARY

Ike en route to West Point for
the first time, a Kansas farm
boy in the big city, Chicago
DWIGHT D. EISENHOWER
LIBRARY

The football team at West Point. Ike is in the second row, third from left; Omar Bradley in
the top row, third from right   U.S. ARMY

The Douds' McCullough Street home in San Antonio, Texas. It was on this porch that Ike courted Mamie NATIONAL PARK SERVICE

Ike and Mamie's wedding portrait, July 1, 1916
DWIGHT D. EISENHOWER LIBRARY

Mamie at the time of her marriage, 1916. The flamboyant signature is hers

Ike and Mamie not long after their marriage, with Mr. and Mrs.
W. T. Gaultney at right and Mrs. Gaultney's sister Dottie at left

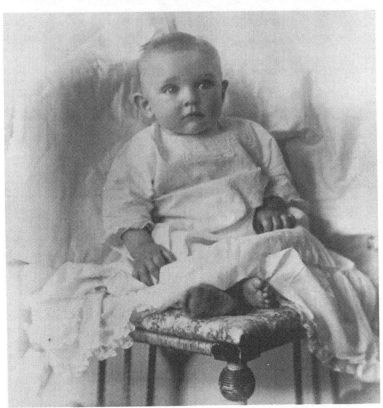

Ikky wearing the christening dress Mamie embroidered for him,
winter 1917, San Antonio, Texas

(Left) Ikky gets a lift from his proud father

(Below left) Mamie and Ikky on the steps of the Alpha Tau Omega house

(Below right) Mamie, Ike, and Ikky at their Spring Street house. All these pictures were taken in Gettysburg in 1918

The army's first transcontinental convoy. Mamie met up with Ike for four days during the cross-country caravan   DWIGHT D. EISENHOWER LIBRARY

En route to the West Coast, Ohio, July 13, 1919: *(from left)* William R. Stuhler, Major Brett, Paul V. Robinson, and Lt. Col. Dwight D. Eisenhower   DWIGHT D. EISENHOWER LIBRARY

Ike with the exotic military technology of its day, the tank, c. 1919–20
DWIGHT D. EISENHOWER LIBRARY

The barracks at Camp Meade that the Eisenhowers shared with the George Pattons and others, 1920
DWIGHT D. EISENHOWER LIBRARY

"Col. Ike" coaching the Tank Corps football team at Camp Meade, 1921
DWIGHT D. EISENHOWER LIBRARY

Mamie en route to Panama and with her sister Mike at the Canal Zone, on the trip she had taken years before. Now she faced its perils anew   PRIVATE COLLECTION

Ikky photographed in Denver less than a year before his death
DWIGHT D. EISENHOWER LIBRARY

Camp Gaillard, Panama, perched on the
Culebra Cut, where Mamie arrived in 1922.
She returned from this place to Denver to
give birth to her second son, John
DWIGHT D. EISENHOWER LIBRARY

Nana and her grandson John in the early fall of
1922 NATIONAL PARK SERVICE

Mamie, gaunt and worn from her years in Panama. "I was down to skin and bones," she later remembered PRIVATE COLLECTION

Mamie with John *(on right)* in Panama
DWIGHT D. EISENHOWER LIBRARY

Mamie *(center)* during an outing on horseback in Panama, about 1924. By now she had recommitted herself to Ike and their army life PRIVATE COLLECTION

Ike as football
coach at Camp
Meade
DWIGHT D.
EISENHOWER
LIBRARY

Mamie, Ike, and Uncle
Joel at 750 Lafayette
Street, 1924–25. Ike's
assignment to Fort Logan
made it easy for them to
get to Denver
PRIVATE COLLECTION

Ike, John, and Mamie on their way to
play a round of golf in Denver, c.
1925–26 PRIVATE COLLECTION

Mamie, John, and Ike, at Fort Logan
PRIVATE COLLECTION

John with Nana in Denver, C. 1924–25 PRIVATE COL-LECTION

Mamie and John's passport to a year of European adventure DWIGHT D. EISENHOW-ER MUSEUM

Photograph of bearer

Description of Bearer

Height 5 feet 4 inches.
Hair Brown
Eyes Blue
Distinguishing marks or features:

Place of birth Boone, Iowa
Date of birth Nov 14, 1896.

the seal of the Department of State is impressed thereon.

Signature of bearer

Ike working on his guide for the Battle Monuments
Commission. History had not yet demonstrated the
value that his intimate knowledge of the European
battlefields would have in the coming war

John in Paris, 1929

John and Mamie with George Horkan at a battlefield memorial in France, 1929. It is possible that Ike took this picture

Nana and Pupah during their tour of World War I battlefields with Ike

(Above) Ike and John "enjoying one last dip" and *(left)* Mamie, too, taking the waters, San Remo, Italy, 1929 DWIGHT D. EISENHOWER LIBRARY

Ike and Mamie with Bill and Helen Gruber, on an Alpine precipice DWIGHT D. EISENHOWER LIBRARY

Dwight Eisenhower during the War Department years

John with Ike's boss, Gen. George Van Horn Moseley *(left)*, and Ike's mentor, Gen. Fox Conner *(right)*, in front of the Wyoming apartments, Washington, early 1930s

The Bonus Marchers' encampment in Washington, July 1932
DWIGHT D. EISENHOWER LIBRARY

The Army intervenes in the Bonus Men's encampment, July 1932
DWIGHT D. EISENHOWER LIBRARY

John, Ike, and Mamie in Rock Creek Park, Washington, just prior to Ike's departure for the Philippines. The separation from his family, Ike wrote the Douds, brought him "nothing but grief" DWIGHT D. EISENHOWER LIBRARY

Mamie on a stopover in Hawaii in 1936 en route to the Philippines, where she would reconnect with Ike after a year's separation. *From left:* Major Potter, Mamie, Col. Wallace McCammon, and Mrs. Potter U.S. ARMY SIGNAL CORPS

Ike in the Philippines
PRIVATE COLLECTION

The family on August 4, 1937, Manila. Mamie had to make many adjustments when she came to live in this strange and beautiful land   PRIVATE COLLECTION

John, in his first dinner jacket, and Mamie at the Manila Hotel
PRIVATE COLLECTION

Mamie and Louise Caffey take tea at the Eisenhowers' apartment in the Manila Hotel DWIGHT D. EISENHOWER LIBRARY

Mamie in Philippine national costume on her way to a party DWIGHT D. EISENHOWER LIBRARY

A gathering of the Doud clan in the summer of 1938 during the
Eisenhowers' home leave from the Philippines. *On the right:* Mamie's sister
Mike and her soon-to-be-estranged husband, Richard Gill, with their sons,
Richard and Michael PRIVATE COLLECTION

The farewell luncheon in the Eisenhowers' honor given by President
Manuel Quezon, who shares a lighthearted moment with Mamie. Ike is at
right, and Gen. Douglas MacArthur, seated, at left.

DWIGHT D. EISENHOWER LIBRARY

At the luncheon, Mamie pins the Philippine Distinguished Service Cross on
Ike as President Quezon looks on   DWIGHT D. EISENHOWER LIBRARY

Mamie and Ike's home at Fort Lewis. Stateside once more DWIGHT D. EISENHOWER LIBRARY

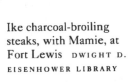

Ike charcoal-broiling steaks, with Mamie, at Fort Lewis DWIGHT D. EISENHOWER LIBRARY

At a fancy dress ball at Fort Lewis, probably in 1940. Mamie wore one of Nana's dresses and Ike an early dress uniform   DWIGHT D. EISENHOWER LIBRARY

Sitting on the front porch of 750 Lafayette Street, Denver, on Mike's wedding day: *(front row)* Ike, Mike, and her new husband, George G. Moore; *(back row)* Mamie, Nana, and Pupah. John was the photographer   DWIGHT D. EISENHOWER LIBRARY

Mamie and Ike *(right)* with Gen.
Walter Krueger and his wife around
the time of the Louisiana
Maneuvers, Fort Sam Houston,
1941   DWIGHT D. EISENHOWER
LIBRARY

Mamie and Kitty Smith at Quarters
#7 just as Ike left to take up his
command in Europe
PRIVATE COLLECTION

Ike in Algiers reading an official memo DWIGHT D. EISENHOWER
LIBRARY

Ike with Arthur Tedder and Gen. Bernard Montgomery inspecting an armored unit in
England, February 1944 U.S. ARMY

Kay Summersby, Pearlie Hargrave
McKeogh, Sue Sarafian, and Capt.
Mattie Pinette, England, 1944
SUE SARAFIAN JEHL

A Fourth of July meeting of Lt.
Gen. Omar Bradley, Ike, and Maj.
Gen. Ire Wyche, at 79th Division
Headquarters in France, 1944
U.S. ARMY

Mamie in uniform during World War II
DWIGHT D. EISENHOWER LIBRARY

Mamie, waiting for Ike during the war. On her piano are
pictures of Ike, Katie Gerow,
and a miniature of Nana
INTERNATIONAL NEWS PHOTO

April 23, 1943, Brooks Field,
San Antonio, Texas: Mamie at
the graduation of the Class of
'43, which she sponsored
AIR CORPS — U.S. ARMY

John took this picture of his
parents at West Point during
Ike's secret visit to the
United States, January 4,
1944 PRIVATE COLLECTION

Mamie, Mrs. Lucius Clay
(Marge), and Mrs. George
Horkan (Mary), at Camp
Lee, Virginia, not long after
the Normandy invasion
DWIGHT D. EISENHOWER
LIBRARY

Mamie and John in 1944, not
long after his return from visiting
Ike at London headquarters
PRIVATE COLLECTION

Mike, Nana, and Mamie in the
summer of 1944 in Denver
EISENHOWER NATIONAL HIS-
TORIC SITE

The Eisenhowers with the
Churchills in England in the
fall of 1946

Mamie and Ike with the
British royal family at
Balmoral Castle

Eisenhower greeting the
enormous multitude of
people who poured out to
welcome him, New York,
1945

Mamie, with Ike holding a sword of honor, a gift from the Netherlands, October 1947. He was celebrated everywhere he went U.S. ARMY

At Mamie's fifty-first birthday party at Fort Myer, Virginia, November 14, 1947. Janie Howard is at right. *(Below right)* Ike and Mamie singing at the birthday party and *(below left)* collapsing with friends after bidding the guests goodbye
DWIGHT D. EISENHOWER LIBRARY

Mamie greeting the children of her husband's aide, Craig Cannon, sometime before the Eisenhowers left for Paris PRIVATE COLLECTION

Mamie tending her garden at Quarters #1, Fort Myer
DWIGHT D. EISENHOWER LIBRARY

Ike's inauguration as president of Columbia University. This academic ceremony, drawing notables from all over the world, had as much pomp and circumstance as any of the many postwar commemorations Ike had attended
DWIGHT D. EISENHOWER LIBRARY

Mamie and Ike take a carriage ride in New York not long after arriving at Columbia

Mamie in the Villa Saint-Pierre, in Marnes-la-Coquette, France, September 1951

SHAPE

Mamie and Ike watch as John's plane heads for Korea. Mamie was sorry they'd been surrounded by photographers and unable to be alone with their "grief"

UNITED PRESS

On November 2, 1952, Ike and Mamie left on a special train for Boston, where Ike was to wind up his campaign with major addresses

UNITED PRESS

On their whistle-stop tour, Mamie and Ike agreed to reenact a dawn greeting for photographers

REPUBLICAN NATIONAL COMMITTEE

Christmas 1952 at 60 Morningside Drive: *From left:* Nana, Mamie, Susan, Ike, David, Anne, and Barbara. John was in Korea DWIGHT D. EISENHOWER LIBRARY

Bess Truman gives the incoming First Lady a tour of the White House. When a journalist asked Mamie about her coat—shortly after Richard Nixon declared that Pat wore "Republican cloth coats"—Mamie replied gaily, "Mink, of course" NATIONAL PARK SERVICE

Uncle Joel presented the new First Lady with "Mamie Eisenhower" orchids developed in Boone, Iowa, by the Kemble-Smith Greenhouses. The charm bracelets, class ring, and sentimental watch would all become part of "the Mamie look"

AP/WASHINGTON POST

Playing bolivia in the White House solarium: Ruth Butcher, Mamie, and Mary Allen (fourth person unknown)
PRIVATE COLLECTION

Mamie and Ike playing Scrabble at Camp David in 1954 u.s. navy

Mamie and Ike a year later, on the day they gave a combined wedding-anniversary and housewarming party at Gettysburg for the White House staff
COURTESY MARY JANE MCCAFREE MONROE

The Gettysburg farm still under construction EISENHOWER NATIONAL HISTORIC SITE

Easter 1956: *(from left)* Susan, the First Lady, and her newest grandchild, Mary Jean

The second inauguration, 1957

Eisenhower in a motorcade in Delhi, where more than a million people thronged to see him

Ike greets Mamie after his arduous round-the-world trip

At the state dinner for Soviet premier Nikita Khrushchev, December 15, 1959

A different kind of White House party, celebrating the birthday of Mamie's lady's maid, Rose Wood, in January 1958. *From left:* A White House usher, Gen. Howard Snyder, the Eisenhowers, Rose, and Mabel Walker, the housekeeper

Mamie made sure that her mother, now bedridden, nonetheless had a proper birthday party, 1958

The last Christmas at the White House, December 24, 1960

The Gettysburg farmhouse, complete with Ike and Mamie's beloved sunporch and three magnificent ash trees   EISENHOWER NATIONAL HISTORIC SITE

Mamie and Ike in a private moment aboard ship, en route to Europe, July 1962 PRIVATE COLLECTION

Ike's photograph of Mamie on the same trip PRIVATE COLLECTION

The cast of two family productions: in *The Sound of Music,* Susan plays Maria, while Nancy Witt, Mary, and Harriet Barriga play the Trapp children. *Young Abe Lincoln* was staged by my mother (playing Abe) as a birthday present for Ike in 1962. Susan is Bill Berry, Anne is the young Abe, and Mary is Anne Rutherford LANE STUDIO

The Tournament of Roses
Parade in 1964. Ike was Grand
Marshal and Mamie wore her
plastic sunglasses, declaring
them the best pair she had ever
owned LESTER NAHAMKIN/
COURTESY EISENHOWER
NATIONAL HISTORIC SITE

Ike as family photographer,
Thanksgiving 1966 PRIVATE
COLLECTION

Ike and Mamie cut their fiftieth-wedding-anniversary cake during a party given at their son's home. Granddaughter Mary looks on BACHRACH INC.

Ike on his last birthday, acknowledging the band and the crowd before his hospital window UPI

President Eisenhower's funeral U.S. ARMY

Mamie at the Pentagon dedicating Eisenhower Corridor, May 15, 1970. She is accompanied by Gen. Omar Bradley and Secretary of Defense Melvin Laird   U.S. ARMY

Mamie launching the USS *Eisenhower*, escorted by Secret Service man Bob Hallman, 1977

Mamie on her eightieth birthday, her rhinestone flag flying. The whole family was there. Here she is surrounded by her son, John *(rear)*, grandson, David *(left)*, granddaughter Susan *(right)*, and great-granddaughters Adriana Echavarria *(left)* and Caroline Bradshaw Mahon *(right)*.

(Below) Mamie reading the little book of reminiscences we gave her, and listening as her son reads his entry aloud; David and his wife, Julie, are at right

Mamie signing copies of *Letters to Mamie* PRIVATE COLLECTION

Mamie in one of her rare speaking appearances, this one at the Eisenhower Medical Center, in Palm Desert, April 12, 1978. Now was the time for mostly memories. A year and a half later she was buried next to Ike in Abilene